THE CRIMINAL PRO
INVESTIGATIONS A

THE CRIMINAL PROCEDURE AND INVESTIGATIONS ACT 1996

Richard Card LL.B, LL.M
Professor of Law and Head of the School of Law
De Montfort University, Leicester

Richard Ward LL.B, Solicitor
Professor of Public Law and Head of the
Department of Law
De Montfort University, Leicester

JORDANS

1996

Published by
Jordan Publishing Limited
21 St Thomas Street
Bristol BS1 6JS

British Library Cataloguing-in-Publication Data
A catalogue record for this book is available from the British Library.

ISBN 0 85308 379 7

Typeset by Mendip Communications Ltd, Frome, Somerset
Printed by Bookcraft (Bath) Ltd, Midsomer Norton

PREFACE

The Criminal Procedure and Investigations Act 1996 is the latest legislative intervention into the criminal justice process. Although not as controversial as the Criminal Justice and Public Order Act 1994, it nevertheless raises broad policy questions as to the balance between prosecution and defence in a criminal case. It also contains a host of detailed changes to criminal procedure.

This book is primarily concerned with providing for practitioners a guide to the provisions of the new Act and their implications. It is not intended to be a review of the policies that underpin them.

Needless to say, we owe thanks to those who have assisted in the preparation of this book, in particular to Kathleen Williamson and Lisa Evans in the School of Law, who assisted in the preparation of the manuscript. Thanks are also due to Richard Hudson, Mollie Dickenson and others at Jordans for their support and speedy production of the book.

The law is stated as at 7 August 1996.

Richard Card
Richard Ward
August 1996

CONTENTS

TABLE OF CASES

TABLE OF STATUTES

References are to paragraph numbers except where they are in *italics* which are references to page numbers.

TABLE OF STATUTORY INSTRUMENTS, CODES OF PRACTICE AND GUIDELINES

References are to paragraph numbers except where they are in *italics* which are references to page numbers.

Chapter 1

INTRODUCTION

1.1 This book is concerned with those provisions in the Criminal Procedure and Investigations Act 1996 which apply to England and Wales.[1] It is divided into two parts: a narrative, followed by the Criminal Procedure and Investigations Act 1996 with annotations thereto. The narrative and the annotated statute have different purposes. The narrative is intended to set out, explain and comment on the provisions of the Act, to give the reasons for them and to set them in the context of the current law. Generally, the text eschews detailed definitions in the Act which are not essential to a basic understanding of the Act and its operation. The purpose of the annotations is to deal with those matters of definition excluded from the narrative and also to provide, where necessary, some explanation of various legal rules underlying particular provisions.

  In both the narrative and the annotations, references to other statutory provisions are to those provisions as amended by legislation other than the new Act. For the sake of simplicity, the amending legislation has not been referred to unless this has been essential to explain the point being made.

---

1 Section 79 prescribes the extent of the Act.

1.2 References are made occasionally to the date on which this book went to press. That date is 12 August 1996. References in this book to 'the Act' or to 'the new Act' or to any section are to the Criminal Procedure and Investigations Act 1996 or to a section of it, unless the contrary is indicated.

1.3 In both parts of this book, references are made to the Parliamentary debates on the Criminal Procedure and Investigations Bill. The Parliamentary progress of the Bill was as follows.

HOUSE OF LORDS
First reading: HL Deb, vol 567, 16 November 1995, col 2.
Second reading: HL Deb, vol 567, 27 November 1995, cols 462–506.
Committee: HL Deb, vol 567, 18 and 19 December 1995, cols 1432–1467, 1480–1504 and 1518–1599.
Report: HL Deb, vol 568, 1 February 1996, cols 1558–1610, and vol 569, 5 February 1996, cols 10–70 and 73–112.
Third reading: HL Deb, vol 569, 19 February 1996, cols 865–912.

HOUSE OF COMMONS
First reading: HC Deb, vol 272, 20 February 1996, col 192.
Second reading: HC Deb, vol 272, 27 February 1996, cols 738–778.
Standing Committee B: The Committee met four times (4 April 1996, and 14, 16 and 21 May 1996). Its deliberations are recorded in cols 1–156 of the Official Report.
Report: HC Deb, vol 279, 12 June 1996, cols 329–398.
Third reading: HC Deb, vol 279, 12 June 1996, col 398.

HOUSE OF LORDS
Consideration of Commons' amendments: HL Deb, vol 573, 26 June 1996, cols 945–1003.

ROYAL ASSENT
4 July 1996.

COMMENCEMENT

1.4   The Act came into force on Royal Assent. Many provisions, however, will apply only to offences, procedures, orders etc on or after an 'appointed day', and some other provisions will not apply in respect of investigations begun before such a day. An 'appointed day' is such day as is appointed for the purposes of the particular provision by the Secretary of State by order made by statutory instrument (s 77(4)). The Secretary of State's power to make an order may be exercised differently in relation to different areas or in relation to other different cases or descriptions of case (s 77(2)). Any order may include such supplementary, incidental, consequential or transitional provisions as appear necessary or expedient to the Secretary of State (s 77(3)). Neither the order nor a draft of it need be laid before Parliament.

It is intended that those provisions not implemented on Royal Assent will be implemented in stages to allow time, where necessary, for the preparation and approval of rules of court and the preparation and provision of guidance and training for the criminal justice agencies which will be concerned with the implementation of the Act. It is the Government's intention that the major procedural changes will be implemented in early 1997.[1]

When this book went to press, no days had been appointed under the Act. To facilitate exposition, however, this book is written on the basis that it is fully operative.

---

1 Baroness Blatch, Minister of State, Home Office, Lords' consideration of Commons' amendments, col 1003; *Home Office Press Notice* 4 July 1996.

OUTLINE OF THE ACT

1.5 Central to the new Act are provisions relating to disclosure of evidence. Part I introduces a new scheme of disclosure of unused material by the prosecution, which is intended to replace the pre-existing common law rules. Part I also introduces an obligation, in cases to be tried on indictment, of defence disclosure, which is part of the trend towards the identification of issues in dispute at an earlier stage in the criminal process. Part II of the Act supplements this statutory framework by enabling the making of a Code of Practice governing the preservation, recording and revelation of material by investigators. A draft of the Code is set out at the end of this book.

This range of measures is completed by certain changes relating to witness summonses, which are a modest attempt to address the problems caused to third parties by disclosure requirements.

1.6 Parts III and IV of the new Act focus on the desirability of settling issues in advance of trial. Part III creates a general power to hold preparatory hearings, and mirrors the more limited provision in the Criminal Justice Act 1987. Part IV enables a binding ruling on any matter of law or admissibility of evidence to be made in advance of trial.

1.7 The new Act makes a variety of changes to the law of criminal procedure. In relation to changes in respect of procedure in magistrates' courts, it repeals the not-yet implemented transfer for trial provisions in the Criminal Justice and Public Order Act 1994 and introduces in their place new procedures for committing cases for trial at the Crown Court, which address the criticisms voiced by the Royal Commission on Criminal Justice.[1] In particular, the new Act abolishes the admissibility of oral evidence and cross-examination at committal proceedings involving consideration of the evidence, and limits the evidence tendered at committal proceedings to that tendered by the prosecution, and it amends the law relating to decisions by magistrates' courts as to the mode of trial of either way offences by requiring that an accused be invited to indicate his intended plea before such a decision is taken and providing that if the intended plea is 'guilty' the case will be dealt with by the magistrates' court (at least, initially).

---

1 (1993) Cm 2263, HMSO.

1.8 Other provisions in the new Act make changes which apply to criminal proceedings in general. Mention may be made here of two of those changes which implement other recommendations of the Royal Commission on Criminal Justice. First, the Act provides a power for the High Court to order a re-trial of a case which has resulted in an acquittal, if the acquittal is tainted by a conviction for an offence involving interference with or intimidation of witnesses or jurors in that case.[1] Secondly, the Act gives judges and magistrates' courts power to restrict the reporting of derogatory assertions made in a speech in mitigation if these are either false or irrelevant.

---

1 This gives effect to the only one of the 27 criminal justice measures announced by Mr Michael Howard, QC, MP, the Home Secretary, at the Conservative Party Conference in October 1993 which remained unimplemented.

1.9 Finally, like the Criminal Justice and Public Order Act 1994 and other modern criminal justice legislation, the Act has been used as a vehicle for a variety of miscellaneous changes. Many of these were added during the Act's Parliamentary passage. The Act started that passage with 49 sections and two Schedules, and ended up with 81 sections and five Schedules. One of these miscellaneous changes, s 63, dealing with the provision of specimens under the drink driving legislation, does not fall neatly into the following chapters of the text. For this reason, its explanation is to be found in the annotations to s 63, and not in the text. Some of these changes, some of them major, were made at quite a late stage in the Parliamentary proceedings, something which is to be deprecated on grounds of the limitation of the opportunity for Parliamentary scrutiny and discussion.

1.10 Despite the implementation of a considerable number of the recommendations for changes to the law made by the Royal Commission on Criminal Justice by the new Act, the Criminal Justice and Public Order Act 1994, and the Criminal Appeal Act 1995, quite a significant number of those recommendations remain unimplemented. As the years pass, there must be increasing doubt as to whether they will ever be implemented. As indicated in para **1.7**, one recommendation made by the Royal Commission, the abolition of committal proceedings (which would have been implemented if the transfer for trial provision of the Criminal Justice and Public Order Act 1994 had been brought into force), is now not to be implemented.

Chapter 2

DISCLOSURE OF EVIDENCE: PROSECUTION AND DEFENCE DISCLOSURE

The pre-existing law – Reasons for change – Primary prosecution disclosure – Defence disclosure – Secondary prosecution disclosure – Sensitive material – Third party material

INTRODUCTION

2.1 Part I of the new Act creates for the first time a statutory framework in respect of the disclosure of unused prosecution material. It also imposes a new obligation on the defence, in a case to be tried on indictment,[1] to disclose the nature of the defence which will be relied on, and imposes an obligation in such a case to indicate the matters on which the accused takes issue with the prosecution. These changes are supplemented by Part II of the Act, which seeks to create a framework in which the disclosure obligations can be properly fulfilled. Part II of the Act empowers the Home Secretary to create a Code of Practice governing the retention and disclosure of material and information identified and acquired during a criminal investigation, and which regulates the way in which disclosable material is to be identified and preserved by an investigator for the prosecutor and for the accused. A draft Code has been published, and its main provisions as at the date of going to press are discussed in Chapter 3. Nevertheless, the workings of the statutory disclosure scheme depend heavily on the detailed provisions of the proposed Code, and reference to it is made at appropriate parts of this chapter.

---

1 Defence disclosure in cases to be tried summarily is voluntary: see s 6 and para **2.53**.

2.2 The changes made by Part I of the new Act draw on the recommendations of the Royal Commission on Criminal Justice.[1] The Report of the Royal Commission recommended that legislation should create a framework for prosecution and defence disclosure, to be supplemented by subordinate legislation or Codes of Practice. The reasons for this are discussed later.[2] The proposed legislation and Code would replace the *Attorney-General's Guidelines*,[3] and the rules of law then currently existing. These recommendations envisaged the introduction of a scheme of disclosure to be undertaken in stages. In broad terms, they were as follows:

(a) Initial prosecution disclosure of all material relevant to the offence or to the offender or to the surrounding circumstances of the case, whether or not the prosecution intended to rely on that material. The prosecution would have had to inform the defence of the existence of any other material obtained in the course of its inquiry, by disclosing the schedules of material prepared by the investigator.

(b) Defence disclosure of the general nature of the defence, perhaps by a solicitor ticking a box on a standard form.

(c) Second stage prosecution disclosure, based on requests by the defence for further disclosure.

---

1 (1993) Cm 2262, HMSO.
2 See para **2.26**.
3 (1982) 74 Cr App R 302.

2.3 In its Consultation Paper on Disclosure,[1] the Government accepted the broad approach recommended by the Royal Commission but rejected its detailed proposals, believing that they would not significantly reduce the disclosure burden imposed by the common law. As seen later,[2] the reduction of what were perceived as undue burdens was one of the primary motivators for changes in the law. The Government also believed that a greater measure of defence disclosure than proposed by the Royal Commission was needed to assist in the narrowing of the issues in dispute. The Consultation Paper therefore proposed a scheme of prosecution and defence disclosure which, in the Government's view, would significantly reduce the volume of material to be disclosed by the prosecution for no good reason, which would protect from disclosure sensitive material which did not really assist the defence case, and which would provide an incentive for a defendant to provide sufficient particulars of his defence.[3] The scheme in Part I of the new Act substantially adopts the detailed recommendations of the Consultation Document, and is set out in summary form at para. **2.11**. Its detail is the subject of this Chapter.

---

1 (1995) Cm 2864, HMSO.
2 Paragraphs **2.25–2.26**.
3 Consultation Paper (1995) Cm 2864, HMSO, Ch 2, para 25.

2.4 The extension of the duty of disclosure to include disclosure of the nature of the defence is a significant change. However, it builds on the trend towards greater disclosure set in train by the Criminal Justice Act 1987 (cases of serious or complex fraud), and also on the principle of greater disclosure inherent in the 'right of silence' provisions of the Criminal Justice and Public Order Act 1994. For these reasons, the principle of defence disclosure has not proved controversial, and was supported both by the responses made to the Government's Consultation Paper[1] and by opposition parties in Parliament. However, whether the framework of disclosure as a whole is practicable, fair or achieves a proper balance between prosecution and defence is more debatable. The Consultation Paper stated:[2]

'This scheme will not increase the risk of a miscarriage of justice. By clarifying the issues before the trial starts, these proposals should help to ensure that those who are guilty are convicted, without prejudicing the acquittal of the innocent. If the defendant is telling the truth in the line of argument he discloses, that will trigger prosecution disclosure of any material which tends to support that defence, and thereby enable the defence to run its case more effectively.'

The provisions relating to prosecution disclosure have attracted criticism. The Criminal Bar Association[3] considered the proposals to be clumsy and too adversarial, and thought that they would inculcate an unhealthy culture into the process of investigation and prosecution, and thought that they were unnecessary, especially in the light of the 'right of silence' provisions of the Criminal Justice and Public Order Act 1994, which made the identification of issues at an early stage much easier. During debate in Parliament on the proposed legislation, criticism was voiced as to the lack of balance between prosecution and defence, and the need to ensure that an 'equality of arms' is achieved.[4] The merits of the detailed proposals, and their likely impact, are considered at the appropriate stages in this chapter.

---

1 See, eg, Criminal Bar Association response, paras 4.1–4.8.
2 (1995) Cm 2864, HMSO, para 27.
3 Op cit, para 3.7.
4. See, eg, Lord McIntosh of Haringey, HL 2nd Reading, col 468. In *X v FRG* (No 1169/61), (1963) YB 520 at 574, the European Court of Human Rights stated that 'equality of arms' is 'an inherent element of a fair trial' for the purposes of art 6(1).

2.5 The need for a fair balance is accentuated by the context provided by the European Convention on Human Rights. Article 6 of the Convention provides for a basic right to a fair trial. A series of decisions by the European Court of Human Rights has confirmed that 'it is a requirement of fairness that prosecuting authorities should disclose all material evidence for or against the accused to the defence. A failure to do this in the instant case can give rise to a defect in the trial proceedings'.[1] Further, the changes in the new Act should not be viewed in isolation. The Court of Human Rights has held that art 6 also includes the right not to be required to incriminate oneself.[2] The new disclosure provisions therefore have to be judged, in combination with the 'right of silence' provisions of the 1994 Act, as to whether the balance between prosecution and defence is such as to be fair or, alternatively, whether it has been tilted in a way that infringes the basic right to a fair trial, and thus infringes art 6.

---

1 *Edwards v United Kingdom* (1992) 15 EHRR 417 (ECHR).
2 *Funke v France* (1993) 16 EHRR 297 (ECHR); *Inbrioscia v Switzerland* (1994) 17 EHRR 441 (ECHR); *Sekannia v Austria* (1994) 17 EHRR 221 (ECHR). For the possible effects of art 6, see Munday, 'Inferences from Silence and European Human Rights Law' [1996] Crim LR 370.

Application of the new disclosure rules

2.6 Part I of the new Act applies in respect of alleged offences into which no criminal investigation has begun before the appointed day (s 1(3)).[1] No day had been appointed when this book went to press. A 'criminal investigation' is an investigation which police officers and other persons have a duty to conduct with a view to it being ascertained:

(a)   whether a person should be charged with an offence; or
(b)   whether a person charged with an offence is guilty of it (s 1(4)).

These disclosure provisions therefore apply to criminal investigations not only by the police, but by others such as Customs & Excise investigators, trading standards officers and persons employed by other investigatory agencies. However, Part II of the new Act, which deals with the Code of Practice, applies only to police officers (s 22(1)). This distinction was the subject of fierce debate,[2] and is discussed further at para **3.15**.

---

1   For the power to appoint a day for this purpose, see s 1(5).
2   See, eg, Mr Alun Michael, MP, HC Committee, cols 95–98.

2.7   The key question for the operation of Part I is the date when a criminal investigation actually begins. Clearly, if an offence is reported to the police, inquiries in response to that report are part of a criminal investigation. However, criminal investigations may take many forms. They often arise from information obtained, or statements made, at times when the police do not know, or do not even necessarily believe, that any offence in fact has been committed, and where inquiries are being conducted for the purpose of determining in fact whether any offence has in fact been committed. It may be that the commission of an offence is suspected, but it is unclear who might have committed it. It is submitted that in each of these cases an investigation has begun. It might be argued that the difference in wording between s 1(3) ('in relation to alleged offences') and s 25(3) ('in relation to suspected or alleged offences') points to a contrary conclusion, and might suggest that investigations into suspected offences, where no offence has been actually alleged, do not fall within the scope of Part I. Arguably, nothing turns on this difference of wording between s 1(3) and s 25(3), which merely reflects the different contexts in which Part I and Part II operate. Part I is concerned essentially with procedures to be followed where a person is to be tried; Part II is concerned with the investigative stage. In any event, to maintain a distinction would lead to absurdity, with common law and statutory obligations existing side by side. This conclusion is also confirmed by para 2.1 of the draft Code, which states as follows:

> 'A criminal investigation is an investigation conducted by police officers with a view to it being ascertained whether a person should be charged with an offence, or whether a person charged with an offence is guilty of it. This will include not only enquiries into undetected crimes, but also investigations which are intelligence-led and begun before a crime is committed, for example when the police keep premises under observation for a period of time and then see a crime being committed.'

However, even if the investigation has begun on or after the appointed day, Part I only applies in the circumstances identified in s 1(1) or s 1(2). By s 1(1), Part I of the new Act applies where:

(a) a person is charged with a summary offence in respect of which a court proceeds to summary trial and in respect of which he pleads not guilty;

(b) a person who has attained the age of 18[1] is charged with an offence which is triable either way, in respect of which a court proceeds to summary trial and in respect of which he pleads not guilty; or

(c) a person under the age of 18[1] is charged with an indictable offence in respect of which a court proceeds to summary trial and in respect of which he pleads not guilty.

---

1 See general annotations.

2.8 By s 1(2), Part I of the new Act also applies where:

(a) a person is charged with an indictable offence (ie an indictable only or either way offence)[1] and he is committed for trial for the offence concerned;[2]

(b) a person is charged with an indictable offence and proceedings for the trial of the person on the charge concerned are transferred to the Crown Court by virtue of a notice of transfer given under s 4 of the Criminal Justice Act 1987 (serious or complex fraud);[1] or

(c) a person is charged with an indictable offence and proceedings for the trial of the person on the charge concerned are transferred to the Crown Court by virtue of a notice of transfer served on a magistrates' court under s 53 of the Criminal Justice Act 1991 (certain cases involving children);[1]

(d) a count charging a person with a summary offence is included in an indictment under the authority of s 40 of the Criminal Justice Act 1988;[1] or

(e) a voluntary bill of indictment charging a person with the indictable offences is preferred under the authority of s 2(2)(b) of the Administration of Justice (Miscellaneous Provisions) Act 1933 (s 1(2)).

---

1 See annotations to s 1.
2 For the new provisions in respect of committal for trial, see s 47 and Sch 1, and Chapter 6.

2.9 Subject to the matters discussed below, the effect of s 21(1) is to ensure that the pre-existing common law duties of disclosure on a prosecutor[1] in such cases end at the same point as the new statutory duties begin.[2] The one exception to this rule is in respect of the rules of common law as to whether disclosure is in the public interest (s 21(2)). This matter continues to be dealt with in accordance with common law principles (see paras **3.57–3.66**).

Accordingly, a clean break between the two sets of rules is achieved as from the relevant time, defined in s 21(3) by reference to the same preconditions as set out in s 1(1) and s 1(2).[3] Thus, the new procedures and law will apply to any case in which the criminal investigation began on or after the appointed day, with the pre-existing case-law ceasing to apply, for example, when a person pleads not guilty on summary trial or is committed for trial on indictment.

By contrast, in cases where the criminal investigation has begun prior to the appointed day, Part I does not apply,[4] and the existing common law rules continue in effect. For this reason, the common law rules discussed at paras **2.23–2.24** continue to be important. Although the existence of two schemes of disclosure might be thought to be inconvenient, this conclusion is confirmed by the terms of s 1(3) which would be meaningless if the contrary were the case. Further, the scheme of disclosure inherent in Part I of the Act presupposes the existence of a Code of Practice governing the preservation and handling of unused material. Such a Code only applies in respect of criminal investigations into suspected or alleged offences commenced after the day when it is brought into effect (s 25(3)); further confirmation, if it were needed, that two schemes of disclosure will continue to operate.

---

1 See para **2.23**. Duties imposed on persons other than the prosecutor are unaffected by the new Act: see para **2.84**. For the meaning of 'prosecutor', see annotations to s 2.
2 Baroness Blatch, Minister of State, Home Office, HL Report, col 1561.
3 See paras **2.7–2.8**
4 See para **2.6**.

GENERAL SCOPE OF THE DISCLOSURE PROVISIONS

2.10 At first sight, Part I of the new Act appears to create a comprehensive statutory scheme governing disclosure, supplemented by the provisions of a Code of Practice. However, what the Act does is to impose certain duties, and it does not, broadly speaking, take away the discretion on the part of the prosecution or the defence to engage in disclosure going beyond those obligations if either wishes to do so.[1] A prosecutor may, subject to the one exception set out below, invite the defence to inspect all the material it has gathered, or an accused may choose to reveal in advance his case in considerable detail. Further, the wider context should be noted. Prosecuting counsel are bound by the Bar's Code of Conduct which sets out that:

> 'Prosecuting counsel should not attempt to obtain a conviction by all means at his command. He should not regard himself as appearing for a party. He should lay before the court fairly and impartially the whole of the facts which comprise the case for the prosecution and should assist the court on all matters of law applicable to the case.'

In the case of a solicitor advocate, the Code of Conduct for Crown Prosecutors may apply, as may any Code adopted by The Law Society for advocates.

In the introduction to that Code of Conduct for Crown Prosecutors, it is provided that 'fair and effective prosecution is essential to the maintenance of law and order', and in the section headed 'General Principles' it stipulates that 'the duty of the CPS is to make sure ... that all relevant facts are given to the court', and that 'Crown Prosecutors must be fair'.

The one exception to the principle that the prosecutor may disclose any material he wishes is in respect of material withheld on the grounds that disclosure is not in the public interest, pursuant to ss 3(6), 7(5) and 8(5), or information withheld because of the fact that it has been intercepted in obedience to a warrant issued under s 2 of the Interception of Communications Act 1985 (ss 3(7), 7(6) and 8(6)). In each of these instances the relevant words used in the subsection are 'must not be disclosed', and therefore no discretion to disclose exists. This is discussed further at para **2.76**.

---

1 See Baroness Blatch, Minister of State, Home Office, HL Committee, col 1486.

SUMMARY OF PROVISION IN CROWN COURT CASES

2.11   In summary, the scheme introduced by Part I of the new Act is as follows:

The *prosecutor* is under a duty to disclose to the defence certain material, during *primary prosecution disclosure*. The material to be disclosed at this stage is material which, in the opinion of the prosecutor, might undermine the prosecution case.[1] The prosecutor also discloses the schedule of non-sensitive material.

The prosecutor is placed in a position to fulfil this duty by the disclosure officer appointed under the Code of Practice.[2] The prosecutor is supplied by the disclosure officer with copies of material relied on, certain other material and a schedule of non-sensitive material obtained during the investigation.

The *accused* is required to engage in *defence disclosure*. A written statement must be supplied to the prosecution, providing sufficient particulars of the defence to identify the issues in dispute before the start of the trial. This process will also enable the prosecution to assess whether it has any additional unused material which might assist the defence case. The more specific the particulars provided by the defence, the more likely that the prosecution will be able accurately to identify any additional material which might be relevant or possibly relevant to an issue identified by the defence.

The *prosecutor* must engage in *secondary prosecution disclosure*. This means that he must disclose any unused material which may assist the particular line of argument disclosed by the defence.[3]

A *failure to disclose the defence* case at the appropriate stage, or an attempt to overcome the limitations on prosecution disclosure by running different lines of argument in succession, may be the subject of comment at trial, and a court or jury may draw such inferences as appear proper from the failure or conduct of the defence in this respect.[4]

Disputes between prosecution and defence as to compliance with the duties of disclosure are to be resolved by a court at a pre-trial hearing.[5] Disputes will be resolved in accordance with criteria which are so drawn as to focus on the issues properly identified by the defence or which might reasonably be expected to be raised at the trial.

The disclosure of sensitive material will continue to be subject to review by the court.[6] Disclosure of relevant sensitive material may only be withheld if a court concludes that it is not in the public interest to disclose material, and orders accordingly.[7]

1 See para **2.34**.
2 See para **3.10**.
3 See para **2.68**.
4 See para **2.67**.
5 For pre-trial rulings, see paras **4.6–4.15**.
6 See para **2.81**.
7 See paras **3.56–3.63**.

APPLICATION TO SUMMARY TRIAL

2.12   Part I of the new Act applies to proceedings which will be tried summarily. The application in summary proceedings of rules relating to prosecution disclosure had been a matter of doubt at common law.

In *Crown Prosecution Service ex parte Warby*,[1] the court decided that the interests of justice required that decisions as to whether material should be disclosed should be restricted to Crown Courts, and were not matters for consideration by magistrates' courts. However, *ex parte Warby* was a case concerned with committal proceedings where the purpose of the proceedings is merely to decide whether or not sufficient evidence exists to justify committal for trial.[2] The case did not determine more generally the extent of common law disclosure obligations in summary trials and, as was later recognised in *Bromley MC ex parte Smith and Wilkins*,[3] different considerations apply to committal proceedings than apply to summary trial itself.

1 (1993) 157 JP 190 (DC).
2 For the new arrangements in respect of committal for trial, see s 47 and Sch 1, and Chapter 6.
3 (1994) 159 JP 251 (DC).

2.13   The exact application of the common law rules relating to disclosure of evidence by the prosecution in summary proceedings was put beyond doubt in *ex parte Smith and Wilkins*, where Simon Brown LJ said:

> 'Common sense and justice alike demand that whether the proceedings are summary or on indictment the same processes with regard to the disclosure of unused material must apply, ie those processes which a series of recent cases have now established are necessary to guard against miscarriages of justice in jury trials. An accused is as much entitled to the safeguard designed to ensure a fair trial in the magistrates' court as in the Crown Court.'

The court concluded that it was not bound by *ex parte Warby*, and that the duty of disclosure applied equally in summary and indictable cases.

Whether, in practical terms, disclosure plays, or will play, much of a role in the vast majority of summary cases is, of course, a very different matter. Nevertheless, the terms of s 1(1)[1] make it clear that the provisions relating to disclosure of material by the prosecution extend to all cases where a person pleads not guilty to an offence being tried summarily, irrespective of whether it is an either way offence or an offence triable only summarily. They also extend to cases where a person under the age of 18[2] pleads not guilty to an indictable offence in respect of which a court proceeds to summary trial (s 1(1)).

---

1 See para **2.7**.
2 See general annotations.

2.14   Two issues are worth specific comment. The first is in respect of defence disclosure. The duty of compulsory disclosure by an accused person, under s 5(1), only applies in the situations identified by s 1(2)[1] (ie where proceedings for an indictable offence are committed or transferred to the Crown Court, a summary offence is included in an indictment under the authority of s 40 of the Criminal Justice Act 1988, or a voluntary bill of indictment is preferred). It does not apply in the circumstances identified in s 1(1) (ie where there is summary trial of a summary or either way offence). However, by s 6(1), in such circumstances an accused may engage in voluntary disclosure by giving a defence statement. Defence representatives will need to consider whether such voluntary disclosure is advantageous. If disclosure is made pursuant to s 6 then the sanction contained in s 11(2)[2] for subsequent reliance at trial on an inconsistent defence, on a different defence or for failing to give particulars of an alibi, will apply. The potential for comment by the trial court, or by any other party at the trial, arises, as does the potential for the drawing of such inferences as appear to a court proper in deciding guilt (s 11(3)). These sanctions and potential do not, of course, arise if no voluntary disclosure has been made.

---

1 See para **2.8**.
2 See para **2.67**.

2.15   Secondly, prosecution disclosure only arises in cases where an offence is being tried summarily where a plea of not guilty has been entered. The Criminal Law Committee of The Law Society has said[1] that, in the future, should any question about the adequacy of the prosecution case arise, a client should be advised to plead not guilty in order to gain access to the prosecution case, and in order that the evidential basis created by the criminal investigation should be revealed by the investigator to the prosecutor.[2] The justification given by the Government for limiting disclosure in cases being tried summarily to cases where a plea of not guilty is tendered is that the prosecutor would otherwise be put to a great deal of work to no useful purpose in the very many cases where the accused intends to plead guilty all along.[3] However, if the advice of The Law Society were to be followed in a widespread way, the possible savings which might otherwise occur in terms of work for the police and investigators would largely be negated, and the courts might end up being clogged with a large number of not guilty cases, in which the plea was entered for tactical reasons.

---

1 See Lord McIntosh, HL Committee, col 1559.
2 For the meaning of these terms, see paras **3.10** and **3.45**.
3 Baroness Blatch, Minister of State, Home Office, HL Committee, col 1562.

2.16 Particular procedural problems may arise in the context of applications in summary cases to withhold material on the grounds that disclosure is not in the public interest.[1] The pre-existing law permitted material to be withheld where disclosure was not in the public interest. The rules relating to non-disclosure in such circumstances remain unaffected by the new Act.[1] As was the case under the pre-existing law,[2] such claims are for a court to adjudicate upon, and, now, ss 3(6), 7(5), 8(5) and 9(8) each empower the court to make such an adjudication if an application is made for that purpose by a prosecutor. Such applications may be made to a magistrates' court in respect of cases being, or to be tried, summarily. Further, s 14(1) provides that after an order that material be withheld has been made, and before the accused is acquitted or convicted or the prosecutor decides not to proceed with the case concerned, the accused may apply to the court for a review of the question whether it is still not in the public interest to disclose material affected by its order. A magistrates' court may therefore have to determine, under these various provisions, applications to withhold otherwise disclosable material, either before the substantive trial commences or during that trial. The issue then arises as to whether or not procedural fairness requires the substantive case to be heard, or re-heard, by a different bench of magistrates. A similar issue arose in *South Worcestershire Magistrates ex parte Lilley*.[3] In that case, the prosecution had served on the defence a schedule of unused material, one item of which was said to be too sensitive to be disclosed, and thus protected by public interest immunity. The justices considered the contents of an envelope handed to them by the prosecution, and excluded the applicant and his solicitor from the proceedings for about 20 minutes. During this period, evidence was heard from the investigating officer and submissions received from the prosecuting solicitor. When the applicant and his solicitor rejoined the court, the justices stated that the sensitive material was immaterial, thereby refusing disclosure and upholding the claim of public interest immunity. The applicant's solicitor thereupon submitted that it was undesirable for the same bench of justices to adjudicate in the trial itself, because the applicant would suspect that the fairness of the proceedings would be prejudiced as a result of what had taken place in his absence. That submission was rejected by the justices. When their decision was challenged in judicial review proceedings, the Divisional Court held that where in a summary trial justices have ruled, after consideration of a public interest immunity claim, that the unused material should not be shown to the defence, they have a discretion in the interests of justice to order that the case be tried by a different bench of justices. On the particular facts of this case, the refusal by the justices who had ruled on the public interest immunity claim to disqualify themselves from hearing the trial was *Wednesbury* unreasonable,[4] and thus invalid.

In each case, therefore, a judgment will have to be made as to whether, as a result of the performance by a magistrates' court of its supervisory and regulatory functions under the new Act, there is an appearance of unfairness which can be overcome only by the matter being dealt with by a different bench.

1 See paras **2.76–2.82**.
2 See *Davis* [1993] 2 All ER 643 (CA); cf *Ward* [1993] 2 All ER 577 (CA).
3 (1995) 159 JP 598 (DC).
4 See *Associated Provincial Picture Houses v Wednesbury Corporation* [1948] 1 KB 223 (CA).

THE PRE-EXISTING LAW AND PRACTICE

Statutory framework

2.17 Unlike the situation in civil proceedings, where discovery is generally available, the duties of pre-trial disclosure in criminal cases have generally been limited. The prosecution has always been under a duty to disclose at committal for trial the evidence upon which it proposes to rely, subject only to the right to call additional evidence in some circumstances and subject to certain conditions. Further, in the case of either way offences which are tried summarily, the Magistrates' Courts (Advance Information) Rules 1985[1] require advance disclosure where it is requested by the defence. By contrast, the defence have never been under a general duty to disclose. The so called 'right of silence' permits the defence at any stage to adduce evidence without notice, and without adverse inferences being drawn in law from that prior non-disclosure, a general rule modified in certain circumstances by statute.[2]

1 SI 1985/601.
2 See, in particular, the Criminal Justice and Public Order Act 1994, ss 34–38, and annotations
  to s 20 and s 44 of the new Act.

2.18 Section 20(1) generally preserves any statutory duties arising under any other enactment with regard to material to be provided to or by the accused or a person representing him, subject to s 20(2) which deals specifically with preparatory hearings held under s 9 of the Criminal Justice Act 1987 (as to which, see below) or under s 31 of the new Act.[1]

The relevant pre-existing statutory provisions are:

(a) *Criminal Justice Act 1967, s 11 (notice of alibi):*[2] this will cease to apply in the case of alleged offences into which no criminal investigation has begun before the appointed day (s 74(5)). In a trial which involves several offences, the investigations into some of which (but not all) commenced before the appointed day, there may therefore be two different sets of rules operating. The impact of this is considered further at para **2.64**.

(b) *PACE, s 81, and Crown Court (Advance Disclosure of Expert Evidence) Rules 1987:*[3] these continue in force (1996 Act, s 20(1)). However, s 20(3) of the new Act empowers the making of rules that may extend advance disclosure of expert evidence to proceedings in magistrates' courts. No such rules have been made as at the date of going to press.

(c) *Criminal Justice Act 1987, s 9 (cases of serious or complex fraud):*[4] the judge may order the defence to provide a statement setting out in general terms the nature of the defence. This remains unaffected by the new Act (s 20(1)).

However, by s 20(2), a judge may, in making an order under s 9 of the 1987 Act, take account of anything which:

(a) has been done;

(b) has been required to be done; or

(c) will be required to be done,

in pursuance of any of the disclosure provisions.

The provisions of ss 34 to 38 of the Criminal Justice and Public Order Act 1994 must also be noted. These do not require the defendant to do anything, but do permit inferences to be drawn if a person in certain circumstances in fact does not mention the matters specified in these sections.[5] These provisions are likewise unaffected by Part I of the new Act.

1 See paras **4.16–4.32**.
2 See para **2.62**, and annotations to s 5.
3 SI 1985/601.
4 See annotations to s 20.
5 See Card and Ward: *Criminal Justice and Public Order Act 1994* (Jordans, 1994), Ch 5. For amendments to these provisions, see s 44.

Attorney-General's Guidelines[1]

2.19 A common law duty of disclosure on the prosecution was recognised in *Bryant and Dickson*,[2] although the precise nature and extent of that duty was a matter of considerable uncertainty and debate, particularly as to whether the duty went beyond disclosure of the name of a witness to include a requirement to disclose any witness statement given to the prosecution by that witness.[3] It was to deal with these uncertainties and ambiguities that, in 1981, the Attorney-General issued Guidelines dealing with the disclosure of the prosecution of unused material. These Guidelines no longer represent accurately the extent of the duty imposed on prosecutors and others by the courts and, in the end, have now come to serve as guidance as to how, in the context of the common law, the duties of disclosure were to be fulfilled.[4] Nevertheless, their value is not simply as guidance, but also to demonstrate the shift both of the common law and of the new statutory disclosure regime.

1 (1981) 74 Cr App R 302 (CA).
2 *Lawson* (1989) 90 Cr App R 107 (CA).
3 (1946) 31 Cr App R 146 (CA).
4 See *Brown* [1995] 1 Cr App R 191 (CA), and para **2.22**.

2.20 The Guidelines state as follows:

(1) 'Unused material' includes all witness statements and documents not included in the committal papers served on the defence, together with the statements of those giving oral evidence at committal, and the edited versions of all statements.

(2) All unused material in cases committed for trial is normally to be made available to the defence if it had some bearing on the offences charged and the surrounding circumstances of the case. Disclosure was to be made

as soon as practicable, if possible before committal proceedings, for the material disclosed might have relevance to the decisions as to how those proceedings are to be conducted, and what form they should take.

(3) Discretion exists to refuse disclosure in certain circumstances:

   (i) where disclosure might lead to an attempt being made to persuade a witness to make a statement retracting an earlier one, to change his story, not to appear in court, or otherwise to intimidate him;

   (ii) a statement (eg from a relative or close friend) is believed to be wholly or partially untrue, and might be of use in cross-examination if the witness should be called by the defence;

   (iii) a statement is favourable to the defence and believed to be substantially true, but there are grounds for fearing that the witness (due to feelings of loyalty or fear) might give the defence solicitor a quite different story;

   (iv) a statement is quite neutral or negative, and there is no reason to doubt its truthfulness, but where there are grounds to believe that the witness may change his story.

In these cases, the defence should have been given the witness's name and address.

   (v) The document is a sensitive statement and it is not in the public interest to disclose it. For example, it may deal with matters relating to national security, or reveal the identity of a member of the security services who, as a result, would be of no further use to them; it might disclose the identity of an informant who might be put in danger, or of a witness who may be in danger of assault or intimidation; it may reveal details which might facilitate the commission of other offences, or alert someone that they may be a suspect.

If doubt existed under the Guidelines the advice of counsel was to be sought.

2.21 The Guidelines identified the fact that a balance needs to be struck between the preservation of the sensitivity of material (on the one hand) and the disclosure of information that might genuinely assist the defence (on the other). They made clear that doubts should be resolved in favour of the defence. However, their status was unclear. The Royal Commission on Criminal Justice stated that 'the Guidelines, although not statutory, to all intents and purposes have the force of law'.[1] Further, in *Saunders*,[2] Henry J stated:

'It seems to me that any defendant must be entitled to approach his trial on the basis that the prosecution will have complied with the Attorney General's Guidelines.'

1 Op cit, p 91, n 20.
2 29 September 1989, unreported (CA).

2.22 However, others took a different view. One writer described the

Guidelines as, 'merely a set of instructions to Crown Prosecution Service lawyers and prosecuting counsel'.[1] This view was confirmed and put beyond doubt by the Court of Appeal in *Brown*.[2] In that case, Steyn LJ concluded that:

> 'Judged simply as a set of instructions to prosecutors, the guidelines would be unobjectionable if they exactly matched the contours of the common law duty of non-disclosure. If they set higher standards of disclosure than the common law, that would equally be unobjectionable. But if the guidelines, judged by the standards of today, reduced the common law duties of the Crown and thus abridge the common law rights of the defendant, they must be pro-tanto unlawful . . . .'

He stated that it is for the court, not prosecuting counsel, to decide on disputed questions as to disclosable materials and decide on any asserted ground to withhold production of relevant material,[3] and the procedure to be adopted to deal with such disputes.[4] For these reasons, he considered the value of the Guidelines to have largely been eroded by the major developments set out below, and also considered that it was in the public interest that this reality should be squarely faced and addressed.

---

1 O'Connor *Prosecution Disclosure: Principle, Practice and Justice* [1992] Crim LR 464 at 468; see also *Re Barlow Clowes Ltd* [1992] Ch 208 at 291.
2 [1995] 1 Cr App R 191 (CA).
3 *Ward* (1993) 96 Cr App R 1 (CA).
4 *Davis, Johnson and Rowe* (1993) 97 Cr App R 110 (CA).

The common law position

2.23   The common law rules relating to disclosure remain important in the context of the general duty of disclosure, of the concept of materiality, and of public interest immunity claims in respect of relevant material. They continue to apply in respect of investigations into offences which commenced prior to the appointed day,[1] continue to define the basis on which public interest grounds for refusal of disclosure are to be judged, and provide the context for an assessment of the significance of the changes.

In *Saunders*,[2] Henry J ruled that 'it is clear the term "unused material" may apply to virtually all material collected during the investigation of a case'. This amounted to a significant extension of the duty of disclosure on the prosecution; the defence thus being entitled to obtain all preparatory material which led to witnesses making statements. The prosecution had no discretion in the matter, as it was a matter for the defence to assess the potential evidential value of the material collected.

As a result of this decision, the term 'unused material' applied to virtually all the material collected during a criminal investigation, thus potentially imposing considerable procedural burdens upon the prosecution, as well as potentially including a wide range of sensitive material.[3]

---

1 See s 20(1), and para **2.9**.
2 29 September 1989, unreported.
3 See para **2.78**.

2.24 In *Keane*,[1] the court adopted the test suggested by Jowitt J in *Melvin and Dingle*,[2] where he said:

> 'I would judge to be material in the realm of disclosure that which can be seen on a sensible appraisal by the prosecution: (1) to be relevant or possibly relevant to an issue in the case; (2) to raise or possibly raise a new issue whose existence is not apparent from the evidence the prosecution proposes to use; (3) to hold out a real (as opposed to fanciful) prospect of providing a lead on evidence which goes to (1) or (2).'

Further, in *Brown*,[3] the court (whilst adopting the tests propounded by Jowitt J) stressed that the phrase 'an issue in the case' must not be construed in the fairly narrow way in which it is used in a civil case but, rather, must be interpreted broadly. It included material not merely going to the actual issues, but also material which may affect the credibility of a prosecution witness. The previous inconsistent statements of prosecution witnesses,[4] the fact that a prosecution witness has made a request for a reward,[5] or that a prosecution witness has previous convictions[6] were all thus disclosable under the common law test. So, too, was the fact that a police officer witness had had disciplinary charges affecting his credit proved against him.[7]

The practical effect of these common law disclosure requirements was to place heavy burdens on investigating and prosecuting authorities, with results which were not always in the interests of justice.[8] In 1993 the Royal Commission on Criminal Justice stated that:

> 'The defence can require the police and prosecution to comb through large masses of material in the hope either of causing delay or of chancing upon something that will induce the prosecution to drop the case rather than have to disclose the material concerned. The defence may do this by successive requests for more material, far beyond the stage at which it could be reasonably claimed that the information was likely to cast a doubt upon the prosecution case. Although it may be time consuming and wasteful of the sources for the police to check all the materials requested, they may have to do so if they are to be sure that it can properly be released.'[9]

---

1 (1994) 99 Cr App R 1 (CA).
2 20 December 1993, unreported (CA).
3 [1995] 1 Cr App R 191 (CA).
4 See *Brown*, op cit. This conclusion is also implicit in *Reading JJ ex parte Berkshire CC* (1995) *The Times*, 5 May (DC); *Derby MC ex parte B* [1995] 4 All ER 526, [1995] 3 WLR 681 (HL).
5 *Taylor* 11 June 1993, unreported (CA); *Rasheed* (1994) *The Times*, 20 May (CA).
6 *Wilson v Police* [1992] 2 NZLR 533 (NZCA). In that case, Cooke P stated: 'As to the kind of conviction within the scope of the duty, the test must be whether a reasonable jury or other tribunal of fact could regard it as tending to shake confidence in the reliability of the witness'. See also *Edwards* [1991] 2 All ER 266.
7 *Edwards* [1991] 2 All ER 266 (CA).
8 Consultation Paper (1993) Cm 2262, HMSO, Ch 2, para 10.
9 Op cit, Ch 6, para 42.

2.25 In one case cited in the Government's Consultation Paper,[1] defence counsel asked to see some 170 surveillance logs and a large quantity of contemporaneous notes of covert audio tapes. The Consultation Paper records that defence counsel did not examine them at all. However, at a pre-trial review in the case, the judge granted a defence request for copies of over 200 audio tapes, with one copy for each of the six defendants. This apparently left the police with the burden of reducing and labelling over 1200 audio tapes within a 21-day deadline. As the Consultation Paper records, 'the current laws oblige the courts to order disclosure in cases where the actual relevance of the sensitive material may be marginal at best, and which in any event does not have to be adequately justified by the defence. An adverse ruling requiring disclosure of the identity of a police informant may damage the public interest in two ways: it may place the informant's life in danger, and it may deter others from coming forward in the future and helping the police'.[2] The Consultation Paper records other instances of where sensitive information has caused difficulties.[3]

However, it should not be forgotten that in each of these instances disclosure will have been at the instance of a court which has concluded that the disputed matter was relevant and material.

1 Consultation Paper (1993) Cm 2262, HMSO, Ch 2, para 13.
2 Op cit, Ch 2, para 14.
3 Op cit, Ch 2, para 15.

REASONS FOR CHANGING THE LAW

2.26 The Government's Consultation Paper noted that the common law requirements 'place heavy burdens' on the investigating and prosecution authorities, with results that may not be in the interest of justice. The requirements could be burdensome in the light of the volume of material which must be disclosed and, as already seen, because of the difficulties concerning sensitive information, such as the identity of police informants or the disclosure of confidential information. By contrast, the defence was not generally required[1] to disclose anything about its case in advance of trial, although the practice of the 'Keane letter' grew up, with the prosecutor identifying the issues believed to exist for the purposes of making decisions as to prosecution disclosure, and inviting the defence to clarify the defence position. The lack of an obligation to disclose in advance of trial, in the view of the Government, created opportunities for 'ambush defences'. In 1994, the Home Secretary, Michael Howard, QC, MP, observed: 'for too long hardened criminals have refused to answer police questions, only to ambush the prosecution by raising a defence at trial for the first time'.[2]

The extent to which ambush defences justified altering the rules regarding defence disclosure is arguable, given that considerable doubt exists as to the extent to which in reality ambush defences create difficulties. In a study for the Royal Commission,[3] Zander and Henderson found that 'last minute' defences were raised in between 7 to 10% of Crown Court trials, but that half of these eventually ended in a conviction. Other research undertaken by Leng[4] found the incidents of ambush defences to be less, and with less significant results. Of course, these research studies were themselves conducted before the effects of ss 34 to 38 of the Criminal Justice and Public Order Act 1994 became apparent: arguably, the effect of those provisions has been to result in greater disclosure by defendants at the investigatory stage.[5] Furthermore, even where disclosure of a defence is not made at the investigatory or pre-trial stage, the nature of the defence often will be obvious.

On the other hand, some supported the proposed greater elements of defence disclosure.[6] Such disclosure might encourage earlier and better preparation for the case, might result in the prosecution being dropped, might result in an earlier resolution of the case through a plea of guilty, and might prevent a defendant withholding his defence until the last minute, thereby evading the investigation of fabricated evidence.

1 Except in the situations discussed at para **2.18**.
2 HC Deb, 11 January 1994, col 26.
3 *Crown Court Study* RCCJ Research Study No 19, HMSO, 1993.
4 *The Right to Silence in Police Interviews* RCCJ Research Study No 10, HMSO, 1993.
5 See *Counsel* Sept–Oct 1995.
6 See, eg, representations by the Criminal Bar Association.

THE NEW LAW – PRIMARY PROSECUTION DISCLOSURE

The duty

2.27 By s 3(1), the prosecutor[1] must:

(a) disclose to the accused any prosecution material which has not been previously disclosed to the accused and which, in the prosecutor's opinion, might undermine the case for the prosecution against the accused; or
(b) give to the accused a written statement that there is no such material.

At the same time, the prosecutor must give to the accused any schedule of non-sensitive material he has received from the disclosure officer (s 4(2)). This duty is imposed on the prosecutor, not the investigating officer or the disclosure officer.[2] No direct sanction applies if the prosecutor fails to comply with this duty but, in such circumstances, the failure may be a ground of challenge by the accused,[3] and no obligation for the accused to engage in defence disclosure arises.

1 See annotations to s 2.
2 See paras **3.10** and **3.53**.
3 See paras **2.44** and **2.75**.

'Material'

2.28 'Material' is defined by s 2(4) as including material of all kinds, including information and objects of all descriptions. The breadth of this definition is such as to include all documents,[1] items of real evidence, and material in the form of information stored on computer disk or in any other way. It includes samples, whether intimate (such as blood) or non-intimate (such as saliva). Any doubt about this was dispelled during the passage of the Act when, in the context of proposed amendments to Part II of the Act, it was confirmed that the widest interpretation was to be placed on this definition, whether in Part I or Part II.[2]

1 See annotations to s 4.
2 See Mr Timothy Kirkhope, MP, Parliamentary Under Secretary of State, Home Office, HC Committee, col 103.

Prosecution material

2.29   The definition of 'material' was noted in para **2.28**. Section 3(2) defines 'prosecution material'. It comprises material:

(a)   which is in the prosecutor's possession,[1] and came into his possession in connection with the case for the prosecution against the accused; or
(b)   which, in pursuance of a code operative under Part II, he has inspected in connection with the case for the prosecution against the accused.

The wording of (a) above is intended to limit the duty to disclose to material that has come into the possession of the prosecutor in connection with the case in issue. Without this formulation, the prosecutor would potentially be under a duty of disclosure, irrespective of whether there is any bearing on the case being prosecuted.[2] It is intended to prevent 'trawling' – the depositing of large bundles of material, which might be material evidence (but frequently is not) in the hands of a judge for decision.[2] For similar reasons, the definition of 'prosecution material' in s 3(2)(b) is limited to material inspected in connection with the case against the accused. On a literal interpretation, s 3(2) does not include material possessed or inspected in connection with the case against a co-accused, even if it puts the prosecution case against the accused himself in a new light. Of course, in the vast majority of cases such evidence is likely to be regarded as fulfilling the requirements of s 3(2).

On a literal interpretation, s 3(2) does not require disclosure of material obtained by the prosecutor for other purposes but which, nevertheless, would clearly undermine the prosecution case. Nor, literally, would disclosure be required under the secondary prosecution disclosure requirements of s 7,[3] because, again, that is an obligation that arises in respect of 'prosecution material'. However, s 3(2) has to be read subject to the basic duty of the prosecutor to act fairly, which surely deals with the point. The problem might have been totally avoided if the new Act had contained a positive duty to disclose material which was likely to assist the defence.[4]

1 See para **2.30**, and annotations to s 3.
2 Sir Derek Spencer, QC, MP, Solicitor-General, HC Committee, cols 41–42.
3 See paras **2.68–2.70**.
4 See amendment proposed by Baroness Mallalieu, HL Committee, col 1445.

In the possession of the prosecutor or inspected by him

2.30 The terms of s 3(2) have already been noted, as have some of the issues that arise. Clearly, the prosecutor should be in possession of material acquired during the investigation stage which falls within the duty of disclosure within the terms of s 3. This is because para 7.3 of the draft Code of Practice requires the disclosure officer not simply to prepare schedules of relevant material not forming part of the prosecution case, but also to supply to the prosecutor a copy of material which it is believed might fall within the test for primary prosecution disclosure. If he does not, the prosecutor can, generally, require a copy.[1] Only if an investigator wrongly believes that material is not disclosable and the prosecutor takes no action, does disclosable material fail to become prosecution material. The remedies available to the accused in such situations are discussed later.[2]

Another question that arises is that of disclosure of material in the hands of third parties. Important material may be held by forensic scientists,[3] doctors or other experts. In some cases, large quantities of relevant material may be held by bodies such as banks, solicitors, accountants, investigators or local authorities. In child abuse cases, highly relevant material relating to the welfare of the child, and the conduct of those charged with the duty of care of that child, may be in the hands of social services. Relevant material may have been acquired by persons working in a counselling or therapeutic capacity with a person later accused. Thus, for example, records may be kept by those who work on behaviour management programmes with sexual offenders. Furthermore, in other instances, there may be notes of interviews or other material in the hands of third party investigators.

---

1 Draft Code, para 7.4. See text, para **3.46**.
2 See para **2.75**.
3 The duty of disclosure on the forensic scientist himself is unaffected by the new Act: see para **2.84**.

2.31 If third party material has been given to the prosecutor, no problems arise in this context: the material falls within s 3(2)(a) ('material in the possession of the prosecutor ...'). Alternatively, the prosecutor may possess a copy of that material, by virtue of the operation of the Code of Practice. Paragraph 4.1 of the draft Code states that 'when information is obtained or inspected in the course of a criminal investigation, it must be recorded at the time it is obtained or inspected or as soon as is practicable after that time'. Therefore, the investigating officer will, or should, have a record of material that has been produced to, or seen by, him. As already noted, the prosecutor will be entitled, under para 7.4 of the draft Code, to inspect material not copied to him by the investigating or disclosure officer, and, if the prosecutor requests a copy, he must be given such a copy.

Thus, the prosecutor can obtain, and therefore disclose to the defence, copies of all relevant material that has in fact been recorded. Material which has been seen by the prosecutor, but not recorded, nevertheless amounts to 'information' within the meaning of s 2(4), and is also disclosable.

Disclosure of information which has not been recorded is achieved by virtue of s 3(4). Section 3(4) provides that, where material consists of information which has not been recorded, the prosecutor discloses it for the purpose of s 3 by securing that it is recorded in such form as he thinks fit and:

(a) by securing that a copy is made of it and that the copy is given to the accused; or

(b) if in the prosecutor's opinion that it is not practicable or not desirable, by allowing the accused to inspect it at a reasonable time and a reasonable place or by taking steps to secure that he is allowed to do so.

The mechanisms therefore exist to ensure that disclosable material originally held by third parties but to which the prosecutor has had access is within the primary prosecution disclosure rules. Plainly, however, a prosecutor cannot disclose that which he has not seen, although the fact that there is relevant material in the hands of a third party might itself be disclosable information. Third party disclosure thus raises wider issues. However, at this stage it should be noted that nothing in the new Act removes any duty of disclosure the law imposes on third parties. Section 2(1)(b) only abrogates rules of common law which applied to the prosecutor. Thus the rules that impose requirements on forensic scientists[1] remain in force.

---

1 *Maguire* [1992] 2 All ER 433 (CA). See para **2.84**.

The pre-condition

2.32 The pre-condition for prosecution disclosure is that the prosecutor must have formed the opinion that material which has not been previously disclosed to the accused might undermine the case for the prosecution against the accused (s 3(2)). There appears to be no duty to disclose material which might undermine the case of the accused.[1] Such material does not meet the test for prosecution disclosure in s 3(2), and thus the new law appears to be the same as the pre-existing position at common law. In *Brown*, the Court of Appeal decided that the prosecution's duty of disclosure did not extend to material which is only relevant to the credibility of a defence witness.[1] The position in respect of material that enhances the credibility of a defence witness is different, in that it is more likely to fulfil the test in s 3(2), although does not inevitably do so.[2]

The use of the term 'prosecutor's opinion' points clearly to the judgment being subjective, not objective.[3] Furthermore, the difference in phraseology between s 3(1)(a) ('prosecutor's opinion') and s 7(2)(a) ('might reasonably be expected to assist the accused's defence') points to the test in the former being purely subjective. If an objective test had been adopted then, in summary cases, judicial review of the decision of the prosecutor would have been available, causing potential for delay in a large number of cases. The provisions of s 29 of the Supreme Court Act 1981 might prevent similar review in the context of the trial on indictment in the Crown Court.[4] For these reasons, the judgment made by the prosecutor under s 3(1) appears at this stage in the proceedings to be beyond challenge.

1 *Brown* [1995] 1 Cr App R 512 (CA): leave to appeal on this issue has been granted by the House of Lords. See also *Seymour* [1996] Crim LR 512 (CA); cf *Philipson* (1990) 91 Cr App R 226.
2 See para **2.35**.
3 See Baroness Blatch, Minister of State, Home Office, HL Committee, col 1440. Attempts during the passage of the new Act to substitute for this subjective test an objective test failed: see Lord McIntosh HL Committee, col 1438.
4 See, eg, *Chester Crown Court ex parte Cheshire CC* [1996] Crim LR 336 (CA); *Manchester Crown Court ex parte DPP* [1993] 1 WLR 1524 (HL). See, further, para **4.7**.

2.33   The subjective nature of the test was the subject of considerable debate and criticism during the passage of the new Act, with one criticism being that the prosecutor may not be the best person to make the judgment that the new Act requires. Further, past experience of failures to comply with disclosure requirements left some lacking in confidence that the subjective approach creates significant safeguards against misjudgment or abuse.[1] Nevertheless, the subjective approach is seen as a key element of the approach taken by the new Act, with the functions to be carried out within a clear framework of professional ethics and of (for Crown Prosecutors) the Code for Crown Prosecutors. It may be that the main criticism of the proposals is not in respect of the subjective element but, rather, the test that the prosecutor is expected to apply. This is discussed at para **2.34**.

1 See, eg, Lord Williams of Mostyn, HL 3rd Reading, col 868; Mr Chris Mullin MP, HC 2nd Reading, cols 767–771; Mr Alun Michael, MP, HC Committee, cols 31–32. The Scott Inquiry found examples where the Government's attitude to disclosure of documents was 'grudging': see *Inquiry into Exports of Defence Equipment and Dual-Use Goods to Iraq and Related Prosecutions* (1996) HC 115, Vol III, para G18.37, and the cases cited therein.

2.34   The material which must be disclosed is that which, in the prosecutor's opinion, might undermine the case for the prosecution against the accused (s 3(1)). This is a narrower test than one which requires disclosure of all relevant material, as existed at common law prior to the passage of the new Act common law, and is intended to be so.[1] A test of relevance, which includes everything which might possibly have a bearing on the case, is very different from whether it actually has a bearing on the case relied on in court. The Royal Commission recommended that '...the prosecution's initial duty should be to supply to the defence copies of all material relevant to the offence or to the offender or to the surrounding circumstances of the case, whether or not the prosecution intend to rely on that material'.[2] This was specifically rejected by the Government, which considered this approach to be too wide.[3] The intention is that the police should less often have to photocopy and deliver large volumes of material, much of it unnecessary in the sense that it is ultimately irrelevant to the actual defence being run. Furthermore, a test of relevance would largely render redundant the provisions relating to secondary prosecution disclosure contained in s 7 of the Act. However, it can equally be argued that the burdens which were inherent in the pre-existing common law position arose not simply because of the quantity of material involved (although that was often an issue), but also because of the difficulties of selection of the material to fulfil the disclosure tests. Because the burden of disclosure imposed by s 3(1) is placed on the prosecutor, the task of selection, and ensuring that the judgments of those who have responsibilities under the draft Code of Practice for investigations or for disclosure[4] are correct ones, will remain an onerous one.

1 Baroness Blatch, Minister of State, Home Office, HL Committee, col 1437.
2 Op cit, Ch 6, para 42.
3 See Mr David MacLean, Minister of State, Home Office, HC Committee, col 40.
4 See para **3.10**.

'Undermine the case for the prosecution'

2.35 The application of this test causes difficulty. Its intent was described as follows:

> 'The test for primary prosecution disclosure is designed to ensure that the prosecutor discloses at the first stage material that, generally speaking, has an adverse effect on the strength of the prosecution case. It is not confined to material raising a fundamental question about the prosecution. If there were a fundamental question about the prosecution, it is unlikely that the prosecutor would proceed with the case. Guilt must be proved beyond reasonable doubt and, as the Code of Practice for Crown Prosecutors makes clear, the prosecutor may not bring proceedings unless there is a realistic prospect of conviction. The disclosure scheme is aimed at undisclosed material that might help the accused, notwithstanding the fact that there is enough evidence to provide a realistic prospect of conviction.'[1]

In other words, any material which significantly weakens the prosecution case must be disclosed, even if a conviction may still be a likely consequence. By contrast, it is submitted that there is no duty to disclose material which weakens peripheral aspects of the prosecution case, but which do not have a significant impact on it.

1 Baroness Blatch, Minister of State, Home Office, HL Committee, cols 866–867.

2.36 These general statements do not wholly assist in determining the scope of the duty placed on the prosecutor. More assistance is gained from specific examples which would fall within the duty of the prosecutor to disclose. Such examples might include the following:

(a) If a part of the prosecution case is a statement by a witness that he saw the accused near the scene of the crime shortly after it was committed, it would be necessary to disclose a statement by another witness that he saw a person of a different description from the accused at the same time and place.

(b) If the accused has told the police in an interview that he was acting in self-defence, it would be necessary to disclose the statement of any witness who supports this but whom the prosecution does not regard as truthful.

(c) If the victim died of a hammer blow and part of the prosecution case is a forensic test showing that the blood stains on a hammer found buried in the accused's back garden matched those of the victim, it will be necessary to disclose a negative test showing that the fingerprints on the hammer did not match those of the accused.

(d) If the prosecution is aware that its main witness has a previous conviction, it must disclose it to the defence since it may affect the weight to be placed on his testimony.[1]

(e) If the prosecution is in possession of a psychiatric report showing that its main witness has a history of psychiatric disorder with a tendency to fantasise, it should disclose the report since it clearly undermines the credibility of that witness.

(f) If the prosecution is aware that a prosecution witness has applied for reward for information leading to the conviction of a person for a criminal offence, it must disclose this to the defence.[2]

(g) If previous versions of witness statements *are* inconsistent with the final version served on the defence they must be disclosed.[3] This should be compared with the test in *Saunders*[4] where Henry J ruled that unused and undisclosed preparatory material *might* reveal inconsistencies upon which the credibility of the witness could be impeached, and should therefore have been disclosed.[5]

It will be noted that these examples encompass a range of matters going to credit as well as to issue, and will include those matters identified by Steyn LJ in *Brown*[6] as disclosable at common law.[7] There is, however, no duty at this stage to disclose material (such as the initial description given by an identification witness) if that is consistent with the prosecution case, even if that material would be of value to the defence in testing credibility.

---

1 Cf *Collister and Warhurst* (1955) 39 Cr App R 100.
2 Cf *Taylor and Taylor* (1994) 98 Cr App R 361.
3 Cf *Baksh* (1958) unreported.
4 29 September 1989, unreported.
5 See Consultation Document, op cit, Ch 4. Examples (a) and (b) were given in addition by Baroness Blatch, Minister of State, Home Office, HL Committee, col 867.
6 [1995] 1 Cr App R 191 (CA).
7 See para **2.24**.

2.37 Difficult issues remain. In cases where the accused has remained silent, there would appear to be no obligation to seek to anticipate what the likely defence might be. The prosecutor in such circumstances will only be required to disclose material which is not being used but which in the prosecutor's judgment would in fact undermine the prosecution case. But even where questions have been answered during the investigation stage, and thus provided some intimation of the likely defence, a prosecutor faces difficult questions as to whether the law requires him to disclose material in his possession. This material may not, in the strict sense, undermine the prosecution case but may, nevertheless, clearly assist the defence. Examples of two types of issue that may arise, and cause prosecutors problems, are set out below.

(a)   Should a prosecutor disclose to the defence previous statements made by a witness on whom he is going to rely irrespective of whether or not they are inconsistent? Should the prosecutor disclose earlier accounts by witnesses which are made in the form of notes by investigators or drafts of statements which are later prepared?[1] In respect of both these matters, para 5.4 of the draft Code is relevant. It will impose a duty on the investigator to retain final versions of witness statements (and draft versions where they differ from the original). If no duty of retention exists, arguably no duty of disclosure arises, and the defence will have no means to ascertaining that these exist. By contrast, if the earlier documents are inconsistent, then they are potentially disclosable. The key question is: what role does the witness play? Is his credit central to the prosecution case. It is in this type of case that the more restrictive test for prosecution disclosure appears to bite, and only if the earlier material casts significant doubt on the credit or reliability of the witness will a duty of disclosure at this stage arise.

(b)   Should the prosecutor reveal information in his possession which demonstrates that the complainant or another witness has been paid or has sought reward for the account that he will give at the trial? Again, if such payments, or solicitation, cast doubt on the credit of a witness on which the prosecution case depends to a significant degree, disclosure obligations arise, unless, of course, the witness was an informant in which case wider public interest issues arise. These might cause the prosecution to collapse.

Questions such as those set out above highlight the difficulties of judging the extent to which the law should impose positive duties on the prosecutor. Some argued during the passage of the new Act[2] that when material is clearly relevant to a defence of which the Crown is aware, then it should be disclosed at an early stage as reasonably possible so the issues could be clarified and the establishment of the truth facilitated. However, by contrast, the Government[3] believes that such an approach would detract from the ordered scheme inherent in the Act. If material points away from the accused, in reality it is very likely to undermine the prosecution case. If the prosecutor tries to guess what the defence might be, the end result may require the disclosure of all sorts of material which may have no bearing at all on the actual defence, resulting in inefficiency and unnecessary disclosure, and a return to the position which existed before the new Act.

---

1   These are types of material which were the subject of disclosure in the *Guinness* trial: see Baroness Mallalieu, HL Commitee, col 1444.
2   Baroness Mallalieu, HL Committee, col 1445.
3   Baroness Blatch, Minister of State, Home Office, HL Committee, col 1448.

Sensitive material

2.38   The prosecutor is under no obligation to disclose at this stage material that might be regarded as sensitive. The term 'sensitive' is not one used in Part I of the Act,[1] but is used in the draft Code of Practice,[2] and defined therein as 'material which an investigator, or the officer in charge of the investigation, or the disclosure officer believes that it is not in the public interest to disclose'. Where a court concludes, on an application by the prosecutor, that non-disclosure on the grounds of public interest is required, it may so order under s 3(6), which is discussed further at para **2.81**. Nor is material to be disclosed under s 3 if it has been intercepted in obedience to a warrant issued under s 2 of the Interception of Communications Act 1985, or it indicates that such a warrant has been issued or that material has been intercepted in obedience to such a warrant (s 3(7)).[3]

1 It is used in Part II: see s 24.
2 See draft Code, para 2.1.
3 See para **2.76**.

Procedure

2.39 The prosecutor has to make a judgment in respect of each item of material as to whether it fulfils the test in s 3(2). He will do this from the schedules prepared by the investigator,[1] a duty of preparation of which is dealt with by paras 6.1–6.10 of the draft Code of Practice,[2] and from the copy material sent to him. The description of each item on that schedule must be such as to identify sufficient detail to enable the prosecutor and the accused to form a judgment as to the significance of that material. Clearly, much turns on the information supplied to the prosecutor by the investigating officer or disclosure officer,[1] and the quality of the judgments made at that stage.

1 See para **3.10**.
2 See paras **3.36–3.40**.

2.40 The mechanics of disclosure are governed by s 3(3) of the new Act. Where material consists of information which has been recorded in any form, the prosecutor discloses it for the purposes of this section:

(a) by making a copy of it and giving the copy to the accused; or
(b) if in the prosecutor's opinion that is not practicable or not desirable, by allowing the accused to inspect it at a reasonable time and a reasonable place or by taking steps to secure that he is allowed to do so.

In addition to the supply of a copy, or the opportunity of inspection, the prosecutor must also supply to the accused a copy of the schedule of non-sensitive material (s 4(2)).

The copy supplied may be in such form as the prosecutor thinks fit, and need not be in the same form as that in which the information has already been recorded. Thus the prosecutor may make a copy available by means of scanning of the original or by computer disk.[1]

'Inspection' includes examination of the material and, despite the definition in s 2(1), is to be interpreted as including inspection by the accused, his legal representative, or by an expert on his behalf.[2] The effect of this is that inspection must surely include the right to analyse that material, for example, by a forensic analyst or other expert, because otherwise this interpretation of the term to include expert examination would be of limited utility. There is no power to prevent inspection of non-sensitive material. Take, for example, a case where an accused person is representing himself on charges relating to sexual offences. It may not be desirable to supply copies of documents which might be misused,[3] but, even in such a case, there is no power to withhold inspection, save, in this context, in respect of local authority child care documents which would be sensitive material and subject to claims of immunity from disclosure. It is submitted that the words of para 10.3 of the Code,[4] give to the person allowing the inspection[5] a discretion as to whether a person is allowed a copy, a conclusion confirmed by the words of s 24(1)(b)[6]. It is, however, difficult to conceive of good reason why a legal representative should be refused a copy of non-sensitive material.

---

1 Sir Derek Spencer, QC, MP, Solicitor-General, HC Committee, col 42.
2 Mr David Maclean, Minister of State, HC Committee, col 30; Lord Mackay LC, HL Report, col 1572.
3 See draft Code, para 10.2.
4 See para **3.54**.
5 Ie the disclosure officer: see para **3.54**.
6 As to which, see para **3.9**.

2.41 Although the question of practicability or desirability appears to be one of the prosecutor's opinion,[1] and thus subjective, the question as to what amounts to a reasonable time or a reasonable place is not qualified by the words 'prosecutor's opinion' and is for this reason objective. The effect of this is that if a court were subsequently to conclude that the time or place offered by the prosecutor was in fact unreasonable, then the prosecution would have failed to comply with its duty of primary disclosure. However, arguably that would amount to purported compliance with s 3 (see s 5(1)(b)), and thus the duty of compulsory disclosure by the accused would remain, despite the unreasonableness of the actions of the prosecutor. Any review of the question of reasonableness would appear to be a matter to be raised at the trial stage, in determining whether or not any comment or inference in respect of failure to disclose the defence should be made or drawn under s 11(3) or, on appeal, by an argument that the failure to state a reasonable time or place amounts to a material irregularity. Disputes as to the need for, content of, or adequacy of disclosure can also, of course, be resolved in a preparatory hearing, where one is held, either under s 29 of the new Act or under s 7 of the Criminal Justice Act 1987,[2] or by way of preliminary ruling under s 39 of the new Act. As the Government observed in its Consultation Paper on Pre-Trial Hearings:[3]

> 'The proposed power for a judge to make binding rulings before the start of the trial would be consistent with the need ... to resolve disputes in a binding way in advance of the trial. It would, for example, be open to either the prosecution or the defence to apply to a judge for a binding ruling on a dispute about the extent of disclosure ... In complex or potentially lengthy cases where a preparatory hearing has already been arranged then that hearing would also resolve disputes about disclosure.'

1 Under para 10.3 of the draft Code; it may, alternatively, be the opinion of the disclosure officer.
2 See, generally, Chapter 4.
3 *Improving the Effectiveness of Pre-Trial Hearings in the Crown Court: A Consultation Document* (1995) Cm 2924, HMSO, Ch 4, para 41.

Timing of disclosure

2.42   The duty of primary prosecution disclosure must be complied with by the prosecutor within the period which is the relevant period for primary prosecution disclosure prescribed by regulation made under s 12 (s 3(8)). These regulations may prescribe the relevant period for this and other purposes, and the regulations to be made may be framed by reference to the nature or volume of the material concerned, or by reference to the prosecutor's belief that the question of non-disclosure on grounds of public interest may arise (s 12(5)). No such regulations have been made as at the date of going to press. Until such regulations are made, s 13(1) applies, and which, for this purpose, creates a new s 3(3). The effect of this is that the prosecutor must comply with his duty under s 3 as soon as practicable after the event which gives rise to the obligation to engage in primary prosecution disclosure.

During the passage of the Act, it was emphasised that 'surely in the interests of both efficiency and justice that primary prosecution disclosure should take place as soon as possible after charge, together with a statement of the case'.[1] Primary prosecution disclosure may further the efficient handling of cases, by encouraging earlier pleas of guilty, earlier preparation of cases, the earlier fixing of dates and, as a result, the lessening of strain on victims. However, some consider it wrong for an accused to be required to disclose even the outline of his defence without being clear of the nature of the offence with which he is charged, and in levels of detail going beyond that contained in the indictment and committal or transfer papers.[2] However, no duty of defence disclosure arises until after the prosecution have served a copy of the indictment and a copy of the set of documents containing the evidence which is the basis of the charge, or the appropriate documentation in respect of notices of transfer in cases of serious or complex fraud[3] or in respect of certain cases involving children[3] has been served (see s 5(2) of the new Act). This meets some, but not all, of the objections of critics. To go further, and require detailed prosecution statements of the case, would be to defeat some of the advantages to be achieved through early prosecution disclosure, and at the cost of significant increased burdens on the Crown Prosecution Service.

1 Viscount Runciman of Doxford, HL 2nd Reading, col 487.
2 See para **2.57**.
3 See annotations to s 1.

2.43   In some cases where large amounts of material have to be considered, or where a ruling in respect of the disclosure of sensitive material is needed (see s 3(6)), it may not be possible to comply with the time-limits prescribed for this purpose. Section 12(3)(a) therefore provides for this, by permitting regulations to be made to allow the prosecutor and the accused to engage in disclosure as required by the new Act within an extended period. No such regulations have been made as at the date of going to press. When made, the regulations may do one or more of the things specified in s 12(3), including specifying the number of applications for extension that may be made, the pre-conditions for the making of an application, or the length of such an extension.

2.44 There is clear potential for real delay. Section 10(2) provides that the failure of the prosecutor to make primary prosecution disclosure within the prescribed period does not of itself constitute grounds for staying proceedings for abuse of process.[1] However, that protection does not apply if the delay by the prosecutor is such as to deny the accused a fair trial (s 10(3)). The new Act gives no guidance as to how a court is to apply this principle, but it is likely that the tests developed in the context of delay being a ground for arguing abuse of process will apply equally here.[1]

1 See annotations to s 10.

Continuing duty of prosecutor to disclose

2.45 The question of whether matters fall within the test for primary prosecution disclosure must be kept under review. Section 9(2) requires the prosecutor to keep under review the question whether at any given time there is prosecution material which:

(a)   in his opinion might undermine the case of the prosecution against the accused; and

(b)   has not been disclosed to the accused;

and if there is such material at any time the prosecutor must disclose it to the accused as soon as is reasonably practicable.

   This duty extends until such time as the accused is acquitted or convicted or the prosecutor decides not to proceed with the case concerned (s 9(1)).[1] This duty to engage in ongoing review is discussed further at para **2.71**.

1 See annotations to s 9.

Confidentiality of material disclosed

2.46 Concern has arisen as to the use to which material disclosed by the prosecution is put. It can be used by an accused to harrass witnesses, or for financial gain, and may have a detrimental affect on the willingness of the public to help the police.[1] In an attempt to overcome these problems the new Act introduces provisions relating to the confidentiality of material disclosed by the prosecution.

   Section 17(1) provides that if an accused is given or allowed to inspect a document or other object under one of the specified provisions of Part I of the new Act, he must not use or disclose it, or any information recorded in it. That general prohibition is subject to various exceptions, but it must be remembered that the potential misuse of a document may also be a basis for refusing to supply a copy of that document to the accused.[2]

1 See Mr David Maclean, MP, Minister of State, Home Office, HC Committee, col 7.
2 See para **3.54**.

2.47 By s 17(2), the accused may use or disclose the object or information:

(a) in connection with the proceedings for whose purposes he was given the object or allowed to inspect it;
(b) with a view to the taking of further criminal proceedings (for instance, by way of appeal) with regard to the matter giving rise to the proceedings mentioned in paragraph (a); or
(c) in connection with the proceedings first mentioned in paragraph (b).

2.48 A further exception to the general rule is provided by s 17(3). The accused may use or disclose:

(a) the object to the extent that it has been displayed to the public in open court; or
(b) the information to the extent that it has been communicated to the public in open court.

The expression 'open court' is not defined. Proceedings remain in open court even if subject to reporting restrictions, and only cease to be so if the public are excluded from those proceedings.[1] Even if proceedings are open, the duty of confidentiality may still exist. A document may simply be read by a judge or magistrate. Alternatively, a document may be put to a witness during cross-examination as a previous inconsistent statement.[2] That document does not necessarily fall within s 17(3), save to the extent that oral reference is made to information therein.

1 See annotations to s 17.
2 See Criminal Procedure Act 1865, s 4.

2.49 The terms of s 17(2) permit the material to be used, without permission, for appellate proceedings, and for the purposes, for example, of a re-trial. The use of the word 'taking' in paragraph (b) suggests that the use of such material in proceedings on other charges is not within s 17(2), and indeed the word 'taking' is not entirely an apt word to use in the context of the example of a re-trial given above. Arguably, to use the material in criminal proceedings on other charges requires permission under s 17(4). That, certainly, would be required prior to the use of that material in civil proceedings, as in, for example, an action brought against the police following an unsuccessful prosecution. Section 18(9) provides that an object or information shall be inadmissible as evidence in civil proceedings if to adduce it would in the opinion of the civil court be likely to constitute a contempt of court under s 18.[1] Because s 18 makes it a contempt of court to use or disclose the object or information without leave, the leave of the criminal court is a precondition to admissibility in the civil proceedings. This may have theoretically anomalous consequences: a public interest immunity claim in respect of certain documents may be sustainable in civil proceedings, because of the nature of the class to which that document belongs, but not in criminal proceedings where the public interest in withholding the document almost always will be counterbalanced by the interests of ensuring a fair trial.[2] It is unclear whether the criminal court deciding on the application for permission will be required to adjudicate on any public interest immunity claims that arise, or whether any permission granted is in effect without prejudice to any further application to a civil court to restrain the use of that material in evidence.

1 See para **2.51**.
2 See para **3.63**.

2.50   Except where a right to disclose arises under either s 17(2) or s 17(3), permission must be sought. Section 17(4) provides that if:

(a)   the accused applies to the court for an order granting permission to use or disclose the object or information; and

(b)   the court makes such an order,

the accused may use or disclose the object or information for the purpose and to the extent specified by the court. There appear to be no limits as to how the court deals with such an application, save only the general intent and purpose of the confidentiality provisions themselves.

Such an application may be made and dealt with at any time, even after acquittal, conviction or discontinuance.[1] It may be governed by rules which may be made under s 19(1). No such rules had been made as at the date of going to press. Such an application may be made to any magistrates' court, when disclosure obligations arise by virtue of s 1(1), or to the Crown Court when they arise by virtue of s 1(2) (s 17(7)), and need not be made to the court of trial. The prosecutor or a person claiming to have an interest in the object or information may apply to be heard by the court, and the court must not make an order granting permission unless that person who has made that application has been given an opportunity to be heard. That does not mean, of course, that that person has in fact to be heard. Although the details of the rules appertaining to applications of the present type have yet to be published, the terms of s 17(6) would appear to be satisfied by serving notice of the intention to make the application under s 17(4) on the prosecutor or other interested party.

1 See annotations to s 9.

Offence

2.51   Unauthorised use of prosecution material amounts to a contempt of court. By s 18, it is a contempt of court for a person knowingly to use or disclose an object or information recorded in it if the use or disclosure is in contravention of s 17. The jurisdiction to deal with the contempt depends on the reason by which Part I applies. If Part I applies by virtue of s 1(1) (ie because the case is to be tried summarily) a magistrates' court has jurisdiction (s 18(2)(a)); if it applies by s 1(2) (ie because the case is to be tried on indictment), it is the Crown Court that has jurisdiction (s 18(2)(b)).

The person who commits the offence is the person who knowingly[1] uses or discloses an object or information in contravention of s 17. The general prohibition against use or disclosure in s 17(1) is placed on the accused. If the accused should use the object or information without leave then he commits the offence under s 18(1). However, that offence is confined in its terms to 'the accused', and it is submitted that the offence does not in its terms extend to unauthorised disclosure by a solicitor or other adviser, because the use or disclosure is not in breach of s 16: the accused has not used or disclosed the material. In the context of criminal liability, the term 'accused' should be construed narrowly, and not in a broad sense to include his representatives. Nor, conversely, is the accused liable in contempt for the actions of his legal representatives: it would be entirely wrong in principle for criminal liability to attach in this way and, in any event, the accused in this situation could not be said to have the requisite knowledge.

Further problems arise in the context of unrepresented accused persons. There is no obligation on a court, or the prosecution, to ensure that such a person is aware of the confidentiality of material disclosed, and it is by no means clear whether the requisite knowledge required by s 18(1) as the mens rea for the contempt extends to the use or disclosure, or, more widely, imports a requirement of mens rea as to the contravention of s 17.

Proceedings for contempt under s 18 may be either by complaint, presumably to be made by a prosecutor or third party aggrieved by disclosure without leave, or begun on the court's own motion. A person who is guilty of a contempt of court under s 18 may be dealt with as follows:

(a)   a magistrates' court may commit him to custody for a specified period not exceeding six months or impose a fine on him, not exceeding £5000, or both;

(b)   the Crown Court may commit him to custody for a specified period not exceeding two years or impose a fine on him, or both (s 18(3)).

---

1 See annotations to s 18.

Forfeiture or destruction

2.52   Section 18 confers powers to order forfeiture or destruction of an object, or a copy of that object (s 18(4) and (7)), the destruction of an object or the taking of an object into the custody of the prosecutor (s 18(5)).

By s 18(4), if:

(a)   a person is guilty of a contempt under s 18; and
(b)   the object concerned is in his possession;[1]

the court finding him guilty may order that the object shall be forfeited and dealt with in such manner as the court may order.

That power appears unlimited, and is wide enough to include an order that an object or information be returned to a third party. It certainly includes a power to order the object to be destroyed or to be given to the prosecutor or to be placed in his custody for such period as the court may specify (s 17(5)). It is less clear whether a court may order that an object in the hands of an accused be given into the possession of his legal advisers. There appears to be no reason why not; forfeiture simply involving the loss of the right to possess. However, before any such order is made, if:

(a)   the court proposes to make a forfeiture order under s 18(4) or s 18(7); and
(b)   the person found guilty, or any other person claiming to have an interest in the object, applies to be heard by the court,

the court must not make the order unless the applicant has been given an opportunity to be heard (s 18(5) and (8)).

---

1 See annotations to s 3.

THE NEW LAW – DEFENCE DISCLOSURE

2.53   Where s 5 of the new Act applies, the accused must give a defence statement to the court and to the prosecutor (s 5(3)). This duty arises where:

(a)   Part I of the Act applies by virtue of s 1(2); and
(b)   the prosecutor complies with s 3 or purports to comply with it (s 5(1)).

It has already been seen[1] that the effect of s 1(2) is that Part I of the new Act applies where a person is charged with an indictable offence and committed for trial, or proceedings for the trial of the person on the charge concerned are transferred to the Crown Court, or where a person is charged with a summary offence which is included in an indictment under the authority of s 40 of the Criminal Justice Act 1988, or where a bill of indictment charging a person with an indictable offence is preferred against that person (s 1(2)). The effect of this is, of course, that compulsory defence disclosure is not required by the new Act in respect of cases to be tried summarily. In such cases, defence disclosure is voluntary. Section 6(2) permits an accused, who is to be tried summarily, to give a defence statement to the prosecutor, within such period as may be prescribed by the Secretary of State by regulations (s 6(4)). It might be thought that s 6 is unnecessary, in that it is always open to an accused to disclose such facts about his defence as he might wish. However, the significance of voluntary disclosure as defined by s 6 is to bring into play the provisions of s 5(6)–(8) (s 6(2)), which set out the nature of the defence statement[2] and which prescribe the detail to be given where alibi evidence is intended to be adduced.[3] Further, it brings into play the terms of s 11(3) where voluntary disclosure has occurred. Section 11 permits a court or other party in certain circumstances to make such comment as appears appropriate or to draw such inferences as appear proper in respect of certain matters. The effect of s 11(2) and s 11(3) cumulatively is to permit a court to draw inferences where there has been inadequate voluntary disclosure.[4]

1 See para **2.8**.
2 See paras **2.57–2.60**.
3 See para **2.64**.
4 See paras **2.66–2.67**.

2.54   In the normal case, where a person is committed for trial in respect of an indictable offence,[1] the duty of defence disclosure arises once the committal has taken place, and the further condition in s 5(1)(b) is satisfied, namely, that the prosecutor has purported to comply with his obligations under s 3. However, in other cases falling within the terms of s 1(2),[1] the further requirements of either s 5(2), s 5(3) or s 5(4) apply. These are as follows:

(a)   that notice of transfer has been given under s 4 of the Criminal Justice Act 1987 (serious or complex fraud)[2] and a copy of the documents containing the evidence has been given to the accused under regulations made under s 5(9) of that Act (s 5(2));

(b)   that a notice of transfer has been served on a magistrates' court under s 53 of the Criminal Justice Act 1991 (certain cases involving children)[2] and a copy of the documents containing the evidence has been given to the accused under regulations made under para 4 of Sch 6 to that Act, (s 5(3)); or

(c)   that s 1(2)(e) applies (preferment of a bill of indictment),[2] and the prosecutor has served on the accused a copy of the indictment and a copy of the set of documents containing the evidence which is the basis of the charge (s 5(4)).

There is no duty to engage in compulsory defence disclosure in respect of cases which fall within s 1(2)(e) of the new Act. It will be recalled that s 1(2)(e) applies in respect of a count charging a person with a summary offence included in an indictment under the authority of s 40 of the Criminal Justice Act 1988. Nor does it appear that voluntary disclosure applies in such a case, because such an offence does not fall within the terms of s 1(1), which is a precondition for the operation of s 6. Such an offence is not being tried summarily for the purposes of s 1(1)(a), and thus voluntary disclosure cannot occur even though that would be permissible if the same offence was in fact being tried summarily. This appears to be a lacuna, albeit one not of any startling significance.

1 See, generally, para **2.8**.
2 See annotations to s 1.

2.55   As already noted, compulsory disclosure is subject to the precondition that the prosecutor complies with s 3 or purports to comply with it. This provision is curious. Section 3(1) is subjective, and requires the prosecutor to disclose to the accused any prosecution material which has not been previously disclosed to the accused and which, in the prosecutor's opinion, might undermine the case for the prosecution against the accused. On a literal interpretation of s 3, any statement given by the prosecutor amounts to compliance with the terms of s 3, because of this subjective nature. It is difficult to see how there can be 'purported compliance' when, by definition, the honest communication of the prosecutor's opinion amounts to 'compliance'. One explanation was given as follows:[1]

> 'This formulation is needed because, although the prosecution may genuinely believe that he has disclosed all material which he thinks undermines the prosecution, he may not in fact have disclosed all such material. There might be some material in the possession of the police which he has not inspected, although he would be entitled to inspect it, and which (if he had inspected it) he might think undermined the prosecution case. In cases where there is this kind of inadvertent non-disclosure the prosecutor does not actually comply with [s 3] but only purports to do so.'

This statement serves to put the earlier statements[2] about the subjectivity of the prosecution's duty of disclosure in a new context.

---

1 Baroness Blatch, Minister of State, Home Office, HL Committee, col 1456.
2 See para **2.32**.

The defence statement

2.56   A defence statement is defined, by s 5(6), as a written statement:

(a)   setting out in general terms the nature of the accused's defence;
(b)   indicating the matters on which he takes issue with the prosecution;
(c)   setting out, in the case of each such matter, the reason why he takes issue with the prosecution.

Additional provisions apply in the case of alibi evidence (s 5(7) and (8)). The defence statement must be served within the relevant period as prescribed by regulations made by the Home Secretary under s 12. These regulations may also provide for a power to apply for an extension of the period for service of the notice (s 12(3)). No such period has been prescribed as at the date of going to press. A defence statement need not be served on any co-accused, although there is nothing to prevent this being done voluntarily.[1] The possible extension of this requirement to include service on a co-accused was rejected by the Government because of the mechanisms, tactical considerations and lack of practical and effective sanctions should non-compliance occur.[2]

---

1 See Sir Derek Spencer, QC, MP, Solicitor-General, HC Committee, col 62.
2 Ibid, cols 61–63.

Nature of the accused's defence

2.57   Problems arise as to the scope of this phrase. A person who puts the prosecution to proof, calling no evidence himself, is not raising a defence in the strict sense. In such a situation, arguably, no defence statement is necessary. Different considerations apply if facts are put to prosecution witnesses in cross-examination, which are accepted as true by those witnesses. In such circumstances, the case-law from Northern Ireland governing the 'right of silence' order suggests, by analogy, that facts are being relied on as part of the defence.[1] In another situation, a defendant may raise the whole question of fitness to plead. Again, strictly speaking, this may not be a defence as such but rather a plea which governs whether, and in what form, the trial may proceed. The difficulty in all these instances is that if no defence statement is served, then the secondary disclosure provisions in s 7 of the new Act will not be triggered, thus depriving the accused of potentially useful prosecution material which might reasonably be expected to assist the accused's defence (see s 7(2)(a)). This point serves only to highlight the difficulties that adoption of the two-stage prosecution disclosure provisions may cause, at any rate in theory. The fact that there is no 'defence' as such may protect the defendant from the consequences identified in s 11, if no defence statement is served, but it will not assist necessarily in achieving full and fair disclosure. For this reason, the failure of the Government to agree to an amendment permitting prosecution disclosure where it is in the interest of justice to do so, or permitting a court to so order, is to be regretted. However, it may be that a court may choose to construe the terms of s 5(4)(a) broadly, and require secondary prosecution disclosure whenever the defence has indicated what its approach at trial will be. This would accord with commonsense, fairness and with the overall justification for the new provisions, namely, that the prosecution should be put into a position where it can judge what it needs to disclose further.[2] On this basis, compulsory defence disclosure might be as to the fact that it is intended to raise the issue that the accused is unfit to plead, or that no evidence is being called and that the prosecution will be put to proof, or that the defence will rely solely on the inadmissibility of evidence.

---

1 *Mclernon* (1992) (unreported, NICA); *Carroll* (1993) (unreported); *Devine* (1992) (unreported, NICA).
2 Sir Derek Spencer, QC, MP, Solicitor-General, HC Committee, col 64.

2.58 Further difficulties arise from the use of the expression 'in general terms'. The Royal Commission had recommended[1] that disclosure should be of a relatively brief type. It reported as follows:

> 'In most cases disclosure of the defence should be a matter capable of being handled by the defendant's solicitor (in the same way that alibi notices are usually dealt with at present). Standard forms could be drawn up to cover the most common offences, with the solicitor having only to tick one or more of a list of possibilities, such as 'accident', 'self-defence', 'consent', 'no dishonest intent', 'no appropriation', 'abandoned goods', 'claim of right', 'mistaken identification' and so on. There will be complex cases which may require the assistance of counsel in formulating the defence.'

The provision in s 5 is intended to go further. The question is: how much further? In the Consultation Paper the Government stated:[2]

> 'the defence would be required to provide sufficient particulars of its case to identify the issues in dispute between the defence and the prosecution before the

commencement of the trial. It would also enable the prosecutor or investigator to access whether they had any additional unused material which might assist that case. The exact details of what would need to be disclosed by the defendant in each case would depend on the particular defence to be advanced. The government envisages that the details will include, as they currently do in an alibi defence, the name and address of any witnesses the defendant proposes to call in support of that defence, or a written statement of fact or opinion which the defendant proposes to adduce as expert evidence, or any evidence which might support a defence of, for example, consent or self-defence or duress.'

1 Op cit, p 99, para 68.
2 Op cit, paras 51–52.

2.59 This level of detail is not, of course, specified by s 5(6), unlike the terms of s 5(7) regarding alibi evidence. This change is significant. The Government reconsidered its position, and concluded that this level of detail was not necessary.[1] However, s 5(6)(c) (which requires the setting out, in the case of matters on which the defence takes issue with the prosecution, of the reason why such issue is taken) does not specify the level of detail to be supplied, unlike s 5(6)(a) which states that the nature of the defence should be set out 'in general terms'. Some fear that an accused will be obliged to reveal his entire argument and line of cross-examination, thereby giving an undue advantage to the prosecution.[2]

Further, an issue of principle arises here if an accused is required to set out, point by point, the reasons why issue is taken. Such a practice might serve to undermine the underlying principles in respect of the burden of proof.[3]

The position is further complicated by comparison with the terms of s 33 (Crown Court rules for preparatory hearings). Section 33(1) states that Crown Court rules governing the disclosure provisions in s 30(6) may provide that 'anything required to be given under s 31 need not disclose who will give evidence'. In one sense this provides confirmation that it is not intended to require defendants generally to disclose to this level of detail. In another sense, it raises the question of the purpose which s 33 serves if an accused is never under an obligation (other than in respect of alibi evidence) to disclose the detail of the witnesses to be called.

1 Sir Derek Spencer, QC, MP, Solicitor-General, HC Committee, col 68.
2 See Mr Alun Michael MP, HC Committee, col 63.
3 See Viscount Runciman of Doxford, HL Committee, col 1459.

2.60 The relationship between s 5(6)(a) and s 5(6)(c), and the level of detail required, was explained by the Solicitor-General as follows:

'In providing a defence statement it is not intended that the accused should have to provide every last detail of the defence, such as the names and addresses of witnesses and so on. That was originally intended by the Consultation document but we have decided that that is not necessary. It is for that reason that subsection [(6)(a)] requires only the general terms of the nature of the defence to be disclosed, self-defence, accident or whatever. Subsection [(6)(c)] ... deals with a much narrower issue. It simply requires the accused to give a reason why he takes issue with a point. There is no suggestion that in giving the reason, details of the evidence to support that reason have to be given. So the fear ... that this might require the defence to set out its oral cross-examination is not well founded. That is not intended at all.'[1]

The intent and purpose of s 5(6) is, he stated, to enable the prosecutor to make secondary prosecution disclosure. The Solicitor-General continued:

'He can only do that if the defence has, to use a colloquialism, set its stall out for the prosecution to be able to say: "That is the issue, that is the issue, and that is the issue. Now what material do I have which I ought to disclose because it might reasonably assist the defence?"'[2]

The Solicitor-General then gave the example of a witness to a shoplifting. A reason for taking issue might be that the witness could not have seen what he said he saw because he was somewhere else. Yet, what of examples where, for instance, the defence simply says, 'the witness is not telling the truth'? Does the defence have to go on and say why? If so, the surprise element in cross-examination is diminished, yet it is submitted that there is a broad obligation to set forward, in outline, why that stance is taken.

---

1 Sir Derek Spencer, QC, MP, Solicitor-General, HC Committee, col 68.
2 Ibid.

Inadequate defence disclosure

2.61 The breadth of the language used in s 5(6) gives to a court of trial a wide discretion as to when to make a comment, or draw an inference, pursuant to s 11(3). It will be for the trial court to determine whether a defence statement has been given at all, or whether the defence being run is inconsistent with that contained in the defence statement. It may be noted, however, that although s 11(1)(e) and s 11(1)(f) make specific provision in respect of the particulars of alibi, or of the witnesses being called in support of an alibi which must be given, no such specific provision is made in respect of other such matters. Nevertheless, the definition of defence statement in s 5(6) is wide enough to encompass not simply the giving of a statement in writing of any sort, but an inadequate statement. On one view, a statement which does not set out in full the general nature of the defence, does not indicate the matters on which issue is taken, or does not set out the reason why issue is taken, does not amount in reality to a defence statement.

Secondary prosecution only occurs after there has been defence disclosure. Unlike prosecution disclosure under s 3, 'purported' defence disclosure is insufficient. However, for a prosecutor to fail to disclose material in secondary prosecution disclosure that is clearly relevant in the light of the, albeit inadequate, defence statement would surely be unfair and wrong, and would, it is submitted, be contrary to the terms of s 7. Arguably, therefore, the broad duty of fairness makes the failure to use that word 'purported' insignificant.

2.62 A further broad issue raised by s 5 is the question of whether or not a fair balance is being achieved between prosecution and defence. Arguably, if defence disclosure of this detail is to be required, it should be preceded not simply by the service of witness statements for the purposes of committal, but by a detailed statement by the prosecution of the facts relied on and the inferences to be drawn. Such case summaries are already prepared in all Class 1 cases, including murder and terrorist cases, in cases in which the gravity or complexity of the case suggests to the Crown Prosecution Service that a judge may find a summary of some assistance,[1] and in cases transferred for trial under the 1987 or 1991 Acts.

However, the Government rejected any change and pointed to the significant increased burden and cost of preparation of such statements. In any event, it is open to a judge on a preparatory hearing under s 30[2] to order such a case statement. An application for a preparatory hearing may be made by the prosecutor, the accused, or a hearing may be ordered by the judge on his own motion.[3]

---

1 Sir Derek Spencer, QC, MP, Solicitor-General, HC Committee, col 59. In 1995 these amounted to some 1652 cases, less than 2% of all Crown Court cases.
2 See para **4.24**.
3 See para **4.25**.

Waiver of defence disclosure

2.63 No discretion exists for a trial judge to waive the requirement for a defence statement contained in s 5(3).[1] However, there are many instances where such waiver might be desirable – where there is an unrepresented defendant, or an illiterate defendant, where both prosecution and defence agree that the defence statement will add nothing (as arises already in some cases in respect of alibi evidence),[2] or where the service of a defence statement may serve to provide opportunities for the intimidation of witnesses. By contrast, the Government believe that, in such cases, the better solution is for there to be no defence statement at all. If a defence statement is inappropriate because of the circumstances, no inference would be drawn in respect of a failure to give one, or comment made as to that failure. Again, however, the result is that no right to receive secondary prosecution disclosure would then arise. It is difficult at first sight to see why there should be an objection of principle to a power to waive the disclosure requirement, save perhaps a desire to avoid disputes which might require resolution by the court.

---

1 This was confirmed by Baroness Blatch, Minister of State, Home Office, HL 3rd Reading, col 884.
2 Lord Williams, HL 3rd Reading, col 882.

Alibi evidence

2.64 Section 11 of the Criminal Justice Act 1967, which ceases to apply in respect of alleged offences into which no criminal investigation has begun before the appointed day,[1] provides that on a trial on indictment a defendant shall not without the leave of the court adduce evidence in support of an alibi[2] unless, before the end of the prescribed period, he gives notice of particulars of the alibi (1967 Act, s 11(1)). Section 11 of the 1967 Act provides for the service of a notice of alibi specifying the name and address of witnesses supporting the alibi, or specifying information of material assistance to the finding of such a witness. It also provides for the procedure to be followed and the power of the court where no notice is served.

The new Act takes a different approach. Henceforth a separate notice of alibi is not required. Instead, s 5(7) provides that, if a defence statement discloses an alibi the accused must give details of that alibi in that statement, including:

(a) the name and address[2] of any witness the accused believes is able to give evidence in support of the alibi, if the name and address are known to the accused when the statement is given;

(b) any information in the accused's possession which might be of material assistance in finding any such witness, if his name and address is not known to the accused when the statement is given.

Section 5(7) mirrors the terms of s 11(2)(a) of the 1967 Act. By contrast, the new Act does not seek to incorporate the provisions of s 11(2)(b),(c) or (d) of the 1967 Act which deal with the ongoing duty to secure that the name and address is ascertained, the duty to notify the name and address of the witness if subsequently discovered, or the duty to supply information to assist in tracing the witness if the prosecutor notifies the accused that the witness has not been traced by the name, or at the address, given. Because none of these duties exist, the position in respect of alibi evidence is therefore the same as in respect of all other types of evidence. The general duty in respect of defence disclosure under s 5 is not an on-going duty.

---

1 See s 74.
2 See annotations to s 5.

2.65 The other significant change is in respect of the sanction that exists in respect of non-compliance. The purpose of requiring leave before alibi evidence, in respect of which no notice had been served, could be adduced was to try to ensure that the prosecution had a proper opportunity to investigate the alibi.[1] Provided that opportunity existed, it was not the intention of Parliament for leave to be refused to punish the accused. Similar justifications underpin the whole concept of defence disclosure under s 5. Where there is failure to disclose, or adequately disclose, s 5 does not create a power to refuse to allow that evidence to be heard. Instead, the broader sanctions of possible comment and inference, discussed in paras **2.66–2.67** apply, and, arguably, they provide sufficient sanction.

---

1 *Sullivan* [1971] 1 KB 253 (CA); cf *Jacks* [1991] Crim LR 611 (CA).

Sanction for non-compliance

2.66 This is provided for by s 11(3), which applies in the circumstances identified either by s 11(1) or by s 11(2).

The circumstances identified by s 11(1) are where the accused:

(a) fails to give the prosecutor a defence statement under s 5;
(b) gives the prosecutor a defence statement under that section but does so after the end of the prescribed period;
(c) sets out inconsistent defences in a defence statement given under s 5;
(d) at his trial, puts forward a defence which is different from any defence set out in a defence statement given under that section;
(e) at his trial, adduces evidence in support of an alibi without having given particulars of the alibi in a defence statement given under that section; or
(f) at his trial, calls a witness to give evidence in support of an alibi without having complied with s 5 as regards the witness in giving a defence statement under that section.

The circumstances identified by s 11(2) are similar. Section 11(2) applies where an accused gives a voluntary defence statement under s 6, and the accused:

(a) gives the statement after the end of the period which is the relevant period for the purposes of s 6;
(b) sets out inconsistent defences in the statement;
(c) at his trial, puts forward a defence which is different from any defence set out in the statement;
(d) at his trial, adduces evidence in support of an alibi without having given particulars of the alibi in the defence statement; or
(e) at his trial, calls a witness to give evidence in support of an alibi without having complied with s 5(7)(a) or (b) (as applied by s 6) as regards the witness in giving the statement.

2.67   Where s 11(3) applies:

(a) the court or, with the leave of the court, any other party may make such comment as appears appropriate;
(b) the court or jury may draw such inferences as appear proper in deciding whether the accused is guilty of the offence concerned (s 11(3)).

Paragraphs (a) and (b) are not mutually exclusive; they are not distinguished by the word 'or' and therefore it is open to a court both to make a comment and to draw such inference as appears to it proper. The terms of s 11(3) are similar to those of s 10 of the Criminal Justice Act 1987,[1] and to those contained in s 34(2) of the new Act relating to preparatory hearings generally. They are also similar to those contained in ss 34 to 38 of the Criminal Justice and Public Order Act 1994, and the arguments and case-law thereon appear relevant by analogy here.[2] The nature of the inference which is permitted to be drawn under s 11(3)(b) is not defined, nor does the new Act impose any particular limits, save only that a person shall not be convicted of an offence solely on an inference drawn under s 11(3) (s 11(5)).

However, s 11 deals with a failure to disclose a defence, or the running of a defence different from that disclosed, or from the failure to give details of the defence being run. This emphasis serves to confirm that an inference cannot be part of the prosecution's prima facie case, despite confusing dicta in *Cowan*[3] that might be taken, in the context of s 35 of the 1994 Act, to suggest the contrary. Whether or not there is that failure, or departure will, after all, only become clear during the defence case, and it is, of course, trite to observe that the defence case will not be reached unless the prosecution has, in fact, established that prima facie case. Such arguments might, in fact, lead to the conclusion that these provisions have no application to cases where the prosecution are simply put to proof or where there is a question of fitness to plead.[4] A comment should be made, or an inference drawn, only where a proper evidential basis for such comment or inference exists. This can be created by the prosecution adducing in evidence the defence statement, or confirmation that no such statement was served. It was held in *Rossborough*[5] that an alibi notice could be used against an accused like any other voluntary statement of his, and that will be the position in future in respect of defence statements.

1 Departure from case disclosed at a preparatory hearing in a case of serious or complex fraud, or a failure to comply with a requirement imposed at such a hearing.
2 *Cowan* [1995] 4 All ER 939 (CA). See annotations to s 11 and, generally, Card and Ward *Criminal Justice and Public Order Act 1994* (Jordans, 1994), Ch 5.
3 [1995] 4 All ER 939 (CA).
4 See para **2.56**.
5 (1985) 81 Cr App R 372 (CA); cf *Watts* (1980) 71 Cr App R 136 (CA).

THE NEW LAW – SECONDARY PROSECUTION DISCLOSURE

2.68 By s 7(1), secondary prosecution disclosure applies where the defence gives a defence statement to the prosecutor under s 5 or s 6. The difference in wording between s 7(1) ('gives a defence statement') and s 5(1)(b) ('complies ... or purports to comply with [the duty of primary prosecution disclosure]') should be noted. The failure to use the expression 'or purports to give a defence statement' lends weight to the argument that secondary disclosure by the prosecutor is only to occur when the defence has properly complied with the requirements of s 5(4) or s 6(2). However, the point is probably more academic than real. The reason for that conclusion is that if the accused has reasonable cause to believe that there is prosecution material which might reasonably be expected to assist defence as disclosed, and that material has not been disclosed to the accused, he may apply to the court under s 8(2) for an order requiring the prosecutor to disclose that material. There is, therefore, a clear benefit to an accused in defining the nature of the defence. Clearly, any dispute as to whether secondary prosecution disclosure should have occurred will be a matter for the court, in an application under s 8, which application might be made as an application for a pre-trial ruling or as part of a preparatory hearing under s 30.[1]

1 See s 31 and para **4.16**.

2.69 The duty of secondary disclosure is defined by s 7(2). The prosecutor must:

(a)   disclose to the accused any prosecution material which has not been previously disclosed to the accused and which might be reasonably expected to assist the accused's defence as disclosed by the defence statement given to the prosecutor under s 5 or s 6; or

(b)   give to the accused a written statement that there is no material of a description mentioned in paragraph (a).

This duty to disclose does not extend to material which the court, on an application by the prosecutor, concludes:

(a)   is not in the public interest to disclose and orders accordingly (s 7(5)); or

(b)   in respect of material which has been intercepted in obedience to a warrant issued under s 2 of the Interception of Communications Act 1985 (s 7(6)); or

(c)   which indicates that such a warrant has been issued (s 7(6)); or

(d)   that material has been intercepted in obedience to such a warrant (s 7(6)).[1]

Secondary disclosure must occur during the relevant period prescribed for this purpose by regulations made by the Home Secretary under s 12 (s 7(7)). No such regulations have been made as at the date of going to press. These regulations may include a power to make applications for an extension of the relevant time-limit. A failure to comply with the time-limits prescribed will not be a ground for seeking a stay on the grounds of abuse of process, unless the delay is such that the accused is denied a fair trial.[2] Until such regulations are made, s 13(2) applies. For this purpose, it creates a new s 7(7). The effect of this is that a prosecutor must comply with his duty under s 7 as soon as practicable after the accused gives a defence statement under s 5 or s 6.

---

1 See paras **2.74** and **2.76**.

2 See annotations to s 10. The mechanics of disclosure are as for primary prosecution disclosure: see para **2.40**. Material disclosed is subject to the duty of confidentiality: see s 17 and para **2.46**.

2.70 The key issue in respect of secondary prosecution disclosure is the question of what might reasonably be expected to assist the accused's defence as disclosed by the defence statement. That is an objective rather than subjective issue.[1] The decision by the prosecutor may therefore be reviewed by a court on an application made under s 8(2). However, such an application presupposes that the accused has reasonable cause to believe that there is such prosecution material which has not been disclosed. There may be a case where there is no evidence upon which a reasonable belief can be founded; if so, there will be no basis for an application under s 8(2). Further, the secondary prosecution disclosure is in respect of the defence as disclosed by the defence statement. On a literal interpretation, there is no obligation to disclose material which might assist another defence. For example, in a murder case unused material might point to provocation rather than the defence of self-defence set out in the defence statement. However, this must be viewed in the context of the provisions of s 9(2) which provide for a continuing duty on the prosecutor to review such issues[2] and also in the context of the basic duty to act fairly, discussed earlier.[3]

1   Cf para **2.34**.
2   See para **2.71**.
3   See para **2.69**.

THE NEW LAW – THE CONTINUING DUTY OF THE PROSECUTOR

2.71   The duty of the prosecutor to disclose is a continuing one. By s 9(1), the prosecutor is under a duty to keep under review disclosure issues from the time there is compliance, or purported compliance, with the terms of s 3 (primary prosecution disclosure) until the accused is acquitted, convicted or the prosecutor decides not to proceed with the case concerned (s 9(1)). The duty of continuing review is defined by s 9(2). No duty arises under s 9(2) if there has not been compliance or purported compliance under s 3. Theoretically, therefore, the prosecutor who does not comply or purport to comply with s 3 need not keep the question of disclosure under review. That conclusion cannot be correct, because of the unfairness that might arise. A prosecutor who does not keep under review the question of disclosure of material surely fails to comply with his basic duty of fairness owed to the accused and to the court. A failure to keep under review may, in some circumstances, amount to an irregularity[1] leading to any conviction that results from a charge being quashed.

1   See Criminal Appeal Act 1995, s 2, which requires the Court of Appeal to allow an appeal against conviction where that conviction is unsafe.

2.72   By s 9(2), the prosecutor must keep under review the question whether at any given time there is prosecution material which:

(a)   in his opinion might undermine the case for the prosecution against the accused; and

(b)   has not been disclosed to the accused.

If there is such material at any time, the prosecutor must disclose it to the accused as soon as is reasonably practicable (s 9(2)). The terms of s 9(2) are couched similarly to those in s 3, and the meanings of the phrases 'undermine the case for the prosecution' and 'disclosed to the accused' are the same.[1] In deciding whether or not there is material which 'undermines the case for the prosecution' the state of affairs existing at the particular time (including the case for the prosecution as it stands at that time) must be taken into account (s 9(3)). Thus, if the prosecution case evolves and is modified, the effect on disclosure must be considered. This duty to keep under review whether or not there is material which undermines the prosecution case ends with the time when the accused is acquitted, convicted or the prosecutor decides not to proceed with the case concerned.[2] There is no duty to keep such matters under review between the time of a conviction and of any appeal. However, under the basic duty of fairness, the prosecutor may well be expected to keep disclosure issues under review if it is known that an appeal is pending which is likely to raise the question of the evidential base of the conviction. Nor does a duty to preserve such material appear to exist, either under the Act or under the draft Code of Practice.[3]

---

1 See paras **2.35** and **2.40**.
2 See annotations to s 8.
3 See para **3.29**.

2.73 A further duty to keep questions of disclosure under review arises by virtue of s 9(5). This applies at all times after the prosecutor complies, or purports to comply, with s 7 (secondary prosecution disclosure) until the time of acquittal, conviction, or the time when the prosecutor decides not to proceed with the case concerned (s 9(4)).[1] This duty amounts to a duty to keep under review the question whether at any given time there is prosecution material which:

(a)   might be reasonably expected to assist the accused's defence as disclosed by the defence statement given to the prosecutor under s 5 or 6; and
(b)   has not been disclosed to the accused (s 9(5)).

If there is such material at any time the prosecutor must disclose it to the accused as soon as is reasonably practicable (s 9(5)). The expression 'might be reasonably expected to assist the accused's defence' bears the same meaning as in s 7.[2] Any material disclosed is subject to the duty of confidentiality created by s 17.[3]

---

1 See annotations to s 9.
2 See para **2.70**.
3 See para **2.46**.

Restrictions on disclosure

2.74   In all cases where there is a duty of continuing review arising by virtue of s 9, there are the restrictions on disclosure which are common to all of the prosecution disclosure provisions.

By s 9(8), material must not be disclosed under s 9 to the extent that the court, on an application by the prosecutor, concludes that it is not in the public interest to disclose it and orders accordingly. Further, by s 9(9), material must not be disclosed under s 9 to the extent that:

(a)   it has been intercepted in obedience to a warrant issued under s 2 of the Interception of Communications Act 1985; or
(b)   that it indicates that such a warrant has been issued or that material has been intercepted in obedience to such a warrant.

Failure to comply with the duty

2.75   Section 9 contains no sanction should the prosecutor fail to comply with this continuing duty to keep under review, or to disclose as soon as reasonably practicable any of the material that should have been disclosed by virtue of s 9. If there was a failure to comply with the duty of primary prosecution disclosure, the remedy the accused has is, of course, to withhold the defence statement. In respect of secondary prosecution disclosure, and the duty of continuing review under s 9, there is, however, no sanction for non-compliance. It is unclear whether the power of an accused to make an application under s 8(2) extends beyond a failure at the secondary prosecution disclosure stage. Section 8(1) states that s 8 applies where the prosecutor complies with s 7 or purports to comply with it or fails to comply with it. Arguably, it is an ongoing duty. Alternatively, it is open to an accused who has reason to believe that the duty has not been discharged at all, or fully, or properly, to make an application for disclosure during a preparatory hearing (if there is one) held under s 29, or, possibly, an application during a pre-trial hearing under s 39.

Questions as to disclosure amount to questions of law for the purposes of s 40. Alternatively, it may be possible to seek challenge by means of an application for judicial review under RSC 1965, Ord 53, provided the matters do not relate to trial on indictment for the purposes of s 29 of the Supreme Court Act 1981. In addition, failure to comply with disclosure provisions may well amount to an irregularity for the purposes of challenge on appeal should a conviction be obtained on a charge consequent to such a failure to disclose.

THE NEW LAW – MATERIAL THAT NEED NOT BE DISCLOSED

2.76 It has already been noted that material must not be disclosed by the prosecution to the extent that:

(a) it has been intercepted in obedience to a warrant issued under s 2 of the Interception of Communications Act 1985;
(b) it indicates that such a warrant has been issued or that material has been intercepted in obedience to such a warrant (s 3(7); s 7(6); s 8(6); s 9(9)).

The purpose of s 2 of the Interception of Communications Act 1985 is to authorise the issue of warrants for the interception of communications, for investigative purposes. This is confirmed by the use of the expression 'preventing and detecting crime' contained in s 2 of the 1985 Act.[1]

---

1 See Lord Mustill in *Preston* [1993] 4 All ER at 666, and the terms of s 9 of the 1985 Act.

2.77 In *Preston*,[1] the House of Lords held that the prosecution was under a duty to disclose to the defence material evidence or information even if it would be inadmissible by the defence under s 9 of the 1985 Act. However, in the light of the 1985 Act, the non-disclosure of the existence of telephone intercepts, and the material contained or derived from them, was an exception to the rule that the prosecution was under a general duty to disclose all unused material to the defence. Therefore, the destruction of that material required by s 6 of the 1985 Act was not a material irregularity in a subsequent trial, because

Parliament could not have intended that an accused person should be able to rely on the absence of that material in order to secure an acquittal. However, Lord Mustill observed, obiter, that nothing in the 1985 Act prevents the prosecution from making disclosure if it chooses to do so.

The terms of the new Act point to a contrary conclusion. The words used in each of s 3(7), s 7(6), s 8(6) and s 9(9) are 'must not be disclosed'. However, in each instance those words are followed by the words 'under this section', and the question therefore arises as to whether or not any power or duty to disclose arises apart from those provisions. It may be, for example, that telephone intercept material points strongly to the weakness of a prosecution case, or to the accused being not guilty of an offence charged. It would be extremely odd, and unfair, if the prosecutor was unable, should such material be discovered, to disclose that material to the defence. Although the effect of s 20 of the new Act is to disapply the rules of common law which pertained prior to the new Act in respect of cases falling within the new rules, the continued duty upon a prosecutor to act fairly remains. For this reason, it is submitted that should such evidence be available, the new Act does not prevent its disclosure on a voluntary basis. However, the reasoning in *Preston* appears to remain good, in the sense that no disclosure can be *required* of the prosecution, and it is this to which the new Act is referring in these provisions. As a result, a defendant cannot, legitimately, justify a failure to give a defence statement under s 5(3) on the grounds that there is undisclosed material relating to telephone intercepts. If disclosure is not possible, because of the sensitivity of the material obtained, it will be the duty of the prosecutor to consider whether the prosecution should proceed further.[2]

---

1 [1993] 4 All ER 638 (HL).
2 See Lord Mustill in *Preston* at p 664.

Withholding of information on the grounds of public interest

2.78   As already noted, s 3(6), s 7(5), s 8(5) and s 9(8) each permit material to be withheld where disclosure would be contrary to the public interest. Such material (hereafter referred to as 'sensitive material')[1] is governed by the pre-existing common law rules. Nothing in the new Act changes the substantive law or rules of evidence that apply to such material. What constitutes sensitive material is the subject of detailed provision in the Code of Practice. For this reason, and for ease of exposition, the substantive law is considered later, in Chapter 3.

---

1 See paras **3.55–3.66**.

2.79   The general question arises: how will the new Act overcome some of the difficulties in relation to sensitive material highlighted by the Government's Consultation Paper?[1] The answer to that question lies in the more restrictive test for prosecution disclosure rather than in any change in the rules of law relating to public interest immunity itself. These rules are being reviewed by the Government, although it may be that the law can better develop on a case-by-case basis, rather than by legislation.[2]

1 See para **2.26**.
2 *Inquiry into the Export of Defence Equipment and Dual-Use Goods to Iraq and related prosecutions*, vol 3, para K 6.1, p 1781. See also Simon Brown LJ in *Brown* [1995] 1 Cr App R 191 (CA).

The procedure to be followed

2.80 In *Davis*,[1] the Court of Appeal set out the following procedure, modifying that outlined in *Ward*:[2]

(a) If the prosecution wishes to rely on public interest immunity or sensitivity to justify non-disclosure then, where possible:
    (i) it has to give notice to the defence that they are applying for a ruling by the court;
    (ii) it has to indicate to the defence the category of the material held;
    (iii) the defence has to be given the opportunity of making representations to the court.

(b) Where to disclose even the category of material in question would in effect reveal that which the Crown contends should not be in the public interest to be revealed, different considerations apply. Although the Crown should still notify the defence that an application would be made, the category of material need not be specified and the application would be ex parte. If the court hearing the application considers that the normal procedure ought to have been followed it will so order; if not, it will rule on the ex parte application.

(c) In highly exceptional and rare cases where disclosure of even the fact that an ex parte application is to be made could defeat the public interest in non-disclosure, the prosecution should apply to the court ex parte without notice to the defence, and if the court hearing the application considers that at least notice of the application should have been given, or even that the normal inter partes procedure should be adopted it will so order.

1 [1993] 2 All ER 643 (CA).
2 [1993] 2 All ER 577 (CA).

2.81 This procedure is to be replaced by procedures to be set out in rules made under s 18(2). No such rules have been made as at the date of going to press.

Section 14 deals with issues of non-disclosure on public interest grounds that arise in summary trials, and s 15 deals with such issues arising in other cases. Section 14 provides for an accused to make to the court an application for a review of the question whether it is still not in the public interest to disclose material affected by an order made under s 3(6), s 7(5), s 8(5) or s 9(8) (s 14(2)). This power to make an application continues until such time as the accused is acquitted, convicted or the prosecutor decides not to proceed with the case concerned.[1] If an application is made the court must review the question as to whether or not it is in the public interest to disclose the material and, if it concludes that it is in the public interest, to disclose material to any extent:

(a) it shall so order; and
(b) it shall take such steps as are reasonable to inform the prosecutor of its
     order (s 14(3)).

The wording of s 14(3) clearly contemplates that such an application need
not be made in the presence of the prosecutor and, presumably, such an
application will be made ex parte without notice having been given. The
provisions of s 14(3) and s 14(4) make no sense unless this is in fact the case.

---

1 See annotations to s 7.

2.82 Section 15 contains similar, but not identical, provisions in respect of
cases to be tried on indictment. The scope of the application of s 15 is the same
as that obtained in respect of s 14; the power of review exists from the time of
the making of the order under s 3(6), s 7(5), s 8(5) or s 9(8), until acquittal,
conviction, or the time the prosecutor decides not to proceed with the case
concerned.

However, the duty in s 15 differs from that in s 14, in that the court itself must
keep under review the question whether at any given time it is still not in the
public interest to disclose material affected by its order (s 15(3)). An
application may be made for this purpose by the accused, such an application
to be subject to the rules referred to above in respect of summary applications.
However, an application by the accused is not essential, because the court must
keep the question under review without the need for an application. It is
unclear from the new Act itself how this duty of ongoing review will in fact be
undertaken.

If the court at any time concludes that it is in the public interest to disclose
material to any extent:

(a) it shall so order; and
(b) it shall take such steps as are reasonable to inform the prosecutor of its
     order.

The prosecutor will then be required to act in accordance with the requirements of Part I of the new Act.

THIRD PARTY DOCUMENTS

2.83 The problems in respect of third party material have already been
noted.[1] If material is in the hands of one part of the same organisation which is
acting as prosecutor, these problems may be overcome by concluding that
material is in the possession of the prosecutor.[1] This is particularly important in
the context of government departments, where problems were highlighted by
the Scott Report.[2] That Report recommended as follows:

(a) that it be accepted as one of the duties of solicitors acting in a prosecution,
     and a counsel for the prosecution once instructed, to consider and advise
     whether any, and if so what, requests for documents should be made to
     other government departments or agencies;

(b) the documents requested should include not only those relevant to the way in which the prosecution puts its case, but also those relevant to the way in which the defence proposes to put its case (if under the extent that it is known or may reasonably be inferred);

(c) every request to other government departments or agencies for documents should be in writing, and in a form settled by solicitors or counsel for the prosecution;

(d) a copy of every such request by the prosecution should be supplied to the defence;

(e) a brief report describing the nature of the search for documents carried out consequent upon each request be prepared by the solicitors for the prosecution. If or to the extent that the search was carried out by the government department or agency itself, that fact should be stated. A copy of the report should be supplied to the defence.

However, in *Blackledge*[3] the Court of Appeal concluded that an organisation could, for the purposes of the disclosure rules, be regarded as indivisible; documents held by one department being in the hands of the Crown in the context of a prosecution being undertaken by another.

---

1 See para **2.30**.
2 Op cit, para K 5.1.
3 (1995) *The Times*, 7 November.

2.84 In other circumstances, third party material may be disclosable by the third party himself, irrespective of any obligation imposed on the prosecutor. In *Maguire*[1] the Court of Appeal concluded that a forensic scientist who is an adviser to the prosecuting authority is under a duty to disclose material of which he knows and which may have 'some bearing on the offence charged and the surrounding circumstances of the case'. That test remains, for this purpose, unaffected by the new Act. Such disclosure is to the person who retains him. Thus a failure to disclose was held to be capable of amounting to a material irregularity.

---

1 [1992] 2 All ER 433 (CA).

2.85 The rationale for this conclusion is that there is no basis to distinguish between members of a prosecuting authority and those advising it in the capacity of a forensic scientist. That reasoning will arguably hold good in respect of any third party being relied on by the prosecutor and, in any event, the prosecutor may well be under a positive duty to make inquiries of that third party. However, such reasoning does not assist in the many cases where third party information cannot be directly linked to the prosecutor in this way. In such cases the proper method of proceeding is, if necessary, to compel the third party to produce material under a witness summons, issued under either s 97 of the Magistrates' Courts Act 1980 (in the case of summary trial), or s 2 of the Criminal Procedure (Attendance of Witnesses) Act 1965 (trial on indictment). Both these provisions are amended by the new Act,[1] the latter extensively so, so as to protect the interests of third parties.[2] However, it should be remembered that the production of documents under either of these provisions is not, and is not intended to be, the same as disclosure by a prosecutor.

---

1 See paras **7.32–7.35**.
2 See para **5.39**.

2.86   In *Derby Magistrates' Court ex parte B*,[1] Lord Taylor CJ sitting in the House of Lords rejected a submission that the test of 'likely to be material evidence' to be found in s 97 of the 1980 Act[2] was to be equated with that of materiality for the purposes of the then common law disclosure rules contained in *Keane*. The effect of this is that material may be non-producable under s 97, even though it may fall within the test for prosecution disclosure. This is because in some cases the documents only attract the classification of material evidence once they are in the hands of the party who wishes to use them. Thus, in the *Derby* case, the accused wished to use the documents to discredit a prosecution witness. If he had had such documents he could have done so, but they only became material evidence once questions had been put to the witness about a previous inconsistent statement which the witness denies making.

These provisions do not, therefore, amount to a general right to obtain evidence from third parties. The tests for the production of such material[3] are restrictive, because of the impositions such claims place on third parties, and the court. In one case, a judge spent some 11 days reading material in order to determine what third party material should be produced.[4] The changes made by the new Act in this context are 'modest',[5] and are to be regarded as a first step. They do not form part of a coherent package of measures equating third party and prosecution disclosure.

---

1 See para **5.34**.
2 [1995] 4 All ER 526. See also *Reading Justices ex parte Berkshire County Council* (1995) *The Times*, 5 May; *Cheltenham Justices ex parte Secretary of State for Trade and Industry* [1977] 1 WLR 95.
3 See para **5.36**.
4 See the judgment of Staughton LJ in *W(G)* (1996) *The Times*, 12 July. It is open to a judge to rely on the assessment of independent counsel appointed by the third party: ibid.
5 Baroness Blatch, Minister of State, Home Office, Lords' consideration of Commons' amendments, col 968.

Chapter 3

DISCLOSURE: THE CODE OF PRACTICE AND RELATED ISSUES

The Code of Practice on disclosure – Recording of material – Retention of material – Revelation and disclosure of material – Sensitive material – Public interest immunity

INTRODUCTION

3.1 In Chapter 2 we examined the provisions of the new Act which impose disclosure obligations on a prosecutor and on an accused. However, by itself this framework is not sufficient to ensure that the overall aim of fairness and 'equality of arms'[1] is achieved. For that to be achieved, proper systems and procedures must be in place, and followed, during the investigation, so that information, documents and objects[2] are properly recorded and retained. Further, if the prosecutor is to comply properly with the obligations which Part I of the new Act imposes on him, he needs to be properly informed about the information and material held by the investigator, and appropriate evidence provided to him. The systems and procedures to ensure the attainment of these objectives are to be contained in a Code of Practice for Criminal Investigation.

---

1 See para **2.4**.
2 See s 2(4), and s 22(1).

3.2 Part II of the Act makes provision for the making and content of such a Code. Under s 23 and s 25 of the new Act, the Home Secretary has the power to prepare such a Code in draft, and, after consultation, to lay it before Parliament. As at the date of going to press no Code has been brought into operation under s 25(2). Nevertheless, various drafts were prepared before and during the passage of the new Act, so as to inform debate, and to inform those likely to be affected by the Code or required to implement it.

References were made in Chapter 2 to aspects of the draft Code, and much of this chapter is concerned with its provisions. References to the draft Code are to the draft as it was published on the date the new Act received Royal Assent. That draft is set out at the end of this book. It may be that further changes will be made. However, the overall approach and content of the Code appear settled.

By s 26(3), the Code will be admissible in evidence in all criminal and civil proceedings, but s 26(2) states that a failure to comply with the Code does not of itself render a person liable to any criminal or civil proceedings.

Interpretation of the Code

3.3 This Code will be a key document which, in the context of disclosure, will identify the duties and functions of investigating officers and disclosure officers. However, like other Codes and, in particular, like the Codes made pursuant to s 67(9) of the Police and Criminal Evidence Act 1984 (PACE), it does not have the direct force of law and, therefore, it should not be construed as if its contents were those of a statute. Rather, it is clear from debate during the passage of the new Act on the application of the Code to persons other than police officers,[1] that the intent of Parliament is that the spirit of the Code should be followed. For that reason, it is submitted that the courts are likely to look at the purposes which the detailed provisions of the Code are intended to serve, and interpret and apply its provisions to give effect to that intent.

---

1 See paras **3.15–3.16**.

The purpose of the Code

3.4 By s 23(1), the Home Secretary is under a duty to prepare a code of practice containing provisions designed to secure certain objectives.
   These are as follows:

(a) That where a criminal investigation is conducted, all reasonable steps are taken for the purposes of the investigation and, in particular, all reasonable lines of inquiry are pursued.

(b) That information[1] which is obtained in the course of a criminal investigation[2] and which may be relevant to the investigation is recorded.

(c) That any record[3] of such information is retained.

(d) That any other material which is obtained in the course of a criminal investigation and may be relevant to the investigation is retained.

(e) That information falling within paragraph (b), and material falling within paragraph (d), is revealed to a person who is involved in the prosecution of criminal proceedings arising out of or relating to the investigation,[4] and who is identified in accordance with prescribed provisions.

(f) That where such a person inspects information or other material in pursuance of a requirement that it be revealed to him, and he requests that it be disclosed to the accused, the accused is allowed to inspect it or is given a copy of it.

(g) That where such a person is given a document indicating the nature of information or other material in pursuance of a requirement that it be revealed to him, and he requests that it be disclosed to the accused, the accused is allowed to inspect it or is given a copy of it.

(h) That the person who is to allow the accused to inspect information or other material or to give him a copy of it,[5] shall decide which of those (inspecting or giving a copy) is appropriate.

(i)   That where the accused is allowed to inspect material as mentioned in paragraph (f) or (g) and he requests a copy, he is given one unless the person allowing the inspection[5] is of opinion that it is not practicable or not desirable to give him one.

(j)   That a person mentioned in paragraph (e) is given a written statement that prescribed activities which the Code requires have been carried out.

---

1 See the definition of material in s 22(2).
2 See s 22(1) and para **3.15**.
3 See annotations to s 23.
4 See annotations to s 2, and para **3.15**.
5 See para **3.47**.

3.5 'Material' is defined by s 22(2) in the same terms as it was defined in Part I of the new Act.[1] It includes material of all kinds and, in particular, includes references to information, and objects of all descriptions. The Code will not apply to material intercepted in obedience to a warrant issued under s 2 of the Interception of Communications Act 1985 (s 23(6)).

---

1 See s 2(4) and para **2.28**.

3.6 The obligation placed on the Home Secretary is to prepare a Code 'designed to secure' the stated objectives. No positive obligation is imposed actually to secure these objectives, but nothing turns on what is essentially a linguistic point. It is those who actually operate the system created by the Code who will actually attain the objectives.[1]

Another definitional point arises in the context of s 23, and the draft Code, where the term 'revealed' is used. No significance attaches to its use rather than the use of the term 'disclosed'. Disclosure is intended to describe the duty that arises between prosecutor and accused. The term 'reveal' and its derivatives describe the duty that arises between investigator and prosecutor.

---

1 See Baroness Blatch, Minister of State, Home Office, HL Committee, col 1540.

3.7 The general terms of s 23(1) are supplemented by further provisions in both s 23 and s 24.

In relation to the former, s 23(2) states that the Code may include provision:

(a)   that a police officer identified in accordance with prescribed provisions must carry out a prescribed activity which the Code requires;

(b)   that a police officer so identified must take steps to secure the carrying out by a person (whether or not a police officer) of a prescribed activity which the Code requires;

(c)   that a duty must be discharged by different people in succession in prescribed circumstances (as when a person dies or retires).

The term 'prescribed' means prescribed by the Code (s 23(8)).

Section 24 gives examples of the kinds of provision that may be included in the Code by virtue of s 23(5). This is dealt with later.[1]

_____

1 See para **3.9**.
_____

3.8   The new Act provides that the Code may include provisions in respect of the form in which information is recorded (s 23(3)), and about the manner and period for which a record of information or other material is to be retained (s 23(4)). In particular, the Code may extend that period beyond the time of a conviction or an acquittal.[1] It may also include provision about the time when, the form in which, the way in which and the extent to which, information or any other material is to be revealed to the prosecutor (s 23(5)).

_____

1 See annotations to s 8.
_____

3.9   Section 24 gives examples of the kind of provision that may be included in the Code by virtue of s 22(5). Although by its very nature, s 24 is, and is intended to be, illustrative, it clearly indicates the intent of Parliament. It is submitted that any Code which failed to address the particular issues identified as illustrations would fail adequately to reflect that intent and would potentially be open to challenge.[1] However, the courts are reluctant on judicial review to intervene in relation to the legality of a document which has been laid before Parliament,[2] and, in any event, the draft Code does, in fact, contain appropriate provisions reflecting the matters given as examples by s 24. The particular examples set out in s 24 are dealt with at the appropriate points in this chapter.

_____

1 *Padfield v Minister of Agriculture, Fisheries and Food* [1968] 1 All ER 694 (HL).
2 *Nottinghamshire County Council v Secretary of State for the Environment* [1986] 1 All ER 199 (HL).
_____

Roles and functions under the draft Code

3.10   Pursuant to s 23(2), the draft Code identifies specific functions and allocates responsibilities. The following are the main functions and responsibilities envisaged in it:[1]

(a)   an *investigator* is any police officer involved in the conduct of a criminal investigation. All investigators have a responsibility for carrying out the duties imposed on them under the draft Code (including, in particular, recording information and retaining records of information and other material);

(b)   the *officer in charge of an investigation* is the police officer responsible for directing a criminal investigation. He is also responsible for ensuring that proper procedures are in place for recording information, and for the retention of records of information and other material acquired during the investigation;

(c)   the *disclosure officer* is the person responsible for examining the records created during the investigation, for revealing material to the prosecutor during the investigation and any criminal proceedings resulting from it, for disclosing it to the accused,[2] and for certifying where necessary that action has been taken in accordance with the requirements of the Code.[3]

1 Draft Code, para 2.1.
2 But see s 3 and para **3.53**.
3 See para **3.51**.

3.11 The draft Code does not define the term 'person who is involved in the prosecution of criminal proceedings ... and who is identified in accordance with prescribed provisions', a term used in s 23(1)(e), and referred to by s 23(1)(f), (g) and (j). Nevertheless, the draft Code consistently uses the term 'prosecutor', and imposes duties on disclosure officers to notify, disclose to and certify to a prosecutor.[1] Arguably, the difference in wording between s 23(1)(e) and the draft Code is merely of linguistic, rather than practical, significance.

1 For the meaning of prosecutor, see annotations to s 2.

3.12 The terms used by para 2.1 of the draft Code are intended to define functions, not specify persons. The functions themselves are separate and distinct. However, whether they are undertaken by one, two or more persons will depend on the complexity of the case and the administrative arrangements within each police force. In a small case of no great complexity, all three functions might be performed by one person. By contrast, in a complex and large investigation almost certainly they will be performed by separate persons. Where they are undertaken by more than one person, close consultation between them will be essential if the duties imposed by the Code are to be performed effectively.[1]

1 See draft Code, para 3.1.

3.13 Each of these functions will be assigned to an identified person. In particular, the role played by the disclosure officer is crucial in ensuring the effectiveness of the disclosure scheme. The chief officer of police[1] for each police force area is responsible for putting in place arrangements to ensure that in every investigation the identity of the disclosure officer is recorded.[2] However, there is no provision in the draft Code which permits the delegation of functions by a disclosure officer to another officer. If the named officer no longer has responsibility for the performance of that function, or becomes unable or unavailable to perform it, someone else must be assigned to perform that duty. Such action is governed by para 3.6 of the draft Code, which appears on its face to permit the assigning of a replacement either by the disclosure officer's supervisor or by the police officer in charge of criminal investigations for the area. Given that the functions of investigating officer and disclosure officer may be performed by the same person, there appears to be no reason in principle why the assignment of a replacement disclosure officer should not be made by either of the officers specified in para 3.6.

1 References to police officers and to the chief officer of police include those employed in a police force as defined in s 3(3) of the Prosecution of Offences Act 1985: see draft Code, para 2.1.
2 Draft Code, para 3.2.

3.14 By contrast to the position in respect of disclosure officers, the officer in charge of an investigation may delegate tasks to another investigator or to civilians employed by the police force, but he remains responsible for ensuring that these have been carried out and for accounting for general policies followed in the investigation.[1] As was the case in respect of disclosure officers, his function may be assigned to another, pursuant to para 3.6 of the draft Code.

1 Draft Code, para 3.2.

Application of the Code

3.15 As is probably the case in respect of Part I of the new Act,[1] the Code will apply to any criminal investigation in relation to suspected or alleged offences which has not begun before the day appointed by the Home Secretary under s 25(2) for the coming into force of Part II of the Act (s 25(3)). The breadth of the expressions 'criminal investigations' and 'begun' have already been noted,[2] and clearly apply to all types of police investigations. However, unlike Part I of the new Act, Part II and the new Code is limited to criminal investigations conducted by *police officers*[3] with a view to it being ascertained:

(a) whether a person should be charged with an offence; or
(b) whether a person charged with an offence is guilty of it (s 22(1)).

The reasons why Part II limits the direct application of the proposed Code to investigations conducted by police officers was the subject of vigorous debate during the passage of the new Act; with some arguing that, because Part I is of application to all criminal prosecutions, the duties imposed by the proposed Code should be imposed on all investigators.[4] This view was not shared by the Government, the Minister of State pointing out that the terms of the draft Code were appropriate for the structures and functions of police forces, and for the relationship between the police and the Crown Prosecution Service.[5] They are not necessarily appropriate for other organisations where both investigatory and prosecution functions are performed within that organisation, or by one person. For this reason, the draft Code has a more limited application than the Codes made pursuant to s 67(9) of PACE.

1 See s 1(2) and para **2.7**, where differences in wording between s 1(2) and s 25(3) were noted.
2 See paras **2.6–2.7**.
3 See annotations to s 1.
4 See Mr Alun Michael, MP, HC Committee, col 88.
5 See Baroness Blatch, Minister of State, Home Office, HL Committee, col 1542.

3.16   Nevertheless, the intention is that the spirit of the Code should be applied by all investigators. Section 26(1) states that a person other than a police officer who is charged with the duty of conducting an investigation with a view to it being ascertained:

(a)   whether a person should be charged with an offence; or
(b)   whether a person charged with an offence is guilty of it,

shall in discharging that duty have regard to any relevant provision of a Code which would apply if the investigation were conducted by police officers.

If a person, other than a police officer, fails to have such regard to the proposed Code, that failure will itself be relevant in deciding issues such as whether an irregularity has occurred sufficient to provide grounds for an appeal,[1] whether evidence is admissible or whether an abuse of process has occurred.[2] Thus the desired result is achieved without the new Code being directly binding on an investigator who is not a police officer. Of course, such a person might in one sense 'have regard' to the Code although declining to follow its provisions. However, the clear intent of Parliament is that the principles of the Code, modified appropriately, should be applied. An investigator who merely paid lip-service to the draft Code should not be treated as having had 'regard' to the Code within the meaning of s 26(1).

---

1 See Criminal Appeal Act 1995, s 2(1).
2 See para **3.18**.

3.17   When a criminal investigation 'begins' was discussed in Chapter 2.[1] It was there submitted that the widest interpretation be placed on that word. This is confirmed by para 2.1 of the draft Code, which brings within the ambit of a criminal investigation not only investigations to decide whether a person should be charged with an offence, or is guilty of it, but also investigations to ascertain whether a crime has been committed, and intelligence-led operations begun even before a crime has been committed, such as the keeping of premises or individuals under observation for a period of time.

---

1 See para **2.7**.

Sanctions for breach of the Code

3.18   No direct sanction for failure to comply with the Code exists. Rather, it is a relevant matter to which regard must be had in determining other issues.

By s 26(4), if it appears to a court or tribunal conducting criminal or civil proceedings that:

(a)   any provision of the Code; or
(b)   any failure by a person (other than a police officer) charged with the duty of conducting an investigation to have regard to any relevant provision of the Code,

is relevant to any question arising in the proceedings, the provision or failure shall be taken into account in deciding the question. The sanctions applicable in the case of non-police investigators have already been discussed,[1] and are of general application. Thus, if questions arise in the context of admissibility of evidence, abuse of process or grounds of appeal, the provisions of the Code, and the nature of any breach, will be relevant. Arguably, the approach taken in respect of the PACE codes, where emphasis has been placed on 'significant and substantial' breaches,[2] is equally pertinent in the context of the new Act and Code.

1 See para **3.16**.
2 *Walsh* (1989) 91 Cr App R 161 (CA).

RECORDING OF INFORMATION

3.19 The proper recording of information obtained during, or for the purposes of, a criminal investigation is a key precondition for the existence of an effective scheme for prosecution disclosure. It has already been seen that s 3(3) defines prosecution disclosure as the giving of a copy of information which has been recorded, or the making available for inspection the record of such information if it is not practicable or desirable to supply a copy. By s 3(4), it is the duty of a prosecutor in respect of information which has not been recorded to ensure that it is, and that a copy is supplied or made available for inspection to the accused. So too with material not consisting of information: it has to be available for inspection by the accused (s 3(5)).

3.20 For these reasons, Part II of the Act, and the draft Code, impose obligations in respect of recording. Section 23(3) provides that the Code may include provision about the form in which information is to be recorded, and the Code may provide for what period records are to be retained (s 23(4)(a)). The draft Code places the obligation to ensure that information is recorded on the officer in charge of the investigation. Of course, this does not mean that that officer actually has to undertake that recording. That duty is placed on all investigators.[1]

If material which may be relevant to the investigation consists of information which is not recorded in any form, he must ensure that it is recorded in a durable or retrievable form (whether in writing, on video or audio tape, or on computer disk [sic]).[1]

1 Draft Code, para 4.1.

3.21 This duty to record is not confined to information that *is* relevant to the investigation, but extends to all material which *may* be relevant. The scope of this duty is therefore wide, and necessarily so if the obligation placed on the disclosure officer by paras 7.1–7.3 of the draft Code is to be met,[1] and the prosecutor thus able to exercise his judgment as required by s 3(1).[2] The definition of relevance for this purpose is to be found in para 2.1 of the draft Code. Material may be relevant to the investigation if it appears to the investigator, or to the officer in charge of an investigation, or to the disclosure officer, that it has some bearing on any offence under investigation or any person being investigated, or to the surrounding circumstances of the case, unless it is incapable of having any impact on the case. In an earlier draft of the Code, enquiries and conversations about a case which were not relevant to the investigation were excluded from the duty to record. This restriction no longer applies, and the general test of relevance of the material obtained will apply.

Despite this change, the final words of para 2.1 of the draft Code ('unless it is incapable of having any impact on the case') serve to confirm that there is no obligation to record information which has no relevance to the investigation. However, arguably, there is a duty to record information obtained in one investigation which is relevant to another. This conclusion is confirmed by the use of the expression 'any offence under investigation'. The point will be important only in cases where investigators know or believe that information which they acquire in one inquiry may be relevant to another. In the converse situation where investigators become aware of information obtained by other investigators, it will be incumbent on those investigators who become so aware to secure the recording of that information.[3]

---

1 See para **3.45**.
2 See para **2.27**.
3 See draft Code, para 4.1.

3.22 The duty to record extends not only to positive information (eg information as to what a witness saw or did, or as to the characteristics of an object or substance), but also to negative information (eg as to what a witness did not see or do, or that an object or substance does not have particular characteristics). Paragraph 4.3 of the draft Code gives the example of a series of persons present in a particular place at a particular time, who state that they saw nothing unusual. This may be relevant to the investigation and should be recorded. Clearly, the extent to which negative information is, or may be, relevant will require judgment. However, the keeping of full records as to what is done as part of an investigation will ensure that a record will exist of what may turn out to be relevant information in the light of the way an inquiry develops, irrespective of whether that information is positive or negative in nature.

3.23 Where information which may be relevant is obtained, it must be recorded at the time it is obtained or as soon as practicable thereafter. This includes, for example, information obtained in house-to-house enquiries, although the requirement to record information promptly does not require an investigator to take a statement from a potential witness where it would not otherwise be taken.[1] The duty to record promptly exists also in respect of material not immediately considered to be, or which might be, relevant, but which later turns out to be so. This conclusion is based on the terms of para 8.2 of the draft Code, which requires new material coming to light to be treated in the same way as earlier material. It would be absurd to treat material which already is known about, but the relevance of which was not appreciated, differently from such new material. A duty to record surely exists once the relevance of material is identified. Such an approach is adopted in respect of the *retention* of material,[2] and is the only approach consistent with the terms of s 23(1)(b) of the new Act, which requires the Code to secure that information which is obtained and which may be relevant, is recorded.

3.24 Information may already be recorded in one form, for example on a database. Clearly, it is desirable evidentially for the initial record to be preserved. However, where it is not practicable to retain the initial record of information because it forms part of a larger record which is to be destroyed, its contents should be transferred verbatim to a durable and more easily stored form before that happens.[1]

1 Draft Code, para 4.2.

RETENTION OF MATERIAL

3.25 Information must not only be recorded, the records made must be retained, as must material comprising matters or objects other than information.[1] Section 23(4) states that the Code may include provision about the manner in which, and the period for which, records of information and other material are to be retained. That period may extend beyond conviction or acquittal[2] for an offence.

1 See the duties of the prosecutor under s 3(3),(4) and (5) of the new Act.
2 See annotations to s 8.

3.26 The investigator must retain material obtained in a criminal investigation which he believes may be relevant to the investigation. This includes not only material coming into the possession of the investigator (such as documents seized in the course of searching premises) but also material generated by him (such as interview records). Material may be retained in the form of a copy rather than the original if the original was supplied to the investigator rather than generated by him and is to be returned to its owner.[1] It should be remembered that the copy supplied to an accused does not need to be in the same form in which it was originally recorded (s 3(3)).

1 Draft Code, para 5.1.

3.27 This duty of retention is, in the case of material seized in the exercise of the powers of seizure conferred by PACE,[1] subject to the provisions on the retention of seized material in s 22 of PACE.[2] In particular, s 22(3) and (4) of PACE impose restrictions on the retention of material in the possession of the police.[3]

1 Powers of seizure are conferred by Part II of PACE (ss 8–23) (Powers of entry, search and seizure), as well as by PACE, s 32 (search on arrest), s 54 (search of detained persons), and s 55 (intimate searches).

2 Draft Code, para 5.2.
3 PACE, s 22(3), states:
   'Nothing seized in the ground that it may be used—
   (a) to cause physical injury to any person;
   (b) to damage property;
   (c) to interfere with evidence; or
   (d) to assist in escape from police detention or lawful custody,
   may be retained when the person from whom it was seized is no longer in police detention
   or the custody of a court or is in the custody of a court but has been released on bail.'

   PACE s 22(4), states:
   'Nothing may be retained for either of the purposes mentioned in subsection (2)(a) ... if a
   photograph or copy would be sufficient for that purpose.'

   The purposes mentioned in s 22(2)(a) are when anything is seized for use as evidence at
   trial, or for forensic examination or for investigation in respect of an offence.

3.28 If the officer in charge of an investigation becomes aware as a result of
developments in the case that material previously examined but not retained
(because it was not thought to be relevant) may now be relevant to the
investigation, he should where practicable take steps to obtain it, or ensure it is
retained for further inspection or for production in court if required.[1] This
could be achieved, for example, by the obtaining of a search warrant or an
appropriate court order.

---

1 Draft Code, para 5.3.

3.29 The draft Code specifically identifies certain types of material as material
that must be retained.[1] These are as follows:

(a) crime reports (including crime report forms, relevant parts of incident
     report books or police officers' notebooks);
(b) records of telephone messages (eg 999 calls) containing descriptions of
     an alleged offence or offender;
(c) final versions of witness statements (and draft versions where they differ in
     any way from the final version), including any exhibits mentioned (unless
     these have been returned to their owner on the understanding that they
     will be produced in court if required);
(d) interview records (written records, or audio or video tapes, of interviews
     with actual or potential witnesses or suspects);
(e) communications between the police and experts such as a forensic
     scientist, reports of work carried out by experts, and schedules of scientific
     material prepared by the expert for the investigator, for the purposes of
     criminal proceedings;
(f) any material casting doubt on the reliability of a confession;
(g) any material casting doubt on the reliability of a witness;
(h) any other material which may fall within the test for primary prosecution
     disclosure of the Act.

The duty to retain material falling into these categories does not extend to
items such as routine exchanges of information or other material which is
purely ancillary to the material in these categories.[2]

3.30 All material of the type described in para **3.29** has the potential to undermine the prosecution case, which is the test for primary prosecution disclosure under s 3(1) of the new Act.[1] Indeed, the duty to retain is drawn broadly and includes draft witness statements which differ in any way from the final version. The wording of this particular provision differs from that originally proposed, and is likely to mean the drafts are retained as a matter of course. By definition, drafts often differ from the final version eventually produced.

Most of the types of material described at para **3.29** relate to matters in issue in an individual case. However, the duty to disclose goes beyond matters going to issue, and extends to matters that affect the credit of a witness which might undermine the prosecution case.[2]

The duty to retain material which casts doubt on the reliability of a witness is wide enough to include not only material that goes beyond questions of reliability on the issue, but also casts doubt on that testimony because of bias, reward, corruption, illusion or whatever. It should be so construed and applied.

1 See para **2.35**.
2 See para **2.36**.

3.31 Also widely drawn under para 5.4 of the draft Code is the duty to retain communications between police and experts, again a provision which changed during the evolution of the draft Code. Patently, the duty to retain is a duty to retain material. Where the communication between police and expert is oral (eg by telephone), there will usually be a duty to record the information discussed, in accordance with the requirements of para 4.1 of the draft Code.[1] Given the importance that forensic evidence often plays, it is of crucial importance that defence advocates can fully test the basis upon which forensic evidence has been obtained,[2] and that information which may place such evidence in a new or different light is available for disclosure to the defence.

However, the obligation described above is subject to para 5.6 of the draft Code. This states that the duty to retain draft versions of witness statements does not extend to draft statements of opinion prepared by expert witnesses: earlier versions tend to be based on incomplete information, and evolve as further information comes to light and additional expert contributions are obtained.

1 See para **3.19**.
2 For the dangers that can arise in the context of forensic evidence, see *Ward* [1993] 2 All ER 577 (CA); *Maguire* [1992] 2 All ER 433 (CA).

3.32 Material may be relevant yet not be in the hands of the police but amount to third party material. If the officer in charge of an investigation or the disclosure officer believes that other investigating agencies may be in possession of material that may be relevant to the investigation, he should inform the agency of the existence of the investigation, and the disclosure officer should inform the prosecutor that the agency has such material. However, the officer in charge of an investigation and the disclosure officer are not required to make speculative enquiries of other investigating agencies: there must be some reason to believe that they must have relevant material.[1]

---

1 Draft Code, para 3.4.

3.33 The term 'other investigating agency' is not defined, but clearly goes beyond police forces. Some guidance may be gained, by analogy, from the interpretation of the words 'charged with the duty of investigating offences' contained in s 67(9) of PACE.[1] However, the use of the term 'agency' might suggest a narrower interpretation, and other questions arise as, for example, the extent to which the security services could be regarded as an 'investigating agency' for this purpose. It is submitted that it would be wrong in principle for the duty in para 3.4 of the draft Code not to apply to a State agency that has a role, albeit often indirect, in law enforcement. It should also be noted that the duty in para 3.4 does not extend to knowledge of relevant materials in the hands of third parties other than investigating agencies. There appears to be no obligation to inform a prosecutor or anyone else of information known to an investigator that relevant material may be held by such third parties, although it should be borne in mind that the draft Code of Practice should be designed to secure 'that where a criminal investigation is conducted all reasonable steps are taken for the purposes of the investigation and, in particular, all reasonable lines of inquiry are pursued' (s 33(1)(a)). However, no specific provisions of the draft Code appear to deal with this point.

---

1 See annotations to s 1.

3.34 If a criminal investigation results in a person being charged with an offence, all relevant material must be retained at least until either:

(a) the prosecutor decides not to proceed with the case;
(b) the case results in an acquittal;
(c) the case results in a conviction, and the time-limit for an appeal has expired with no appeal being lodged; or
(d) an appeal against conviction is determined, in cases where the appeal is lodged within time.[1]

There is no duty to retain material even in circumstances where it is known that a conviction is being re-opened. Theoretically, such material could be destroyed. This conclusion is consistent with the terms of s 9(2), which deals with the duty of the prosecutor to keep under review his duty of disclosure,[2] and is driven by practicalities. Clearly, material cannot be retained indefinitely, and the likelihood of material knowingly being destroyed in such circumstances is, arguably, slight.

1 Draft Code, para 5.8.
2 See para **2.71**.

3.35   The chief officer of police for each police force area must develop a policy on the length of time for which material is retained if a criminal investigation does not result in charges and also after the conclusion of any criminal proceedings if the investigation has resulted in charges.[1] In developing the policy, he may take into account the following criteria among others:

(a)   the seriousness of the offence;
(b)   the plea entered by the accused;
(c)   whether a re-trial is likely, if the proceedings resulted in an acquittal;
(d)   the length of any custodial or community sentence imposed, if the proceedings resulted in a conviction;
(e)   whether an appeal against conviction or sentence is pending or is expected;
(f)   the possibility that a complaint or civil action against the police might follow (particularly if an investigation has not resulted in charges);
(g)   the practice of his force in relation to the retention of material, at the time the policy is developed;
(h)   the retention policies developed or likely to be developed by chief officers of police in other force areas;
(i)   any statutory requirements for the retention of material imposed other than under the Code.

It is open to the chief officer of police to decide either to retain all material for a certain period, or to set differing retention periods according to the criteria set out above.[2] There is no indication of any national policy on these matters, which is, perhaps, somewhat surprising.

1 Draft Code, para 5.9.
2 Ibid, para 5.10.

PREPARATION OF MATERIAL FOR PROSECUTOR

3.36   By s 23(5), the Code may include provision about the time when, the form in which, and the extent to which, information or any other material is to be revealed to the person mentioned in s 23(1)(e). That person is a person 'who is involved in the prosecution of criminal proceedings arising out of or relating to the investigation and who is identified in accordance with prescribed provisions'.[1] The term 'prescribed' means 'prescribed by the code' (s 23(8)).

1 See para **3.11**.

3.37 The detailed provisions of the new Act, and of the draft Code, dealing with the preparation of material by the disclosure officer and with the actual revelation of material by him, draw distinctions between sensitive and non-sensitive material. Material is 'sensitive' to the extent that its disclosure under Part I would be contrary to the public interest (s 24(8)). It has already been seen[1] that various provisions of Part I of the new Act permit, or require, a court to consider whether material should be withheld in the public interest. The nature of that material, and the substantive rules which govern such claims, are discussed later.[2]

1 See ss 3(6), 7(5), 8(5), 9(8), 13(3) and 14(3).
2 See paras **3.56–3.65**.

3.38 In addition to the general provision contained in s 23(5), more detail as to the duties of preparation and revelation is given, by way of example, by s 24:

(a) If a person is required by the Code to reveal material which is, respectively, sensitive or non-sensitive, he must give a document which:
   (i) indicates the nature of that material; and
   (ii) which states that (as the case may be) he believes that material to be sensitive or non-sensitive (s 24(2) and (3)).
   In short, separate schedules in respect of sensitive and non-sensitive material must be prepared for the prosecutor.
(b) The Code may require the person required to reveal material to supply copies of that material to persons prescribed by the Code. These subsections again differentiate between the production of sensitive and non-sensitive material (s 24(4),(5) and (6)).

3.39 This statutory framework is amplified by the detailed provisions in the draft Code. The draft Code places the responsibility for performance of these duties on the disclosure officer. It is his duty to prepare schedules of sensitive and non-sensitive material. These schedules must list material which has been retained and which does not form part of the case against the accused.[1] The term 'material' means material of any kind, including information and objects,[2] which is obtained in the course of a criminal investigation and which may be relevant to the investigation.[3]

1 Draft Code, para 6.1.
2 Ibid, para 2.1 and the new Act, s 22.
3 Draft Code, para 2.1. For the meaning of this provision, see text, para **3.21**.

3.40 The duty to prepare these schedules arises in the circumstances identified by para 6.1 of the draft Code. These reflect the circumstances when prosecution disclosure is likely to be required by s 1 of the new Act. The circumstances are as follows:

(a)   the accused is charged with an offence which is triable only on indictment;
(b)   the accused is charged with an offence which is triable either way, and it is considered either that the case is likely to be tried on indictment or that the accused is likely to plead not guilty at a summary trial;
(c)   the accused is charged with a summary offence, and it is considered that he is likely to plead not guilty.

In deciding whether a schedule is likely to be needed in the circumstances identified in (b) and (c) above, the existence or non-existence of an admission to the offence, and the fact that a police officer witnessed the offence are to be regarded as relevant considerations.[1] However, there is nothing in the draft Code to suggest that they are the only, or the determining, considerations, and the disclosure officer (whose decision it is) will need to consider the circumstances as a whole, given the desirability, on the one hand, of early disclosure and, on the other, the desirability of avoiding unnecessary work and administration.

---

1 Draft Code, para 6.2.

3.41   If it is believed that the court will proceed to summary trial and that the accused is likely to plead guilty, it is not necessary to prepare schedules in advance. If, contrary to this belief, it is decided that the offence is to be tried on indictment, or the court proceeds to summary trial and the accused pleads not guilty, the disclosure officer must ensure that a schedule is prepared as soon as is reasonably practicable after that happens.[1] Of course, it needs to be borne in mind that the timescale for prosecution disclosure is to be set by regulations made pursuant to s 12,[2] and that presupposes that the schedules of unused material have been prepared and revealed to the prosecutor. It remains to be seen how, in summary cases, these procedures can be made to work in the way envisaged by Part I of the new Act while avoiding unnecessary adjournments, and avoiding significant numbers of applications for extensions of time under regulations made to fulfil s 12(3)(b) of the new Act.

---

1 Draft Code, para 6.3.
2 Unless no such regulations have been made, in which case s 13 of the new Act will apply. See para **2.42**.

3.42   The disclosure officer should ensure that each item of material is listed separately on the schedule, and is numbered consecutively. The description of each item should make clear the nature of the item and should contain sufficient detail to enable the prosecutor to form a judgment on whether the material needs to be disclosed.[1]

In some enquiries it may not be practicable to list each item of material separately. For example, there may be many items of a similar or repetitive nature. These may be listed in a block and described by quantity and generic title,[2] not simply in major inquiries but in any inquiry where such material is acquired. However, even if some material is listed in a block, the disclosure officer must ensure that any items of material which might meet the test for disclosure[3] are listed and described individually.[4] The wording of this last provision is rather unclear. The test for primary prosecution disclosure is subjective, and depends on the prosecutor's opinion. No such subjective wording is included in the wording of para 6.7 of the draft Code, which is phrased in objective terms.

Although, clearly, a judgment has to be made as to whether the potential for the material to undermine the case for the prosecution exists, arguably, no further judgment or decision by the disclosure officer is required or desirable. That judgment, as to whether such material might in all the circumstances undermine the prosecution case, is for the prosecutor to make, not the disclosure officer. Any other conclusion would significantly undermine the scheme of prosecution disclosure created by Part I of the new Act, and result in prosecutors perhaps being left unaware of potentially disclosable material.

---

1 Draft Code, para 6.5.
2 Ibid, para 6.6.
3 See s 3, and para **2.27**.
4 Draft Code, para 6.7.

3.43 Clearly, when the schedules are prepared, the disclosure officer will not know what defence an accused may subsequently set out in a defence statement under s 5 or s 6 of the new Act.[1] It is not his duty at the time of the preparation of the schedules to seek to anticipate these or speculate as to what the defence might be. Rather, subsequent action may become necessary, a duty discussed later.[1]

---

1 See para **3.49**.

3.44 It has already been noted that the duty to prepare schedules includes a schedule in respect of sensitive material. The meaning of this term was noted at para **3.37**, and is discussed further at para **3.56**. Paragraph 6.4 of the draft Code states that any material which is believed to be sensitive must be either listed on a schedule of sensitive material[1] or, in exceptional circumstances, revealed to the prosecutor separately.[2]

---

1 Draft Code, para 6.8.
2 Ibid, para 6.9. See also text, para **3.68**.

REVELATION OF MATERIAL TO PROSECUTOR

3.45 The draft Code places on the disclosure officer the duty to reveal to the prosecutor certain items. In summary, that officer must take the following action:

(a)   supply to the prosecutor the material which forms part of the prosecution case;

(b)   send the schedules of sensitive and non-sensitive material to the prosecutor.[1] The schedules should be signed and dated by the disclosure officer.[1] Wherever practicable, these schedules should be sent at the same time as the disclosure officer sends the file containing the material for the prosecution case (or as soon as possible after the decision on mode of trial or the plea);[2]

(c)   send to the prosecutor copies of certain material, set out in para 7.3 of the draft Code. This is dealt with at para **3.46**.

---

1 Draft Code, para 7.1.
2 See, ibid, para 6.1, and text, para **3.41**.

3.46   In addition to listing material on the schedule, by para 7.3 of the draft Code the disclosure officer must give the prosecutor, at the same time as he gives him the schedule, a copy of any material which falls into the following categories:

(a)   records of the first description of a suspect given to the police by a potential witness whether or not the description differs from that of the alleged offender. This formulation is wider than that originally proposed, which confined itself to descriptions which differed from that of the accused, and is clearly intended to ensure that cases which wholly or mainly turn on disputed identification evidence can proceed in a fair way, with material being available to the prosecutor which will enable a judgment to be made as to the cogency of the identification being relied on by the prosecution. Clearly, however, there will be no obligation on the prosecutor under s 3 of the new Act to disclose to the accused the first description of the alleged offender if it does not differ from that being relied upon, because such material will not 'undermine the case for the prosecution';

(b)   information provided by an accused person which indicates an explanation for the offence with which he has been charged. This may, or may not, fall within the test for primary prosecution disclosure, and may in any event be part of the prosecution case for the purposes of potential inferences under s 34, s 36 or s 37 of the Criminal Justice and Public Order Act 1994. However, it also provides the prosecutor with the context in which to assess the extent to which the investigation has pursued or dealt with all aspects of the case;

(c)   any material casting doubt on the reliability of a confession. This is clearly disclosable material;[1]

(d)   any material casting doubt on the reliability of a witness. Again, this is disclosable material;[1]

(e)   any other material which the investigator believes may fall within the test for primary prosecution disclosure in the Act. This judgment is that of the investigator, not the disclosure officer, but it is surely inconceivable that a disclosure officer would not forward copies of material known to him and considered by him as potentially undermining the case for the prosecution, even if not identified as such by the investigator.

---

1 See para **2.36**.

3.47 If the prosecutor asks to inspect material which has not already been copied to him, the disclosure officer must allow him to inspect it.[1] If the prosecutor asks him for a copy of material which has not already been copied to him, the disclosure officer must give him a copy. However, this does not apply where the officer in charge of an investigation or the disclosure officer believes that the material is too sensitive to be copied and can only be inspected.[1] This power to deny the prosecutor a copy appears to be vested in either of the two persons identified. No doubt, any disagreements that might arise would be resolved informally through force procedures in liaison with prosecutors. There appears to be no mechanism for the prosecutor to challenge this judgment, save through the making of decisions as to whether, and in what way, to proceed with a prosecution in the light of the situation then appertaining.

---

1 Draft Code, para 7.4.

3.48 If material consists of information which is recorded other than in writing, whether it should be given to the prosecutor in its original form as a whole, or by way of relevant extracts recorded in the same form, or in the form of a transcript, is a matter for agreement between the disclosure officer and the prosecutor.[1] Again, no mechanism exists for the resolution of any disputes.

---

1 Draft Code, para 7.5.

SUBSEQUENT ACTION BY OFFICER IN CHARGE OF INVESTIGATION AND DISCLOSURE OFFICER

3.49 As already noted,[1] at the time a schedule is prepared, the officer in charge of an investigation or disclosure officer will not know what defence the accused is to set out in a defence statement under Part I of the Act. After a defence statement has been given, the disclosure officer must look again at the material which has been retained and must draw the attention of the prosecutor to any material which might reasonably be expected to assist the defence disclosed by the accused. He must reveal it to him in accordance with paras 7.4 and 7.5 of the draft Code.[2]

---

1 See para **3.43**.
2 Draft Code, para 8.1. For paras 7.4 and 7.5 of the draft Code, see text, paras **3.47** and **3.48** respectively.

3.50 The new Act imposes a continuing duty on the prosecutor, for the duration of criminal proceedings against the accused, to disclose material which meets the tests for disclosure[1] (subject to public interest considerations). To enable him to do this, any new material coming to light should be treated in the same way as the earlier material.[2]

---

1 For this continuing duty, see para **2.71**.
2 Draft Code, para 8.2

3.51 The disclosure officer must certify to the prosecutor that, to the best of his knowledge and belief, the duties imposed under the code have been complied with. It will be necessary to do this not only at the time when the schedules and accompanying material are submitted to the prosecutor, but also when material which has been retained is reconsidered after the accused has given a defence statement. This is because the prosecutor must, at the stages of both primary and secondary prosecution disclosure, either disclose material to the accused or give him a written statement that there is no material that meets the test for disclosure.[1]

Where an investigation has been conducted jointly by police officers and officers of another investigating agency, the disclosure officer will be able to certify only in relation to the activities of the police officers.[2]

---

1 Draft Code, para 9.1.
2 Ibid, para 9.2.

DISCLOSURE OF MATERIAL TO ACCUSED

3.52 It will be recalled that Part I of the new Act places the duty of disclosure of material to an accused on the prosecutor. Subsections (3), (4) and (5) of s 3 of the new Act require the prosecutor to disclose material or information either by the supply of a copy or, in certain circumstances, by allowing the accused to inspect the material or record of information.[1]

Paragraph 10.1 of the draft Code states that if material has not already been copied to the prosecutor, and he requests its disclosure to the accused, the disclosure officer must disclose it to the accused in the following circumstances:

(a) if, in the opinion of the prosecutor, the material might undermine the prosecution case; or
(b) the accused has given the prosecutor a defence statement, and the material might reasonably be expected to assist the defence which the accused has disclosed; or
(c) the court has ordered the disclosure of the material after considering an application from the accused under Part I of the Act.

The judgment to be made in respect of (b) above is clearly to be made by the prosecutor rather than the disclosure officer, although the draft Code does not say so explicitly.

1 See para **2.40**.

3.53 In respect of material which has been supplied to the prosecutor, the choice exists as to whether disclosure is made by the prosecutor or the disclosure officer. Paragraph 10.2 of the draft Code says that, in such circumstances, who discloses is a matter for agreement between them. The main significance of the decision appears to lie in the question as to whose judgment determines whether it is practicable or desirable for an accused to receive a copy of material. The provisions of Part I of the new Act[1] confer the power to make this judgment on the prosecutor. However, if disclosure is being effected by the disclosure officer (even at the instance of a prosecutor), the terms of paras 10.3 and 10.4 of the draft Code (discussed below) tend to suggest that that judgment is that of the disclosure officer, a rather surprising conclusion given that the *duty* of disclosure is placed by the new Act firmly on the prosecutor. It must surely be correct to argue that the prosecutor ought to have the final say, although, of course, any disputes must ultimately be resolved by the court. Against that, the terms of paras 10.3 and 10.4 clearly are based on the objective set out in s 24(1)(h) and (i) of the new Act. Those subsections clearly envisage the choice being that of the person allowing the inspection.

1 See s 3(3).

3.54 Paragraph 10.2 of the draft Code provides that the disclosure officer must disclose material to the accused either by giving him a copy or by allowing him to inspect it. If the accused person asks for a copy of any material which he has been allowed to inspect, the disclosure officer must give it to him unless, in the opinion of the disclosure officer, that is either not practicable (eg because the material consists of an object which cannot be copied) or not desirable (eg because the material is a statement by a child witness in relation to a sexual offence, and it is believed that the accused may give the statement to persons unconnected with the proceedings).

Further, by para 10.4, if material which the accused has been allowed to inspect consists of information which is recorded other than in writing, whether it should be given to the accused in its original form or in the form of a transcript is a matter for the discretion of the disclosure officer. If the material is transcribed, the disclosure officer must certify to the accused that the transcript is a verbatim record of the material which has been transcribed. Again, these provisions appear to confer the power to make such judgments on the disclosure officer, even if inspection is occurring at the instigation or request of the prosecutor.

3.55 Paragraph 10.5 of the draft Code deals with the mechanics of disclosure of sensitive material. For the purposes of the draft Code, 'sensitive material' is defined as material which an investigator, or the officer in charge of the investigations, believes it is not in the public interest to disclose.[1] It will be recalled that a court may conclude that it is in the public interest that an item of sensitive material be disclosed to the accused.[2] If it does so, clearly it will be necessary to disclose the material if the case is to proceed. This does not mean that sensitive documents must always be disclosed in their original form; for example, the court may agree that sensitive details still requiring protection should be blacked out, or that documents may be summarised, or that the prosecutor may make an admission about the substance of the material under s 10 of the Criminal Justice Act 1967.[3]

---

1 See draft Code, para 2.1.
2 See para **2.78**.
3 Draft Code, para 10.5.

SENSITIVE MATERIAL – WITHHOLDING IN THE PUBLIC INTEREST

3.56 The broad duties placed on disclosure officers in respect of sensitive material have already been noted.[1] The term 'sensitive material' is used in s 24 of the new Act, and in the draft Code of Practice. It is not used in Part I of the Act which, in various provisions,[2] permits a court, on an application by a prosecutor, to conclude that disclosure is not in the public interest. In either context, therefore, the key considerations are the circumstances when material can be withheld in the public interest. For this reason, the substantive rules relating to public interest immunity claims in criminal cases provide an essential background, and are therefore dealt with in this section of the book.

---

1 See para **3.38**. For the definition of sensitive material, see para **3.55**.
2 See s 3(6), s 7(5), s 8(5), s 9(8).

Withholding documents and information in the public interest – public interest immunity

3.57 The law has for many years sought to protect certain types of information and material obtained during, or relevant to, a criminal investigation. Well-established rules of law prohibited the disclosure at trial of the identity of police informers,[1] although exceptions to that principle existed where disclosure was necessary for the purposes of making a defence to a criminal charge.[2] If a judge considered that the lack of information as to the identity of an informer would cause a miscarriage of justice, he was under a duty to admit it. Similar considerations applied in the context of the identities and locations of police observation posts.[3]

---

1 *Marks v Beyfus* (1890) 25 QB 494 (QBD); *Hallett* [1986] Crim LR 462 (CA); *Hennessey* (1979) 68 Cr App R 419 (CA).
2 *Hallett*, op cit; *Agar* [1990] Crim LR 183 (CA).
3 *Hallett*, op cit; *Johnson* [1989] 1 All ER 121 (CA); *Rankine* [1986] 2 All ER 566 (CA).

3.58 However, the principles set out above recognised that the overriding duty was to ensure a fair trial, with the result that, on occasion, criminal proceedings had to be dropped to protect certain sensitive material.[1] Furthermore, although public interest immunity claims could be made by those in possession of documents to resist the production of documents,[2] these claims could not prevent the ordering of production of documents essential for a fair trial of an accused. It was not until the judgment of Mann LJ in *Governor of Brixton Prison ex parte Osman*,[3] that it became clear that the doctrine of public interest immunity which, if a claim is sustained, prevents the production of documents or information irrespective of the needs of the proceedings in which the claim is made, might apply not only in the context of the civil law relating to discovery, but also to criminal cases.

---

1 See, eg *Langford* [1990] Crim LR 653 (CA).
2 See, eg *Thompson* (1992) unreported, an application under s 2 of the Criminal Procedure (Attendance of Witnesses) Act 1965, where the balance fell clearly in favour of disclosure of social work documents notwithstanding their confidentiality, and the desirability of maintaining the confidentiality of the child care process.
3 [1991] 1 WLR 281 (CA).

3.59 The doctrine of public interest immunity is primarily a doctrine designed to resist discovery of documents, and information, in civil cases. In *Conway v Rimmer*,[1] the House of Lords clearly established:

(a) that claims of immunity were ultimately a matter for the court to decide, not for a Minister of the Crown or other executive body;
(b) that public interest immunity might be claimed on either contents grounds or on the basis on the class of document to which the material thought to be withheld belongs; and
(c) that confidentiality of itself was insufficient to found a claim of public interest immunity, although it was a relevant consideration.

The House of Lords in *Conway v Rimmer* did not address the issue of the applicability of the doctrine in criminal cases. In *ex parte Osman*,[2] Mann LJ characterised the habeas corpus proceeding before him as being criminal in nature, but it is not clear that he intended the principles that he was accepting as applying as being equally applicable to 'criminal proceedings properly so called'.[3] Nevertheless, he observed that he could see no reason why the doctrine should not apply in criminal cases, although the weight to be given to the interests of justice in the balancing process would be very great.

---

1 [1968] AC 910 (HL). See also: *Burmah Oil v Bank of England* [1980] AC 1090 (HL); *Air Canada v Secretary of State for Trade* [1983] 1 All ER 910 (HL); *Makanjuola v Commissioner of Police for the Metropolis* [1992] 3 All ER 617 (CA).
2 [1991] 1 WLR 281 (CA).
3 Ibid, at p 298.

3.60 The concept of a balancing exercise in a criminal case is not an easy one. It involves an acceptance that there may be a public interest in non-disclosure, even at the risk of a miscarriage of justice. Despite the dicta in *ex parte Osman*, and in *Clowes*,[1] the balance of these authorities tended to suggest that if the contents of the documents were material, then the documents would have to be produced. As the Scott Report observed:[2]

> 'there is ... no reported criminal case in which the judge has concluded that documents would be of assistance to the defendant that has nonetheless declined on PII grounds to order them to be disclosed. The firm conclusion is, in my opinion justified that in criminal cases the only question should be whether the documents might be of assistance to the defendant. This is not a "balancing exercise". The issue does not depend on the weight of the PII factors that are being evoked.'

1 [1992] 3 All ER 440.
2 Op cit, Vol III, para G 18.79.

3.61 The first consideration in such cases is whether or not the document in principle qualifies for disclosure. In *Chief Constable of the West Midlands Police ex parte Wiley*,[1] Lord Templeman observed as follows:

> 'if a document is not relevant and material it need not be disclosed and public interest immunity will not arise. In case of doubt as to relevance and materiality the directions of the court can be obtained before trial; a pre-trial conference can help to define the issues and the scope of discovery. If a document is relevant and material then it must be disclosed unless it is confidential and unless a breach of confidentiality will cause harm to the public interest which outweighs the harm to the interests of justice caused by non-disclosure.'

1 [1994] 3 All ER 420 (HL).

3.62 It is at this stage that the issue arises as to whether a claim should be made. The judgment of the court in *Makanjuola v Commissioner of Police for the Metropolis*[1] was understood for some time as requiring a claim of immunity to be made by a minister or other body without a subjective judgment being made. This view was rejected by the House of Lords in *ex parte Wiley*, where Lord Woolf said:

> 'the principle was not that it was for the courts to impose immunity where, after due consideration, no immunity was claimed by the appropriate authority. What was inherent in the reasoning of the house in [*Conway v Rimmer*] was that because of the conflict which could exist between the two aspects of the public interest involved, the courts, which have final responsibility for upholding the rule of law, must equally have final responsibility for deciding what evidence should be available to the courts of law in order to enable them to do justice. As far as contents of documents are concerned, I cannot conceive that their Lordships in *Conway v Rimmer* would have anticipated that their decision could be used, except in the most exceptional circumstances so that a Department of State was prevented by the courts from disclosing documents which it considered it was appropriate to disclose.'

1 [1992] 3 All ER 617 (CA).

3.63 It is only at this stage that any question of withholding the documents arises. In this context, it is now that the balance must be struck, but it is clear from the judgments in *Keane*[1] and *Brown*[2] that any balance 'comes down resoundingly in favour of [disclosure]'[3] where material may prove the defendant's innocence or avoid a miscarriage of justice.

1 (1994) 99 Cr App R 1 (CA).
2 [1995] 1 Cr App R 191 (CA).
3 (1994) 99 Cr App R 1, at 9, per Lord Taylor CJ.

3.64 By contrast, as noted by the Scott Report, the balancing function is more apposite in respect of documents which do not appear to have the potential to assist the defence, but which might fall within the criteria of relevance. It is in respect of this last type of material that the provisions of the new Act may have some effect, in the light of the narrowing of the scope for disclosure. One example is given by the Government Consultation Paper:

'At present, where the defence can deduce from disclosed material that there is an informant in the case, then they put forward the defence that the defendant was coerced to participate in the crime by the informant, and demand disclosure of the informant's name. Under the new scheme, this approach might be counter-productive for the defence if they decided to run a different line of argument at trial, since an inference could then be drawn from this.'[1]

1 Op cit, Ch 7, para 67.

3.65 The Scott Report summarised the currrent state of the law as follows (para 16.18):

'(1) If documents are not within the criteria of relevance established by Keane and Brown they need not be disclosed.

(2) PII claims on a class basis should not in future be made. PII contents claims should not be made in respect of documents which it is apparent are documents which might be of assistance to the defence.

(3) Before making a PII claim on a contents basis, consideration should be given to the use of redactions. The PII claim can then be confirmed to the redacted parts of the documents.

(4) PII claims on a contents basis should not be made unless in the opinion of the minister or person putting forward the claim "disclosure will cause substantial harm".

(5) A PII claim should not be made if the responsible minister forms the opinion that notwithstanding the sensitivity of the documents of public interest which requires that the documents should be disclosed.

(6) Save where the circumstances render it impracticable a minister who is asked to sign a PII certificate should always be given adequate time to reflect upon the weight of the public interest as alleged to require that the documents in question be not disclosed.

(7) If a disclosure issue in respect of documents the subject of a PII claim is referred to the judge, the judge should, unless the parties are in agreement on the point, be invited to rule, first, whether the documents are within the criteria of materiality so as to be disclosable.

(8) If the documents are within the criteria of relevance established by *Keane* and *Brown* the judge should be asked to decide whether the documents might be of assistance to the defence. If a document satisfies this test, the document

ought not to be withheld from a defendant on PII grounds. There is no true balance to be struck. The weight of public interest factors underlined in the PII claim is immaterial. However, existing authority with its apparent endorsement of the 'balancing exercise' while at the same time requiring the disclosure of any document which 'may prove the defendant's innocence or avoid a miscarriage of justice' suffers, in my opinion, from some degree of ambiguity it would be important, in my opinion, if disclosure of a material document is to be withheld, that the defendant should know whether the decision was based on the Judge's conclusion that the document would not be of any assistance to the defence or on the Judge's conclusion that despite meeting that test, the weight of the public interest factors precludes disclosure. The latter conclusion would, in my opinion, be wrong in principle and contrary to authority.

(9)   For the purpose of any argument on the assistance that a document might give the defence, the defendant should specify the line or lines of defence which, in the defendant's contention, give the document its requisite materiality.

(10) If the documents, although relevant and prima facie disclosable, do not appear to be documents that might assist the defence, the Judge may conclude that in view of the public interest factors underlined the PII claim the documents need not be disclosed.'

Further, the Scott Report clearly rejected any necessity for claims of public interest immunity to be based on a class claim. It observed:

'I find particularly bizarre and unacceptable that in respect of documents that are prima facie disclosable and whose contents do not justify any PII contents claim, the Government can properly put forward a PII class objection to their disclosure to a defendant seeking to establish his innocence in a criminal trial.'

Documents in the hands of a third party

3.66   It should be noted that documents in the hands of a third party will be subject to claims for non-production by that third party, a claim that may be made by the prosecution itself, in resistance to orders requiring the production of that document or information pursuant to s 2 of the Criminal Procedure (Attendance of Witnesses) Act 1965, or s 97 of the Magistrates' Courts Act 1980.[1]

Authorities suggest that the courts will seek to protect the confidentiality of third party information in a variety of contexts. Thus, local authority records of child care investigations are generally immune from disclosure,[2] but will on occasion be outweighed by the interests of a fair trial for an accused[3] provided, of course, that the tests of specificity and materiality can be satisfied.[4] So too with other types of confidential material. Thus, in *Clowes*[5] the confidentiality of transcripts of interviews with liquidators was highly relevant, but ultimately outweighed by the competing interests of justice.

---

1 See, further, para **5.38**.
2 See *Re D (Infants)* [1970] 1 All ER 1088; *Re M* (1989) 88 LGR 841; *R v K (Trevor Douglas)* (1993) 97 Cr App R 342.
3 See *Thompson*, (1992) (unreported).
4 *K*, op cit; *W(G)* (1996) *The Times*, 12 July.
5 [1992] 3 All ER 440 (CA).

The role of the disclosure officer

3.67 Clearly, the judgments to be made described above are those for a prosecutor, not the disclosure officer. Material may be sensitive notwithstanding the fact that a claim for immunity might not be made, or, if made, unlikely to succeed.

Paragraph 6.8 of the draft Code requires the disclosure officer to list on the sensitive schedule any material which he or the officer in charge of an investigation believes it is not in the public interest to disclose, and the reasons for that belief. Depending on the circumstances, examples of such material may include the following:

(a) material relating to national security;

(b) material received from the intelligence and security agencies;

(c) material relating to intelligence from foreign sources which reveals sensitive intelligence gathering methods;

(d) material such as telephone subscriber checks and itemised billing which is supplied to an investigator for intelligence purposes only;

(e) material given in confidence;

(f) material relating to the identity or activities of informants, or undercover police officers, or other persons supplying information to the police who may be in danger if their identities are revealed;

(g) material revealing the location of premises or other place used for police surveillance, or the identity of any person allowing a police officer to use them for surveillance;

(h) material revealing, either directly or indirectly, techniques and methods relied upon by a police officer in the course of a criminal investigation, for example covert surveillance techniques, or other methods of detecting crime;

(i) material whose disclosure might facilitate the commission of other offences or hinder the prevention and detection of crime;

(j) internal police communications such as management minutes;

(k) material upon the strength of which search warrants were obtained;

(l) material containing details of persons taking part in identification parades;

(m) material supplied to an investigator during a criminal investigation which has been generated by an official of a body concerned with the regulation or supervision of bodies corporate or of persons engaged in financial activities;

(n) material supplied to an investigator during a criminal investigation which relates to a child witness and which has been generated by a local authority social services department or other party contacted by the investigator during the investigation.

An accused will not receive copies of sensitive material, nor of the schedule of sensitive material prepared and sent to the prosecutor. However, the prosecutor will be able to judge from the defence statement given under s 5 or s 6 of the new Act what sensitive material ought to be disclosed, if that is not apparent at the initial stage of prosecution disclosure under s 3.

3.68 Where the officer in charge of an investigation believes that material is so sensitive that its revelation to the prosecutor by means of an entry on the sensitive schedule is inappropriate, the existence of the material must be revealed to the prosecutor separately of the existence of the material. The draft Code gives the example of where, if the material were compromised, that would be likely to lead directly to the loss of life, or directly threaten national security.

In such circumstances, the responsibility for informing the prosecutor lies with the investigator who knows the detail of the sensitive material. The investigator should act as soon as reasonably practicable after the file containing the prosecution case is sent to the prosecutor. The investigator must also ensure that the prosecutor is able to inspect the material so that he can assess whether it needs to be brought before a court for a ruling on disclosure.

Chapter 4

PRE-TRIAL RULINGS AND PREPARATORY HEARINGS

Pre-trial rulings – Preparatory hearings – Preparatory hearings in cases of serious or complex fraud

INTRODUCTION

4.1   Part IV of the new Act introduces a scheme which will permit the making of rulings on matters of law and evidence prior to trial on indictment. Part III introduces a general scheme for preliminary hearings (where appropriate) in respect of cases to be tried on indictment, basing itself substantially on the provisions in the Criminal Justice Act 1987 and which have permitted preliminary hearings in cases of serious or complex fraud. Those provisions remain in force, albeit with some amendments made by s 72 of and Sch 3 to the new Act.

4.2   Pre-trial hearings in respect of criminal proceedings to be tried on indictment have existed on an informal basis for some years. In 1994 a more general approach was taken, with the Lord Chief Justice issuing a Practice Direction creating a framework for a scheme of pleas and directions hearings, which would operate at Crown Courts. These pleas and directions hearings are short, and are intended to occur between four and six weeks after a case is committed for trial by a magistrates' court, or transferred for trial. At such a hearing, pleas are taken and, where a not guilty plea is entered, the hearing may identify the issues likely to be raised at trial, and defence and prosecution may agree certain facts, all with the aim of enabling the case to be listed for trial as soon as possible. However, their value is limited.[1] They are not suitable vehicles for the consideration of pre-trial issues in detail, and a judge at a pleas and directions hearing has no power to make binding rulings in advance of trial. That inability to make a binding ruling on a matter of law or evidence remains the case, even if a judge ordered a further preliminary hearing, so as to facilitate the consideration of pre-trial issues in more detail.

---

1 See Royal Commission on Criminal Justice, Research Study no 14, *The Investigation, Prosecution and Trial of Serious Fraud*, at p 89, where, in the context of fraud cases, the study observes that very few of the people interviewed for the purposes of that study defended pre-trial hearings in cases not transferred for trial under the Criminal Justice Act 1987, s 4.

4.3   The one exception to the general arrangement described in para **4.2** is in respect of cases of serious or complex fraud. Sections 7–11 of the Criminal Justice Act 1987 were introduced to give effect to the recommendations of the Roskill Report,[1] and a scheme for preparatory hearings in such cases has existed since 1987. The new power to order preparatory hearings will not apply to cases that fall within the terms of the 1987 Act,[2] and these provisions, as amended,[3] remain in force.

1 Report of the Fraud Trials Committee, 1986.
2 See para **4.18**.
3 See paras **4.33–4.36**.

4.4   In 1993 the Royal Commission on Criminal Justice[1] concluded that existing arrangements for the pre-trial review of cases in the Crown Court were ineffective, and recognised the potential for preparatory hearings to improve the position. It recommended that in potentially long or complex cases, or where agreement could not be reached between the parties on a pre-trial issue, a preparatory hearing should be held. However, in less complex cases the Commission considered that a pre-trial exchange of papers between the parties was sufficient.

It envisaged that preparatory hearings would occur only in a minority of cases, because it considered that the potential for a judge to make binding rulings would itself act as an incentive to the prosecution and defence to reach agreement. On the question of continuity of the trial judge, and of counsel, the Commission recognised the desirability of achieving this, but doubted whether its achievement was feasible. In the view of the Royal Commission, the way forward was to grant power to trial judges to make binding rulings at preparatory hearings, with counsel being prohibited from re-opening matters which were the subject of a binding ruling. It considered that there might be a need for a scheme of interlocutory appeals, and recognised that consideration would need to be given as to what incentives and sanctions existed to ensure that counsel achieved a proper balance between the undertaking of preparatory work and the advocacy at the trial itself.

1 (1993) Cm 2262, HMSO.

4.5   In a Consultation Paper in 1995,[1] the Government recognised the desirability of achieving the objectives identified by the Royal Commission, namely the achievement of shorter and more efficient trials. However, it did not adopt the Commission's proposals for a pre-trial exchange of papers in less complex cases. Instead, the Government considered the way forward to be the creation of a system based on a mixture of binding rulings at pleas and directions hearings, coupled with preparatory hearings to be held in complex or potentially lengthy cases. In relation to preparatory hearings, the Government recognised that little information in fact exists as to whether the extension of the preparatory hearing system beyond its existing context of cases of serious or complex fraud would achieve those objectives. In particular, preparatory hearings in fraud cases have not speeded up the processing of cases as much as had been hoped. The Roskill Commmittee had recommended that 'a full day should be set aside for preparatory hearings';[2] in one, admittedly complex fraud case,[3] preparatory hearings took some three months.

The new Act provides a legislative framework for the implementation of the Government's Consultation Paper proposals. However, that Consultation Paper makes clear that the legislative framework in respect of preparatory hearings is a preliminary to a pilot scheme being adopted to 'rigorously test' the view that only a small proportion of cases would require such a hearing.[4]

1 *Improving the Effectiveness of Pre-Trial Hearings in the Crown Court* (1995) Cm 2924, HMSO.
2 Op cit, recommendation 48.
3 The *Guinness* case.
4 Op cit, para 27.

PRE-TRIAL RULINGS

4.6 By s 40, a judge may make at a pre-trial hearing a binding ruling as to:

(a)   any question as to the admissibility of evidence;
(b)   any other question of law relating to the case concerned.

Such a ruling may be made under s 40 either on an application by a party to the case or of the judge's own motion (s 40(2)). There is no power for a person who is not a party to the case to make such an application.

4.7 The precondition for the making of a binding ruling is that there is a pre-trial hearing. This is defined by s 39.

Section 39(1) states that a hearing is a pre-trial hearing if it relates to a trial on indictment, and it takes place:

(a)   after the accused has been committed for trial, or the case has been transferred for trial to the Crown Court;[1] and
(b)   before the start of the trial.

A hearing is also a pre-trial hearing if it relates to a trial on indictment to be held pursuant to a bill of indictment which has been preferred under s 2(2)(b) of the Administration of Justice (Miscellaneous Provisions) Act 1933,[1] and it takes place after the bill of indictment has been preferred and before the start of the trial (s 39(2)).

1 See annotations to s 1.

4.8 The term 'relates to a trial on indictment' is a wide one, and would appear to bear the same meaning as similar words to be found in s 29(3) of the Supreme Court Act 1981, which prevents judicial review of such matters. In *Smalley v Crown Court at Warwick*,[1] Lord Bridge stressed the need to proceed on a case-by-case basis and adopted a working test: does the decision affect the conduct of a trial on indictment? However, it is the words of the statute that are crucial,[2] and matters such as the forfeiture of a recognisance,[3] an application for a stay on the grounds of abuse of process,[4] and the quashing of an indictmemt, or counts on it,[5] will all fall within the ambit of trial on indictment. Cases will not if they relate to a person other than a party to the case, for example, application for the forfeiture of a recognisance of a third party,[6] or where the court is acting under a different jurisdiction, for example binding over a third party.[7]

1 [1985] 1 All ER 769 (HL).
2 *Sampson v Crown Court at Croydon* [1987] 1 All ER 609, per Lord Bridge.
3 *Smalley v Crown Court at Warwick*, op cit.
4 *Manchester Crown Court ex parte Director of Public Prosecutions* [1994] AC 9 (HL).
5 *DPP v Crown Court at Manchester and Huckfield* [1993] NLJR 1711 (3 December 1993).
6 *Smalley v Crown Court at Warwick*, op cit.
7 *Crown Court at Inner London ex parte Benjamin* (1986) 85 Cr App R 267 (DC).

4.9   In both situations defined by s 39(1), a ruling has to be made at a hearing before 'the start of the trial'. This is, for this purpose, defined by s 39(3), which states that 'the start of a trial on indictment occurs when a jury is sworn to consider the issue of guilt or fitness to plead or, if the court excepts a plea of guilty before a jury is sworn, when that plea is excepted; but this is subject to s 8 of the Criminal Justice Act of 1987 and s 29 of this Act (preparatory hearings)'. This definition of the 'start' of a trial on indictment is identical to that in s 22(11A) of the Prosecution of Offences Act 1985, which is inserted therein by s 71 of the new Act. The effect of the adoption of this definition is that, by s 30 of the new Act[1] and by s 8 of the 1987 Act, if and when a judge orders a preparatory hearing the trial is to be regarded as starting with that hearing. In short, the result appears to be that the power to make a pre-trial ruling under this provision ceases where a preparatory hearing occurs. Clearly, however, it would be extremely odd if the power to rule on matters of law or admissibility was less in some cases than in others. For that reason, it is submitted that the intent of Parliament is that matters of law or admissibility which, prior to the holding of a preparatory hearing, would be within the pre-trial ruling procedure, are to be dealt with during a preparatory hearing; the purpose of the legislation on this point being to avoid two separate systems operating in the same case.

1 See para **4.23**.

4.10   The ruling that may be made under s 40 is one in respect of any matter relating to the admissibility of evidence or any other question of law relating to the case concerned. These provisions should be construed broadly. Questions of admissibility include questions not only as to whether evidence is legally admissible, but also as to whether admissible evidence should be excluded, for example under s 78 of PACE or under a common law discretion.

The phrase 'question of law relating to the case' is likewise broad, but one which, in the context of the terms of s 9(3) of the Criminal Justice Act 1987 relating to the powers of a judge on a preparatory hearing, has caused some difficulty.[1] It is intended to include decisions as to whether material is disclosable under the new disclosure provisions,[2] and extends to decisions as to the meaning of statutory provisions, such as s 4 of the Contempt of Court Act

1981, and the quashing of an indictment or counts on it. By contrast, issues that are essentially factual in nature may not necessarily be within the scope of s 39.

---

1 See, generally, Jones, 'The Decline and Fall of the Preparatory Hearing' [1996] Crim LR 460. See para **4.21**.
2 Consultation Paper, op cit, Ch 4, para 41. See, generally, para **2.41**.

Effect of ruling

4.11 By s 40(3), where a ruling has been made it has binding effect from the time it is made until the case against the accused or, if there is more than one, against each of them is disposed of; and the case against an accused is disposed of if:

(a) he is acquitted or convicted; or
(b) the prosecutor decides not to proceed with the case against him.

The binding nature of the ruling is, of course, only in respect of the person in respect of whom the ruling is made. In cases of multiple defendants, a trial judge will need to take care to ensure that any ruling that is made defines precisely to whom it is to apply. However, that is a principle of general application, and not one which arises specifically out of the power conferred by s 40.

4.12 The binding nature of the ruling is subject to one proviso. By s 40(4), a judge may discharge or vary (or further vary) a ruling made under the section if it appears to him that it is in the interests of justice to do so; and a judge may so act under s 40(4):

(a) on an application by a party to the case; or
(b) of his own motion.

The judge who makes the order of discharge or variance (or further variance, for nothing in the section prevents ongoing reconsideration or rulings) need not be the judge who made the initial ruling or the ruling to be varied if that is different (s 40(6)).

4.13 Nothing in s 40 imposes a constraint as to the order a judge may make on an application to discharge, vary, or further vary, a ruling. The matter appears to be at large subject only to the overall limitation contained in s 40 that the matter must be one of admissibility of evidence or be a question of law. However, by s 40(5), no application may be made under s 40(4)(a) unless there has been a material change of circumstances since the ruling was made or, if a previous application has been made, since the application (or last application) was made. This restriction does not apply in respect of discharge or variance under s 40(4)(b). A judge may, therefore, reconsider of his own motion, irrespective of whether there has, or has not, been a change of circumstances.

No definition is given as to what amounts to a 'material change of circumstances'. In the Consultation Paper,[1] the Government expressed the view that it would not be open to either party to reopen rulings on the basis of the same information. This suggests that it is intended that the phrase 'change of circumstances' should relate to the information on which the ruling was based, a conclusion that has the practical advantage of limiting the opportunities to reopen decided questions. The whole purpose of a binding ruling procedure would be undermined if issues or law or admissibility were being reviewed.

---

1 Improving the Effectiveness of Pre-Trial Hearings in the Crown Court (1995) Cm 2924, HMSO.

Restrictions on reporting

4.14 Section 41 provides for restrictions on reporting of certain matters which are defined by s 41(2). The following matters fall within that subsection:

(a) a ruling made under s 40;
(b) proceedings on an application for a ruling to be made under s 40;
(c) an order that a ruling made under s 40 be discharged or varied or further varied;
(d) proceedings on an application for a ruling made under s 40 to be discharged or varied or further varied.

This general prohibition is subject to a power, vested in a trial judge by s 41(3), which permits him to order that the prohibition shall not apply, or shall not apply to a specified extent, to a report of the matter. Such an order shall be made if (and only if) the judge is satisfied after hearing the representations of the accused that it is in the interests of justice to do so; and if the order is made it shall not apply to the extent that a report deals with any such objection or representations (s 41(4)). Where there are two or more accused and one or more of them objects to the making of an order under s 41(3), the judge shall only make the order if (and only if) satisfied after hearing the representations of each of the accused that it is in the interest of justice to do so.

4.15 The prohibition contained in s 41 does not apply to publication of a report of such matters or inclusion in a relevant programme[1] of a report of such matters, at the conclusion of the trial of the accused or of the last of the accused to be tried (s 41(6)). Nothing in s 41 affects any other prohibition or restriction imposed by any other enactment (s 41(7)).

---

1 See general annotations.

Offence

4.16 Where there is a publication or inclusion in a relevant programme of any report, in contravention of s 41, a summary offence is committed (s 42(1)). Where such conduct occurs, each of the following persons is guilty of that offence:

(a) in the case of a publication of a written report as part of a newspaper or periodical, any proprietor, editor or publisher of the newspaper or periodical;
(b) in the case of a publication of a written report otherwise than as part of a newspaper or periodical, the person who publishes it;

(c)   in the case of the inclusion of a report in a relevant programme, any body corporate which is engaged in providing the service in which the programme is included and any person having functions in relation to the programme corresponding to those of an editor of a newspaper.

Proceedings for such an offence are not to be instituted otherwise than by or with the consent of the Attorney-General (s 42(3)). A person found guilty of such an offence is liable to a fine of an amount not exceeding level 5 on the standard scale[1] (s 42(2)).

---

1 See general annotations.

PREPARATORY HEARINGS

4.17   As noted at para **4.1**, Part III of the Act creates a general power for a court to order that a preparatory hearing be held. Hitherto, the power to do so only extended to cases of serious or complex fraud under the Criminal Justice Act 1987, s 7.[1] Those provisions remain but are amended by s 72 and Sch 3 to the new Act. Part III will not apply to cases that fall within the scope of the 1987 Act. Section 29(3) of the new Act states that no order under s 29 is to be made where it appears to a judge of the Crown Court that the evidence on an indictment reveals a case of fraud of such seriousness or complexity as is mentioned in s 7 of the 1987 Act. Thus, such cases fall within the pre-existing provisions of the 1987 Act, as amended.

---

1 For the application of the 1987 Act, see annotations to s 1.

Application of Part III

4.18   Part III of the new Act applies to any offence for which a person is committed to the Crown Court for trial on the charge concerned on or after the appointed day, the case is transferred for trial[1] after the appointed day or a bill of indictment is preferred[1] on or after the appointed day (s 28). No such day had been appointed as at the date of going to press.

---

1 See annotations to s 1.

Power to order preparatory hearing

4.19   By s 29(1), where it appears to a judge of the Crown Court that an indictment reveals a case of such complexity, or a case whose trial is likely to be of such length, that substantial benefits are likely to accrue from a hearing:

(a)   before the jury are sworn; and
(b)   for any of the purposes mentioned in subsection (2),

he may order that a preparatory hearing be held.

A judge may make such an order on the application of the prosecutor, the accused (or, if more than one, any of them) or on his own motion (s 29(4)). No such order can be made if the case falls within the provisions of the Criminal Justice Act 1987, s 7 (s 29(3)). At the time of the making of an order for a preparatory hearing, a judge may also make any order he could make at that hearing (s 32(2)).

4.20 The purposes mentioned in s 29(2) are crucial to the operation of the preparatory hearing regime. The equivalent provisions in s 7 of the 1987 Act have been held to define and limit the exercise of the powers conferred by s 9(3) of the 1987 Act,[1] and the terms of s 29(2) are likely to similarly limit what can be done pursuant to s 31(3) of the new Act.

Section 29(2) sets out several purposes for the preparatory hearing. These are:

(a)   identifying issues which are likely to be material to the verdict of the jury;
(b)   assisting their comprehension of any such issues;
(c)   expediting the proceedings before the jury;
(d)   assisting the judge's management of the trial.

---

1 *Gunawardena and others* (1990) 91 Cr App R 55 (CA). For discussion of the authorities, see Jones, 'The Decline and Fall of the Preparatory Hearing' [1996] Crim LR 460.

4.21   In *Gunawardena and others*,[1] the Court of Appeal decided that the purpose of a preliminary hearing under the 1987 Act was limited to those set out in s 7(1)(a), (b), (c) or (d) of that Act. It was not the intention of Parliament to permit judges to 'range around' all manner of issues not perceived to be related to those purposes. The fact that a matter might have the consequence of incidentally achieving one of those purposes was irrelevant: that did not suffice to bring the matter within a s 7 preparatory hearing.[2] It is clear that confusion exists in the authorities,[3] but clearly a court must intend to act within the specified purposes. If there is any doubt as to the purpose, that is itself a preliminary question of law which is to be determined by the court and, if necessary, to be the subject of an interlocutory appeal under the terms of s 35 of the new Act, or s 9 of the 1987 Act.

---

1 (1990) 91 Cr App R 55 (CA).
2 *Moore* 5 February 1991, unreported. See also: *Jennings and others* (1994) 98 Cr App R 308.
3 See Jones, op cit.

4.22   The question remains as to how these principles are to be applied. The authorities suggest that applications to stay proceedings on the grounds of abuse of process,[1] applications to postpone reporting under s 4(2) of the Contempt of Court Act 1981,[2] applications to discharge witness summonses,[3] and applications to sever the counts of an indictment are each outside the purposes of s 7 of the 1987 Act and, presumably, s 29 of the new Act. Each of such matters could, arguably, be part of a ruling under s 39 of the new Act, subject, however, to the point made at para **4.9**, namely, that the effect of s 39(3) is to prevent a preliminary ruling being given after a preparatory hearing commences. Arguably, the position is that a judge may determine in a binding way a question of law, but, if such matter is not within the purposes set out in s 29, no interlocutory appeal will arise.

1 *Gunawardena,* op cit (CA).
2 *Saunders* 5 February 1990, unreported (CA).
3 *Clowes* (1991) 95 Cr App R 440 (CA); *Jennings* (1994) 98 Cr App R 308 (CA).

Powers and duties of judge at preparatory hearing

4.23 The judge must arraign the accused at the commencement of the preparatory hearing, unless arraignment has already occurred (s 30). Such a hearing may be adjourned from time to time (s 31(2)), and the powers of the judge extend to making rulings as to the admissibility of evidence or other question of law relating to the case (s 31(3)). However, as already noted, that is subject to the overall parameters of the legislation, discussed at para **4.22**.

4.24 By s 31(4), the judge may order the prosecutor:

(1) to give the court and the accused (or each of them) a written statement (a case statement) of the matters falling within s 31(5). The matters that fall within s 31(5) are:
  (a) the principal facts of the case for the prosecution;
  (b) the witnesses who will speak to those facts;
  (c) any exhibits relevant to those facts;
  (d) any proposition of law on which the prosecutor proposes to rely;
  (e) the consequences in relation to any of the counts in the indictment that appear to the prosecutor to flow from the matters falling within paras (a) to (d) of s 31(5);
(2) to prepare the prosecution evidence and any explanatory material in such a form as form to the court and to the accused (or each of them);
(3) to give the court and the accused (or each of them) written notice of documents the truth of the contents of which ought, in the prosecutor's view, to be admitted and of any other matters which in his view ought to be agreed;
(4) to make any amendments of any case statement given in pursuance of an order under paragraph (a) that appear to the judge to be appropriate, having regard to objections made by the accused or, if there is more than one, by any of them.

This power to require the prosecution to provide a statement of evidence may tend to lead prosecution teams to prepare cases with vigour, and with an eye to evidential strengths and weaknesses of the case, and provide a basis for the defence to reassess the plea to be tendered in the light of knowledge of the detailed case going beyond the material used for committal or transfer purposes. On the other hand, it may prove expensive and time-consuming.[1]

1 See RCCP Research Study No 14, *The Investigation, Prosecution and Trial of Serious Fraud.*

4.25 By s 31(6), the judge may order the accused (or each of them) to do certain things. These are set out at para **4.26**. This power to make an order in respect of the accused (or each of them) only exists where the prosecutor has been ordered to give a case statement under s 31(4)(a), and the prosecutor has complied with that order.

The new Act does not define the term 'complied'. Clearly, a total failure to produce the matters the subject of a s 31(4) order amounts to non-compliance. More difficult is inadequate compliance. It is submitted that, should any dispute arise, that will be a matter for the judge who made the order. What amounts to compliance is, presumably, a matter of law, because it is a precondition to a requirement being imposed on the accused by order. It is not open to a judge to make an order under s 31(4) and s 31(6) at the same time: compliance with the former is a precondition to the power to make the latter.

4.26   By s 31(6), the accused (or each of them) may be ordered:

(a)   to give the court and the prosecutor a written statement setting out in general terms the nature of his defence and indicating the principal matters on which he takes issue with the prosecution;

(b)   to give the court and the prosecutor written notice of any objections that he has to the case statement;

(c)   to give the court and the prosecutor written notice of any point of law (including any point as to the admissibility of evidence) which he wishes to take, and any authority on which he intends to rely for that purpose.

These provisions cannot be viewed in isolation, but must be considered in the context of the defence disclosure provisions contained in s 5 of the new Act. The provisions in s 31(6) go further that those in s 5, in particular in respect of the detail required to be given by s 31(6)(b) and (c), which amount to levels of detail not expected in a defence statement under s 5. However, it should be noted that nothing in s 31(6) requires an accused to disclose who will give evidence. That will only be required if it is so required either by the Crown Court (Advance Disclosure of Expert Evidence) Rules[1] or by s 5.[2]

---

1 See annotations to s 20.
2 See paras **2.53–2.67**.

4.27   By s 31(7), the accused (or each of them) may be ordered to respond to a written notice given by the prosecutor under s 31(4)(c) (matters to be agreed or admitted). Where such notice has been given, the judge may order the accused (or each of them) to give to the court and the prosecutor a written notice stating:

(a)   the extent to which he agrees with the prosecutor as to documents and other matters to which the notice under s 31(4)(c) relates; and

(b)   the reason for any disagreement.

The judge may order the giving of further or better reasons where the reasons given appear inadequate (s 31(9)).

Consequences of non-compliance or departure from case disclosed

4.28   The sanction against the prosecutor for non-compliance or, arguably, insufficient compliance, with requirements imposed on him has already been noted: no obligation can in law be imposed on the accused (or each of them) (s 31(6)). The sanction in respect of non-compliance by the accused is dealt with by s 34. By s 31(8), the judge shall, at the time of making an order under s 31(6) or s 31(7), warn the accused (or each of them) of the possible consequences of non-compliance. Section 33 permits any party to depart from the case he disclosed in pursuance of a requirement under s 31, a provision that is plainly essential if an accused is to be able to adequately, and fairly, defend himself in the light of a case as it evolves. However, it is submitted that if a formal admission of a fact or facts has been made on behalf of an accused, that is governed by the normal rules governing such admissions.

Where a party departs from the case disclosed under any requirement imposed under s 31, or fails to comply with such a requirement, the judge or, with leave of the judge, any other party may make such comment as appears to the judge or the other party (as the case may be) to be appropriate and the jury may draw such inference as appears proper (s 34(2)). In deciding whether to grant leave the judge shall have regard:

(a) to the extent of the departure or failure; and
(b) to whether there was any justification for it (s 34(3)).

4.29 This provision is similar in terms to that contained in s 10 of the 1987 Act.[1] In respect of that provision it has been held that the prosecution is entitled to put into evidence the defence statement to show that departure, although case statements should not be put into evidence as a matter of routine or course.[2] The terms of s 34(3) also reflect similar terminology in s 11 of the new Act (failure to disclose by an accused) and, indeed, the provisions in ss 34 to 38 of the Criminal Justice and Public Order Act 1994. Arguably, principles developed in that context are of equal validity and utility here. Nowhere in s 34(3) is there any limitation placed on a court as to the purpose an inference may serve. However, it is submitted that it should be the duty of the prosecution to establish its prima facie case independently from any inference to be drawn under s 34. The justification for this conclusion is that the justification for requiring disclosure of the matters the subject of the s 31 order, is to enable the prosecution to assess the nature of the defence and its weight. Arguably, therefore, any failure ought to reflect on those matters and not go to bolster a weak prosecution case.

---

1 See para **4.36**.
2 *Mayhew* (1991) (unreported) (CA).

4.30 The statement given by the accused under s 31(6)(a), or any information relating to the case for the accused (or any of them) given under s 31, is not to be disclosed at a stage in the trial after the jury have been sworn without the consent of the accused concerned (s 34(4)). However, that is subject to the provisions of s 34 relating to departure from the case disclosed, and the comment and inference potentially available to prosecutor or judge.

APPEALS

4.31   An appeal from any ruling of a judge lies, with leave of the judge or of the Court of Appeal, to the Court of Appeal (s 35). A further appeal lies to the House of Lords, on limited grounds (s 36(1)). Where leave to appeal has been granted, a preparatory hearing may continue, but no jury shall be sworn until that appeal has been determined or abandoned (s 35(2)).

It should, however, be noted that these powers of appeal only arise in the context of a valid preparatory hearing, in the sense of a preparatory hearing which fulfils or, possibly, is intended to fulfil, the purposes set out in s 29 of the new Act. It was noted earlier that the rulings a court may make must be for the general purposes identified by s 30 or by s 7 of the 1987 Act.[1] If a matter of law does not fall within those purposes, no right of appeal at an interlocutory stage exists.[2]

---

1 See para **4.19**.
2 See *Saunders*, (1990) (unreported); *Gunawardena* (1990) 91 Cr App R 55 (CA); *Moore* (1991) (unreported) (CA).

Restrictions on reporting

4.32   Section 37 provides that, except as provided therein:

(a)   no written report of a preparatory hearing, of an application for leave to appeal in relation to such a hearing, or of an appeal in respect of such a hearing;

(b)   no report of such hearings,

shall be included in a relevant programme[1] for reception in Great Britain.[1]

The matters which are exceptions to this general prohibition are set out by s 37(9), as follows (unless falling within any other prohibition or restriction):[2]

(a)   the identity of the court and the name of the judge;
(b)   the names, ages, home addresses and occupations of the accused and witnesses;
(c)   the offence or offences, or a summary of them, with which the accused is or are charged;
(d)   the name of counsel and solicitors in the proceedings;
(e)   where the proceedings are adjourned, the date and place to which they are adjourned;
(f)   any arrangements as to bail;
(g)   whether legal aid was granted to the accused (or any of them).

In addition, the judge may order that the prohibition shall not apply, or not apply to a specified extent (s 37(3)). Such an order shall not be made if the accused (or any of them) objects, unless the judge is satisfied after hearing the representations of the accused (or each of them) that it is in the interests of justice to do so (s 37(3)–(7)).

---

1 See general annotations.

Offence

4.33 By s 38(1), if a report is published or included in a relevant programme in contravention of s 37, the persons specified in s 38 are each guilty of a summary offence, and liable on conviction to a fine not exceeding level 5 on the standard scale.[1] No proceedings may be instituted otherwise than by or with the consent of the Attorney-General.

The persons specified in s 38(1) are:

(a) in the case of a publication of a written report as part of a newspaper or periodical, any proprietor, editor or publisher of the newspaper or periodical;

(b) in the case of a publication of a written report otherwise than as part of a newspaper or periodical, the person who publishes it;

(c) in the case of the inclusion of a report in a relevant programme, any body corporate which is engaged in providing the service in which the programme is included and any person having functions in relation to the programme corresponding to those of an editor of a newspaper.

1 See general annotations.

PREPARATORY HEARINGS: CASES OF SERIOUS OR COMPLEX FRAUD

4.34 The new Act makes significant amends to the provisions of the 1987 Act governing preparatory hearings in cases of serious or complex fraud (s 72 and Sch 2). The changes, although lengthy, do not raise new questions of principle beyond those already discussed in this chapter. Rather, the intent is to bring the regimes that will exist under the 1987 and 1996 Acts so far as possible into line. The amended provisions will apply in relation to an offence transferred to the Crown Court on or after the appropriate day, or in respect of which a bill of indictment is preferred after the appointed day.

4.35 Paragraph 2 of Sch 3 omits s 7(3), (4) and (5) from the 1987 Act. These provisions had dealt with the requirement of service of documents by prosecution or defence at the time of ordering a preparatory hearing. These provisions are no longer necessary in the light of a new s 9A to the 1987 Act, created by para 4 of Sch 3. The new s 9A permits a judge when ordering a preparatory hearing to make any order he could make at that hearing. This change is itself intended to reflect a similar power to be found in s 32 of the new Act.

4.36 Paragraph 5 of Sch 2 creates a new s 10 of the 1987 Act. The new s 10 deals with the later stages of trial and, in terms, is identical in provision (other than in respect of the cross references to other sections) to s 34 of the new Act.[1]

---

1 See para **4.19**.

4.37　　Paragraph 6 of Sch 2 creates a new s 11 and a new s 11A of the 1987 Act. These together deal with reporting restrictions, and offences arising in respect thereof, in identical terms to those found in s 37 and s 38 of the new Act.[1]

---

1 See paras **4.32–4.33**.

Chapter 5

MISCELLANEOUS PROCEDURAL PROVISIONS

*Tainted acquittals – Derogatory assertions in mitigation etc: reporting restrictions –
Custody time-limits: preliminary stage of criminal proceedings – Witness orders and
summonses – Checks against fingerprints – Television links and video-recorded evidence*

TAINTED ACQUITTALS

5.1 Hitherto there has been no way that an acquittal could be challenged on
the ground that it is tainted by bribery, threats or other interference with a
witness or juror. This has been part of an approach whereby, with the exception
of an appeal against an acquittal in the magistrates' court by case stated to the
Divisional Court of the Queen's Bench Division[1] on the ground that it is wrong
in law or in excess of jurisdiction, there is no right of appeal against an acquittal.

---

1 Magistrates' Courts Act 1980, s 111.

5.2 The Royal Commission on Criminal Justice[1] thought that this was
unsatisfactory and recommended that, where a person was convicted of
conspiracy to pervert the course of justice on the ground that he or she
interfered with a member of the jury in a case which led to the acquittal of the
accused, the trial at which that jury returned that verdict should be regarded as
a nullity. If practicable, the acquitted accused should be prosecuted again for
the same offence.[2]

---

1 (1993) Cm 2263, HMSO.
2 Ibid, Ch 10, para 74.

5.3 The Commission's recommendation is implemented, with important
modifications, by s 54. In particular, the new provisions extend to cases where
the interference has been with a witness (or potential witness) and to acquittals
in a magistrates' court. The first modification is in line with the offence under
s 51(1) of the Criminal Justice and Public Order Act 1994 which, inter alia,
punishes those who intimidate a witness (or potential witness) or juror with
intent to cause the course of justice to be perverted.[1] Although there are no
reliable statistics to indicate the extent of the problem, it is clear from anecdotal
evidence that interference with witnesses or jurors by bribery, violence, threats
or other improper behaviour can be a serious problem in some cases.

Section 54 only applies in relation to acquittals in respect of offences alleged to be committed on or after the day appointed by the Home Secretary (s 54(7) and (8)).[2] No day had been appointed when this book went to press.

---

1 The offence is described and discussed in Card and Ward, *Criminal Justice and Public Order Act 1994* (Jordans, 1994), paras 4.45–4.56.
2 See annotations to s 54.

When does section 54 apply?

5.4   Section 54 applies where:

(a)   a person has been acquitted of an offence; and
(b)   a person has been convicted of an administration of justice offence involving interference with or intimidation of a juror or a witness (or potential witness) in any proceedings which led to the acquittal (s 54(1)). That person could be the person acquitted referred to in (a) above.

The importance of a person being convicted of an administration of justice offence must be noted. If a person, who has undoubtedly committed such an offence in proceedings which led to the acquittal, is not convicted of it, because he has died or become permanently unfit to plead or has fled the country and cannot be found or extradited, s 54 cannot operate.

The following fall within the definition of an 'administration of justice offence':

(a)   the common law offence of perverting the course of justice, which is triable only on indictment;
(b)   the either way offence under s 51(1) of the Criminal Justice and Public Order Act 1994 (intimidation of a witness, potential witness or juror);
(c)   an offence of aiding, abetting, counselling, procuring, suborning or inciting another person to commit perjury, which offences are triable only on indictment (s 54(6)).[1]

It is worthy of note that conspiracy to commit one of the above substantive offences is not an 'administration of justice offence', even though the substantive offence is committed.

It must be emphasised that it is not enough that someone has been convicted of one of the above administration of justice offences. In addition, the offence must have involved interference with or intimidation of a juror or a witness (or potential witness) in any proceedings which led to the acquittal. 'Intimidation' clearly refers to threats (whether to the person or property of the person threatened or another), and 'interference' covers bribery and other forms of persuasion or encouragement.

In the light of the way that s 54(1) is drafted, it is not surprising that the definition of an 'administration of justice offence' does not include the perpetration of the offence of perjury. The perpetration of perjury could not conceivably involve interference with or intimidation of a juror or witness, unlike aiding or abetting etc perjury where the aider or abetter etc may well have threatened or otherwise persuaded or encouraged the witness who perpetrates perjury.

Nevertheless, the fact that the new provisions were not drafted in such a way as to encompass acquittals following the perpetration of perjury by a witness of his own volition seems unfortunate.

The Government resisted extending the new provisions to include the perpetration of perjury on the ground that it would extend too far the inroad into the finality of criminal proceedings, despite its suspicions as to the frequency of perjury in criminal trials. It saw a valid distinction between acts done outside the criminal trial and acts (of perjury) done during the giving of evidence at the trial.[2] The validity of this distinction is doubtful. The perpetration of perjury at a trial is liable to be more likely to taint an acquittal than the conduct covered by s 54.

---

1 See annotations to s 54.
2 Lord Mackay of Drumadoon, Lord Advocate, HL Report, cols 79–81.

Procedure under section 54

5.5 Where s 54 applies, the procedure under it is instituted by the court before whom the person convicted of an administration of justice offence was convicted (s 54(2)). That court can only institute the procedure if it appears to it that there was a real possibility (and not simply a mere possibility) that, but for the interference or intimidation, the acquitted person would not have been acquitted (s 54(2)(a)). The fact of the conviction for an administration of justice offence is therefore not enough. There must appear to exist a real possibility of a causal connection between the interference or intimidation and the acquittal. In particular, where the interference or intimidation has been directed at a witness, the mere fact that a person has been convicted of an administration of justice offence will not necessarily indicate a real possibility that, but for the interference or intimidation, the acquitted person would not have been acquitted. It will all depend on the circumstances. As Baroness Blatch, Minister of State, Home Office, stated:

> 'It may be that the witness who was intimidated gave evidence which was merely of peripheral relevance to the case. In such circumstances, the judge, who will have heard the details of what happened during the trial of the intimidation offence, may well conclude that there are no grounds for interfering with the original verdict. In other cases, it may be clear to the judge that the witness's evidence was so central to the case that the acquittal is unsafe.'[1]

---

1 HL 2nd Reading, col 503.

5.6 Even if this requirement is satisfied, the court cannot act if, because of lapse of time or for any other reason, it would be contrary to the interests of justice to take proceedings against the acquitted person for the offence of which he was acquitted (s 54(2) and (5)). 'Other reasons' why it might be contrary to the interests of justice to take proceedings might be that crucial witnesses in the original trial had since died or perhaps that the accused himself was already serving a lengthy sentence for some other offence.[1]

---

1 These examples were given by Baroness Blatch, Minister of State, Home Office, HL 2nd
reading, col 503.

5.7   Where it appears to the court before which the person convicted of the
administration of justice offence that:

(a)   there is a real possibility that, but for the interference or intimidation, the
acquitted person would not have been acquitted; and

(b)   s 54(5) (lapse of time etc) does not apply,

the court must certify that it so appears (s 54(2)).

5.8   Once a certificate has been made, an application may be made to the
High Court for an order quashing the acquittal (s 54(3)). No doubt, normally,
the application will be made by the Crown Prosecution Service, but there is no
limitation in the Act on who may apply. The court must make the order if the
following four conditions are satisfied, but otherwise it must not do so
(s 54(3)). The four conditions are provided by s 55.

The first condition is that it appears to the High Court likely (and not merely
seriously possible, as under s 54(2)) that, but for the interference or
intimidation, the acquitted person would not have been acquitted (s 55(1)).

The second condition is that it does not appear to the High Court that,
because of lapse of time or for any other reason, it would be contrary to the
interests of justice to take proceedings against the acquitted person for the
offence of which he was acquitted (s 55(2)).

The third condition is that it appears to the High Court that the acquitted
person has been given a reasonable opportunity to make written
representations to the court (s 55(3)).

The fourth condition is that it appears to the High Court that the conviction
for the administration of justice offence will stand (s 55(4)).

In considering this, the court must take into account all the information
before it, but it must ignore the possibility of new factors coming to light
(s 55(5)). The fourth condition has the effect that the court must not make an
order quashing the acquittal if, for instance, it appears to the court that any
time allowed for giving notice of appeal has not expired or that an appeal is
pending (s 55(6)).

Effect of an order under section 54

5.9   Where the High Court makes an order under s 54(3) quashing an
acquittal, proceedings may be taken against the acquitted person for the
offence of which he was acquitted (s 54(4)). The word 'may' must be
emphasised. There is no requirement that proceedings must be taken. It would
appear from the provisions as to time-limits mentioned below, that the
proceedings are to be instituted *de novo*, ie a fresh prosecution must be brought.
The effect of an order under s 54(3) can be contrasted with the situation where,
acting under s 7 of the Criminal Appeal Act 1968, the Court of Appeal
(Criminal Division) orders a re-trial when allowing an appeal against
conviction on indictment; there the re-trial is on a fresh indictment preferred

by direction of the Court of Appeal.[1] It can also be contrasted with the power of the Divisional Court on an appeal by case stated to order a re-hearing.[2]

If there is a statutory time-limit on the taking of proceedings, calculated by reference to the commission of that offence, that time-limit has effect as if the period was, instead, one calculated by reference to the time that the order under s 54(3) is made (s 56(1)). This applies however the enactment is expressed (s 56(2)). Thus, for example, it applies in the case of:

(a) a 12-month time-limit running from the offence charged in respect of the offence of unlawful intercourse with a girl under 16 years old (or an attempt to commit it) (Sexual Offences Act 1956, s 37 and Sch 2, para 10);

(b) the prohibition on a magistrates' court trying an information which has not been laid within six months from the time when the offence was committed (Magistrates' Courts Act 1980, s 127(1));

(c) a statutory time-limit imposed only in certain circumstances (as where proceedings are not instituted by or with the consent of the Director of Public Prosecutions) (s 56(2)).

---

1 Criminal Appeal Act 1968, s 8(1). Cf the effect of a writ of *venire de novo: Blackstone's Criminal Practice* (1996), D21.33.

2 *Griffiths v Jenkins* [1992] AC 76, [1992] 1 All ER 65 (HL).

Section 54 and double jeopardy

5.10 The above provisions, hedged around with restrictions as they are, are clearly an infringement on the rule against double jeopardy. However, balanced against that it cannot be acceptable that an accused who has been acquitted should not be capable of being re-tried when it is proved that his acquittal was due to jury-nobbling or witness-nobbling. To confer an immunity from re-trial in such a case serves as an encouragement to nobbling. In view of the required effect of the interference or intimidation on the outcome of the trial, it could be argued that the accused was not, in the full sense, in jeopardy at his first trial and that the above provisions are on a par with other exceptions to the double jeopardy rule, where the accused was not truly in jeopardy at the first trial.[1]

The complex provisions described above seem to provide adequate safeguards against oppressive use or misuse of s 54.

---

1 This argument was put forward by Lord Taylor of Gosforth, HL 2nd reading, col 479. An example of such an exception is an acquittal after a trial on a defective indictment.

Supplementary provisions

5.11 Section 57 makes supplementary provision in two respects.

5.12 The first relates to acquittals in a magistrates' court in respect of a charge of common assault or common battery. Section 44 of the Offences against the

Person Act 1861 provides that, where criminal proceedings are taken in respect of a common assault or common battery by or on behalf of the person aggrieved, and the magistrates deem the offence not to be proved,[1] and accordingly dismiss the information, they must issue a certificate of dismissal. By s 45 of the 1861 Act, if a certificate is granted, the accused is released from all other proceedings, civil or criminal, for the same cause. Section 57(1) of the new Act qualifies this by stating that s 45 is subject to s 54(4) of the new Act, whereby if an order quashing an acquittal is made, criminal proceedings may be taken against the acquitted person for the offence for which he was acquitted. Civil proceedings remain barred under s 45 of the 1861 Act where it applies.

---

1 Or to have been justified or to be so trifling as not to merit any punishment.

5.13   The second respect in which supplementary provision is made relates to the Contempt of Court Act 1981. This is amended in two ways.

5.14   The 'strict liability rule', whereby a 'publication' may be treated as a contempt of court as tending to interfere with the course of justice in particular legal proceedings regardless of intent to do so, if it creates a substantial risk that the course of justice in those proceedings will be seriously prejudiced, applies only if the proceedings in question are active (Contempt of Court Act 1981, s 2(3)). Criminal proceedings are active from the relevant initial step, namely:

(a)   arrest without warrant;
(b)   the issue of a warrant for arrest;
(c)   the issue of a summons;
(d)   the service of an indictment or other document specifying the charge; or
(e)   oral charge (1981 Act, Sch 1, para 4),

until concluded:

(a)   by acquittal or, as the case may be, by sentence;
(b)   by any other verdict, finding, order or decision putting an end to the proceedings; or
(c)   by discontinuance by operation of law (1981 Act, Sch 1, para 5).

As enacted, the list of initial steps does not cover the case where proceedings are brought under s 54 following a tainted acquittal. For this reason, a new paragraph, 4A, is added to Sch 1 to the 1981 Act by s 57(4). This provides that the initial step in such a case is the certification under s 54(2) to the effect that there is a real possibility that, but for interference or intimidation involved, the acquitted person would not have been acquitted.

5.15   The other amendment to the 1981 Act relates to s 4 of that Act. Section 4(1) provides that a person is not guilty of contempt under the strict liability rule in respect of a fair and accurate report of legal proceedings held in public, published contemporaneously and in good faith. Section 4(1) is, however, subject to s 4(2), which empowers a court to postpone publication of reports of proceedings before it. Section 4(2) provides that in legal proceedings held in public the court may order that the publication of a report of them (or part of them) be postponed for such a period as it thinks necessary where it appears to be necessary in order to avoid a substantial risk of prejudice to the administration of justice in those proceedings, or in any other proceedings pending or imminent.

Knowingly to disregard an order under s 4(2) amounts to a contempt of court, regardless of whether the publication creates any risk of prejudice to current, pending or imminent proceedings.[1] If there is such a risk, there may be liability under the strict liability rule regardless of the absence of knowledge. Section 4 of the 1981 Act is amended by s 57(3) of the new Act so as to adopt the operation of s 4(2) to the provisions relating to tainted acquittals. A new s 4(2A) is added, which provides that where in proceedings for an 'administration of justice offence' it appears to the courts that there is a possibility that proceedings may be taken against a person for an offence of which he has been acquitted, s 4(2) of the 1981 Act applies as if those proceedings were pending or imminent.

---

1 *Horsham JJ ex parte Farquharson* [1982] QB 762, [1982] 2 All ER 269 (CA).

DEROGATORY ASSERTIONS IN MITIGATION ETC: REPORTING RESTRICTIONS

5.16 The Royal Commission on Criminal Justice received evidence that, particularly if a guilty plea has been entered, the victim of an offence may have slurs cast upon him during the defence speech in mitigation, perhaps in an attempt to obtain a reduced sentence. As the Commission noted,[1] such assertions are privileged[2] and may be reported with impunity by the press, with no opportunity for the victim to obtain redress, despite the distress which they may cause. In addition, such assertions can be distressing to the relatives of a victim. This is particularly important when the victim has died. The accused's advocate is obliged to carry out his client's instructions, but the prosecution can intervene to prevent unfair attacks on the victim or witness (or even some other third party who has not appeared at the trial at all). The Royal Commission noted that such a course cannot be embarked on lightly since there may have to be a separate hearing, following an adjournment, if the defence persists in its version of the facts. It believed that, if the prosecution advocate intervened more often, the accused would be less prone to launching unsubstantiated attacks on the character of a victim or a third party, since such attacks would be likely to be counter-productive when it came to sentence.

The Royal Commission went further and recommended that a judge should have the power to prohibit the reporting of unsupported derogatory assertions made during a speech in mitigation.[1] It envisaged this power to be used in the last resort in the extreme case of an accused apparently using the speech in mitigation or a chance to do as much as possible to harm the reputation of a victim or third party, without any risk of legal retaliation.[1]

---

1 (1993) Cm 2263, HMSO, Ch 8, para 47.
2 A fair and accurate report in any newspaper of proceedings publicly heard before any court exercising judicial authority is, if published contemporaneously with those proceedings,

absolutely privileged, by virtue of the Law of Libel Amendment Act 1888, s 3, which is not affected by the provisions described below (s 61(4)). Section 3 of the 1988 Act also applies to broadcast reports by radio or television within the United Kingdom (Defamation Act 1952, s 9(2); Broadcasting Act 1990, s 203 and Sch 20, para 2). If the terms of s 3 are not satisfied, because the report is not contemporaneous or is not contained in a newspaper or broadcast, there may be qualified privilege at common law, provided the report is a fair and accurate one. The defence of qualified privilege will fail if the defendant was actuated by malice. As to privilege, see Howarth, *Textbook on Tort* (Butterworths, 1995), pp 578–581 and 584.

5.17 The Royal Commission's recommendation is implemented, with modifications, by s 58. As noted in para **5.18**, the power to prohibit extends to a wider range of situations than that recommended by the Commission.

To what does section 58 apply?

5.18 Section 58 applies where a person has been convicted of an offence and a speech in mitigation is made by him or on his behalf before:

(a) a court determining what sentence should be passed on him in respect of the offence; or

(b) a magistrates' court determining whether he should be committed to the Crown Court for sentence (s 58(1)).

Section 58 also applies where a sentence has been passed on a person in respect of an offence and a submission relating to the sentence is made by him or on his behalf before:

(a) a court hearing an appeal against or reviewing[1] the sentence; or

(b) a court determining whether to grant leave to appeal against the sentence (s 58(2)).

Section 58 does not apply to derogatory assertions in another context, cross-examination, where it may occur.

Section 58 only applies where the offence of which a person has been convicted is committed[2] on or after a day to be appointed by the Home Secretary (s 61(1) and (2)).[2] At the time when this book went to press no day had been appointed.

---

1 Ie under the Criminal Justice Act 1988, s 36 (Court of Appeal's power to review lenient sentences).

2 See annotations to s 61.

The order

5.19 In the circumstances outlined below, the court may make an interim order or a full order in relation to an assertion (s 59(1)) (which, presumably, must be specified in the order). The effect of either type of order is that, as long as it is in force, the assertion must not:

(a) be published in Great Britain[1] in a written[2] publication available to the public; or

(b) be included in a programme included in a programme service[3] for reception in Great Britain (s 59(1) and (2)).

It is noteworthy that, although the power to make an order under s 58 is only available to an English or Welsh court (s 79), an order under s 58 extends to Scotland, as well as to England and Wales.

In (a) above, 'written publication' includes a film, a sound track and any other record in permanent form but does not include an indictment or other document prepared for use in particular legal proceedings (s 59(2)).

For the purposes of s 59, an assertion is published or included in a programme if the material published or included:

(a)   names the person about whom the assertion is made or, *without naming him, contains enough to make it likely that members of the public will identify him as the person about whom it is made*; and

(b)   reproduces the actual wording of the matter asserted or *contains its substance* (s 59(3)).

---

1 See general annotations.
2 See annotations to s 2.
3 Within the meaning of the Broadcasting Act 1990 (s 57(2)); see general annotations.

At what point can an order be made?

5.20   A full order may only be made after the court has made 'a determination with regard to sentencing' (s 58(8)(a)). For the purposes of s 58, the court makes such a determination:

(a)   in the case of a court determining what sentence should be passed, when it determines that sentence;

(b)   in the case of a magistrates' court determining whether a convicted person should be committed for sentence, when it determines whether the person should be committed;

(c)   in the case of a court hearing an appeal or reviewing the sentence, when it determines what the sentence should be;

(d)   in the case of a court determining whether to grant leave to appeal against a sentence, when it determines whether to grant leave (s 58(9)).

A full order may only be made if it is made as soon as is reasonably practicable[1] after the making of the determination (s 58(8)(a)). If it is not, it would seem that it would be invalid.

A full order may be revoked at any time by the court (s 58(8)(b)), ie the court which made it. If not previously revoked, it ceases to have effect at the end of a 12-month period[1] beginning on the day on which it is made (s 58(8)(c)).

---

1 See annotations to s 58.

5.21   An interim order can be made at any time before the court has made a 'determination with regard to sentencing', as defined by s 58(9)[1] (s 58(7)(a)). It can be revoked at any time by the court (s 58(7)(b)) and automatically ceases to have effect when the court makes a determination with regard to sentencing (s 58(7)(c)). Clearly, an interim order is made available in order to permit a court to make an immediate 'gagging order' as soon as a derogatory assertion of the requisite type is made. Because of this, the order may be made without time for full receipt of the speech in mitigation, proper argument, inquiry and reflection. It is for this reason that the duration of an order is limited. Because the order ceases to have effect when the court makes a determination with regard to sentencing, a court should consider whether to make a full order at that point of time. If it does decide to make a full order, it should make it there and then. If it delays doing so, there will be a 'window of opportunity' for publication without legal retaliation.

No doubt, normally, a full order will be made after an interim order but it is not a requirement for a full order that an interim order has been made (s 58(8)(d)). On the other hand, having heard the rest of the mitigation and argument, the court may decide that a full order is not justified.

---

1 See para **5.20**.

Criteria for an order

5.22   The court may make a *full* order in relation to an assertion where there are substantial grounds for believing:

(a)   that an assertion forming part of the speech or submission is derogatory[1] to a person's character (for instance, because it suggests that his conduct is or has been criminal, immoral or improper); and

(b)   that the assertion is false or (although it is not false) that the facts asserted are irrelevant to the sentence (s 58(4)).

Thus, a full order can be made even if the matters in (a) and (b) have not been established, provided that there are substantial grounds for believing that they are satisfied.

The court may make an *interim* order in relation to an assertion where it appears to it that there is a real possibility (a lower test than 'substantial grounds for believing') that a full order will be made in relation to the assertion at the appropriate time (s 58(3)).

The new Act does not indicate who should raise the question of whether an order should be made under s 58. Presumably, the matter is left to be raised by the judge in the Crown Court, or the bench in a magistrates' court, of his or its own motion. In a magistrates' court, the clerk will play an important role in alerting lay magistrates to their powers under s 58.

A full or interim order must not be made in relation to an assertion if it appears to the court that the assertion was previously made:

(a)   at the trial at which the person was convicted of the offence; or

(b)   during any other proceedings relating to the offence (s 58(5)).

The phrase 'it appears' is intended to limit the burden on the court of establishing whether an assertion, which might be the subject of an order, has been made in earlier proceedings.[2]

---

1 Ie tending to detract, disparage or belittle a person's character: *Collins English Dictionary.*
2 Baroness Blatch, Minister of State, Home Office, HL Committee, col 1586.

Appeal against order

5.23 A person aggrieved by a full or interim order under s 58 made by the Crown Court as the court of trial may appeal against the order to the Court of Appeal (Criminal Division) with its leave (s 61(6)).[1] In the case of a person aggrieved by a full or interim order made by a magistrates' court or by the Crown Court in its appellate capacity, the order may be challenged by an application for judicial review. Judicial review is not available in respect of 'matters relating to trial on indictment',[2] a phrase which has been held to include other types of order restricting publication made by the Crown Court as a trial court.[3]

There appears to be no right of appeal where the order is made by the Court of Appeal hearing an appeal against or reviewing sentence or determining whether to grant leave to appeal against sentence.

---

1 Amending the Criminal Justice Act 1988, s 159. Under the 1988 Act, s 159(1), the Court of Appeal's decision is final.
2 Supreme Court Act 1981, s 29(3).
3 *Central Criminal Court ex parte Cook* (1984) *The Times,* 8 November (DC).

Breach of an order

5.24 If an assertion is published or included in a programme included in a programme service[1] in Great Britain in contravention of a full or interim order under s 58, each of the following persons[2] is guilty of an offence:

(a) in the case of publication in a newspaper or periodical, any proprietor, any editor and any publisher of the newspaper or periodical;
(b) in the case of publication in any other form, the person publishing the assertion;
(c) in the case of an assertion included in a programme, any body corporate engaged in providing the service in which the programme is included and any person having functions in relation to the programme corresponding to those of an editor of a newspaper (s 60(1)).

Breach in Scotland of an order made by a court in England or Wales under s 58 is an offence within the jurisdiction of an English or Welsh court, in the same way as is such a breach in England and Wales.

An offence under s 60(1) is only triable summarily (s 60(2)). It is not punishable with imprisonment; the maximum penalty is a fine not exceeding level 5 on the standard scale[3] (s 60(2)).

1 These terms bear the same meaning as in s 59 (s 60(6)); para **5.19**; see general annotations.
2 See annotations to s 60.
3 See general annotations.

5.25   The prosecution does not have to prove that a person[1] charged with an offence under s 60 was aware, or even had reason to suspect, either that an order had effect at that time or that the publication or programme contained the assertion in question. Instead, the accused has a defence if he proves[1] that at the time of the alleged offence:

(a)   he was not aware, and neither suspected nor had reason to suspect, that a full or interim order under s 58 had been made at that time; or

(b)   he was not aware, and neither suspected[1] nor had reason to suspect,[1] that the publication or programme in question was of, or (as the case may be) included, the assertion in question.

Where an accused is a corporate body, it would seem in principle that it will suffice if it proves lack of awareness etc. on the part of any 'controlling officer' of the body corporate, whose acts and state of mind can be identified with it, such as a director or an editor or employee to whom the directors have delegated full power in the running of the corporation's affairs or part of its affairs.[2]

1 See annotations to s 60.
2 *Tesco Supermarkets Ltd v Nattrass* [1972] AC 153, [1971] 2 All ER 127 (HL). The surprising decision in *Tesco Stores Ltd v London Borough of Brent* [1993] 2 All ER 718 (DC), where it was held in relation to a similar defence that it was irrelevant that the company's controlling officers lacked awareness etc if the junior employee who had committed the offence did, is of no relevance here. The reason is that, where the commission of the offence under s 60 by a corporation is in issue, it is only the conduct of controlling officers which could constitute the commission of the offence within its terms.

5.26   As is common with modern criminal legislation, s 60(4) provides a 'directors clause' whose wording is in standard form. Section 60(4) provides that, where an offence under this section committed by a body corporate is proved to have been committed with the consent or connivance of, or to be attributable to any neglect on the part of:

(a)   a director,[1] manager, secretary or other similar officer of the body corporate; or

(b)   a person purporting to act in any such capacity,

he as well as the body corporate is guilty of the offence and liable to be proceeded against and punished accordingly.[2]

1 In relation to a body corporate whose affairs are managed by its members (ie shareholders in the case of a company), 'director' in s 60(4) means a member of the body corporate (s 60(5)).
2 See annotations to s 60.

CUSTODY TIME-LIMITS: MEANING OF PRELIMINARY STAGE OF CRIMINAL PROCEEDINGS

5.27 By s 22(1) of the Prosecution of Offences Act 1985, the Home Secretary is empowered to make regulations to make provision, with respect to any specified 'preliminary stage' of proceedings for an offence, as to the maximum period:

(a)   to be allowed to the prosecution to complete that stage;
(b)   during which the accused may, while awaiting completion of that stage, be kept in custody.

Although, as indicated by (a), the regulations may prescribe an overall time-limit within which the prosecution must complete the preliminary stage of the proceedings in question, no such regulations have been made.

Regulations have, however, been made in respect of (b), imposing maximum periods for which an accused may be remanded in custody while the preliminary stage in question is being completed. These are the Prosecution of Offences (Custody Time Limits) Regulations 1987,[1] which relate only to indictable offences.

---

1 SI 1987/299.

5.28   As enacted, s 22(11) of the 1985 Act defined 'preliminary stage', in relation to any proceedings, as not including 'any stage of the proceedings after the accused has been arraigned in the Crown Court or, in the case of a summary trial, the magistrates' court has begun to hear evidence for the prosecution at the trial'. In line with the first half of this definition, reg 5 of the Regulations provides that the maximum period in which an accused may be remanded in custody between the time when he is committed for trial[1] (or a voluntary bill of indictment is preferred) and his arraignment is 112 days, and not the start of the trial (which may not immediately follow the arraignment, and indeed may not do so for some time).

---

1 Or a notice of transfer is given under the Criminal Justice Act 1987, ss 4–6, or under the Criminal Justice Act 1991, s 53.

5.29   The first part of the definition of 'preliminary stage' has given rise to problems for two reasons. First, there have been instances of arraignments being conducted for no reason other than to deprive an accused of the benefit of the expiration of a custody time-limit. The Divisional Court has held in *Crown Court at Maidstone ex parte Hollstein*[1] and in *Crown Court at Maidstone ex parte Clark*[2] that such a sham arraignment can be quashed in proceedings for judicial review, but in a subsequent case, *Crown Court at Leeds ex parte Hussain*,[3] the Divisional Court expressed the view that the two previous decisions were wrong in so far as they decided that a sham arraignment could be so quashed. The difference of opinion centred around the question of whether a sham arraignment is a matter 'relating to trial on indictment'. If it is, it will not be susceptible to judicial review because of the prohibition on judicial review being available in relation to the jurisdiction of the Crown Court in respect to matters relating to trial on indictment.[4]

It was held in *Crown Court at Maidstone ex parte Clark* that, even if judicial review is not available to quash a sham arraignment, habeas corpus is available as a remedy to rectify the wrong. In *Crown Court at Leeds ex parte Hussain*, no reference was made to the availability of habeas corpus in the case of sham arraignments, but the arraignment in that case had not been a sham.

1 [1995] 3 All ER 503 (DC).
2 [1995] 3 All ER 513 (DC).
3 [1995] 3 All ER 527 (DC).
4 Supreme Court Act 1981, s 29(3).

5.30 The second problem which the first part of the definition of 'preliminary stage' gives rise to is that an accused who is awaiting trial in the Crown Court and who has been released on bail following the expiry of the custody time-limit is only entitled to bail under the Act and Regulations until arraignment, as opposed to the start of the trial. While this is the clear effect of the definition, some uncertainty was caused by the wording of reg 6(6) of the Regulations, which provides that:

> 'The Crown Court, on being notified that an accused who is in custody pending trial there has the benefit of a custody time limit . . . and that the time limit is about to expire, shall grant him bail . . . as from the expiry of the time limit . . . subject to a duty to appear before the Crown Court for trial.'

Taken literally, these words seem to extend the protection of a custody time-limit to a period after arraignment where a trial did not immediately follow, in which case they would be ultra vires and of no effect, although it might be in the spirit of the rules about custody time-limits. However, in *Croydon Crown Court ex parte Lewis*[1] the Divisional Court held that reg 6(6) should be construed so as not to be ultra vires, since it did not state expressly that bail must continue until trial but merely made the bail granted subject to a duty to appear before the Crown Court for trial. Therefore, reg 6(6) on its true construction did not conflict with the clear statement in s 22 of the 1985 Act that the Home Secretary might make regulations with respect to a preliminary stage of proceedings down to but not beyond the date of arraignment, specifying the maximum period which the accused might be in custody pending arraignment.

1 [1995] Crim LR 44 (DC).

5.31 Now that an accused can be arraigned at a plea and directions hearing some time, often a long time, before the start of the trial, the undoubted intention of Parliament that custody time-limits should operate up to the start of the trial proper (as is expressly provided in the second half of the definition of 'preliminary stage', relating to summary proceedings) was thwarted. For this reason, the definition of 'preliminary stage' in s 22(11) of the 1985 Act is amended by s 71(2) so as to provide that ' "preliminary stage", in relation to any proceedings, does not include any stage after the start of the trial (within the meaning given by subs (11A)and (11B) below [which are inserted by s 71(3) of the new Act].'

5.32   Section 22(11A) and (11B) clarify what is meant by the 'start of the trial'. Section 22(11A) of the 1985 Act provides that, for the purposes of s 22, the start of a trial on indictment is to be taken to occur when a jury is sworn to consider the issue of guilt or fitness to plead or, if the court accepts a plea of guilty before a jury is sworn, when that plea is accepted. This, however, is subject to a qualification where the judge orders a preparatory hearing in a case covered by s 8 of the Criminal Justice Act 1987[1] or s 30 of the new Act.[2] There, the trial starts with the preparatory hearing, as provided by those sections.

Section 22(11B) provides that, for the purposes of s 22, the start of a summary trial is to be taken to occur:

(a)   when the court begins to hear evidence for the prosecution at the trial or to consider whether to exercise its power (under s 37(3) of the Mental Health Act 1983) to make a hospital order without convicting the accused; or

(b)   if the court accepts a guilty plea without proceeding as described in (a), when that plea is accepted.

---

1 See annotations to s 39.
2 See para **4.23**.

5.33   Section 71(4) makes consequential amendments to the Prosecution of Offences (Custody Time Limits) Regulations 1987.[1]

---

1 See s 71(4) and annotations thereto.

5.34   With one exception, the changes made by s 71 apply to:

(a)   any time-limit which begins to run on or after a day to be appointed by the Home Secretary; and

(b)   any time-limit which has begun to run and has not expired before that day (s 71(5) and (6)).

When this book went to press, a day had not been appointed for this purpose.

The exception is that s 71 does not apply to proceedings for an offence for which the accused has been duly arraigned in the Crown Court before the appointed day (s 71(5)).

WITNESS ORDERS AND SUMMONSES

5.35   Section 66 of the new Act substitutes a new s 2 of the Criminal Procedure (Attendance of Witnesses) Act 1965 for the pre-existing s 2, and inserts new ss 2A, 2B, 2C and 2D. It also textually amends s 4 of the 1965 Act to reflect the substantive changes made,[1] and omits from the 1965 Act the pre-existing Sch 1. All of these changes apply as from a day to be appointed.[2] No such day had been appointed as at the date of going to press.

The purpose of these changes is to introduce revised witness summons procedures designed to relieve some of the burdens that are imposed on third parties by accused persons seeking the widescale production of documents held by them, and which may sometimes amount to nothing more than a 'fishing expedition'. The changes, although technical in nature, are part and parcel of the change in approach to disclosure of material, and are the first, 'modest'[3] steps towards changes in the disclosure of third party material.[4]

---

1 See annotations to s 67.
2 See general annotations.
3 Baroness Blatch, Minister of State, Home Office, Lords' consideration of Commons' amendments, col 968.
4 See para **2.87**.

5.36   The pre-existing s 2 permitted a Crown Court, or the High Court, to issue automatically a witness summons requiring the person to whom it was directed to attend the Crown Court to give evidence or to produce any document or thing specified in the summons. The person so directed could challenge that summons, by hearing,[1] and could do so on one of three grounds. These were that the witness summons was insufficiently specific as to what was to be produced;[2] that that person did not have material evidence to give or produce;[3] or by a claim of public interest immunity in respect of that evidence or document.[4]

---

1 See Crown Court Rules 1982, r 23 (SI 1982/1109).
2 *Miller* (5 July 1993) (unreported) (CA); *W(G)* (1996) *The Times*, 12 July.
3 *Cheltenham JJ ex parte Secretary of State for Trade* [1977] 1 WLR 95 (DC); *Clowes* (1992) 95 Cr App R 440 (CA); *Greenwich Juvenile Court ex parte Greenwich LBC* (1977) 76 LGR 99 (DC); *Skegness Magistrates' Court ex parte Cardy* [1988] RTR 49 (DC); *Coventry Magistrates' Court ex parte Perks* [1985] RTR 74 (DC); *Derby Magistrates' Court ex parte B* [1995] 4 All ER 526 (HL); *Reading Justices ex parte Berkshire County Council* (1995) *The Times*, 5 May (DC). These cases involve the Magistrates Courts' Act 1980, s 97, but the concept of materiality is common to both.
4 *Clowes*, op cit; *K* (1992) *The Times*, 8 December (CA); cf *Thompson* (1992) (unreported) (CA).

5.37   Such issues often arose in contexts such as child care records held by local authority social services departments, and third parties might often face real difficulties to decide what material, if any, should be disclosed, what material public interest immunity might properly be claimed for, and whether the requirement for production of document was specific and well-founded, or merely speculative.

In its Consultation Paper on Disclosure[1] the Government proposed changes, so that the issues raised by third party disclosure are raised at an early stage, and in a careful and structured way 'designed to elicit clearly the real ways in which the defence might be assisted, and to enable these to be properly balanced against the often highly sensitive responsibilities and duties of third parties such as doctors, social workers and others who may hold sensitive information about a person which has been obtained as the result of a relationship based on privacy and confidentiality.'[2] The new s 2 of the 1965 Act is designed to achieve this objective.

---

1 (1995) Cm 2864, HMSO.
2 Ibid, Ch 8, para 80.

5.38 The new s 2 of the 1965 Act applies where the Crown Court is satisfied that:

(a) a person is likely to be able to give evidence likely to be material evidence, or produce the document or thing likely to be material evidence, for the purposes of any criminal proceedings before the Crown Court; and

(b) the person will not voluntarily attend as a witness or will not voluntarily produce the document or thing (1965 Act, s 2(1)).

Where the court is so satisfied, it shall issue a witness summons directed to the person concerned and require him to attend before the Crown Court at the time and place stated and give the evidence or produce the document or thing. However, the issue of a summons is subject to an application being made (1965 Act, s 2(3)). The Crown Court may refuse to issue a summons if the requirements relating to the application for a summons are not met.

Thus, the significant change is that no longer is the issue of the summons automatic. It should also be noted that a summons may be issued by a Crown Court of its own motion (1965 Act, s 2D).

5.39 An application for a witness summons under s 2(1) of the 1965 Act must be made as soon as practicable[1] after committal or transfer for trial, or after the preferment of a bill of indictment (1965 Act, s 2(4),(5),(6)). The procedural requirements governing such applications will be governed by Crown Court rules (1965 Act, s 2(7) and (8)). No such rules had been made as at the date of going to press. However, such rules may, in particular, require such an application to be supported by affidavit (1965 Act, s 2(8)c)) and may, in particular, require that affidavit to:

(a) set out any charge on which the proceedings are based;

(b) specify any stipulated evidence, document or thing in such a way as to enable the directed person to identify it;

(c) specify grounds for believing that any stipulated evidence is likely to be material evidence;

(d) specify grounds for believing that any stipulated document or thing is likely to be material evidence (1965 Act, s 2(9)).

'Stipulated evidence, document or thing' and 'directed person' are to be taken as references to the matters or person referred to in the proposed witness summons (1965 Act, s 2(10)).

The intent behind this change is to ensure that the applicant specifically identifies the evidence document or thing required, and to state reasons why it is material.[2]

---

1 See annotations to s 58.
2 For documents to be 'material' for this purpose they must not only be relevant to the issues arising in the criminal proceedings, but also admissible in evidence: *Reading Justices ex parte Berkshire CC* (5 May 1995) (unreported). A witness summons is not available simply to secure the use of documents for use in cross-examination: *Cheltenham JJ ex parte Secretary of State for Trade* [1977 1 All ER 460 (DC); *Derby Magistrates' Court ex parte B* [1995] 4 All ER 526 (HL). The test is not the same as that of materiality for the purposes of the common law disclosure rules. The fact that documents are useful to the defence does not make them material for the purposes of s 2.

Production in advance of Crown Court hearing

5.40   If issued, a witness summons may not only require the person directed to produce a document or thing at the Crown Court to do so, but may also require him to produce it:

(a)   at a place stated in the summons; and
(b)   at a time which is so stated, and precedes the time when such production at the Crown Court is required,

for inspection by the person applying for the summons (1965 Act, s 2A).

Disobedience to such a requirement will amount to a contempt of court, punishable summarily as if the contempt had been committed in the face of the court (1965 Act, s 3(1A), inserted by the new Act, s 66(3)).

Thus, the person seeking production can have sight of the document or thing at an early stage, prior to trial. Following that inspection, it may be the case that the applicant for the summons no longer requires production at trial. Section 2B(1) of the 1965 Act permits him in such circumstances to apply to the Crown Court for a direction that the summons be of no further effect, and the court may direct accordingly. There is nothing in s 2B(1) that requires him to make such an application. Any application that is made is to be governed by Crown Court rules (1965 Act, s 2B(2) and (3)). No such rules had been made as at the date of going to press.

Application for discharge

5.41   If a witness summons is directed to a person who:

(a)   applies to the Crown Court;
(b)   satisfies the court that he was not served with notice of the application to issue the summons and that he was neither present nor represented at the hearing of the application; and
(c)   satisfies the court that he cannot give any evidence likely to be material evidence or, as the case may be, produce any document or thing likely to be material evidence,

the court may direct that the summons shall be of no effect (1965 Act, s 2C(1)).

A similar application may be made, under s 2E of the 1965 Act, in respect of a summons issued of the court's own motion, under s 2D.

An application under s 2C will be governed by Crown Court rules, which may provide for the production of the document or thing at the hearing of the application (1965 Act, s 2C(7)). No such rules had been made as at the date of going to press. Because no rules about any of the applications discussed have been made, it is impossible to say whether such rules, made under the 1965 Act, s 2(8), will require notice of the application for a summons to be served on the person the subject of the summons. It is for that reason that s 2C(2) makes clear that whether service is required under such rules is irrelevant to the grounds of application under s 2C(b).

Section 2C(8) provides some sanction against the seeking of a witness summons on tenuous or unnecessary grounds. If an application for discharge under s 2C(1) succeeds, the person on whose application the summons was issued may be ordered to pay the whole or any part of the costs of the application for discharge. Taxation and enforcement of payment of such costs are dealt with by s 2C(9), which treats them as a civil debt.

Abolition of witness orders

5.42 Section 1 of the 1965 Act required a magistrates' court acting as examining justices to make a witness order in respect of each witness examined by the court, requiring him to attend and give evidence before the Crown Court.

Section 47 of and Sch 1 to the new Act amend significantly the provisions relating to committal for trial,[1] with the consequence that there will be, after the new provisions come into operation, no examination of witnesses on committal. Instead, committals will be based on the written evidence identified by Sch 1, para 3. By s 68 and Sch 2, such written statements will be admissible at trial if the precondition contained in Sch 2, para 1(2) or 2(1) apply.

---

1 See Chapter 6.

5.43 The need for s 1 of the 1965 Act thus disappears, and it is omitted from the 1965 Act by s 65(1) of the new Act. Consequential amendments are made by s 65(2) to s 3 and s 4 of the 1965 Act,[1] and by s 65(3) to s 145 of the Magistrates' Courts Act 1980. The provisions of s 65 are to be brought into effect by an order made by the Home Secretary (s 65(3)). No such order has been made as at the date of going to press.

---

1 See annotations to s 66.

Witness summonses: issue of power of arrest

5.44 The power in s 4(1) of the 1965 Act to issue a warrant to arrest a witness in respect of whom a witness summons is in force, and who is unlikely to comply with the summons, has hitherto been vested in any judge of the High Court.

The witness summons is, of course, to compel attendance at the Crown Court, and there appears no cogent reason why the power to issue such a warrant should not be vested in a circuit judge. Section 67 of the new Act makes that change, to come into effect on the making of an order by the Home Secretary. No such order had been made as at the date of going to press.

CHECKS AGAINST FINGERPRINTS

5.45   Section 56 of the Police and Criminal Evidence Act 1994 introduced a new s 63A into the Police and Criminal Evidence Act 1984 (PACE). That new section permitted fingerprints[1] or samples or the information derived from samples taken under any power conferred by Part V of PACE from a person who had been arrested on suspicion of being involved in a recordable offence[1] to be checked against other fingerprints or samples or the information derived from other samples held by or on behalf of the police or held in connection with or as a result of an investigation of an offence. Such comparisons are important generally, and particularly in the context of the development and use of a DNA database.

---

1 See annotations to s 64.

5.46   Certain gaps existed in that new section. For that reason, s 64 of the new Act substitutes a new s 63A(1) for the pre-existing s 63A(1) created by the 1994 Act. The new s 63A(1) came into effect on Royal Assent (4 July 1996) and applies where a person:

(a)   is arrested on suspicion of being involved in a recordable offence;[1]
(b)   is charged with a recordable offence; or
(c)   is informed that he will be reported for a recordable offence (1996 Act, s 67(2)).

---

1 See annotations to s 1.

5.47   The pre-existing s 63A(1) only applied where the fingerprints, etc, had been taken from a person who had been arrested. However, the powers to take samples under s 62 and s 63 of PACE were not so confined. The new s 63A(1) applies not only where a person has been arrested, but also where he has been charged with a recordable offence or informed that he will be prosecuted for such an offence.

5.48   A second change is in respect of the material against which the check may be made. Under the pre-existing s 63A(1) the check could be made only against fingerprints, samples or the information dervied from other samples contained in records held by or on behalf of the police. This is widened by the new s 63A(1)(a) to include all fingerprints or samples to which the person seeking to check has access and which are held by a police force (widely defined by s 63A(1A)), or are held in connection with or as a result of an investigation of an offence. Thus if the police have access to samples held by a third party, but not covered by legal professional privilege, the check may be made against that material.

A check may also be made against information derived from other samples contained in records to which the person seeking to check has access and which are held as mentioned by s 63A(1)(a) (s 63A(1)(b)).

TELEVISION LINKS AND VIDEO-RECORDED EVIDENCE

5.49 Section 32 and s 32A of the Criminal Justice Act 1988 provide for certain evidence of children to be given by live television link and video-recording respectively.[1]

The objective of these provisions is to try to avoid a child suffering the trauma of giving evidence in open court, but difficulties have arisen where expectations of the respective processes being followed have not been met.

To overcome this, s 62 of the new Act amends both s 32 and s 32A of the 1988 Act by the addition of new subsections. Where leave is granted for the giving of evidence by live television link or video-recording, the child witness shall not give evidence otherwise than by those means (s 32(3C), s 32A(6A)). Permission to do otherwise may be granted by a court on an application by a party to the case or on the court's own motion, if it appears to the court in the interests of justice to do so (s 32A(3D), s 32A(6B)). However, no application is to be made unless there has been a material change of circumstances since the original leave to permit the child to give evidence by live television link or video-recording was granted (s 32(3E), s 32A(6B)).

These provisions come into effect when the leave concerned is given on or after the appointed day.[1] No such day had been appointed as at the date of going to press.

---

1 See annotations to s 62.

5.50 A minor change to the words of s 32A(10) of the 1988 Act is made by Sch 1, para 33, to the new Act. The change made is consequential on the abolition of committal proceedings, described in Chapter 6, whereby witnesses are no longer called.

Chapter 6

COMMITTAL PROCEEDINGS

Non-implementation of provisions relating to transfer for trial – Changes to committal proceedings – Changes relating to post-committal stage

NON-IMPLEMENTATION OF PROVISIONS RELATING TO TRANSFER FOR TRIAL

6.1 In recent years, committal proceedings have been the subject of considerable scrutiny. Fundamental change was made by the Criminal Justice Act 1967 permitting committal without consideration of the evidence,[1] but in 1981 the Royal Commission on Criminal Procedure[2] doubted that committal proceedings acted as an effective filter to prevent weak cases being committed for trial to the Crown Court. It saw no case for the retention of committals without consideration of the evidence, and recommended the creation of a new procedure to be known as an 'application for discharge' to replace committal hearings on consideration of the evidence. Under this proposal the defence would have had the option of a hearing before magistrates at which to make a submission of no case to answer after the prosecution case had been disclosed in writing. No action was taken to implement that recommendation at that time, but in 1986 the Roskill Committee[3] recommended an interim procedural reform in respect of serious fraud cases, until such time as action might be taken by the Government to implement the Royal Commission recommendations. The resulting changes were introduced by the Criminal Justice Act 1987.

---

1 Re-enacted by s 6(2) of the Magistrates' Courts Act 1980.
2 (1981) Cmnd 8092, HMSO, paras 8.24–8.31.
3 Report of the Fraud Trials Committee (1986).

6.2 More recently, the Royal Commission on Criminal Justice[1] received evidence that a significant number of acquittals occur as a result of a direction by the judge to the jury to acquit, thus casting some doubt upon the effectiveness of the committal process as a filter. It considered that committal proceedings involving consideration of the evidence, which constitute about 7% of committals, were cumbersome and exposed vulnerable witnesses to the double ordeal of having to give evidence and being cross-examined at committal proceedings as well as at the trial itself. The Commission concluded that committal proceedings, whether with consideration of the evidence or without consideration of the evidence, served little useful purpose. It recommended that both types of committal proceedings should be abolished.

It also recommended, however, that an accused should have the opportunity to make a submission of no case to answer to a stipendiary magistrate after a mode of trial decision in favour of trial in the Crown Court in the case of an either way offence, or to the Crown Court in the case of an 'indictable only' offence. This submission would be considered on the papers, although the accused would be able to advance oral arguments in support and the prosecution would be able to reply. Witnesses would not be called.

---

1   (1993) Cm 2263, HMSO, Ch 6, paras 20–32.

6.3   Section 44 of the Criminal Justice and Public Order Act 1994 abolished committal proceedings. Section 44 of and Sch 4 to the 1994 Act replaced them with provisions for a system of transfer for trial, which had some similarity with the recommendations of the Royal Commission on Criminal Justice. Under this system, a person charged before a magistrates' court with an indictable offence, in relation to whom the prosecution had served a notice of the prosecution case on the magistrates' court, would have been transferred by the magistrates' court to the Crown Court for trial, unless he had made a successful application for dismissal. Unless the case was one of complexity or difficulty (where the court could grant an oral hearing), an application by a legally represented accused could only be made in writing.

6.4   It had been intended that the new provisions would come into effect in 1995, but the implementation date was postponed on three occasions because the delegated legislation required to develop the Act's provisions had not been completed. In seeking to complete that task, it became apparent to the Government that there were some areas where primary legislation would be helpful in improving the operational effectiveness of the new procedures. For this reason, it inserted into the Bill a number of provisions to deal with eventualities not previously dealt with. The combined result of the original provisions and the Bill's provisions, coupled with draft regulations, was a structure which was costly, bureaucratic, slow and cumbersome, something which the transfer system had been intended to avoid. It also involved the automatic discharge of an accused if the prosecution did not serve the notice of its case within the prescribed period (or any extended period). As a result of pressure from The Law Society, the Bar and the Justices' Clerks' Society, new provisions were introduced into the Bill at the Committee stage in the House of Commons, which repeal the relevant provisions in the 1994 Act (s 44(2), s 80 and Sch 5).

The repeal of the transfer provisions under the 1994 Act does not affect the provisions for the transfer of a case after a notice of transfer has been served[1] (and committal proceedings by-passed) in cases of serious or complex fraud (under ss 4 to 6 of the Criminal Justice Act 1987) or in certain cases involving children (under s 53 of the Criminal Justice Act 1991),[2] which would have survived the introduction of the transfer provisions under the 1994 Act anyway. On the other hand, the notice of transfer provisions under Sch 1 to the War

Crimes Act 1991, which would have been repealed when those transfer provisions came into force,[3] are repealed by the new Act (see s 46, s 80 and Sch 5).[4]

---

1 By the DPP (or by certain other designated authorities in the case of serious or complex fraud).

2 These provisions have been amended by the new Act, see paras **7.1–7.3**.

3 Criminal Justice and Public Order Act 1994, s 167(3) and Sch 11. The repeal provision in the 1994 Act is omitted from it but repealed by the new Act, see s 44(5)(m) and Sch 5 respectively.

4 Section 46 also contains a number of consequential amendments.

6.5 Instead of the transfer scheme described in para **6.4**, the new Act seeks to achieve the objectives of improved efficiency and protection of witnesses by modifying the form of committal proceedings. Modifications are contained in Sch 1 to the Act, which will have effect in accordance with provision made by the Home Secretary by order (Sch 1, para 39). At the time that this book went to press no order had been made. The new provisions are largely in line with proposals made by The Law Society. In essence, committal proceedings involving the receipt of oral evidence, evidence from the defence and cross-examination of witnesses are to be abolished. The evidence at a contested committal will be limited to documentary evidence and exhibits tendered by the prosecution. However, the magistrates will be able to consider any representations by the defence or the prosecution, in addition to the prosecution evidence, to help them to reach their decision on whether to commit for trial or to discharge the accused.

6.6 The provisions differ from those of The Law Society in one significant respect. The Law Society's proposal envisaged streamlining uncontested committals where the accused was legally represented by allowing cases to proceed to the Crown Court for trial without the attendance of the parties at the magistrates' court, at the discretion of the defence. Under the proposal, a court would have set a committal date and, no later than a specified date before that date (14 days was proposed), the prosecutor would have been required to serve written statements by witnesses on the defence. No later than seven days before the committal date, the accused's legal representative would have sent a certificate of agreement requesting that the attendance of all parties be dispensed with. The next stage would have been that, no later than three days before the committal date, the court would have had to send a notice to the accused or his legal representative and the prosecutor excusing the parties from attending. At the committal date, the case would have been committed to the Crown Court by a justices' clerk or a delegated member of staff.

The new provisions do not adopt this proposal because of the substantial administrative arrangements which would have been required to underpin the various requirements for notices to be given, which was one of the reasons why the transfer provisions were abandoned. In addition, the proposal would also have posed problems where (as happens in about two-thirds of cases) the court has to deal with ancillary matters at a hearing. Cases where issues relating to bail have to be resolved are one example. Another example are cases where charges are amended, added or substituted. If the accused was not present at committal the court would be unable to proceed in such a case and there would have been further delay.[1]

---

1 Mr David Maclean MP, Minister of State, Home Office, HC Committee, cols 118–121.

COMMITTAL PROCEEDINGS: THE NEW LAW

6.7   Committal proceedings will continue to be capable of being conducted by a single justice,[1] sitting in open court (MCA 1980, s 4(1) and (2)).

---

1 Or by the justices' clerk, or a member of his staff duly authorised, in the case of a committal for trial under MCA 1980, s 6(2), in the circumstances specified in the Justices' Clerks Rules 1970 (SI 1970/231), Sch 1 (Justices' Clerks Rules 1970, rr 3 and 4 and Sch 1).

Admissible evidence

6.8   Section 5A of the 1980 Act, introduced by Sch 1, para 3, to the new Act, deals with evidence which is admissible in committal proceedings. Section 5A(1) and (2) provides that only evidence tendered by or on behalf of the prosecutor is admissible, and even that evidence is *only admissible* if it falls within one of the following *six* categories limited to documentary evidence and exhibits set out in s 5A(3) (s 5A(2)). Rules which conflict with these provisions have been amended.

Section 30 of the Criminal Justice Act 1988, which provides that an expert report is admissible as evidence in criminal proceedings, *whether or not the person making it attends to give oral evidence in them, and that, where it is proposed that the maker of an expert report should not give oral evidence, the written report is only admissible with leave of the court*, is amended by Sch 1, para 32, to the new Act so that the words italicised do not apply to committal proceedings. Other conflicting rules which have been amended are referred to later in this chapter.

1. Written statements complying with s 5B of the 1980 Act (MCA 1980, s 5A (3)(a))

6.9   Section 5B of the 1980 Act, which is also introduced by Sch 1, para 3 to the new Act, replaces s 102 of the 1980 Act[1] (written statements before examining justices) in generally similar terms. Section 5B provides that a written statement complies with it if the following conditions are met:

(a)   the statement purports to be signed by the person who made it;
(b)   the statement contains a declaration by that person to the effect that it is true to the best of his knowledge and belief and that he made the statement knowing that, if it were tendered in evidence, he would be liable to prosecution if he wilfully stated in it anything which he knew to be false or did not believe to be true;[2] and

(c)   before the statement is tendered in evidence a copy of the statement is given, by or on behalf of the prosecutor, to each of the other parties to the proceedings (s 5B(1) and (2)).

However, unlike s 102, none of the other parties can render the statement inadmissible by objecting to it being tendered before it is tendered in evidence, nor does the court have power to require a person who has made it to attend before the court and give evidence.

---

1 MCA 1980, s 102, is omitted from the Act by Sch 1, para 9, and repealed by Sch 5.
2 If, and when (if ever), the Children and Young Persons Act 1969, Sch 5, para 55, as amended by the new Act, Sch 1, para 21, is brought into force, a different rule will apply where a statement indicates that the person making it has not attained 14. In such a case, the question will not be whether the declarant knew that he would be liable to imprisonment if he wilfully stated something which he knew to be false or did not believe to be true, but whether he understood the importance of telling the truth. This amendment is consequential on the, as yet, unimplemented provisions in the 1969 Act, s 4, whereby a person cannot be charged with an offence, except homicide, by reason of anything done or omitted while he was a child. The implementation of this provision is now most unlikely.

6.10   Where the statement is made by a person aged under 18,[1] it must give his age, otherwise it is inadmissible (s 5B(1) and (3)(a)). Likewise, if the statement is made by someone who cannot read it, it will be inadmissible unless it is read to him before he signs it and it is accompanied by a declaration by the person who has read it that it was so read (s 5B(1) and (3)(b)).

Where the statement refers to any other document as an exhibit, the copy given to any other party to the proceedings must be accompanied by a copy of that document or by such information as may be necessary to enable the party to whom it is given to inspect that document or a copy of it (s 5B(1) and (3)(c)).

Essentially, these provisions replicate s 102(3) of the 1980 Act. The only change is in the age limit in respect of which a maker of a statement must give his age, which is reduced from 21 to 18. Section 5B(3) also replaces s 105 of the 1980 Act, the general effect of which was to permit a witness who was too ill ever to be likely to attend court and testify to make a deposition.[2]

---

1 See annotations to s 1.
2 Schedule 1, para 11, and Sch 5. The Criminal Law Act 1867, ss 6 and 7, which stated the conditions to be satisfied for such a deposition to be tendered at committal proceedings (or at the trial on indictment if there was a committal) is omitted from the Act by Sch 1, para 14, and repealed by Sch 5.

6.11   The provisions of ss 5A and 5B of the 1980 Act relating to written statements and to documents or other exhibits referred to in them, and to their admissibility in committal proceedings, apply where written statements are made in Scotland or Northern Ireland as well as where written statements are made in England and Wales (Criminal Justice Act 1972, s 46(1A), inserted by Sch 1, para 22, to the new Act).

The same provisions apply[1] where written statements are made outside the United Kingdom[2] with two exceptions. The first is that the requirements in s 5B for the statement to contain a declaration that it is true to the best of the declarant's knowledge and belief and that he knew that, if it was tendered in evidence, he would be liable to prosecution if he wilfully stated in it anything which he knew to be false, or did not believe to be true, does not apply to a statement made outside the United Kingdom. The second is that sub-s '(3A)' of s 5B does not apply to such a statement. This creates a problem, because there is no such subsection. Presumably, Parliament meant to refer to sub-s (3)(a) of s 5B, which requires that a statement made by a person aged under 18 must give his age.

---

1 Criminal Justice Act 1972, s 46(1B) and (1C), inserted by Sch 1, para 22, to the new Act. Corresponding, but not identical, provisions in the Criminal Justice Act 1972, s 46, in respect of written statements under the repealed MCA 1980, s 102, are omitted by the new Act, Sch 1, para 22, and repealed by Sch 5.
2 See general annotations.

6.12   By s 106 of the 1980 Act, as amended by Sch 1, para 12, to the new Act, a person who, in a written statement admitted in evidence by virtue of s 5B wilfully makes a statement material in those proceedings which he knows to be false or does not believe to be true, commits an either way offence (maximum punishment two years' imprisonment and/or a fine on conviction on indictment), just as is currently the case with a statement tendered by virtue of s 102. Schedule 1, para 22, to the new Act, however, amends s 46 of the Criminal Justice Act 1972 so as to extend the offence under s 106 of the 1980 Act to written statements made in Scotland or Northern Ireland as well as those made in England and Wales.

2. Documents or other exhibits (if any) referred to in the statements described in 1 (MCA 1980, s 5A(3)(b))

6.13   Any document or other object referred to as an exhibit and identified in a statement admitted in evidence by virtue of s 5B must be treated as if it had been produced as an exhibit and identified in court by the maker of the statement (s 5(B)(5)). There was a similar requirement in s 102(6) of the 1980 Act.

3. Depositions complying with s 5C of the 1980 Act (MCA 1980, s 5A(3)(c))

4. Documents or other exhibits (if any) referred to in the depositions falling within 3 (MCA 1980, s 5A(3)(d))

6.14   A deposition complies with s 5C if:

(a)   a copy of it is sent to the prosecutor by the clerk of the court under s 97A(9) of the 1980 Act (see below) (MCA 1980, s 5C(1)(a)); and

(b)   before the magistrates' court begins to inquire into the offence concerned as examining justices, a copy of the deposition is given, by or on behalf of the prosecutor, to each of the other parties to the proceedings (ibid, s 5C(1)(b) and (2)); and

(c)   where the deposition refers to any other document as an exhibit, the copy given to the other party to the proceedings under (b) above is accompanied by a copy of that document or by such information as may be necessary to enable the person to whom it is given to inspect that document or a copy of it (ibid, s 5C(1)(c) and (3)).

6.15 Any document or other object referred to as an exhibit and identified in a deposition admitted in evidence by virtue of s 5C of the 1980 Act must be treated as if it had been produced as an exhibit and identified in court by the person whose evidence is taken as the deposition (MCA 1980, s 5C(5)).

6.16 Since a deposition is a written record of a witness's sworn statement, the witness will be guilty of the offence of perjury, contrary to s 1 of the Perjury Act 1911, if he wilfully makes a statement material in the committal proceedings which he knows to be false or does not believe to be true. This offence is triable only on indictment and has a maximum penalty of seven years' imprisonment.

6.17 Depositions of the present type will be used where a witness will not voluntarily make a written statement. A new section, s 97A, is added to the 1980 Act by Sch 1, para 8, to the new Act to provide for the taking of them. The section also provides a procedure to deal with those who are unwilling to produce a document or other exhibit.

Section 97A(2) provides that, where a justice of the peace for any commission area is satisfied that three conditions are fulfilled in relation to a particular person, he shall issue a summons requiring that person to attend before a justice at the time and place appointed in the summons to have his evidence taken as a deposition or to produce the document or other exhibit. Where a summons is issued with a view to taking a deposition, the time appointed must be such as to enable the evidence to be taken as a deposition before a magistrates' court begins to inquire into the offence concerned as examining justices (MCA 1980, s 97A(6)). By virtue of the Justices' Clerks Rules 1970, the summons may be issued by the justices' clerk[1] or by a member of his staff to whom he has delegated this power.[2]

The three conditions referred to above are set out in s 97A(1). They are that:

'(a) any person in England or Wales is likely to be able to make on behalf of the prosecutor a written statement containing material evidence, or produce on behalf of the prosecutor a document or other exhibit likely to be material evidence, for the purposes of proceedings before a magistrates' court inquiring into an offence as examining justices;

(b) the person will not voluntarily make the statement or produce the document or other exhibit; and

(c) the magistrates' court mentioned in paragraph (a) above is a court for the commission area concerned.'

The person against whom the deposition is to be tendered is not entitled to the opportunity of attending at the taking of the deposition and of cross-examining the witness.[3]

---

1 SI 1970/231, r 1 and Sch.
2 The delegation must be in accordance with r 4.
3 Cf the repealed provisions for the taking of a deposition from a witness too ill ever to attend court under the repealed MCA 1980, s 105 (para **6.10**).

6.18   Some unwilling witnesses may be more unwilling than others. If a justice of the peace is satisfied by evidence on oath that the conditions set out in s 97A(1) of the 1980 Act are fulfilled, and also that it is probable that a summons under subsection (2) above would not procure the result required by it, the justice may instead of issuing a summons issue a warrant to arrest the person concerned and bring him before a justice at the time and place specified in the warrant (MCA 1980, s 97A(3)). Where the warrant is issued with a view to taking a deposition, the time specified must be such as to enable the evidence to be taken as a deposition before a magistrates' court begins to inquire into the offence concerned as examining justices (MCA 1980, s 97A(6)). Unlike a summons under s 97A(2), a warrant cannot be issued under s 97A(3) unless the justice is satisfied by evidence on oath that the person concerned is in England and Wales (MCA 1980, s 97A(4)).

6.19   If a summons under s 97A has been issued but the person summonsed fails to attend before a justice in answer to the summons, and:

(a)   the justice is satisfied by evidence on oath that he is likely to be able to make a statement or produce a document or other exhibit as mentioned in s 97A(1)(a) above;

(b)   it is proved on oath, or in such other manner as may be prescribed, that he has been duly served with the summons and that a reasonable sum has been paid or tendered to him for costs and expenses; and

(c)   it appears to the justice that there is no just excuse for the failure,

the justice may issue a warrant to arrest him and bring him before a justice at a time and place specified in the warrant (MCA 1980, s 97A(5)).

These are the same conditions as apply under s 97 of the 1980 Act for the issue of an arrest warrant in respect of the non-attendance of a person summonsed under that section to appear before the court as a witness at a trial. Where the warrant is issued with a view to taking a deposition, the time specified in the warrant must be such as to enable the evidence to be taken as a deposition before a magistrates' court begins to inquire into the offence concerned as examining justices (MCA 1980, s 97A(6)).

6.20   If someone attending or brought before a justice under s 97A refuses without just excuse to have his evidence taken as a deposition, or to produce the document or other exhibit, the justice may commit him to custody for such period not exceeding one month as may be specified in the summons or warrant, or impose a fine up to £2,500, or both (MCA 1980, s 97A(7)).

6.21   What happens to a deposition taken or to an exhibit produced under s 97A? The answer is that where a person:

(a)   has his evidence taken as a deposition; or

(b)   produces an exhibit which is a document,

under s 97A, the clerk to the justices must as soon as is reasonably practicable[1] send a copy of it to the prosecutor (MCA 1980, s 97A(9) and (10)).

Secondly, where, under s 97A, a person produces an exhibit which is not a document, the clerk to the justices must as soon as is reasonably practicable[1] inform the prosecutor of the fact and the nature of the exhibit (MCA 1980, s 97A(11)).

---

1 See annotations to s 58.

---

5. Statements complying with s 5D of the MCA 1980 (MCA 1980, s 5A(3)(e))

6.22 We are concerned here, of course, with statements in documents. For such a statement to comply with s 5D, three conditions must be satisfied (MCA 1980, s 5D(1)).

6.23 First, before committal proceedings are begun, the prosecutor must notify the magistrates' court and each of the parties to the proceedings that he believes:

(a) that the statement might by virtue of s 23 or s 24 of the Criminal Justice Act 1988[1] be admissible as evidence *if the case came to trial*; and

(b) that the statement would not be admissible otherwise than by virtue of s 23 or s 24 if the case came to trial (MCA 1980, s 5D(2)).

Although neither s 23 nor s 24 of the 1988 Act directly govern the question of compliance with s 5D of the 1980 Act, the fact that the prosecutor must have the specified belief under paragraph (a) that the requirements of one or other of them might be satisfied means that their terms must be understood. Under both sections, a statement made by a person in a document[2] is admissible in criminal proceedings (other than committal proceedings)[1] as evidence of any fact of which direct oral evidence by him would be admissible if specified requirements are satisfied.

---

1 By Sch 1, paras 28 and 29, to the new Act, ss 23 and 24 are amended so that they no longer apply to committal proceedings. Likewise, s 26 of the 1988 Act, under which a court must not admit a statement satisfying s 23 or s 24 unless it concludes (having considered the factors in s 26) that it should be admitted in the interests of justice, is amended by Sch 1, para 30, so that it no longer applies to committal proceedings. This brings s 26 into line with s 25 of the 1988 Act, under which a court must admit a statement satisfying s 23 or s 24 unless it concludes (having considered the factors in s 25) that in the interests of the administration of justice it should not be admitted; s 25 is already limited to trial and appellate proceedings. Also consequential on the amendment to ss 23 and 24, s 27 of the 1988 Act, which deals with the way in which a statement in a document which is admissible as evidence may be proved, is amended by Sch 1, para 31, so that it no longer applies to committal proceedings.
2 See annotations to s 4.

6.24 Under s 23 of the 1988 Act, the requirements are that:

(a) the maker of the statement is dead or by reason of his bodily or mental condition unfit to attend as a witness[1], or is outside the United Kingdom and it is not reasonably practicable to secure his attendance, or cannot be found despite all reasonable steps to find him; or

(b)   the statement was made to a police officer or some other person charged
        with the duty of investigating offences or charging offenders, and the
        person who made it does not give oral evidence through fear[2] or because
        he is kept out of the way.

---

1 *Setz-Dempsey* (1994) 98 Cr App Rep 23 (CA).
2 *Acton Justices ex parte McCullen* (1991) 92 Cr App Rep 98 (DC); *Ashford Magistrates' Court ex parte Hilden* (1993) 96 Cr App Rep 92 (DC).

6.25   Under s 24 of the 1988 Act, the requirements are that the document was
created or received by a person in the course of an occupation or as the holder
of a paid or unpaid office, and that the information in the document was
supplied by someone (whether or not the maker of the statement) who had, or
may reasonably be supposed to have had, personal knowledge of the matters
dealt with. If the information was supplied indirectly, each person through
whom it was supplied received it in the course of an occupation or as the holder
of a paid or unpaid office (Criminal Justice Act 1988, s 24(2)).

6.26   If a statement produced by a computer is to be admitted under s 23 or
s 24 it must also comply with the requirements of s 69 of PACE. Section 69
requires that such a statement is not admissible as evidence of any fact stated
therein unless it is shown that there are no reasonable grounds for believing
that the statement is inaccurate because of improper use of the computer, that
at all material times the computer was operating properly, or, if not, that any
respect in which it was not operating properly was not such as to affect the
production of the document or the accuracy of its contents, and that any
conditions specified in rules of court are satisfied. Schedule 3, para 8, to the
1984 Act states that, where it is decided to give a statement in accordance with
s 69, a certificate dealing with specified matters is evidence of anything
contained in it. Schedule 3, para 9, however, provides that notwithstanding
this, a court may require oral evidence to be given of anything of which
evidence could be given under such a certificate. This is amended by Sch 1,
para 27, to the new Act so as not to apply to committal proceedings.

6.27   It must be emphasised that it is not enough merely for the prosecutor to
have the specified belief that the requirements of s 23 or s 24 of the 1988 Act
might be satisfied. The prosecutor must also believe that the statement in the
document would not be admissible if the case came to trial otherwise than by
virtue of s 23 or s 24.

6.28   The second condition for a statement to comply with s 5D is that:

(a)   the prosecutor's belief is based on information available to him at the time
        that he makes the notification referred to in para **6.23**;
(b)   he has reasonable grounds for his belief; and
(c)   he gives the reasons for his belief when he makes the notification (MCA
        1980, s 5D(3)).

6.29   The third condition is that when the court or a party is so notified, a copy
of the statement is given, by or on behalf of the prosecutor, to the court or the
party concerned (MCA 1980, s 5D(4)).

6. Documents falling within s 5E of the 1980 Act (MCA 1980, s 5A(3)(f))

6.30 These are documents of the following types:

(a) any document which by virtue of any enactment is evidence in proceedings before a magistrates' court inquiring into an offence as examining justices;

(b) any document which by virtue of any enactment is admissible, or may be used, or is to be admitted or received, in or as evidence in such proceedings;

(c) any document which by virtue of any enactment may be considered in such proceedings;

(d) any document whose production constitutes proof in such proceedings by virtue of any enactment;

(e) any document by the production of which evidence may be given in such proceedings by virtue of any enactment.

Three of these categories under s 5E require further explanation.

ANY DOCUMENT WHICH BY VIRTUE OF ANY ENACTMENT IS EVIDENCE IN
COMMITTAL PROCEEDINGS (MCA 1980, s 5E(1)(a))

6.31 Within this category is evidence admissible under the Bankers' Book Evidence Act 1879, s 3 which provides that: 'Subject to the provisions in this Act, a copy of any entry in a bankers' book[1] shall in all legal proceedings be received as prima facie evidence of such entry, and of the matters, transactions, and accounts therein recorded'. Section 4 of the 1879 Act provides that the book in question must have been one of the ordinary books of the bank, that the entry was made in the usual and ordinary course of business, and that the book is in the custody or control of the bank.[2] Section 4 permits such proof to be given only by a partner or officer of the bank, and normally it permits it to be given orally or by an affidavit sworn before any commissioner or person authorised to take affidavits. This last provision is amended by Sch 1, para 15, to the new Act, so as to provide that, where the proceedings in question are committal proceedings, proof by a partner or officer of the bank may only be given by an affidavit, and not orally. Section 5 of the 1879 Act goes on to provide that a copy of an entry in a bankers' book must not be received in evidence unless it is further proved that the copy has been examined with the original entry and is correct. The section requires such proof to be given by a person who has examined the copy with the original entry. Normally, as in the case of s 4, s 5 permits that proof to be given orally or by an affidavit sworn before a commissioner or person authorised to take affidavits. This provision is amended by Sch 1, para 16, to the new Act in the same way as in the case of s 4. Consequently, in the case of committal proceedings, proof under s 5 can only be given by an affidavit.

---

1 As defined by the Bankers' Book Evidence Act 1879, s 9(2).
2 ibid, s 9(1).

6.32 A further example of a document in the present category of documents falling within s 5E of the 1980 Act is provided by s 41 of the Criminal Justice Act 1948. Section 41(1) states that, in any criminal proceedings, a certificate purporting to be signed by a constable, or by a person having the prescribed qualification,[1] and certifying that a plan or drawing exhibited thereto is a plan or drawing by him of the place or object specified in the certificate, and that the plan or drawing is correctly drawn to a scale so specified, is evidence of the relative position of the things shown on the plan or drawing. Section 41(4) provides that nothing in s 41 is deemed to make a certificate admissible as evidence except in a case where and to the extent to which oral evidence to the like effect would have been admissible in the proceedings. This would render s 41 inapplicable to committal proceedings. Consequently, Sch 1, para 18, to the new Act provides that s 41(4) does not apply to such proceedings. For the same reason, Sch 1, para 18, amends s 41(5), a provision similar to those described above. Section 41(5) states that a certificate is not admissible under s 41:

(a)   unless a copy of it has, not less than seven days before the hearing or trial, been served in the prescribed manner on the accused; or

(b)   if the accused, not later than three days before the hearing or trial or within such further time as the court may allow, serves notice in the prescribed form and manner on the prosecutor requiring the attendance at the *trial* (sic) of the person who signed the certificate.

Presumably, on the basis that the word 'trial' italicised above embraces a hearing as well, Sch 1, para 18, to the new Act provides that paragraph (b) does not apply to committal proceedings. The requirement of the witness's attendance at the proceedings is clearly incompatible with the new nature of committal proceedings.

---

1 See the Evidence by Certificate Rules 1961 (SI 1961/248).

ANY DOCUMENT WHICH BY VIRTUE OF ANY ENACTMENT IS ADMISSIBLE, OR MAY BE USED, OR IS TO BE ADMITTED OR RECEIVED, IN OR AS EVIDENCE IN COMMITTAL PROCEEDINGS (MCA 1980, s 5E(1)(b))

6.33   Within this provision is evidence admissible under s 27(4) of the Theft Act 1968. This provides that, in any proceedings for the theft of anything in the course of transmission (by post or otherwise), or for handling stolen goods from such a theft, a statutory declaration by any person that he dispatched or received or failed to receive any goods or postal packet, or that any goods or postal packets when dispatched or received by him were in a particular state or condition, is admissible as evidence of the facts stated in the declaration.

Normally, such a statutory declaration is only admissible under s 27(4) where, and to the extent to which, oral evidence to the like effect would have been admissible in the proceedings, and only if at least seven days before the hearing or trial a copy of it has been given to the person charged, and he has not, at least three days before the hearing or trial (or within such further time as the court may allow), given the prosecutor written notice requiring the attendance at the hearing or trial of the person making the declaration. As in the case of the provision just mentioned above, the references to the extent to which oral evidence would have been admissible in the proceedings and to the requirement of the witness's attendance at the proceedings are incompatible with the new nature of committal proceedings. Consequently, Sch 1, para 19, to the new Act adds sub-s (4A) to s 27 of the 1968 Act, which provides that, where the proceedings in question are committal proceedings, these requirements do not apply. Probably, by way of oversight, the wording of sub-s (4A) is such as also to disapply the requirement that a copy of the declaration be given seven days before the hearing. This requirement has not been disapplied in the amendments of similar provision referred to in this chapter.

6.34 Also within this category is a statement by a child witness in a child abuse case or the like. Section 103(1) of the 1980 Act, as amended by Sch 1, para 10, to the new Act provides that, in committal proceedings relating to an offence to which the section applies (various offences involving children), a statement made in writing by, or taken in writing from, a child[1] is admissible in evidence of any matter. Hitherto, such a statement has not been admissible in writing:

(a) where the prosecutor required the attendance of the child to establish someone's identity; or

(b) where the court had discontinued a summary trial and changed to committal proceedings.

These exclusions, contained in s 103(3) of the 1980 Act, have been omitted by Sch 1, para 10, and repealed by Sch 5, to the new Act.

Instead of being in the form of a written statement, the statement which the prosecution tenders under s 103 may be in the form of a video recording which it is proposed to adduce at trial (Criminal Justice Act 1988, s 32A(10), as amended by Sch 1, para 33).

---

1 As defined by the Criminal Justice Act 1991, s 53 (MCA 1980, s 103(5)).

6.35 Another example is provided by s 11 of the Road Traffic Offenders Act 1988. Section 11(1) provides that in any proceedings for one of the wide range of offences to which the section applies, a certificate in the prescribed form, purporting to be signed by a constable and certifying that a person specified in the certificate stated to the constable that a particular vehicle:

(a) was being driven or used by, or belonged to, that person on a particular occasion; or

(b) on a particular occasion was used by, or belonged to, a firm (or a corporation) and that he was a partner in that firm (or, as the case may be, a director, officer or employer of that corporation),

is admissible as evidence for the purpose of determining by whom the vehicle was being driven or used, or to whom it belonged, as the case may be, on that occasion.

6.36 Normally, a certificate under s 11(1) is only admissible where, and to the extent that, oral evidence to the like effect would have been admissible (Road Traffic Offenders Act 1988, s 11(2)), and is not admissible if a copy has not been served on the person charged at least seven days before the trial or hearing or if the person charged has, not later than three days before the hearing or trial (or such further time as the court permits), required attendance at the trial of the constable who signed the certificate (ibid, s 11(3)).

These provisions are incompatible with the nature of the new committal proceedings. Consequently, Sch 1, para 35, to the new Act amends s 11 in relation to committal proceedings, so that in that respect s 11(2) will not apply, nor will that part of s 11(3) which gives the person charged the opportunity to require the attendance of the certifying constable to give oral evidence, although the seven days' notice requirement will.

6.37   Another provision within the present category is s 13 of the Road Traffic Offenders Act 1988. This deals with statements in documents purporting to be a part of the records maintained by the Secretary of State in respect of driving licences or of vehicles, or a copy of a document forming part of those records, or a note of any information contained in them. Section 13(2) provides that a statement of this type is admissible in any proceedings as evidence of any fact stated in it 'to the same extent as oral evidence of that fact is admissible in those proceedings'. By Sch 1, para 36, to the new Act, s 13 is amended to the effect that the words just quoted do not apply where the proceedings in question are committal proceedings. This is another amendment consequential on the changed nature of committal proceedings. So are two other amendments, which relate to s 13(4) of the 1988 Act, which is concerned with proceedings in which the statement is produced for an offence involving obligatory or discretionary disqualification. Section 13(4) provides that, where the statement specifies an alleged previous conviction of the accused or any order made on the conviction, the court may take account of the previous conviction 'as if the accused had appeared and admitted it', provided it is satisfied that not less than seven days before the statement is so produced a notice was served on the accused, in the prescribed form and manner, specifying the previous conviction or order and stating that it is proposed to bring it to the notice of the court in the event of or, as the case may be, in view of his conviction, and provided the accused is absent from court when the statement is produced. These provisions are amended by Sch 1, para 36, to the new Act to the effect that in relation to committal proceedings the words quoted and the two requirements referred to do not apply.

ANY DOCUMENT BY THE PRODUCTION OF WHICH EVIDENCE MAY BE GIVEN IN COMMITTAL PROCEEDINGS BY VIRTUE OF ANY ENACTMENT (MCA 1980, s 5E(1)(e))

6.38   Within this third category of documents falling within s 5E of the 1980 Act, come ss 16 and 20 of the Road Traffic Offenders Act 1988.

Section 16(1) of the Road Traffic Offenders Act 1988 provides that evidence of the proportion of alcohol or a drug in a specimen of breath, blood or urine may (provided certain conditions are satisfied) be given by the production of a document or documents purporting to be whichever of the following is appropriate, namely:

(a) a statement automatically produced by the device by which the proportion of alcohol in a breath specimen was measured and a certificate signed by a constable that the statement relates to the specimen provided by the accused at the date and time shown in the statement; and
(b) a certificate signed by an authorised analyst as to the proportion of alcohol or any drug found in a specimen of blood or urine identified in the certificate.

6.39 Section 16(1) of the 1988 Act applies in respect of proceedings for an offence under s 3A, 4 or 5 of the Road Traffic Act 1988 (RTOA 1988, s 15(1)). One of the conditions which must be satisfied in order that a document purporting to be a statement or certificate of the type referred to in s 16(1) be admissible on behalf of the prosecution is that a copy of it must have been served on the accused not later than seven days before the hearing (RTOA 1988, s 16(3)). Normally, a document purporting to be a *certificate* is not admissible if the accused, not later than three days before the hearing or within such further time as the court may in special circumstances allow, has served notice on the prosecutor requiring the attendance at the hearing of the person by whom the document purports to be signed (RTOA 1988, s 16(4)). Schedule 1, para 37 to the new Act amends s 16 of the 1988 Act so as to provide that this requirement shall not apply to proceedings where the proceedings in question are committal proceedings. This amendment is of importance only where the proceedings relate to the offence under s 3A of the Road Traffic Act 1988 of careless driving under the influence of alcohol or drugs, since the other offences to which s 15 (and hence s 16) apply are summary only.

The amendment could, however, be relevant in respect of an offence under s 4 or s 5 of the 1988 Act if the prosecution, in committal proceedings for an either way offence, tendered evidence in relation to that summary offence when the committal for trial of the accused under s 41 of the Criminal Justice Act 1988 for that offence, as being linked with the either way offence, was under consideration.[1]

---

1 The tendering of evidence in respect of the summary offence is unlikely. The 1988 Act, s 41(1), states that evidence of it need not be disclosed in the evidence relied on by the prosecution to secure the committal for trial of the either way offence. Consequently, there seems to be no need for the prosecution to tender evidence of the summary offence. It appears that the prosecution need do no more than make representations to the examining justices explaining how the two offences are linked so as to fall within the section. See *Blackstone's Criminal Practice* (1996), para D 6.31.

6.40 Section 20(1) of the Road Traffic Offenders Act 1988 provides that evidence of a fact relevant to proceedings for an offence to which s 20 of that Act applies may be given by the production of:

(a) a record produced by a prescribed device; and
(b) a certificate as to the circumstances in which the record was produced signed by a constable or authorised person.

As in the case of similar provisions under ss 11, 13 and 16 of the 1988 Act, a document is not admissible under s 20 as evidence unless a copy of it has, not less than seven days before the hearing or trial, been served on the accused. If not less than three days before the hearing or trial (or such further time as the court may allow), the accused serves a notice on the prosecutor requiring attendance at the hearing or trial of the signatory of the document, it is not admissible as evidence of anything other than the matters shown on a record produced by a prescribed device (RTOA 1988, s 20(8)). This provision enables the accused to challenge the validity or accuracy of the documents. Schedule 1, para 38, to the new Act amends s 20 of the 1988 Act to the effect that this last provision (right of accused to serve a counter-notice) does not apply to committal proceedings. This amendment is initially puzzling, since the offences to which s 20 currently applies (speeding offences and failing to comply with automatic traffic lights) are summary only. Moreover, the possibility of the application of s 41 of the Criminal Justice Act 1988 seems remote. However, the Secretary of State has power to add to the list of specified offences (RTOA 1988, s 20(3)), and the amendment would be of relevance if any additional offence was indictable.

General

6.41   For the purposes of the above provisions, 'document' means anything in which information of any description is *recorded* (MCA 1980, ss 5A(4), 5B(6), 5C(6) and 5E(4)).[1] Thus, it includes not only something in writing but also a map or plan, a photograph, a disk, tape, sound track or other device in which sound or data are embodied so as to be capable of being reproduced.

Where a statement, deposition or document is admissible in evidence by virtue of s 5B, s 5C, s 5D or s 5E of the 1980 Act, it may be proved by the production of:

(a)   the statement, deposition or document; or
(b)   a copy[2] of it, or the material part of it (whether or not the statement, deposition or document still exists) (MCA 1980, s 5F(1) and (2)).

It is immaterial how many removes there are between a copy and the original (MCA 1980, s 5F(3)), so that copies of copies are admissible.

---

1 This definition can also be found in the Civil Evidence Act 1995, s 13.
2 Ie anything onto which information recorded in the statement, deposition or document has
   been copied by whatever means and whether directly or indirectly (MCA 1980, s 5F(4)).

Presence of the accused

6.42   Section 4(3) of the 1980 Act currently provides that, subject to s 4(4) (below) and s 102 of the Act, evidence given before the examining justices must be given in the presence of the accused, and that the defence may put questions to any witness. Schedule 1, para 2, to the new Act substitutes a new s 4(3) whereby, subject to s 4(4), evidence (of the admissible types referred to above) *tendered* before examining justices must be tendered in the accused's presence.

The entitlement of the defence to put questions to a witness is not, of course, preserved.

Section 4(4), as consequentially amended by Sch 1, para 2, will continue in force, with the result that examining justices continue to have a power to allow evidence to be tendered in the absence of the accused if they consider that, by reason of his disorderly conduct before them, it is not practicable for the evidence to be tendered in his presence, or if he cannot be present for reasons of health but is legally represented and has consented to the evidence being given.

Magistrates' court's power of adjournment

6.43 A magistrates' court's power under s 5 of the 1980 Act to adjourn committal proceedings before or during them will remain and is not amended by the Act.

Types of committal procedures

6.44 Section 6(1) and (2) of the 1980 Act, which respectively provide for committal proceedings involving consideration of the evidence and for committal proceedings without consideration of the evidence, are substituted by a new s 6(1) and (2), by Sch 1, para 4, to the new Act. The new s 6(1) streamlines committals on consideration of the evidence, but the law under s 6(2) relating to uncontested committals (committals without consideration of the evidence) is essentially unchanged.

6.45 The new s 6(1) provides that a magistrates' court inquiring into an offence as examining justices must on consideration of the evidence (ie the evidence tendered by or on behalf of the *prosecutor* which falls within s 5A(3) of the 1980 Act, above):

(a) commit the accused for trial if it is of opinion that there is sufficient evidence to put him on trial by jury for any indictable offence;

(b) discharge him if it is not of that opinion and he is in custody for no other cause than the offence under enquiry.

As in the case of s 102, so much of any statement as is admitted in evidence in proceedings under s 6(1) by virtue of s 5B of the 1980 Act must, unless the court otherwise directs, be read aloud at the hearing; and where the court so directs an account must be given orally of so much of any statement as is not read aloud (MCA 1980, s 5B(4)). An identical provision applies to so much of any deposition, of any statement as is in writing or of any document as is admitted in evidence by virtue of s 5C, s 5D or s 5E, respectively, of the 1980 Act (MCA 1980, ss 5C(4), 5D(5) and 5E(3)).

Although no express reference is made in the new s 6(1), it will continue to be possible for a submission of no case to answer to be made in proceedings under s 6(1). This is assumed by the new s 6(2) of the 1980 Act.

Consequent on the substitution of a new s 6(1), a change is made to Sch 3 to the 1980 Act which, inter alia, makes provision in respect of the committal for trial of a corporation. As enacted, Sch 3, para 2(a), provided that 'a representative may on behalf of a corporation make a statement before examining magistrates in answer to the charge'. For this there is substituted by Sch 1, para 13, to the new Act a provision that 'a representative may on behalf of a corporation make before examining justices such representations as could be made by an accused who is not a corporation'. In other words, the representative can make a submission of no case to answer but can no longer give evidence, consistent with the amendment to committal proceedings in general.

6.46 By the new s 6(2), a magistrates' court inquiring into the evidence as examining magistrates may in certain circumstances commit the accused for trial without consideration of the contents of any statements, depositions or other documents, and without consideration of any exhibits which are not documents. The circumstances are as follows:

(a) the court must be satisfied that all the evidence tendered by or on behalf of the prosecutor falls within one of the six categories in s 5A(3) of the 1980 Act, above;

(b) the accused or one of the accused has a legal representative (sic) acting for him in the case; and

(c) there is no submission by a legal representative (sic) for the accused or one of the accused, as the case may be, that there is no case to answer.

It is noteworthy that in (b) and (c) 'legal representative' is used, and not 'solicitor' or 'solicitor or counsel', respectively, as in the corresponding paragraphs in the old s 6(2). This change of wording recognises that, although currently only barristers and solicitors have a right of audience in magistrates' courts, other bodies may be authorised under the Courts and Legal Services Act 1990 to grant such a right of audience.

As in the case of s 102, a statement admitted in evidence in proceedings under s 6(2) by virtue of s 5B of the 1980 Act is not required to be read aloud at the hearing or summarised. Nor is a deposition complying with s 5C.

Ancillary provisions

6.47 The rest of s 6 of the 1980 Act (bail and public notice of committal) are not affected by the Act. Nor is s 7 (specification of the Crown Court centre at which the trial is to take place). Section 8 (restrictions on reports of committal proceedings) continues to apply.

Other evidential changes relating to committal proceedings

6.48 Section 71 of PACE provides that in any proceedings the contents of a document may be proved by the production of an enlargement of a microfilm copy of that document or of the material part of it, authenticated in such manner as the court may approve. In respect of committal proceedings, s 71 is amended by Sch 1, para 24, to the new Act, so as not to require authentication of the document.

6.49 Section 76(1) of PACE which provides that, in any proceedings, a confession made by an accused may be given in evidence insofar as it is material and not excluded by the court under other provisions is amended by Sch 1, para 25, to the new Act to the effect that in committal proceedings the reference to exclusion by the court and the provisions of the section relating to this do not apply.

6.50 Likewise, the provisions in s 78 of PACE as to the exclusion of unfair evidence do not apply henceforth to committal proceedings (new Act, Sch 1, para 26).

6.51 Section 2 of the Sexual Offences (Amendment) Act 1976 lays down a restriction on evidence and on cross-examination of the victim at a *trial* involving a rape offence.[1] Section 2(1) provides that if at a trial a person is charged with a rape offence, to which he pleads not guilty, then, except with the leave of the judge, no evidence and no question in cross-examination shall be adduced or asked at the trial by the defence about any sexual experience of a complainant with a person other than the accused.

---

1 'Rape offence' means any of the following: rape, attempted rape, secondary participation in rape or attempted rape, incitement to rape, conspiracy to rape and burglary with intent to rape (Sexual Offences (Amendment) Act 1976, s 7(2)).

6.52 Section 3(1) of the 1976 Act lays down a corresponding restriction in respect of committal proceedings. As enacted, it provided that where a magistrates' court inquired into a rape offence as examining justices, then, except with the consent of the court, *evidence could not be adduced and a question could not be asked at the inquiry which could not be adduced or asked without leave under s 2(1)*. Section 3(1) has had to be amended in the light of the fact that the new-style committal proceedings do not involve evidence adduced by the defence or cross-examination of witnesses.

As amended by Sch 1, para 23, the words italicised in the above account of the 'old' s 3(1) are replaced by the terms italicised in the following two sentences. The 'new' s 3(1) of the 1976 Act provides that where a magistrates' court is inquiring into a rape offence as examining justices then, except with the consent of the court, *no restricted matter shall be raised. A 'restricted matter' is a matter as regards which evidence could not be adduced and a question could not be asked without leave in pursuance of s 2 of the 1976 Act if:*

(a) *the inquiry were a trial at which a person is charged with a rape offence to which he pleads not guilty; and*

(b) *each of the accused at the inquiry were charged at the trial with the offence or offences of which he is accused at the inquiry.*

6.53 Section 3(2) is consequentially amended by Sch 1, para 23, so as to provide that, on an application for consent for any restricted matter to be raised, the court must:

(a) refuse the consent unless it is satisfied that leave in respect of the matter would be likely to be given at a relevant trial; and

(b) give the consent if so satisfied.

CHANGES RELATING TO THE POST-COMMITTAL STAGE

Written statements and depositions as evidence at Crown Court trial

6.54 The changes made to the types of evidence admissible at committal proceedings have necessitated changes to the rules whereby, as exceptions to the general rule that a witness must give his evidence orally in court, a written statement or deposition may be read to the jury as evidence, so that there is no need to call its maker as a witness.

6.55 As the law stood before the new Act, a deposition taken at committal proceedings could without further proof be read as evidence at the trial of the accused if the witness was subject to a conditional witness order, or if the witness was dead or insane, or too ill to travel, or if the witness was kept out of the way by means of the procurement of the accused or on his behalf (provided, in each case, that the correct procedures for the taking of depositions were followed at the magistrates' court). These provisions were contained in s 13(3) of the Criminal Justice Act 1925. They were extended to written statements tendered under s 102 of the MCA 1980 in respect of the same types of case by s 102(7). In their discretion, the courts could exclude evidence admissible under s 13(3) of the 1925 Act.[1] As already indicated, oral evidence will no longer be taken at committal proceedings (so that depositions will no longer be taken at them). As a result, s 13(3) of the 1925 Act and s 7 of the 1967 Act are omitted by Sch 2, para 6, and repealed by Sch 5 to the new Act. The repeal of s 102 of the 1980 Act has already been mentioned.

---

1 See *Blackstone's Criminal Practice* (1996), F.16.23.

6.56 Provision is, however, made by Sch 2 to the new Act for written statements complying with s 5B of the 1980 Act, and depositions complying with s 5C,[1] which have been admitted as evidence at the committal proceedings, to be read at the trial in the Crown Court following those proceedings (Sch 2, paras 1 and 2). As we saw in para **6.8**, these written statements and depositions will have been tendered by the prosecution only. The aim of the new provision is to facilitate the conduct of the trial, and to avoid the unnecessary and wasteful use of time at it, by allowing for written statements or depositions to be admitted at the trial where all parties agree,[2] as they are likely to do if none of them disputes the evidence in question. It is not, however, limited to cases where the parties agree.

Schedule 2 provides that such a written statement or deposition purporting to be signed by a justice of the peace[3] may without further proof be read as evidence on the trial of the accused, whether for the offence for which he was committed for trial or 'for any other offence arising out of the same transaction or set of circumstances' (Sch 2, paras 1 and 2). The effect of the words just quoted, which also appeared in s 13(3) of the 1925 Act, is to allow a written statement complying with s 5B of the 1980 Act or a deposition complying with s 5C to be read at the accused's trial for an offence which is not the one for which he was committed for trial but which arises from the same transaction or set of circumstances as that offence.

Thus, for example, where a person has been committed for trial on a charge of wounding with intent, and the victim later dies, with the result that a charge of murder is preferred by a voluntary bill of indictment, a written statement tendered at the committal proceedings for wounding with intent may be read at the murder trial.

It will be noted that, unlike the provisions replaced, the reading of written statements or depositions is not limited to specified situations. However, the new provisions do not apply, and a witness will have to give oral evidence, if:

(a) it is proved that the statement or deposition was not signed by the justice of the peace by whom it purports to have been signed;

(b) the trial court at its discretion order that the relevant provision shall not apply; or

(c) a party to the proceedings objects[4] to the relevant provision applying, except that the trial court may override the objection and order that the objection shall have no effect if it considers it to be in the interests of justice so to order (Sch 2, paras 1 and 2).

The above provisions do not apply to written statements made outside the United Kingdom[5] (Criminal Justice Act 1972, s 46(1C), inserted by Sch 1, para 22). Depositions, of course, are only taken in England and Wales.[5]

---

1 The written statement or deposition must comply with s 5B or s 5C, as appropriate, prior to the committal proceedings (Sch 2, paras 1 and 2).

2 Baroness Blatch, Minister of State, Home Office, Lords' consideration of Commons' amendments, col 949.

3 Schedule 2, paras 1 and 2. In the case of a deposition, it must purport to be signed by the justice before whom it was taken. A justice who signs a certificate authenticating one or more statements or depositions is treated as signing the statement or deposition or (as the case may be) each of them (Sch 2, para 3). The Criminal Justice Act 1967, s 7, which is superseded by this provision is omitted by Sch 2, para 7, and repealed by Sch 5).

4 A time-limit for objection may be prescribed by rules made under the Supreme Court Act 1981, s 84, and so may a power for the trial court to waive such a limit (Sch 2, para 4).

5 See general annotations.

6.57 The potential danger in admitting written statements or depositions as evidence at the trial is obvious. A written statement will normally have been taken by a police officer, and the form of a written statement 'very substantially depends on the person who took it. That is inevitable – it is not a criticism of any police officer who takes the statement and is simply the way life is'.[1] A person who makes a written statement or deposition will not have been cross-examined at the committal proceedings, nor will the witness be cross-examinable at the trial if the written statement or deposition is admitted at it. Moreover, the jury will be denied the possibility of assessing a witness's demeanour if such evidence is admitted.

The safeguards are contained in (b) and (c) of para **6.56**, namely, the trial court's discretion to order that the relevant provision shall not apply (ie to exclude the reading of the written statement or deposition), and the accused's entitlement to object to the application of the relevant provision (subject to the trial court's power to override the objection). Whether or not these safeguards prove to be strong enough in practice will depend on how the courts exercise their discretion to exclude the reading of a written statement or deposition or their discretion to override an accused's objection to its being read as evidence at the trial.

---

1 Lord Williams of Mostyn, Lords' consideration of Commons' amendments, col 947.

6.58   The *discretion to override the accused's objection to a written statement etc being read as evidence* is required to be exercised by reference to the 'interests of justice'. It is submitted that the courts will exercise this discretion by reference to those factors to which s 26 of the Criminal Justice Act 1988 says a court must have regard in considering whether to exercise its discretion to give leave for a written statement admissible under s 23 or s 24[1] of that Act to be given in evidence, just as the courts have previously done in exercising their discretion to exclude evidence admissible under s 13(3) of the Criminal Justice Act 1925.[2]

Section 26 of the 1988 Act states that a court must not give leave unless it is of the opinion that the written statement ought to be admitted in the interests of justice, and that, in considering the interests of justice, the court must have regard to:

(a)   the contents of the statement;

(b)   any risk that its admission or exclusion will result in unfairness to the accused; and

(c)   any other relevant circumstances.

Among these circumstances are the importance of the statement sought to be admitted in the context of the case as a whole,[3] and the quality of the evidence in the statement; the poorer that quality, the less likely a court is to exercise discretion in favour of admitting the written statement.[4]

---

1 Paragraphs **6.23–6.25**.
2 *Cole* [1990] 2 All ER 108 (CA).
3 *Cole* [1990] 2 All ER 108 (CA); *French* (1993) 97 Cr App Rep 421 (CA); *Grattan* [1995] Crim LR 61 (CA). Cf Archbold *Criminal Pleading, Evidence and Practice* (1995), vol 1, paras 10.51–10.58.
4 *Cole* [1990] 2 All ER 108 (CA); *Scott v R* [1989] AC 1242, [1989] 2 All ER 305 (PC); *Patel* (1993) 97 Cr App Rep 294 (CA); *Irish* [1994] Crim LR 922 (CA).

6.59   Although the court's *discretion to exclude the reading of a written statement or deposition* is not required by Sch 2, paras 1 and 2, to be exercised by reference to the 'interests of justice', the better view is that, despite the absence of such a reference and despite the specification of such a reference in respect of the other discretion in Sch 2, paras 1 and 2, this discretion should also be exercised by reference to the interests of justice and that, in considering those interests, the court should have regard to the factors listed in s 25 of the Criminal Justice Act 1988 which gives a court a discretion to refuse to admit evidence contained in a written statement admissible under s 23 or s 24 of that Act if, having regard to all the circumstances, it is of the opinion that in the interests of justice the statement should not be admitted. If this was not the case the court would have no criterion by which to exercise its discretion. In addition, it would be unfortunate if the discretion was exercisable in a different way from the discretion under ss 25 and 26 of the Criminal Justice Act 1988 to exclude or admit written statements admissible under s 23 or s 24 of that Act.

6.60 In respect of the arguments in both paras **6.58** and **6.59**, it is noteworthy that the Government anticipated that in exercising either of the above discretions the courts would apply the 'interests of justice' test as laid down in the Criminal Justice Act 1988 and in the light of the case-law on it.[1]

---

1 Baroness Blatch, Minister of State, Home Office, Lords' consideration of Commons' amendments, cols 951–952.

6.61 Where a re-trial takes place in the Crown Court, Sch 2, paras 1 and 2, do not apply to any written statement or deposition. Instead, a transcript of the record of the evidence given by any witness at the original trial may, with the leave of the judge, be read as evidence:

(a) by agreement between the prosecution and the defence; or
(b) if the judge is satisfied that the witness is dead or unfit to give evidence or to attend for that purpose, or that all reasonable efforts to find him or to secure his attendance have failed,

and, in either case, may be so read without further proof, if verified in accordance with rules of court (Criminal Appeal Act 1968, Sch 2, para 1, as amended by the new Act, Sch 2, para 5).

This simply replicates the previous law relating to depositions and written statements read to the court under s 13(3) of the Criminal Justice Act 1925. It is noteworthy that the provision has not been extended to other situations in general.

6.62 Reference has already been made (paras **6.23–6.25**) to the admissibility at trial of written statements falling within the terms of ss 23 and 24 of the Criminal Justice Act 1988. Also admissible at a trial in the Crown Court are the various categories of evidence in writing of the types referred to in paras **6.31–6.40**.

6.63 Section 28(1) of the Theft Act 1968 provides that, where goods have been stolen, and an offender is convicted of an offence with reference to the theft (or has such an offence taken into consideration), the court may order anyone having possession or control of the goods to restore them to any person entitled to recover them from him. 'Stolen goods' include goods obtained by deception or by blackmail, contrary to ss 15 and 21 of the 1968 Act respectively (Theft Act 1968, s 24(1) and (4)), and an 'offence with reference to theft' includes handling stolen goods and, possibly, conspiracy to steal or assisting an offender (in respect of the thief).

6.64 Section 28(4) provides that the court must not make a restitution order under s 28 unless in its opinion the relevant facts sufficiently appear from evidence given at the trial or the 'available documents', together with admissions made by or on behalf of any person in connection with any proposed order. Schedule 1, para 20, to the new Act amends the definition of 'available documents' in s 28(4). Hitherto, that term has been defined by s 28(4) to mean 'any written statements or admissions which were made for use, and would have been admissible, as evidence at the trial, *the depositions taken at any committal proceedings and any written statements or admissions used as evidence in those proceedings*'. Consequential on the amendment of committal proceedings and the evidence admissible at them, the words italicised have been replaced by the following: '*and such written statements, depositions and other documents as were tendered by or on behalf of the prosecutor at any committal proceedings*'.

Substituted or additional charges in bill of indictment

6.65 Section 2(2) of the Administration of Justice (Miscellaneous Provisions) Act 1933 is amended consequential on the new nature of committal proceedings so as to provide that, where the accused has been committed for trial, the bill of indictment against him may include, either in substitution for or in addition to counts charging the offence for which he was committed, any counts founded on facts or evidence disclosed to the magistrates' court inquiring into that offence as examining justices. This amendment is made by Sch 1, para 17.

Power to join in indictment a count for common assault etc

6.66 Section 40 of the Criminal Justice Act 1988[1] provides that, where the accused is committed for trial on indictment, it is possible in certain circumstances for the prosecution to include a specified summary-only offence in the indictment for trial at the Crown Court. The specified offences are common assault or battery, assault on a prison custody officer, assault on a secure training centre custody officer, taking a motor vehicle (sic) without consent, driving while disqualified, and criminal damage of a value not exceeding £5,000 (CJA 1988, s 40(3)).

A count charging one of these offences can only be included in the indictment if the charge of the summary offence is either:

(a) founded on the same facts or evidence as a count charging an indictable offence; or

(b) is part of a series of offences of the same or similar character (CJA 1988, s 40(1)).

In addition, as enacted, s 40(1) of the 1988 Act required (in either case) that the facts or evidence relating to the offence must have been disclosed in an examination or deposition taken before a justice in the presence of the person charged. This requirement has been amended by Sch 1, para 34, so as to accord with the new style of committal proceedings. The amended requirement is that the facts or evidence relating to the summary offence must have been disclosed (by the documentary evidence tendered by the prosecution) to the magistrates' court inquiring into the indictable offence as examining magistrates.

---

1 The section is set out in full, as amended, in annotations to s 1.

Chapter 7

OTHER PROCEDURAL CHANGES RELATING TO MAGISTRATES' COURTS

Notices of transfer: documentary requirements – Either way offences: accused's intention as to plea – Change in decision relating to mode of trial: adjournment – Non-appearance of accused: issue of warrant of arrest – Witness summonses: miscellaneous amendments – Remand: juveniles – Enforcement of payment of fines – Attachment of earnings – Separate stages: differently constituted courts – Indemnification of justices and justices' clerks

NOTICES OF TRANSFER: DOCUMENTARY REQUIREMENTS

7.1 Section 45 makes a minor amendment to the provisions relating to notices of transfer under ss 4 to 6 of the Criminal Justice Act 1987 (cases of serious or complex fraud) or s 53 of the Criminal Justice Act 1991 (certain cases involving children).[1]

Both sets of provisions empower the Attorney-General to make regulations concerning the giving of notice of transfer (CJA 1987, s 9; CJA 1991, Sch 6, para 4). Inter alia, the relevant provisions, as enacted, require the Attorney-General to make regulations requiring the giving of a notice of transfer, together with *a statement of the evidence* on which any charge to which it relates is based:

(a)   to any person to whom the notice of transfer relates; and
(b)   to the Crown Court sitting at the proposed place of trial (CJA 1987, s 5(9)(a); CJA 1991, Sch 6, para 4(1)(a)).

Pursuant to this, the regulations which have been made require the copy of a notice of transfer to be accompanied by a statement of the evidence on which any charge to which the notice relates is based.[2]

---

1 See annotations to s 1.
2 Notice of Transfer Regulations 1988 (SI 1988/1691), regs 4 and 5; Criminal Justice Act 1991 (Notice of Transfer) Regulations 1992 (SI 1992/1670), regs 3 and 5.

7.2   The preparation of the statement of evidence is a time-consuming task, and an unnecessary one in view of the function of notices of transfer. For these reasons the amendments next described would seem to be unobjectionable.

The respective provisions relating to a requirement on the Attorney-General to make regulations set out above are amended, so as to oblige the regulations under s 5(9)(a) of the 1987 Act and Sch 6, para 4(1)(a) to the 1991 Act to require the giving of a notice of transfer to be accompanied by 'copies of the documents containing the evidence (including oral evidence)'[1] (s 45(2) and (5)). In addition, s 45(3) and (6) add a new provision[1] to each of the respective provisions whereby the regulations under s 5(9)(a) of the 1987 Act and Sch 6, para 4 to the 1991 Act 'may provide that there shall be no requirement for copies of documents to accompany the copy of the notice of transfer if they are referred to, in documents sent with the notice of transfer, as having already been supplied'.

---

1 CJA 1987, s 5(9A); CJA 1991, Sch 6, para 4(1A).

7.3 These amendments apply where a notice of transfer is given under s 4 of the 1987 Act or s 53 of the 1991 Act (as the case may be) on or after a day to be appointed (s 45(8) and (9)).[1] When this book went to press the existing regulations had not been amended, nor had a day been appointed for the above purpose.

---

1 See annotations to s 45.

EITHER WAY OFFENCES: ACCUSED'S INTENTION AS TO PLEA

Background

7.4 In the 1980s there was a large increase in the proportion of cases involving either way offences which were committed to the Crown Court for trial. In relation to accused persons aged 17 or over, the proportion rose from 15% (59,600 accused) in 1980 to 23% in 1987 (93,100) before falling to 17% (73,800) in 1992.[1]

Of these, the proportion who were committed to the Crown Court because the magistrates declined jurisdiction rose from 47% in 1987 to 64% in 1991 and then fell to 63% (46,500) in 1992.[1] The increase in committals contributed to an increase in the remand and sentenced prison population, as well as having significant implications for the police, the CPS, the courts and the Legal Aid fund.

---

1 *Mode of Trial: A Consultation Paper* (1995) Cm 2908, HMSO, para 2.

7.5 It was for these resource-driven reasons that a Home Office Consultation Paper on the Mode of Trial[1] sought views on three options, which were not mutually exclusive, for ensuring that cases capable of being properly dealt with in a magistrates' court are retained there. The first option related to recommendations by the Royal Commission on Criminal Justice[2] that a person accused of an either way offence should no longer be entitled to insist on trial in the Crown Court (but that the mode of trial should be a matter of agreement between the accused and the CPS and, failing that, a matter to be decided by the magistrates.) This option is not taken up by the new Act, although it may be in the future, nor is the second option, that there could be a re-classification of the mode of trial of minor thefts and certain other offences.

1 Op cit, paras 15–18.
2 (1993) Cm 2263, HMSO, Chapter 6, paras 4–15.

7.6 The third option concerned the two-thirds of cases of those accused of either way offences in respect of which the magistrates currently decline jurisdiction, and not the one-third who elect for trial in the Crown Court. It related to a system whereby a person accused of an either way offence would be obliged to enter a plea before the mode of trial decision was taken, before the magistrates decide whether to deal with the case themselves or to transfer jurisdiction to the Crown Court.

7.7 Behind this option was a concern that magistrates have to make mode of trial decisions in the absence of any knowledge of how the accused intends to plead at his trial. Often, magistrates decide to send a case on for trial in the Crown Court, only for the accused to plead guilty when arraigned and to be given a sentence which the magistrates could have imposed. In the Consultation Paper on Mode of Trial,[1] it was estimated that in the year ended June 1993 there were 38,000 accused in this category. It was also stated in the paper that there was 'considerable evidence' that a 'significant proportion' of those accused would be prepared to plead guilty in a magistrates' court to an either way charge and be dealt with by the magistrates. Of the 73,800 persons accused of either way offences who were committed for trial in 1992, 63% (46,500) were sent there because the magistrates declined jurisdiction. A Home Office research study showed that 65% of those committed for trial (25,000 plus) might have been willing to plead guilty at the magistrates' court if they had had the opportunity.

By enabling magistrates' courts to make their mode of trial decisions in the full knowledge of the accused's plea and to retain jurisdiction in appropriate cases where the accused pleaded guilty, the third option has the potential to retain a larger amount of business for magistrates' courts, as well as thereby according with the wishes of many people charged with either way offences and avoiding the delay and extended anxiety for victims and witnesses which a committal to the Crown Court could cause.

1 Op cit, paras 23 and 24.

The new provisions

7.8   The third option in the Consultation Paper is given effect by s 49 of the new Act, which introduces three new sections (ss 17A, 17B and 17C) into the Magistrates' Courts Act 1980.

7.9   The 'new provisions' only apply where a person who has attained 18 appears or is brought before a magistrates' court on an information charging him with an either way offence[1] (MCA 1980, ss 17A(1) and 17B(1)).

---

1   See annotations to s 1.

7.10   The new provisions only apply where a person appears or is brought before a magistrates' court on or after a day to be appointed by the Home Secretary (s 49(6) and (7)).[1] No day had been appointed when this book went to press. The new provisions will not apply, however, if the accused has already appeared or been brought before a magistrates' court in respect of the same offence (ie same facts and same offence) on a previous occasion before the appointed day (s 49(6)).

---

1   See annotations to s 49.

7.11   The new provisions do not affect the current arrangements insofar as they allow an accused to choose his venue for trial of an intended not guilty plea. They impact, however, on an accused who accepts the case against him and intends to plead guilty. Under the current arrangements, the magistrates cannot be made aware of this and will commit for trial if the offence appears sufficiently serious or the accused elects committal (in which case the accused is selecting the sentencing form). The effect of the new provision is to reserve the Crown Court for those not initially admitting the offence charged and those whose offence is so serious that, despite a guilty plea, the Crown Court is the only appropriate sentencing forum. The new provisions have the potential to retain a larger amount of cases in the magistrates' court than any limitation on the accused's right to elect trial in the Crown Court.

7.12   Section 17A of the 1980 Act provides a new procedure in respect of ascertaining the accused's intentions as to plea. It provides that, where the accused appears or is brought before a magistrates' court charged with an either way offence, the court must cause the charge to be written down, if this has not already been done, and to be read to the accused (MCA 1980, s 17A(3)).

7.13   The court must then explain to the accused in ordinary language that he may indicate whether (if the offence were to proceed to trial) he would plead guilty or not guilty (MCA 1980, s 17A(4)). The court must also explain to the accused in ordinary language that if he indicates that he would plead guilty:

(a)   the court must proceed as if the proceedings constituted ab initio the summary trial of the information, and the court had asked him whether he had pleaded guilty or not guilty; and

(b) he may be committed for sentence to the Crown Court under s 38 of the 1980 Act if the court is of the opinion that one of the grounds under s 38(2) exists (MCA, s 17A(4)).

The court must then ask the accused whether (if the offence were to proceed to trial) he would plead guilty or not guilty (MCA 1980, s 17A(5)).

7.14 As already indicated, if the accused indicates that he would plead guilty the court must proceed as if the proceedings constituted from the beginning the summary trial of the information, and it had asked him whether he had pleaded guilty or not guilty (MCA 1980, s 17A(6)). By s 38(2) of the 1980 Act, if the magistrates' court is of the opinion:

(a) that the offence or combination of the offence and other offences associated with it was so serious that greater punishment should be inflicted for the offence than the court has power to impose; or
(b) in the case of a violent or sexual offence, that a sentence of imprisonment for a term longer than the court has power to impose is necessary to protect the public from serious harm from him,

the court may commit the offence in custody or on bail to the Crown Court for sentence.

However, subject to s 17A(6), asking the accused under s 17A how (if the offence were to proceed to trial) he would plead, and an indication by him of how he would plead, do not for any purpose constitute the taking of a plea (MCA 1980, s 17A(9)). Consequently, for example, an indication of an intention to plead not guilty does not constitute the taking of a plea in the Crown Court, if the case is subsequently transferred for trial, or in the magistrates' court, if it is not. In the relevant court after mode of trial proceedings have been completed, a fresh plea must be taken.

7.15 If the accused indicates that he would plead not guilty, ss 19 to 23 of the 1980 Act apply, ie subject to those provisions, mode of trial proceedings will take place (MCA 1980, s 17A(7)). If the accused fails to indicate how he would plead, he is to be taken to indicate that he would plead not guilty, with the same result (MCA 1980, s 17A(8)).

7.16 The provisions of s 17A apply whether or not the accused is legally represented.

7.17 The disclosure provisions in Part I of the Act do not apply at the stage where the accused indicates his intended plea, since this situation falls outside those in s 1(1) and (2) to which Part I applies.

The absent accused

7.18 The above procedure depends on the accused being present. Just as in the case of mode of trial proceedings, however, special (albeit different) provision is made for the court to proceed in the absence of the accused if he is disorderly. The special provision, made by s 17B of the Magistrates' Courts Act 1980, applies where an accused appears or is brought before a magistrates' court on an information charging him with an either way offence, and:

(a)   the accused is represented by a *legal representative;*[1]
(b)   the court considers that by reason of the accused's disorderly conduct before the court it is not practicable[2] for proceedings under s 17A above to be conducted in his presence; and
(c)   the court considers that it should proceed in the absence of the accused (MCA 1980, s 17B(1)).

---

1 See para **6.26**.
2 See annotations to s 58.

7.19   The following special procedure applies in such a case. First, the court must cause the charge to be written down (if not already done so) and to be read to the legal representative (s 17B(2)(a)). The court must ask the representative whether (if the offence were to proceed to trial) the accused would plead guilty or not guilty (s 17B(2)(b)).

If the representative indicates that the accused would plead guilty the court must proceed as if the proceedings constituted ab initio the summary trial of the information as the accused had pleaded guilty (s 17B(2)(c)). However, subject to this, asking the representative how the accused would plead, or an indication of how the representative of the accused would plead, do not constitute the taking of a plea (s 17B(4)).

If the representative indicates that the accused would plead not guilty, ss 19 to 23 of the 1980 Act apply, see above.

If the legal representative does not indicate how the accused would plead, he is to be taken to indicate that the accused would plead not guilty (MCA 1980, s 17B(3)).

The new procedure does not operate if a disorderly accused does not have a legal representative or if an accused is absent for some other reason. In these cases there will have to be an adjournment until the accused can be present, because (as explained in para **7.22**) mode of trial proceedings cannot take place unless, and until, an indication of an intended plea of not guilty has been given.

Adjournment
7.20   A magistrates' court proceeding under s 17A or s 17B of the 1980 Act may adjourn the proceedings at any time (MCA 1980, s 17C). If the accused is present when it does so, the court may remand him in custody (ibid). Moreover, it must remand an accused who is present if:

(a)   when he first appeared, or was brought, before the court to answer to the information he was in custody or, having been released on bail, surrendered to the custody of the court; or
(b)   he has been remanded at any time in the course of proceedings on the information (ibid).

Where the court remands the accused, the time fixed for the resumption of proceedings shall be that at which he is required to appear or be brought before the court in pursuance of the remand or would be required to be brought before the court but for the provisions of s 128(3A) of the 1980 Act, which permit the court in certain circumstances further to remand in custody a person who has not been remanded in custody under s 128A of the 1980 Act for a period exceeding eight clear days (MCA 1980, s 17C).

7.21 The provisions of s 128 of the 1980 Act, which apply to other remands, in respect of explaining to a legally represented adult accused the provisions of s 128(3A) and (3B) about further remands, of s 128(3A) itself, of s 128(3C) about further remands, and of s 128(3E) about the procedure to be adopted where it appears after a remand in absence that the accused ought not to have been so remanded, are extended to a remand under s 17C (s 49(5)). So are the provisions of s 130 of the 1980 Act concerning the transfer of remand hearings (s 49(5)).[1]

---

1 See annotations to s 49.

7.22 Section 18(1) of the 1980 Act, which provides that ss 19 to 23 thereof (provisions relating to choice of mode of trial) have effect if an adult appears or is brought before a magistrates' court on an information charging him with an either way offence, is amended so as to apply only where:

(a) the accused indicates under s 17A above that (if the offence were to proceed to trial) he would plead not guilty; or

(b) his representative indicates under s 17B above that (if the offence were to proceed to trial) he would plead not guilty (s 49(3)).

This means that, unless, and until, an intention to plead not guilty has been indicated under s 17A or s 17B, mode of trial proceedings cannot be held.

Likewise, since an indication of intended plea will already have been made, the requirement in s 19(2) of the 1980 Act that, before considering whether the offence appears more suitable for summary trial or trial on indictment the court must cause the charge to be written down, if not previously done, and read to the accused is repealed (s 49(4)).

7.23 The new provisions are far from foolproof. There will still be 'cracked trials' because, for a variety of reasons, there will be accused who intend ultimately to plead guilty, who indicate a not guilty plea and elect for trial by jury.

The successful operation of the new provisions is going to depend on the prosecution having its case fully prepared and disclosed to the accused in time for an informed plea to be entered before the magistrates. It will also depend on the CPS finalising charges at an early stage.

CHANGE IN DECISION RELATING TO MODE OF TRIAL: ADJOURNMENT

7.24 Consequential on the changes made to committal proceedings, Sch 1, para 5, amends s 25 of the 1980 Act in respect of a change to committal proceedings from a summary trial of an either way offence. Section 25(2) (accused aged 18 or over) and s 25(6) (accused aged under 18) provide that the magistrates' court may at any time discontinue the summary trial and proceed with a view to committal for trial. Prior to their amendment, both provisions stated that, on discontinuing the summary trial, the court 'may adjourn the proceedings without remanding the accused'.

Both provisions are amended in two ways. First, there is substituted in them a duty to adjourn the hearing on discontinuing the summary trial (Sch 1, para 5). This amendment is unavoidable, given that committal proceedings are required to proceed only on the basis of written evidence and exhibits. It will no longer be possible to use the oral evidence given at the trial at the committal proceedings.[1] Secondly, a new provision, s 25(8), inserted by Sch 1, para 6, provides that, if the court adjourns the hearing under s 25(2) or (6), 'it may (if it thinks fit) do so without remanding the accused'. Schedule 1, paras 5 and 6, are to come into force in accordance with provisions made by the Home Secretary by order (Sch 1, para 39).

---

1 MCA 1980, s 28, which provided that evidence given at committal proceedings was deemed to have been given for purposes of the summary trial and need not be repeated at the summary trial is omitted by Sch 1, para 28, and repealed by Sch 5, consequent on the exclusion from committal proceedings of oral evidence. If the prosecution wishes to use the evidence contained in a written statement or deposition tendered at committal proceedings for the summary trial, he will have to call its maker as a witness.

NON-APPEARANCE OF ACCUSED: ISSUE OF WARRANT OF ARREST

7.25　Section 48 amends the relevant law relating to the non-appearance for summary trial of an accused who has not 'pleaded guilty by post' under s 12 of the 1980 Act. The amendment is in line with the recommendations of the review of magistrates' courts procedure in 1992.[1]

---

1 *Review of Magistrates' Courts Procedure* (1992), Home Office.

7.26　If an accused fails to appear for summary trial or an adjourned summary trial, the magistrates' court has a discretion to proceed in his absence under s 11(1) of the Magistrates' Courts Act 1980. Its discretion is, however, subject to some limitation where the prosecution is commenced by virtue of a summons, since in this type of case the magistrates may only proceed in the accused's absence if it is proved to its satisfaction that either the summons was served a reasonable time before the hearing or that the accused has appeared on a previous occasion to answer the information (MCA 1980, s 11(2)). The rationale for this limitation is that whereas an accused who has been arrested is necessarily aware of the charge against him, a person who has merely been summonsed may not be and it would be unfair to proceed against him in his absence if he was not aware of that charge.

7.27 If the court decides to adjourn or further adjourn the trial of an information rather than proceeding in the accused's absence, it may issue a warrant for his arrest, provided the information has been substantiated on oath and, in the case of an adult, the offence is punishable with imprisonment or the court, having convicted the accused of a road traffic offence, proposes to impose a disqualification on him (MCA 1980, s 13(1) and (3)).[1]

---

1 Where the accused was on bail and has failed to surrender to custody in answer to his bail, the more usual course, if the court wishes to issue an arrest warrant, will be to issue a warrant under the Bail Act 1976, s 7.

7.28 In addition, for the same reasons as in the case of the limitation on proceeding in the accused's absence, s 13(2) of the Magistrates' Courts Act 1980, as enacted, provided that, where a summons had been issued, the court could not issue a warrant under s 13 unless it was *either* proved to its satisfaction, on oath 'or in such other manner as may be prescribed', that the summons had been served on the accused within what appeared to it to be a reasonable time before the trial or adjourned trial *or* the accused had appeared on a previous occasion in answer to the information.

7.29 Section 13(2) of the 1980 Act is amended, so that a magistrates' court cannot issue a warrant under s 13 unless one or other of two conditions, set out in new sub-s (2A) and (2B), is fulfilled (s 48(3)). The first condition replicates the first of the two conditions in s 13(2) as enacted, namely, that it is proved to the satisfaction of the court, on oath or in such other manner as may be prescribed, that the summons was served on the accused within what appears to the court to be a reasonable time before the trial or adjourned trial.

The alternative condition (set out in sub-s (2B)) replaces the second of the two conditions in s 13(2), as enacted. Whereas under that condition the court could issue a warrant in respect of an absent accused simply because he had appeared on a previous occasion in answer to the information, the new condition is that:

(a) the adjournment now being made is a second or subsequent adjournment of the trial;

(b) the accused was present on the last (or only) occasion when the trial was adjourned; and

(c) on that occasion the court determined the time for the hearing at which the adjournment is now being made.

7.30 This amendment applies where the court proposes to issue a warrant under s 13 on or after a day to be appointed by the Home Secretary (s 48(4) and (5)).[1] No day had been appointed when this book went to press.

---

1 See annotations to s 48.

WITNESS SUMMONSES: MISCELLANEOUS AMENDMENTS

7.31   The Act amends s 97 of the Magistrates' Courts Act 1980, whereby, if the prosecution or defence are apprehensive that a witness whom they wish to call may not attend court voluntarily to give oral evidence or to produce documentary evidence, they may apply for a witness summons. A witness summons under s 97 of the 1980 Act is not simply the means by which reluctant witnesses are brought to court to give oral evidence or to tender documentary evidence in criminal cases. It is also the means used to achieve third party disclosure in such cases.[1]

---

1 See para **2.86**.

7.32   As enacted, s 97(1) of the 1980 Act required a justice of the peace,[1] if satisfied that any person in England or Wales 'is likely to be able to give material evidence, or produce any document or thing likely to be material evidence' at committal proceedings or at summary trial of an information or hearing of a complaint by a magistrates' court, and that 'that person will not voluntarily attend as a witness or will not voluntarily produce the document or thing,[1] to issue a summons requiring that person to give evidence or to produce the document or thing'. Consequent on the new regime for committal proceedings whereby oral evidence is not admissible at them, the reference to committal proceedings is deleted by Sch 5 to the new Act. A new provision, s 97A of the 1980 Act, referred to in para **6.17**, deals with summonses in respect of witnesses who are required to attend at committal proceedings to produce a document or other exhibit. The upshot of all this is that a summons under s 97 can only be issued in respect of the attendance of a witness or person to produce a document or other exhibit at a summary trial or the hearing of a complaint. This repeal will take effect in accordance with provisions made by the Home Secretary (Sch 1, para 7). Presumably, this will be the date when the new style committal proceedings come into operation.

---

1 Or justices' clerk or a member of the clerk's staff to whom the clerk has delegated the power to issue a summons (Justices' Clerks Rules 1970 (SI 1970/231, rr 3, 4 and Sch).

7.33   Section 51 further amends s 97. The amendments which it makes are intended to improve arrangements for third party disclosure in criminal proceedings.[1] As enacted, s 97 did not require a justice to be satisfied that the application for a summons under s 97(1) was made by a party to the case as soon as reasonably practicable after the accused pleaded not guilty. This is changed by s 51(1) of the new Act, which adds a new subsection, (2B), to s 97 to the effect that a justice may refuse to issue a summons under s 97(1) in relation to the summary trial of an information if he is not so satisfied. This amendment is designed to encourage earlier applications, without penalising those who have good reason for a later application.[1]

1 Baroness Blatch, Minister of State, Home Office, Lords' consideration of Commons' amendments, col 968.

7.34　If a justice[1] is satisfied by evidence on oath of the matters mentioned in s 97(1), and also that it is probable that a summons issued under s 97(1) would not procure the attendance of the person concerned, he may instead of issuing a summons issue a warrant of arrest (s 97(2)). The requirements of s 97(2) are altered in consequence of another new provision, sub-s (2C), added to s 97 by s 51(1). This provides that, in relation to the summary trial of an information, s 97(1) shall have effect as if the references to the matters mentioned in s 97(1) included a reference to the matter mentioned in s 97(2B), with the result that a justice may refuse to issue a warrant under s 97(2) of the 1980 Act in relation to the summary trial of an information if he is not satisfied that the application was made by a party to the case as soon as reasonably practicable after the accused pleaded not guilty.

1 But not a justices' clerk.

7.35　These amendments will apply in relation to any proceedings for the purpose of which no summons has been issued under s 97(1), and no warrant has been issued under s 97(2), before a day to be appointed by the Home Secretary (s 51(2) and (3)).[1] At the time that this book went to press no day had been appointed.

1 See annotations to s 51.

REMAND: JUVENILES

7.36　Section 52 is another provision in line with the recommendations of the review of magistrates' courts procedure in 1992.[1] It abolishes the minimum age limit of 17 in respect of the application of various provisions under the Magistrates' Courts Act 1980 relating to a remand in custody, which will apply whatever the age of the accused (s 52(1) and (2)), namely:

(a)　Section 128(1A) – This requires a court which proposes to remand or further remand in custody a legally represented person who is before it to explain to him the possibility of a further remand being made in his absence if he consents under s 128(3A) and (3B). It also requires the court to inform him that, notwithstanding the procedure for a remand in absentia, he will be brought before the court for the hearing and determination of at least every fourth application for his remand, and of every application when he has no solicitor acting for him in the case.

(b)　Section 128(3A) – The basic effect of this provision is to allow the accused to consent to being remanded in custody for up to one month without attending court. Section 128(3A) provides that, where a person who has a solicitor acting for him (s 128(3B)) has been remanded in custody and the remand is not a remand under s 128A (below) for a period exceeding eight clear days, the court may further remand him on an adjournment without his being brought before a court, if he gave his consent to the hearing and determination in his absence of any application for his remand on an adjournment of the case. The court can only act in this way if the person concerned has not been remanded under s 128(3A) without being brought before the court on more than two occasions immediately preceding the application in question, and provided that he has not withdrawn his original consent.

(c)   Section 128A – This gives a court power to remand an accused in custody for a period exceeding eight clear days, whether or not he consents, if it has previously remanded him in custody for the same offence, he is before the court, and it has set a date on which it expects that it will be possible for the next stage (other than a hearing in relation to a further remand) to take place. In such a case the remand in custody must only be for a period ending not later than that date or for 28 days, whichever is less.

The extension of the power to remand for up to 28 days is sensible in the light of the severe shortage of secure local authority accommodation for juveniles. In many cases, a juvenile may be remanded to secure accommodation hundreds of miles from the court in which he is to appear, with the consequent cost of escorting that person back and forwards to it.[2]

---

1 *Review of Magistrates' Courts Procedure* (1992), Home Office.
2 Mr Jack Straw MP, HC 2nd Reading, col 751.

7.37   In respect of s 128(1A) and (3A) of the 1980 Act, the amendment applies only where the offence with which the person concerned is charged is alleged to be committed[1] on or after the day to be appointed by the Home Secretary (s 52(3) and (4)).[2] No day had been appointed when this book went to press.

The amendment to s 128A had immediate effect on Royal Assent.

---

1 See s 75.
2 See annotations to s 52.

7.38   The accused will remain free to make bail applications if circumstances change. The Government is to issue guidance to remind courts and local authorities of the need to consider the welfare of the 'child' and to be alert to changes in circumstances which may justify an application for bail.[1]

---

1 Baroness Blatch, Minister of State, Home Office, HL 2nd Reading, col 66.

ENFORCEMENT OF PAYMENT OF FINES

7.39   Section 87(1) of the Magistrates' Courts Act 1980 provides for the enforcement by the High Court or a county court of payment of fines imposed by a magistrates' court, as if the sum were due to the clerk of the magistrates' court in pursuance of a judgment or order of the High Court or county court, as the case may be. The effect of this provision is that the clerk is deemed to be a judgment creditor, with all the rights of such a person, and can use methods of recovery of a fine which are not available in a magistrates' court, such as a garnishee order.

Proceedings to recover the sum in question are taken by the clerk of the magistrates' court. Section 87(3) of the 1980 Act provided that the clerk could not take such proceedings 'unless authorised to do so by the court after an inquiry [by it] under s 82 [of that Act] into that person's means'. Section 50(1) of the new Act removes the requirement of authorisation by the court, so that the clerk can act of his own motion, but adds that the clerk must not take proceedings unless there has been an inquiry under s 82 of the 1980 Act into the person's means and he appeared to the magistrates' court to have sufficient means to pay the sum forthwith.[1] This amendment applies where the clerk proposes to take proceedings by virtue of s 87(1) on or after a day to be appointed by the Home Secretary (s 50(2) and (3)).[1] No day had been appointed when this book went to press.

---

1 See annotations to s 50.

ATTACHMENT OF EARNINGS

7.40 Section 53 is the third provision in the Act which implements a recommendation in the review of magistrates' courts procedure in 1992.[1] It amends s 3 of the Attachment of Earnings Act 1971, in respect of fines and of compensation orders under s 35 of the Powers of Criminal Courts Act 1973.

---

1 *Review of Magistrates' Courts Procedure* (1992), Home Office.

7.41 Hitherto, an attachment of earnings order in respect of a fine, a compensation order, an order for costs or forfeited recognisances could not be made, otherwise than on the application of the debtor, unless it appeared to the court that the debtor had failed to make one or more payments required by the relevant adjudication (1971 Act, s 3(3)). This remains the case in respect of an order for costs or forfeited recognisances. However, in respect of a fine or compensation order, s 53(1) adds two subsections, (3B) and (3C), to s 3 of the 1971 Act. These provide respectively that at the time that a court imposes a fine or makes a compensation order it may make an attachment of earnings order to secure payments of the fine or compensation order, as the case may be. The court may only do so where the person consents to an order being made under the relevant subsection. There is no need for an application for the order to be made.[1]

The good sense of providing in advance for a breach of an order to pay a fine or compensation is obvious.

---

1 The relevant parts of the 1971 Act, s 3, are set out in the annotations to s 53.

7.42 The new provisions apply in relation to fines imposed in respect of offences committed on or after a day to be appointed by the Home Secretary, and to compensation orders made on convictions for offences committed on or after that day (s 53(2) and (3)).[1] No day had been appointed when this book went to press.

---

1 See annotations to s 53.

SEPARATE STAGES: DIFFERENTLY CONSTITUTED COURTS

7.43 Where the proceedings in a magistrates' court involve separate procedural stages, the magistrates' court for a later stage need not normally be composed of the same justices as constituted in the court for an earlier stage. This is necessary because, the great majority of justices being part-time, it may be impracticable for the same bench to deal with each stage of the proceedings. The principle is provided by s 148(2) of the 1980 Act in the following terms:

> 'Except where the contrary is expressed, anything authorised or required by *this Act*[1] to be done by, to or before the magistrates' court by, to or before which any other thing was done, or is to be done, may be done by, to or before any magistrates' court acting for the same petty sessions area as that court.'

Section 76 of the new Act makes a technical amendment to s 148(2) by providing that the reference to 'this Act' includes a reference to the new Act.

---

1 Italics supplied.

INDEMNIFICATION OF JUSTICES AND JUSTICES' CLERKS

7.44 A justice of the peace or a justices' clerk may be liable in damages for acts or omissions in the purported execution of his duty as such a justice, or as such a clerk when exercising any of the functions of a single justice,[1] but with respect to a matter outside his jurisdiction, provided it is proved that he acted in bad faith (Justices of the Peace Act 1979, s 45). Otherwise he is immune from an action for damages (ibid), just as he is in any event in respect of a matter within his jurisdiction (ibid, s 44). There is no similar immunity for a justices' clerk in respect of administrative acts performed by him, nor is there any immunity for any member of his staff in any respect. Such persons may, of course, also be ordered personally to pay costs in respect of proceedings for damages, or in respect of other proceedings, such as case stated or judicial review proceedings in the High Court,[2] to which they are parties.[3] In addition, they may personally incur expense in settling any proceedings against them.

---

1 Under the Justices' Clerks Rules 1970.
2 Under the Supreme Court Act 1981, ss 28A and 51B, respectively.
3 An order for costs can be made against justices etc who are parties to the proceedings even if

they do not appear before the court but merely file an affidavit (see, for example, *Newcastle-under-Lyme JJ and Stoke-on-Trent JJ, ex parte Massey* [1995] 1 All ER 120 at 126). Likewise, an order for costs can be made against justices in civil proceedings who refuse to give their consent (via a consent order) to an appeal against a decision of theirs being allowed; in this case the costs will be limited to the costs of unnecessary representation at a hearing, and not the costs of the proceedings generally. (*Newcastle-under-Lyme JJ and Stoke-on-Trent JJ ex parte Massey*).

7.45   Section 53(1) of the 1979 Act mitigated the rigour of the liability to pay costs and other sums by providing that

'a justice of the peace [including a stipendiary magistrate or acting stipendiary magistrate[1]] or justices' clerk [or a member of his staff[2]] may be indemnified out of local funds in respect of—

(a)   any costs reasonably incurred by him in or in connection with proceedings against him in respect of anything done or omitted in the exercise or purported exercise of the duty of his office, or in taking steps to dispute any claim which might be made in such proceedings;
(b)   any damages awarded against him or costs ordered to be paid by him in any such proceedings; or
(c)   any sums payable by him in connection with a reasonable settlement of any such proceedings or claim;

and shall be entitled to be so indemnified if, in respect of the matters giving rise to the proceedings or claim, he acted reasonably and in good faith.'[3]

What constitutes acting reasonably may be a matter of dispute and more easily determined with the benefit of hindsight, and there is a risk that any decision by justices reversed on appeal may be categorised as 'unreasonable' no matter how genuinely and carefully they dealt with the case.

It will be noted that this provision does not provide for immunity from liability, but simply for indemnification (ie the making good a loss suffered by a justice or justice's clerk). It has caused considerable anxiety among justices etc who have feared that the discretion to indemnify might not be exercised in their favour or, in respect of the obligation to indemnify, that they might be unable to prove that they acted reasonably and in good faith. In some cases, justices etc have feared being made bankrupt. As an indication of the prevalence of costs orders against justices etc, during the period 1 January 1994 to 1 November 1995, 8% of court areas outside central London had costs orders made against justices etc in them.

Quite apart from the above concerns, a clear point of principle is involved as to whether it is appropriate for justices etc to have to pay the costs of proceedings to which they are parties, when they were only seeking to carry out their official function.

The points referred to above were crystallised in a paper produced by the Justices' Clerks' Society in November 1994.[4] The paper made a number of proposals for reform in respect of the award of costs against justices and their clerks. The principal proposal was that justices and their clerks should be immune from the court's power to award costs against a party. A secondary proposal was that, if this was not acceptable, an award of costs against them should only be possible where bad faith was established. The justices' clerks' second proposal has succeeded to some extent, as we shall explain, and its principal proposal may succeed in due course.

1 Justices of the Peace Act 1979, ss 15(2A) and 34(2A).
2 Ibid, s 53(5).
3 Any question whether, and to what extent, a person is to be indemnified under the 1979 Act, s 53, is determined by the magistrates' courts committee for the area for which the person claiming to be indemnified acted at the material time (1979 Act, s 53(2)). There is a right of appeal from the magistrates' courts committee's decision by the person concerned or by the local authority responsible for funding the magistrates' courts in question. Appeal lies to a person appointed for the purpose by the Lord Chancellor (ibid, s 53(3)).
4 *A Paper on the Award of Costs against Justices, including Proposals for Reform.*

7.46 At the Committee stage in the House of Lords, Lord Ackner successfully introduced an amendment to s 53 of the 1979 Act to strengthen the position of justices and justice's clerks etc in respect of indemnification.[1] The amendment was initially resisted by the Government on the ground that it was premature before the outcome of a planned consultation exercise relating to the possible introduction of an immunity against costs orders for justices and justice's clerks,[2] but, at the Third Reading in the House of Lords, the Government acceded to it in somewhat altered terms, which are now s 70 of the new Act.

1 HL Report, cols 63–70.
2 Baroness Blatch, Minister of State, Home Office, ibid, col 68.

7.47 Section 70 amends s 53 of the 1979 Act, but it only does so in relation to orders for costs etc against justices or their clerks etc, or other expenditure incurred by them, in respect of proceedings against them concerning their conduct relating to criminal matters (ie relating to the exercise of their criminal jurisdiction).[1] Where an order etc relates to a civil matter, s 53 of the 1979 Act remains unamended as set out above. The amendment had to be restricted to criminal matters because to have included civil ones would have taken it outside the scope of the Act. The amendment is a stop gap pending the outcome of the consultation exercise referred to above; a consultation paper is to be issued in the summer of 1996.[2]

1 See annotations to s 70.
2 Baroness Blatch, Minister of State, Home Office, HL 3rd Reading, cols 895–897.

7.48 The amendment is contained in a new s 53(1A) of the 1979 Act, inserted by s 70(1), which provides that so far as s 53(1) of the 1979 Act relates to criminal matters it shall have the effect that a justice or justice's clerk etc must be indemnified out of local funds in respect of the orders or expenditure referred to in paras (a) to (c) of s 53(1), set out in para **7.45**, unless it is proved,[1] in respect of the matters giving rise to the proceedings or claim, that he acted in bad faith. The important changes are that in respect of orders etc relating to criminal matters there is always a duty to indemnify a justice of the peace or justice's clerk etc out of local funds, unless in respect of the proceedings bad faith is proven against him (presumably, by the relevant magistrates' courts committee), whereas where an order etc relates to civil matters (ie cases arising from the magistrates' civil jurisdiction) it remains the situation that there is generally no duty to indemnify (only a discretion) and a duty only arises where the justice etc proves not only that in respect of the proceedings he did not act in bad faith but also that he acted reasonably. Section 70 brings the test of whether indemnity should be given to justices and justice's clerks in respect of orders etc relating to criminal matters into line with the test for civil liability for acting in excess of jurisdiction under s 45 of the 1979 Act.

1 See annotations to s 70.

7.49 The above amendment applies in relation to things done or omitted on or after a day to be appointed by the Home Secretary (s 70(2) and (3)).[1] No such day had been appointed when this book went to press. The fixing of the date will depend on any financial implications for magistrates' courts committees being sorted out.[2]

1 See annotations to s 70.
2 Baroness Blatch, Minister of State, Home Office, HL 3rd Reading, cols 896–897.

APPENDIX 1

Criminal Procedure and Investigations Act 1996 (1996 c. 25)

ARRANGEMENT OF SECTIONS

PART I
DISCLOSURE

Introduction

PART V
COMMITTAL, TRANSFER, ETC.

PART VI
MAGISTRATES' COURTS

PART VII
MISCELLANEOUS AND GENERAL

Tainted acquittals

Derogatory assertions

Evidence: special provisions

Witness orders and summonses

An Act to make provision about criminal procedure and criminal investigations.

[4 July 1996]

GENERAL ANNOTATIONS

Certain frequently recurring terms are annotated here, and cross-reference is made to these annotations at the appropriate place.

Great Britain—Ie England, Scotland and Wales Union with Scotland Act 1706, preamble, art 1; Wales and Berwick Act 1746, s 3.

'England' means, subject to any alteration of boundaries under Part IV of the Local Government Act 1972, the area consisting of the counties established by s 1 and (as originally enacted) 20 of that Act (subject, in the case of Wales, to any alteration made under s 73 of that Act), Greater London and the Isles of Scilly (Interpretation Act 1978, s 5 and Sch 1).

'Wales' means the combined area of the counties created by the Local Government Act 1972, as originally enacted, but subject to any alteration made under the 1972 Act, s 73 (consequential alteration of boundary following alteration of watercourse).

Programme service, within the meaning of the Broadcasting Act 1990—The Broadcasting Act 1990, s 202(1) provides that '"programme" includes an advertisement and, in relation to any service, includes any item included in that service'.

By the 1990 Act, s 201(1), a 'programme service', for the purposes of that Act is defined as meaning:

'any of the following services (whether or not it is, or it requires to be, licensed under this Act), namely—
   (a) any television broadcasting service or other television programme service (within the meaning of Part I of this Act);
   (b) any sound broadcasting service or licensable sound programme service (within the meaning of Part III of this Act);
   (c) any other service which consists in the sending, by means of a telecommunication system, of sounds or visual images or both either—
      (i) for reception at two or more places in the United Kingdom (whether they are so sent for simultaneous reception or at different times in response to requests made by different users of the service); or
      (ii) for reception at a place in the United Kingdom for the purpose of being presented there to members of the public or to any group of persons.

'(2) Subsection (1)(c) does not apply to—

   (a) a local delivery service (within the meaning of Part II of this Act);
   (b) a service where the running of the telecommunication system does not require to be licensed under Part II of the Telecommunications Act 1984; or
   (c) a two-way service (as defined by section 46(2)(c) [of the 1990 Act]).'

Standard scale—The 'standard scale' of fines applies only to offences which are only triable summarily. The meaning of the standard scale is that given by the Criminal Justice Act 1982, s 37 and to Interpretation Act 1978, Sch 1. When this book went to press the standard scale was as follows:

level 1   £200
level 2   £500
level 3   £1,000
level 4   £2,500
level 5   £5,000

(Criminal Justice Act 1991, s 17). The Home Secretary has power by order to change the amounts specified in the standard scale in the light of a change in the value of money (Magistrates' Courts Act 1980, s 143(1) as amended by the Criminal Justice Act 1982, s 48). An order under s 143(1) must be made by statutory instrument subject to annulment in pursuance of a resolution of either House of Parliament, and may be revoked by a subsequent order thereunder; it does not affect the punishment for an offence committed before it comes into force (MCA 1980, s 143(6)).

United Kingdom—Ie Great Britain and Northern Ireland (Interpretation Act 1978, s 5 and Sch 1).

PART I
DISCLOSURE

Introduction

1 Application of this Part

(1) This Part applies where—

   (a) a person is charged with a summary offence in respect of which a court proceeds to summary trial and in respect of which he pleads not guilty,
   (b) a person who has attained the age of 18 is charged with an offence which is triable either way, in respect of which a court proceeds to summary trial and in respect of which he pleads not guilty, or

(c) a person under the age of 18 is charged with an indictable offence in respect of which a court proceeds to summary trial and in respect of which he pleads not guilty.

(2) This Part also applies where—

(a) a person is charged with an indictable offence and he is committed for trial for the offence concerned,

(b) a person is charged with an indictable offence and proceedings for the trial of the person on the charge concerned are transferred to the Crown Court by virtue of a notice of transfer given under section 4 of the Criminal Justice Act 1987 (serious or complex fraud),

(c) a person is charged with an indictable offence and proceedings for the trial of the person on the charge concerned are transferred to the Crown Court by virtue of a notice of transfer served on a magistrates' court under section 53 of the Criminal Justice Act 1991 (certain cases involving children),

(d) a count charging a person with a summary offence is included in an indictment under the authority of section 40 of the Criminal Justice Act 1988 (common assault etc.), or

(e) a bill of indictment charging a person with an indictable offence is preferred under the authority of section 2(2)(b) of the Administration of Justice (Miscellaneous Provisions) Act 1933 (bill preferred by direction of Court of Appeal, or by direction or with consent of a judge).

(3) This Part applies in relation to alleged offences into which no criminal investigation has begun before the appointed day.

(4) For the purposes of this section a criminal investigation is an investigation which police officers or other persons have a duty to conduct with a view to it being ascertained—

(a) whether a person should be charged with an offence, or

(b) whether a person charged with an offence is guilty of it.

(5) The reference in subsection (3) to the appointed day is to such day as is appointed for the purposes of this Part by the Secretary of State by order.

Explanatory text—See paras 2.7–2.8.

Commencement—On Royal Assent (4 July 1996), but see subs (5).

Summary offence, offence triable either way, indictable offence (subss (1) and (2))—'Summary offence' means an offence which, if committed by an adult, is triable summarily only (Interpretation Act 1978, s 5 and Sch 1).

An 'offence triable either way' means an offence, other than an offence triable on indictment only by virtue of Part V of the Criminal Justice Act 1988 (which empowers the Crown Court to try a summary offence on indictment in certain cases if it is related to an indictable offence charged in the indictment) which, if committed by an adult, is triable either on indictment or summarily (Interpretation Act 1978, s 5 and Sch 1).

'Indictable offence' means an offence which, if committed by an adult, is triable on indictment, whether it is exclusively so triable or triable either way (Interpretation Act 1978, s 5 and Sch 1).

Age (subs (1))—A person attains 18 years of age at the commencement of the eighteenth anniversary of his (or her) birth (Family Law Reform Act 1969, s 9).

In respect of which a court proceeds to summary trial (subs (1))— This will comprise offences which are triable only summarily and those offences which are either way offences where a magistrates' court has determined, pursuant to Magistrates' Courts Act 1980, that it shall be tried summarily. For the definition of an either way offence, see Magistrates' Courts Act 1980, s 17 and Sch 1.

'Pleads not guilty' (subs (1))—This includes not only cases where a plea of not guilty is tendered by the accused, but also where a plea of not guilty is entered by the court on his behalf, because the accused wilfully stays silent on arraignment, enters a plea which is ambiguous or fails to give a direct answer to the charge (see Criminal Law Act 1967, s 6(1)).

Section 4 of the Criminal Justice Act 1987 (subs (2))—Section 4 of the 1987 Act deals with the notice of transfer procedure in certain cases of fraud. Where the designated authority is of the opinion:

(a) that the evidence of the offence charged would be sufficient for proceedings against the person to be transferred for trial; and
(b) reveals a case of fraud of such seriousness or complexity that it is appropriate that the management of the case should without delay be taken over by the Crown Court,

that authority may give to a magistrates' court a notice of transfer.

'Designated authority' for this purpose is defined by the Criminal Justice Act 1987, s 4(2), as the Director of Public Prosecutions, Director of Serious Fraud Office, Commissioners of Inland Revenue, Commissioners of Customs and Excise, and the Home Secretary.

The service of notice of transfer under the Criminal Justice Act 1987, s 4, has the effect of removing the jurisdiction of the court, subject to certain residual powers in respect of bail and legal aid.

Section 53 of the Criminal Justice Act 1991 (subs (2))—The offences to which this section apply are specified in the Criminal Justice Act 1988, s 32(2). These are as follows:

(a) an offence which involved an assault on, or injury or threat of injury to, a person;
(b) an offence under the Children and Young Persons Act 1933, s 1 (cruelty to persons under the age of 16);
(c) an offence under the Sexual Offences Act 1956, Indecency with Children Act 1960, Sexual Offences Act 1967, Criminal Law Act 1977, s 54, or Protection of Children Act 1978; and
(d) an offence which consists of any attempting or conspiring to commit, or of aiding, abetting, counselling, procuring or inciting the commission of any of the above offences.

Where Criminal Justice Act 1991, s 53, does apply, then where the Director of Public Prosecutions is of the opinion—

(a) that the evidence of the offence would be sufficient for proceedings against the person to be transferred for trial;
(b) that a child who is alleged:
   (i) to be a person against whom the offence was committed, or
   (ii) to have witnessed the commission of the offence,
   will be called to give evidence at the trial; and
(c) that for the purposes of avoiding any prejudice to the welfare of the child, the case should be taken over and proceeded with without delay by the Crown Court,

the Director may serve a notice of transfer. This has the effect of depriving the magistrates' court of jurisdiction, save in regard to bail and legal aid.

Included in an indictment under . . . section 40 of the Criminal Justice Act 1988 (subs (2))—Section 40 provides as follows:

'(1) A count charging a person with a summary offence to which this section applies may be included in an indictment if the charge—

(a) is founded on the same facts or evidence as a count charging an indictable offence; or
(b) is part of a series of offences of the same or similar character as an indictable offence which is also charged,

but only (in either case) if the facts or evidence relating to the offence were disclosed to a magistrates' court inquiring into the offence as examining magistrates.

(2) Where a count charging an offence to which this section applies is included in an indictment, the offence shall be tried in the same manner as if it were an indictable offence; but the Crown Court may only deal with the offender in respect of it in a manner in which a magistrates' court could have dealt with him.

(3) The offences to which this section applies are—

    (a) common assault;

  (aa) an offence under section 90(1) of the Criminal Justice Act 1991 (assaulting a prison custody officer);

  (ab) an offence under section 13(1) of the Criminal Justice and Public Order Act 1994 (assaulting a prison custody officer).

    (b) an offence under section 12(1) of the Theft Act 1968 (taking motor vehicle or other conveyance without authority etc);

    (c) an offence under section 103(1)(b) of the Road Traffic Act 1988 (driving a motor vehicle while disqualified);

    (d) an offence [of criminal damage etc] which would otherwise be triable only summarily by virtue of section 22(2) of [Magistrates' Courts Act 1980]; and

    (e) any summary offence specified under subsection (4) below.

(4) The Secretary of State may by order made by statutory instrument specify for the purposes of this section any summary offence which is punishable with imprisonment or involves obligatory or discretionary disqualification from driving.'

The offence in (3)(a) includes a common battery: *Lynsey* [1995] 3 All ER 654 (CA).

Bill of indictment ... under ... section 2(2)(b) of the Administration of Justice (Miscellaneous Provisions) Act 1933 (subs (2))—Section 2(2)(b) provides that a bill of indictment may be preferred 'by the direction or with the consent of a judge of the High Court'. The procedure to be followed is set out in Indictments (Procedure) Rules) 1971 (SI 1971/2084), rr 6–10, and in *Practice Direction (Crime: Voluntary Bills)* [1990] 1 WLR 1633. The voluntary bill of indictment procedure is unaffected by the changes made in respect of transfers for trial.

Criminal investigation (subs (3))—This will include not only investigations conducted into reported and undetected crimes, but also investigations which are intelligence-led and which begin before an offence actually is committed: draft Code of Practice, para 2.1. For discussion, see paras **2.6** and **2.7**, and, for the status of the Code of Practice, s 26 and para **3.18**.

Appointed day (subss (3) and (5))—No day had been appointed when this book went to press.

Police officers or other persons have a duty to investigate (subs (4))—The term 'police officer' would for this purpose appear to be synonymous with 'constable', and includes all those who hold the office of constable pursuant to the Police Act 1964, s 19, including special constables (1964 Act, s 19) and those who hold office as police officers under police forces established for specific purposes: see, eg British Transport police (Transport Act 1962, s 69), Civil Aviation police (Civil Aviation Act 1982, s 57), Ministry of Defence police (Ministry of Defence Police Act 1987). It will include those whose geographical jurisdiction is limited (see, eg Port of London Act 1968, s 2(1)), which limit jurisdiction of officers to the docks, landing places and land vested in, belonging to or administered by the Port of London Authority. It does not extend to persons who have, for limited purposes, the powers of constables (see, eg water bailiffs, pursuant to Salmon and Freshwater Fisheries Act 1975, s 36, and fisheries officers pursuant to Sea Fisheries Regulation Act 1966, s 10(3). The definition is probably not vital for the purposes of s 1 in the light of the extension of the definition to include 'other persons'. Cf s 15, which refers only to 'police officers'.

    The phrase 'other persons ...' is similar to that found in the Police and Criminal Evidence Act 1984, s 67(9) ('charged with the duty of investigating offences or charging offenders'). Persons who fall within the scope of that phrase include Customs and Excise officials, commercial investigators employed by a company to investigate possible crimes (*Thwaites* (1991) 92 Cr App R 106 (CA), trading standards officers (*Dudley MBC ex parte Debenhams plc* (1994) 159 JP 18 (DC) and might include others such as store detectives (*Joy v Federation Against Copyright Theft Ltd* [1993]

Crim LR 588. It does not include Department of Trade and Industry investigators acting pursuant to the Companies Acts (*Seelig, Spens* (1992) 94 Cr App R 17 (CA). In each case, it is a question of fact (*Bayliss* [1994] Crim LR 687 (CA). See also: *Smith* (1993) 99 Cr App R 233 (CA), where the fact that the Bank of England has investigative powers did not impose a duty to investigate offences on the bank official concerned.

By order (subs (5))—The order must be made by statutory instrument; see s 77(1)–(4).

2 General interpretation

(1) References to the accused are to the person mentioned in section 1(1) or (2).

(2) Where there is more than one accused in any proceedings this Part applies separately in relation to each of the accused.

(3) References to the prosecutor are to any person acting as prosecutor, whether an individual or a body.

(4) References to material are to material of all kinds, and in particular include references to—

(a) information, and
(b) objects of all descriptions.

(5) References to recording information are to putting it in a durable or retrievable form (such as writing or tape).

(6) This section applies for the purposes of this Part.

Explanatory text—See para **2.28**.

Commencement—On Royal Assent (4 July 1996), but see s 1(5).

'Person acting as prosecutor, whether an individual or a body' (subs (3))—In *Malz v Rosen* [1966] 2 All ER 10, it was held that an individual who signed a charge sheet at the invitation of the police, who subsequently instructed counsel and solicitor in the prosecution, was, nevertheless to be regarded as the prosecutor for the purposes of the tort of malicious prosecution.

The word 'prosecutor' certainly relates to the person who has brought the prosecution. The draft Code of Practice issued pursuant to Part II of the 1996 Act (as to which, see para **3.4**) states (in para 2.1 of that draft Code) that the 'prosecutor' is 'the authority responsible for directing a criminal investigation on behalf of the Crown. Particular duties may in practice fall to individuals acting on behalf of the prosecuting authority'.

Documents which are in the hands of counsel etc, will remain within the possession of the prosecutor even if those who present the case in court are not to be regarded as the 'prosecutor' for this purpose: see annotations to s 3. Further, counsel or solicitor presenting the case in court will be under their own duties in respect of obligations to other parties and the court by reference to the relevant Codes of Conduct. For discussion of these points, see para **2.10**.

The term 'body' includes the Crown, as well as bodies created by statute (eg Crown Prosecution Service, created by Prosecution of Offences Act 1987).

Tape (subs (5))—This term is not defined, but clearly includes audio and video tape.

Writing (subs (5))—Includes printing, lithography, photography and other mode of representing or reproducing words in a visible form, and expressions referring to writing are to be construed accordingly (Interpretation Act 1978, s 5 and Sch 1). The use, in s 2(5), of the term 'retrievable' suggests that the term 'writing' should be given the widest interpretation, and should not be confined to representations or reproductions which are 'visible'. On this basis, it will include information which is stored in a computer's memory, whether permanent memory (ROM) or temporary memory (RAM).

The main provisions

3 Primary disclosure by prosecutor

(1) The prosecutor must—

(a) disclose to the accused any prosecution material which has not previously been disclosed to the accused and which in the prosecutor's opinion might undermine the case for the prosecution against the accused, or
(b) give to the accused a written statement that there is no material of a description mentioned in paragraph (1).

(2) For the purposes of this section prosecution material is material—

(a) which is in the prosecutor's possession, and came into his possession in connection with the case for the prosecution against the accused, or
(b) which, in pursuance of a code operative under Part II, he has inspected in connection with the case for the prosecution against the accused.

(3) Where material consists of information which has been recorded in any form the prosecutor discloses it for the purposes of this section—

(a) by securing that a copy is made of it and that the copy is given to the accused, or
(b) if in the prosecutor's opinion that is not practicable or not desirable, by allowing the accused to inspect it at a reasonable time and a reasonable place or by taking steps to secure that he is allowed to do so;

and a copy may be in such form as the prosecutor thinks fit and need not be in the same form as that in which the information has already been recorded.

(4) Where material consists of information which has not been recorded the prosecutor discloses it for the purposes of this section by securing that it is recorded in such form as he thinks fit and—

(a) by securing that a copy is made of it and that the copy is given to the accused, or
(b) if in the prosecutor's opinion that is not practicable or not desirable, by allowing the accused to inspect it at a reasonable time and a reasonable place or by taking steps to secure that he is allowed to do so.

(5) Where material does not consist of information the prosecutor discloses it for the purposes of this section by allowing the accused to inspect it at a reasonable time and a reasonable place or by taking steps to secure that he is allowed to do so.

(6) Material must not be disclosed under this section to the extent that the court, on an application by the prosecutor, concludes it is not in the public interest to disclose it and orders accordingly.

(7) Material must not be disclosed under this section to the extent that—

(a) it has been intercepted in obedience to a warrant issued under section 2 of the Interception of Communications Act 1985, or
(b) it indicates that such a warrant has been issued or that material has been intercepted in obedience to such a warrant.

(8) The prosecutor must act under this section during the period which, by virtue of section 12, is the relevant period for this section.

Explanatory text—See paras **2.27–2.44.**

Commencements—On Royal Assent (4 July 1996), but see s 1(5).

Prosecutor (subss (1),(2),(3),(4),(5),(6) and (8))—See annotations to s 2.

Accused (subss (1),(2),(3),(4) and (5))—See s 2(1).

Undermine the case for the prosecution (subs (1))—Whether this is so is a matter for the judgment of the prosecutor. Some limited guidance as to its meaning may be gleaned by analogy with the case-law dealing with cross-examination of co-accused persons under the Criminal Evidence Act 1898, s 1(f)(iii). The key phrase in s 1(f)(iii) is 'give evidence against', which has been construed as meaning, inter alia, the giving of evidence which undermines the case for the defence: *Murdoch v Taylor* [1965] AC 574 (HL). This has been held to mean evidence which makes the acquittal of the accused less likely. See *Bruce* [1975] 1 WLR 1252 (CA), but cf *Hatton* (1976) 64 Cr App R 88 (CA).

Possession (subs (2))—This term is used in statutes in a disparate range of contexts. It is a term used particularly in the context of possession of an article or substance as the actus reus of a criminal offence. See, generally, *Warner v Metropolitan Police Commissioner* [1969] 2 AC 256, [1968] 2 All ER 356 (HL). Its precise meaning depends on the context in which it is used, and the intent and purpose of Parliament in the use of the term, which, in the case of disclosure provisions, is to ensure that evidence collected by the prosecution is made available to the defence if relevant and not being used. In this context, it is submitted that possession includes all matters under the control or direction of the prosecutor, irrespective of whether they are physically in the custody of the prosecutor (see, analogously, *Lockyer v Gibb* [1967] 2 QB 243, [1966] 2 All ER 653 (DC)). Thus, articles will be in the possession of the prosecutor even if, eg, sent to a laboratory for analysis. It is submitted that the authorities such as *Ashton-Rickhardt* [1978] 1 WLR 37, [1978] 1 All ER 173 (CA) in respect of possession of items of which an individual is unaware are of limited value in this context. The fact that the prosecutor is unaware that material has come into his possession, believes that it is no longer in his possession (cf *Buswell* 1 WLR 64 (CA)) or believes that it relates to the instant case, affects the judgment he is entitled to make under s 3(1), but it is unlikely that such matters will be regarded as outside the possession of the prosecutor for the purpose of the new Act. Further, it is submitted that an article in the possession of one person who is employed by an organisation, or by one department of a large organisation, is in the possession of that organisation for all purposes. In *Blackledge and Others* (1995) *The Times*, 7 November (CA), it was held that documents in the hands of one or another of a number of Government departments involved in consideration of the issue of licences allowing the exportation of armaments to Iraq were to be regarded as being in the possession of the Crown as an indivisible entity.

Code operative under Part II (subs (2))—See para **3.4**.

Recorded (s 3(3))—See s 2(5), and annotations thereto.

Not in the public interest to disclose (subs (6))—See paras **3.56–3.66**.

Section 2 of the Interception of Communications Act 1985 (s 3(7))—Section 2(1) of the 1985 Act empowers the Secretary of State to issue a warrant requiring the person to whom it is addressed to intercept, in the course of their transmission by post or by means of a public telecommunication system, such communications as are described in the warrant; and such a warrant may also require the person to whom it is addressed to disclose the intercepted material to such persons and in such manner as are described in the warrant. A warrant may not be issued of the interception of communications by cordless telephone, if the method of interception involves the interception of impulses passing between handset and base unit. They are not being passed through the public telecommunications system at that point, because it amounts to a private system connected to the public system: *Effick* [1994] 3 WLR 583, [1994] 3 All ER 458 (HL).

The pre-conditions for the issue of a warrant are that the Secretary of State considers that the warrant is necessary: (a) in the interests of national security; (b) for the purpose of preventing or detecting serious crime; or (c) for the purposes of safeguarding the economic well-being of the United Kingdom (1985 Act, s 2(2)). The Secretary of State must have regard to whether the information which is considered necessary to acquire could reasonably be acquired by other means (1985 Act, s 2(3)), but a warrant shall not be issued on ground (c) above unless the information relates to the acts or intentions of persons outside the British Isles (1985 Act, s 2(4)).

Relevant period (subs (8))—See s 12 and paras **2.42–2.43**.

4 Primary disclosure: further provisions

(1) This section applies where—

(a) the prosecutor acts under section 3, and
(b) before so doing he was given a document in pursuance of provision included, by virtue of section 24(3), in a code operative under Part II.

(2) In such a case the prosecutor must give the document to the accused at the same time as the prosecutor acts under section 3.

Explanatory text—See para **2.40**

Commencement—On Royal Assent (4 July 1996), but see s 1(5).

Prosecutor (subss (1) and (2))—See annotations to s 2.

Code operative under Part II (subs (1))—See para **3.4**.

Document (subss (1) and (2))—The new Act does not define 'document', and definitions in other statutes must be read in the context in which they appear. However, the definition of 'document' in the Civil Evidence Act 1968, s 10, has been adopted in the criminal context (see, eg Criminal Justice Act 1988, s 27) and is almost certainly an appropriate definition for the purposes of the new Act.

Section 10(1) of the 1968 Act states:

'In this part of this Act—

. . .

"document" includes, in addition to a document in writing—

(a) any map, plan, graph or drawing;
(b) any photograph;
(c) any disc, tape, soundtrack or other device in which sounds or other data (not being visible images) are embodied so as to be capable (with or without the aid of some other equipment) of being reproduced therefrom . . .'.

Section 10(2) of the 1968 Act provides that any reference to any copy of a document includes—

'(a) in the case of a document falling within paragraph (c) but not (d) of the definition of document . . . a transcript of the sounds or other data embodied therein;
(b) in the case of a document falling within paragraph (d) but not (c) of that definition, a reproduction or still reproduction of the image or images embodied therein, whether enlarged or not;
(c) in the case of a document falling within both of those paragraphs, such a transcript together with such a still reproduction; and
(d) in the case of a document not falling within the said paragraph (d) of which a visual image is embodied in a document falling within that paragraph, a reproduction of that image, whether enlarged or not . . .'.

This definition of 'document' is wide enough to include the making of statements by computer transmission (E-mail).

This provision survives the passage of the Civil Evidence Act 1995. Section 13 of the 1995 Act defines 'document' as meaning 'anything in which information of any description is recorded', and 'copy' in relation to a document means 'anything onto which information recorded in the document has been copied by whatever means and whether directly or indirectly.'

Accused (subs (2))—See s 2(1).

5 Compulsory disclosure by accused

(1) Subject to subsections (2) to (4), this section applies where—

(a) this Part applies by virtue of section 1(2), and
(b) the prosecutor complies with seciton 3 or purports to comply with it.

(2) Where this Part applies by virtue of section 1(2)(b), this section does not apply unless—

(a) a copy of the notice of transfer, and
(b) copies of the documents containing the evidence,

have been given to the accused under regulations made under section 5(9) of the Criminal Justice Act 1987.

(3) Where this Part applies by virtue of section 1(2)(c), this section does not apply unless—

(a) a copy of the notice of transfer, and
(b) copies of the documents containing the evidence,

have been given to the accused under regulations made under paragraph 4 of Schedule 6 to the Criminal Justice Act 1991.

(4) Where this Part applies by virtue of section 1(2)(e), this section does not apply unless the prosecutor has served on the accused a copy of the indictment and a copy of the set of documents containing the evidence which is the basis of the charge.

(5) Where this section applies, the accused must give a defence statement to the court and the prosecutor.

(6) For the purposes of this section a defence statement is a written statement—

(a) setting out in general terms the nature of the accused's defence,
(b) indicating the matters on which he takes issue with the prosecution, and
(c) setting out, in the case of each such matter, the reason why he takes issue with the prosecution.

(7) If the defence statement discloses an alibi the accused must give particulars of the alibi in the statement, including—

(a) the name and address of any witness the accused believes is able to give evidence in support of the alibi, if the name and address are known to the accused when the statement is given;
(b) any information in the accused's possession which might be of material assistance in finding any such witness, if his name or address is not known to the accused when the statement is given.

(8) For the purposes of this section evidence in support of an alibi is evidence tending to show that by reason of the presence of the accused at a particular place or in a particular area at a particular time he was not, or was unlikely to have been, at the place where the offence is alleged to have been committed at the time of its alleged commission.

(9) The accused must give a defence statement under this section during the period which, by virtue of section 12, is the relevant period for this section.

Explanatory text—See paras **2.53–2.65**.

Commencement—On Royal Assent (4 July 1996), but see s 1(5).

Prosecutor (subss (1) and (5))—See annotations to s 2.

Accused (subss (2),(3),(4),(5),(6),(7),(8) and (9))—See s 2(1).

Written statement (subs (6))—See s 2 and annotations thereto.

Alibi (subss (7) and (8))—An alibi is a defence that, because of the presence of the accused at a particular place, or area, at a particular time, he did not commit the offence charged. Section 5(8) defines 'evidence in support of an alibi' in such terms, and it follows from this that the prosecution must allege an offence at a particular place, or in a particular area, at a particular time: *Hassan* [1970] 1 QB 423 (CA).

There is no 'evidence in support of an alibi' if the accused simply denies presence at the place, or area, of commission of the offence: *Johnson* [1994] Crim LR 949. On the other hand, evidence of the presence of the accused at a particular place at a particular time is evidence in support of an alibi, even though the time in question is different from that of the commission of the offence, provided that presence is being relied on to show that the accused did not commit the offence: *Fields and Adams* [1991] Crim LR 38 (CA); cf *Lewis* [1969] 2 QB 1 (CA).

Evidence that the accused has served notice of alibi should normally be adduced as part of the prosecution case: *Rossborough* (1985) 81 Cr App R 372 (CA). Where an alibi is shown to be false, this can, in some circumstances, go to the issue of guilt. The lies (ie the false alibi) must be deliberate, relate to a material issue, and the jury must be satisfied that there was no innocent motive for the lies: *Broadhurst v R* [1964] AC 441, [1964] 1 All ER 111 (PC); *Lucas* [1981] QB 720, [1981] 2 All ER 1008 (CA); *Richens* [1993] 4 All ER 877 (CA); *Goodway* [1993] 4 All ER 895 (CA). Subject to the application of similar principles, an alibi that is shown to be false can support a disputed identification: *Turnbull* [1977] QB 224, [1976] 3 All ER 549 (CA); *Mills v R* [1995] Crim LR 884 (PC); *Mussell* [1995] Crim LR 887 (CA); *Fergus* (1993) 98 Cr App R 313 (CA); *Lesley* [1995] Crim LR 946. Failure to give notice of an alibi later relied on at trial in the Crown Court meant that no evidence in support of that alibi could be adduced save with leave of the court: Criminal Justice Act 1967, s 11. Section 11 is repealed by the new Act, s 80 and Sch 5. For the sanction in respect of failure to disclose details of alibi, see para **2.65**.

Address (subs (7))—'Address' is capable of more than one meaning. In one sense, it can refer to a postal address. In another, to the place where a person resides. In *Bishop* [1959] 2 All ER 787 (CCA) the court construed the (now repealed) Prison Act 1952, s 29 provision that required the specified persons to register their 'addresses' with the police. B had no fixed abode. In the context of a statutory provision which gave a wide meaning to the term 'residence' (1952 Act, Sch 1, para 2), the court was of the opinion that the obligation under the statute could be fulfilled properly by the giving of a reasonable description of such a place, not necessarily a postal address but something which described or identified the place where they resided with reasonable clarity. In the light of the terms of s 5(7)(b), it may be that the narrower interpretation would be given by a court. The point is probably unimportant, because the combined effect of s 5(5)(a) and (b) is to require an accused to give the prosecutor whatever information he has which will assist in the location of the witness.

Possession (subs (7))—See annotations to s 3.

Relevant period (subs (8))—See s 12 and para **2.56**.

6 Voluntary disclosure by accused

(1) This section applies where—

    (a) this Part applies by virtue of section 1(1), and
    (b) the prosecutor complies with section 3 or purports to comply with it.

(2) The accused—

    (a) may give a defence statement to the prosecutor, and
    (b) if he does so, must also give such a statement to the court.

(3) Subsections (6) to (8) of section 5 apply for the purposes of this section as they apply for the purposes of that.

(4) If the accused gives a defence statement under this section he must give it during the period which, by virtue of section 12, is the relevant period for this section.

Explanatory text—See para **2.53**.

Commencement—On Royal Assent (4 July 1996), but see s 1(5).

Prosecutor (subss (1) and (2))—See annotations to s 2.

Accused (subss (2) and (4))—See s 2.

Relevant period (subs (4))—See s 12 and para **2.56**.

7 Secondary disclosure by prosecutor

(1) This section applies where the accused gives a defence statement under section 5 or 6.

(2) The prosecutor must—

(a) disclose to the accused any prosecution material which has not previously been disclosed to the accused and which might be reasonably expected to assist the accused's defence as disclosed by the defence statement given under section 5 or 6, or

(b) give to the accused a written statement that there is no material of a description mentioned in paragraph (a).

(3) For the purposes of this section prosecution material is material—

(a) which is in the prosecutor's possession and came into his possession in connection with the case for the prosecution against the accused, or

(b) which, in pursuance of a code operative under Part II, he has inspected in connection with the case for the prosecution against the accused.

(4) Subsections (3) to (5) of section 3 (method by which prosecutor discloses) apply for the purposes of this section as they apply for the purposes of that.

(5) Material must not be disclosed under this section to the extent that the court, on an application by the prosecutor, concludes it is not in the public interest to disclose it and orders accordingly.

(6) Material must not be disclosed under this section to the extent that—

(a) it has been intercepted in obedience to a warrant issued under section 2 of the Interception of Communications Act 1985, or

(b) it indicates that such a warrant has been issued or that material has been intercepted in obedience to such a warrant.

(7) The prosecutor must act under this section during the period which, by virtue of section 12, is the relevant period for this section.

Explanatory text—See paras **2.58–2.70**.

Commencement—On Royal Assent (4 July 1996), but see s 1(5).

Accused (subss (1) and (2))—See s 2(1).

Prosecutor (subss (2),(3),(4),(5) and (7))—See annotations to s 2.

Material (subss (2),(3),(5) and (6))—See s 2(2).

Possession (subs (3))—See annotations to s 5.

Not in the public interest to disclose (subs (3))—See paras **3.55–3.65**.

Section 2 of the Interception of Communications Act 1985 (subs (6))—See annotations to s 3.

8 Application by accused for disclosure

(1) This section applies where the accused gives a defence statement under section 5 or 6 and the prosecutor complies with section 7 or purports to comply with it or fails to comply with it.

(2) If the accused has at any time reasonable cause to believe that—

(a) there is prosecution material which might be reasonably expected to assist the accused's defence as disclosed by the defence statement given under section 5 or 6, and

(b) the material has not been disclosed to the accused,

the accused may apply to the court for an order requiring the prosecutor to disclose such material to the accused.

(3) For the purposes of this section prosecution material is material—

(a) which is in the prosecutor's possession and came into his possession in connection with the case for the prosecution against the accused,

(b) which, in pursuance of a code operative under Part II, he has inspected in connection with the case for the prosecution against the accused, or

(c) which falls within subsection (4).

(4) Material falls within this subsection if in pursuance of a code operative under Part II the prosecutor must, if he asks for the material, be given a copy of it or be allowed to inspect it in connection with the case for the prosecution against the accused.

(5) Material must not be disclosed under this section to the extent that the court, on an application by the prosecutor, concludes it is not in the public interest to disclose it and orders accordingly.

(6) Material must not be disclosed under this section to the extent that—

(a) it has been intercepted in obedience to a warrant issued under section 2 of the Interception of Communications Act 1985, or

(b) it indicates that such a warrant has been issued or that material has been intercepted in obedience to such a warrant.

Explanatory text—See para **2.70**.

Commencement—On Royal Assent (4 July 1996), but see s 1(5).

Accused (subss (1),(2) and (3))—See s 2.

Prosecutor (subss (1),(2),(3),(4) and (5))—See annotations to s 2.

Reasonable cause to believe (subs (2))—'Belief' refers to the state of mind of someone who does not know for certain that the facts believed exist, but who considers that there is no substantial doubt that they do: *Hall* (1985) 81 Cr App R 260 (CA). A 'reasonable cause to believe' indicates that that belief must be held reasonably ie on evidence. The existence of reasonable grounds, and of the belief which is founded on them, is a matter to be decided on the basis of the evidence available, and can be reviewed by the court. The grounds on which the person concerned held that belief must be sufficient to induce in a reasonable person the prescribed belief. See: *McCardle v Egan* (1933) 150 LT 412 (CA); *Nakkuda Ali v Jayarante* [1951] AC 66 (PC); *IRC ex parte Rossminster Ltd* [1980] AC 952, [1980] 1 All ER 80, at 84, 92, 103 and 104 (HL); *Castorina v Chief Constable of Surrey* (1988) 138 NLJ 180 (CA).

Material (subss (2),(3),(4),(5) and (6))—See s 2(2).

Possession (subs (3))—See annotations to s 5.

Code operative under Part II (subs (3))—See para **3.4**.

Not in the public interest to disclose (subs (5))—See paras **3.55–3.65**.

Section 2 of the Interception of Communications Act 1985 (subs (6))—See annotations to s 3.

9 Continuing duty of prosecutor to disclose

(1) Subsection (2) applies at all times—

    (a) after the prosecutor complies with section 3 or purports to comply with it, and

    (b) before the accused is acquitted or convicted or the prosecutor decides not to proceed with the case concerned.

(2) The prosecutor must keep under review the question whether at any given time there is prosecution material which—

    (a) in his opinion might undermine the case for the prosecution against the accused, and

    (b) has not been disclosed to the accused;

and if there is such material at any time the prosecutor must disclose it to the accused as soon as is reasonably practicable.

(3) In applying subsection (2) by reference to any given time the state of affairs at that time (including the case for the prosecution as it stands at that time) must be taken into account.

(4) Subsection (5) applies at all times—

    (a) after the prosecutor complies with section 7 or purports to comply with it, and

    (b) before the accused is acquitted or convicted or the prosecutor decides not to proceed with the case concerned.

(5) The prosecutor must keep under review the question whether at any given time there is prosecution material which—

    (a) might be reasonably expected to assist the accused's defence as disclosed by the defence statement given under section 5 or 6, and

    (b) has not been disclosed to the accused;

and if there is such material at any time the prosecutor must disclose it to the accused as soon as is reasonably practicable.

(6) For the purposes of this section prosecution material is material—

    (a) which is in the prosecutor's possession and came into his possession in connection with the case for the prosecution against the accused, or

    (b) which, in pursuance of a code operative under Part II, he has inspected in connection with the case for the prosecution against the accused.

(7) Subsections (3) to (5) of section 3 (method by which prosecutor discloses) apply for the purposes of this section as they apply for the purposes of that.

(8) Material must not be disclosed under this section to the extent that the court, on an application by the prosecutor, concludes it is not in the public interest to disclose it and orders accordingly.

(9) Material must not be disclosed under this section to the extent that—

    (a) it has been intercepted in obedience to a warrant issued under section 2 of the Interception of Communications Act 1985, or

    (b) it indicates that such a warrant has been issued or that material has been intercepted in obedience to such a warrant.

Explanatory text—See paras **2.71–2.73**.

Commencement—On Royal Assent (4 July 1996), but see s 1(5).

Accused (subss (1),(2),(4),(5) and (6))—See s 2.

Prosecutor (subss (1),(2),(4),(5),(6),(7) and (8))—See annotations to s 2.

Before accused is acquitted or convicted or the prosecutor decides not to proceed (sub (1))—The terms 'acquit' and 'convict' can be interpreted simply as referring to the making of a finding of not guilty or guilty. In respect of the doctrines of autrefois acquit and autrefois convict, Lord Bridge in *Richard v R* [1993] AC 217, [1992] 4 All ER 807 observed:

> 'With respect to the central issue there is a curious conflict of authority which their Lordships must now resolve. It has been said many times that the word "conviction" is ambiguous and it has sometimes been construed in a statutory context as referring to nothing more than a finding of guilt. But, in the absence of something in the context which suggests that narrower meaning, the authorities in the nineteenth century and earlier all seem to point to the conclusion that the requirement to establish a conviction requires proof not only of the finding of guilt but also of the court's final adjudication by sentence or some other order.'

In that case the accused pleaded guilty to manslaughter, but had not been sentenced. At a resumed hearing the prosecution was halted, and the accused was subsequently tried and sentenced for murder. In dismissing an appeal against conviction, the Privy Council concluded that the doctrine of autrefois convict did not assist the accused, because the adjudication was not in fact complete.

However, the context may require a more narrow approach: see, eg *Blaby* [1894] 2 QB 170, [1891–4] All ER Rep 715 (DC) where the person subject to a finding of guilt under the Coinage Offences Act 1861, s 6 and s 9, was held to have been convicted. See also *Miles* (1890) 24 QBD 423, [1886–90] All ER Rep 715. It is submitted that the context in the new Act is one where it is appropriate to regard the acquittal or conviction as occurring on the making of a finding, given that the intent is to provide ongoing review of disclosure decisions whilst criminal liability is a live issue before the court.

The interpretation of these terms to mirror the law relating to the doctrines of autrefois acquit and autrefois convict would greatly extend the review duty. However, note the terms of para 8.2 of the draft Code of Practice issued pursuant to Part II of the new Act:

> 'The Act imposes a continuing duty on the prosecutor, for the duration of criminal proceedings against the accused, ...'.

For the doctrine of autrefois acquit and autrefois convict, see: *Connolly v DPP* [1964] AC 1254, [1964] 2 All ER 401 (HL); *Dabhade* [1993] QB 329, [1992] 4 All ER 796 (CA).

The prosecutor decides not to proceed with the case (sub (1))—Such a decision can be implemented by the offering of no evidence, which will lead to an acquittal. The Prosecution of Offences Act 1985, s 23(3), permits the Director of Public Prosecutions at any time during the preliminary stages of proceedings to serve on the clerk of the court that he does not want the proceedings to continue.

The 'preliminary stage' of proceedings does not include—

(a) in the case of a summary offence, any stage of the proceedings after the court has begun to hear evidence for the prosecution at the trial;
(b) in the case of an indictable offence, any stage of the proceedings after:
  (i) the accused has been committed for trial; or
  (ii) the court has begun to hear evidence for the prosecution at a summary trial of the offence.

Such powers are exercisable by Crown Prosecutors: *Liverpool Crown Court ex parte Bray* [1987] Crim LR 51.

Not in the public interest to disclose (subs (8))—See paras 3.55–3.65.

Undermine the case for the prosecution (subs (2))—See annotations to s 3.

Material (subss (2),(5),(6),(8) and (9))—See s 2(2).

Possession (subs (6))—See annotations to s 3.

Code operative under Part II (subs (6))—See para **3.4**.

Section 2 of the Interception of Communications Act 1985 (subs (9))—See annotations to s 3.

10 Prosecutor's failure to observe time limits

(1) This section applies if the prosecutor—

- (a) purports to act under section 3 after the end of the period which, by virtue of section 12, is the relevant period for section 3, or
- (b) purports to act under section 7 after the end of the period which, by virtue of section 12, is the relevant period for section 7.

(2) Subject to subsection (3), the failure to act during the period concerned does not on its own constitute grounds for staying the proceedings for abuse of process.

(3) Subsection (2) does not prevent the failure constituting such grounds if it involves such delay by the prosecutor that the accused is denied a fair trial.

Explanatory text—See para **2.44**.

Commencement—On Royal Assent (4 July 1996), but see s 1(5).

Prosecutor (subss (1),(3))—See s 2.

Abuse of process (sub (2))—A court can, as part of its inherent power, order a stay to prevent an abuse of process occasioned, inter alia, by delay: *Connolly v DPP* [1964] AC 1254 (HL). It is a power that is, on the grounds of delay, exercisable by either Crown Court or magistrates' court: *Horseferry Road Magistrates Court ex parte Bennett* [1994] 1 AC 42 (HL). In *DPP v Humphreys* [1976] 2 All ER 497, Viscount Dilhorne warned that this power should be used only 'in the most exceptional circumstances'.

The leading statement of principles to be applied on applications based on delay is that of Lord Lane CJ in *Attorney-General's Reference (No 1 of 1990)* [1992] 3 All ER 169. Even if delay is unjustifiable, the imposition of a stay should be the exception rather than the rule. It will be rare that a stay will be justified in the absence of fault on the part of complainant or prosecution. In assessing whether delay is likely to cause prejudice to the extent that no fair trial is possible, regard should be had to the ability of the judge to regulate the admissibility of evidence, to whether all factual issues can be put before the court, and the power of the trial judge to direct the jury appropriately.

The fact that complexity of a case leads to delay is not of itself sufficient to justify a stay: *Holyoake* (1990, unreported). Delay in a case based primarily on contemporary documents is less likely to lead to a stay being justified: *Telford Justices ex parte Badham* (1991) 93 Cr App R 171. By contrast, a stay may be more justifiable if the delay has been based on improper use of procedures by the prosecutor, or by inefficiency: see *Brentford Justices ex parte Wong* 73 Cr App R 65; *Oxford Justices ex parte Smith* 75 Cr App R 200 (DC).

Accused (subs (3))—See s 2(1).

11 Faults in disclosure by accused

(1) This section applies where section 5 applies and the accused—

- (a) fails to give a defence statement under that section,
- (b) gives a defence statement under that section but does so after the end of the period which, by virtue of section 12, is the relevant period for section 5,
- (c) sets out inconsistent defences in a defence statement given under section 5,
- (d) at his trial puts forward a defence which is different from any defence set out in a defence statement given under section 5,
- (e) at his trial adduces evidence in support of an alibi without having given particulars of the alibi in a defence statement given under section 5, or

(f) at his trial calls a witness to give evidence in support of an alibi without having complied with subsection (7)(a) or (b) of section 5 as regards the witness in giving a defence statement under that section.

(2) This section also applies where section 6 applies, the accused gives a defence statement under that section, and the accused—

(a) gives the statement after the end of the period which, by virtue of section 12, is the relevant period for section 6,
(b) sets out inconsistent defences in the statement,
(c) at his trial puts forward a defence which is different from any defence set out in the statement,
(d) at his trial adduces evidence in support of an alibi without having given particulars of the alibi in the statement, or
(e) at his trial calls a witness to give evidence in support of an alibi without having complied with subsection (7)(a) or (b) of section 5 (as applied by section 6) as regards the witness in giving the statement.

(3) Where this section applies—

(a) the court or, with the leave of the court, any other party may make such comment as appears appropriate;
(b) the court or jury may draw such inferences as appear proper in deciding whether the accused is guilty of the offence concerned.

(4) Where the accused puts forward a defence which is different from any defence set out in a defence statement given under section 5 or 6, in doing anything under subsection (3) or in deciding whether to do anything under it the court shall have regard—

(a) to the extent of the difference in the defences, and
(b) to whether there is any justification for it.

(5) A person shall not be convicted of an offence solely on an inference drawn under subsection (3).

(6) Any reference in this section to evidence in support of an alibi shall be construed in accordance with section 5.

Explanatory text—See paras **2.66–2.67**.

Commencement—On Royal Assent (4 July 1996), but see s 1(5).

Accused (subss (1) and (2))—See s 2(1).

Alibi (subss (1),(2) and (6))—See annotations to s 5.

Relevant period (subss (1) and (2))—See s 12 and para **2.56**.

May draw such inferences as appear proper (subs (3)); Shall not ... be convicted of an offence ... solely on an inference (subs (5))—These provisions are similar to those contained in the Criminal Justice and Public Order Act 1994, s 35(3) and s 38(3), which were the subject of consideration in *Cowan* [1995] 4 All ER 939 (CA). See annotations to s 44.

Time limits

12 Time limits

(1) This section has effect for the purpose of determining the relevant period for sections 3, 5, 6 and 7.

(2) Subject to subsection (3), the relevant period is a period beginning and ending with such days as the Secretary of State prescribes by regulations for the purposes of the section concerned.

(3) The regulations may do one or more of the following—

(a) provide that the relevant period for any section shall if the court so orders be extended (or further extended) by so many days as the court specifies;

(b) provide that the court may only make such an order if an application is made by a prescribed person and if any other prescribed conditions are fulfilled;

(c) provide that an application may only be made if prescribed conditions are fulfilled;

(d) provide that the number of days by which a period may be extended shall be entirely at the court's discretion;

(e) provide that the number of days by which a period may be extended shall not exceed a prescribed number;

(f) provide that there shall be no limit on the number of applications that may be made to extend a period;

(g) provide that no more than a prescribed number of applications may be made to extend a period;

and references to the relevant period for a section shall be construed accordingly.

(4) Conditions mentioned in subsection (3) may be framed by reference to such factors as the Secretary of State thinks fit.

(5) Without prejudice to the generality of subsection (4), so far as the relevant period for section 3 or 7 is concerned—

(a) conditions may be framed by reference to the nature or volume of the material concerned;

(b) the nature of material may be defined by reference to the prosecutor's belief that the question of non-disclosure on grounds of public interest may arise.

(6) In subsection (3) 'prescribed' means prescribed by regulations under this section.

Explanatory text—See paras **2.42**, **2.56** and **2.69**.

Commencement—On Royal Assent (4 July 1996), but see s 1(5).

Regulations (subss (2), (3) and (6))—The regulations must be made by statutory instrument; see s 77(1)–(4) and (6).

Day (subss (2),(3) and (4))—'The term "day" is, like the term year and "month" used in more senses than one. A day is strictly the period of time which begins with one midnight and ends with the next. It may also denote the period of 24 hours, and again it may denote the period of time between sunrise and sunset' (45 Halsburys Laws (4th edn Revised, para 1113). Only the first of these three meanings is appropriate to the use of the term 'day' in this context.

Public interest (subs (5))—See paras **3.55–3.65**.

13 Time limits: transitional

(1) As regards a case in relation to which no regulations under section 12 have come into force for the purposes of section 3, section 3(8) shall have effect as if it read—

"(8) The prosecutor must act under this section as soon as is reasonably practicable after—

(a) the accused pleads not guilty (where this Part applies by virtue of section 1(1)),

(b) the accused is committed for trial (where this Part applies by virtue of section 1(2)(a)),

(c) the proceedings are transferred (where this Part applies by virtue of section 1(2)(b) or (c)),

(d) the count is included in the indictment (where this Part applies by virtue of section 1(2)(d)), or

(e) the bill of indictment is preferred (where this Part applies by virtue of section 1(2)(e))."

(2) As regards a case in relation to which no regulations under section 12 have come into force for the purposes of section 7, section 7(1) shall have effect as if it read—

"(7) The prosecutor must act under this section as soon as is reasonably practicable after the accused gives a defence statement under section 5 or 6."

Explanatory text—See paras **2.42**, **2.56** and **2.69**.

Commencement—On Royal Assent (4 July 1996), but see s 1(5).

Prosecutor (subss (1) and (2))—See annotations to s 2.

Pleads not guilty (subs (1)); Proceedings are transferred (subs (1)); Included in the indictment (subs (1)); Bill of indictment is preferred (subs (1))—See annotations to s 1.

Regulations (subs (1))—See annotations to s 12.

Public interest

14 Public interest: review for summary trials

(1) This section applies where this Part applies by virtue of section 1(1).

(2) At any time—

(a) after a court makes an order under section 3(6), 7(5), 8(5) or 9(8), and

(b) before the accused is acquitted or convicted or the prosecutor decides not to proceed with the case concerned,

the accused may apply to the court for a review of the question whether it is still not in the public interest to disclose material affected by its order.

(3) In such a case the court must review that question, and if it concludes that it is in the public interest to disclose material to any extent—

(a) it shall so order, and

(b) it shall take such steps as are reasonable to inform the prosecutor of its order.

(4) Where the prosecutor is informed of an order made under subsection (3) he must act accordingly having regard to the provisions of this Part (unless he decides not to proceed with the case concerned).

Explanatory text—See para **2.81**.

Commencement—On Royal Assent (4 July 1996), but see s 1(5).

Prosecutor (subss (2),(3) and (4))—See annotations to s 2.

The accused is acquitted or convicted (subs (2))—See annotations to s 9.

The prosecutor decides not to proceed with the case (subss (2) and (4))—See annotations to s 9.

Public interest (subss (2) and (3))—See paras **3.55–3.65**.

Material (subss (2) and (3))—See annotations to s 2(2).

15 Public interest: review in other cases

(1) This section applies where this Part applies by virtue of section 1(2).

(2) This section applies at all times—

- (a) after a court makes an order under section 3(6), 7(5), 8(5) or 9(8), and
- (b) before the accused is acquitted or convicted or the prosecutor decides not to proceed with the case concerned.

(3) The court must keep under review the question whether at any given time it is still not in the public interest to disclose material affected by its order.

(4) The court must keep the question mentioned in subsection (3) under review without the need for an application; but the accused may apply to the court for a review of that question.

(5) If the court at any time concludes that it is in the public interest to disclose material to any extent—

- (a) it shall so order, and
- (b) it shall take such steps as are reasonable to inform the prosecutor of its order.

(6) Where the prosecutor is informed of an order made under subsection (5) he must act accordingly having regard to the provisions of this Part (unless he decides not to proceed with the case concerned).

Explanatory text—See para **2.82**.

Commencement—On Royal Assent (4 July 1996), but see s 1(5).

Prosecutor (subss (2),(5)and (6))—See annotations to s 2.

Before accused is acquitted or convicted or the prosecutor decides not to proceed (subss (2) and (5))—See annotations to s 9.

Material (subss (3) and (5))—See s 2(2).

Public interest (subs (5))—See paras **3.55–3.65**.

16 Applications: opportunity to be heard

Where—

- (a) an application is made under section 3(6), 7(5), 8(5), 9(8), 14(2) or 15(4),
- (b) a person claiming to have an interest in the material applies to be heard by the court, and
- (c) he shows that he was involved (whether alone or with others and whether directly or indirectly) in the prosecutor's attention being brought to the material,

the court must not make an order under section 3(6), 7(5), 8(5), 9(8), 14(3) or 15(5) (as the case may be) unless the person applying under paragraph (b) has been given an opportunity to be heard.

Explanatory text—See para **2.81**.

Commencement—On Royal Assent (4 July 1996), but see s 1(5).

Material—See s 2.

Confidentiality

17 Confidentiality of disclosed information

(1) If the accused is given or allowed to inspect a document or other object under—

    (a) section 3, 4, 7, 9, 14 or 15, or

    (b) an order under section 8,

then, subject to subsections (2) to (4), he must not use or disclose it or any information recorded in it.

(2) The accused may use or disclose the object or information—

    (a) in connection with the proceedings for whose purposes he was given the object or allowed to inspect it,

    (b) with a view to the taking of further criminal proceedings (for instance, by way of appeal) with regard to the matter giving rise to the proceedings mentioned in paragraph (a), or

    (c) in connection with the proceedings first mentioned in paragraph (b).

(3) The accused may use or disclose—

    (a) the object to the extent that it has been displayed to the public in open court, or

    (b) the information to the extent that it has been communicated to the public in open court;

but the preceding provisions of this subsection do not apply if the object is displayed or the information is communicated in proceedings to deal with a contempt of court under section 18.

(4) If—

    (a) the accused applies to the court for an order granting permission to use or disclose the object or information, and

    (b) the court makes such an order,

the accused may use or disclose the object or information for the purpose and to the extent specified by the court.

(5) An application under subsection (4) may be made and dealt with at any time, and in particular after the accused has been acquitted or convicted or the prosecutor has decided not to proceed with the case concerned; but this is subject to rules made by virtue of section 19(2).

(6) Where—

    (a) an application is made under subsection (4), and

    (b) the prosecutor or a person claiming to have an interest in the object or information applies to be heard by the court,

the court must not make an order granting permission unless the person applying under paragraph (b) has been given an opportunity to be heard.

(7) References in this section to the court are to—

    (a) a magistrates' court, where this Part applies by virtue of section 1(1);

(b) the Crown Court, where this Part applies by virtue of section 1(2).

(8) Nothing in this section affects any other restriction or prohibition on the use or disclosure of an object or information, whether the restriction or prohibition arises under an enactment (whenever passed) or otherwise.

Explanatory text—See paras **2.46–2.50**.

Commencement—On Royal Assent (4 July 1996), but see s 1(5).

Document (subs (1))—See annotations to s 5.

Open Court (subss (3), (4))—In *Denbigh Justices ex parte Williams* [1974] QB 759, Lord Widgery CJ stated as follows, in the context of a submission that a hearing had not been in open court:

> 'The trial should be "public" in the ordinary common-sense acceptation of that term. The doors of the courtroom are expected to be kept open, the public are entitled to be admitted, and the trial is to be public in all respects ... with due regard to the size of the courtroom, the conveniences of the court, the right to exclude objectionable characters and youth of tender years, and to do other things which may facilitate the proper conduct of the trial.'

A trial is conducted in open court even if reporting restrictions under the Contempt of Court Act 1981, s 4 or s 11, or other enactments, are in force.

Acquitted or convicted or the prosecutor has decided not to proceed with the case (subs (5))—See annotations to s 7.

18 Confidentiality: contravention

(1) It is a contempt of court for a person knowingly to use or disclose an object or information recorded in it if the use or disclosure is in contravention of section 17.

(2) The following courts have jurisdiction to deal with a person who is guilty of a contempt under this section—

(a) a magistrates' court, where this Part applies by virtue of section 1(1);
(b) the Crown Court, where this Part applies by virtue of section 1(2).

(3) A person who is guilty of a contempt under this section may be dealt with as follows—

(a) a magistrates' court may commit him to custody for a specified period not exceeding six months or impose on him a fine not exceeding £5,000 or both;
(b) the Crown Court may commit him to custody for a specified period not exceeding two years or impose a fine on him or both.

(4) If—

(a) a person is guilty of a contempt under this section, and
(b) the object concerned is in his possession,

the court finding him guilty may order that the object shall be forfeited and dealt with in such manner as the court may order.

(5) The power of the court under subsection (4) includes power to order the object to be destroyed or to be given to the prosecutor or to be placed in his custody for such period as the court may specify.

(6) If—

(a) the court proposes to make an order under subsection (4), and
(b) the person found guilty, or any other person claiming to have an interest in the object, applies to be heard by the court,

the court must not make the order unless the applicant has been given an opportunity to be heard.

(7) If—

(a) a person is guilty of a contempt under this section, and
(b) a copy of the object concerned is in his possession,

the court finding him guilty may order that the copy shall be forfeited and dealt with in such manner as the court may order.

(8) Subsections (5) and (6) apply for the purposes of subsection (7) as they apply for the purposes of subsection (4), but as if references to the object were references to the copy.

(9) An object or information shall be inadmissible as evidence in civil proceedings if to adduce it would in the opinion of the court be likely to constitute a contempt under this section; and "the court" here means the court before which the civil proceedings are being taken.

(10) The powers of a magistrates' court under this section may be exercised either of the court's own motion or by order on complaint.

Explanatory text—See para **2.51**.

Commencement—On Royal Assent (4 July 1996), but see s 1(5).

Knowingly (subs (1))—'Knowing' does not limit the mens rea to actual knowledge since it also includes 'wilful blindness'. In *Ross v Moss* [1965] 2 QB 396, [1965] 3 All ER 145 (DC), Lord Parker CJ had this to say about the adverbial form of the word:

'[It] covers the case of shutting one's eyes to what is going on, and still more, covers the case where one intends what occurs to go on, but deliberately looks the other way.'

See also *Roper v Taylor's Central Garages (Exeter) Ltd* [1951] 2 TLR 284 (DC); *Vane v Yiannopoullos* [1965] AC 486 at 505 and 509, [1964] 3 All ER 820 (HL); *Westminster City Council v Croyalgrange Ltd* [1986] 2 All ER 353, [1986] 1 WLR 674 (HL).

Possession (subs (7))—See annotations to s 3.

Other provisions

19 Rules of court

(1) Without prejudice to the generality of subsection (1) of—

(a) section 144 of the Magistrates' Courts Act 1980 (magistrates' court rules), and
(b) section 84 of the Supreme Court Act 1981 (rules of court),

the power to make rules under each of those sections includes power to make provision mentioned in subsection (2).

(2) The provision is provision as to the practice and procedure to be followed in relation to—

(a) proceedings to deal with a contempt of court under section 18;
(b) an application under section 3(6), 7(5), 8(2) or (5), 9(8), 14(2), 15(4), 16(b), 17(4) or (6)(b) or 18(6);
(c) an application under regulations made under section 12;
(d) an order under section 3(6), 7(5), 8(2) or (5), 9(8), 14(3), 17(4) or 18(4) or (7);
(e) an order under section 15(5) (whether or not an application is made under section 15(4));
(f) an order under regulations made under section 12.

(3) Rules made under section 144 of the Magistrates' Courts Act 1980 by virtue of subsection (2)(a) above may contain or include provision equivalent to Schedule 3 to

the Contempt of Court Act 1981 (proceedings for disobeying magistrates' court order) with any modifications which the Lord Chancellor considers appropriate on the advice of or after consultation with the rule committee for magistrates' courts.

(4) Rules made by virtue of subsection (2)(b) in relation to an application under section 17(4) may include provision—

(a) that an application to a magistrates' court must be made to a particular magistrates' court;
(b) that an application to the Crown Court must be made to the Crown Court sitting at a particular place;
(c) requiring persons to be notified of an application.

(5) Rules made by virtue of this section may make different provision for different cases or classes of case.

Explanatory text—See para **2.50**.

Commencement—On Royal Assent (4 July 1996), but see s 1(5).

Section 144 of the Magistrates' Courts Act 1980 (subss (1) and (3))—The Magistrates' Courts Act 1980, s 144, empowers the Lord Chancellor, on the advice of or after consultation with the rule committee, to make rules for regulating and prescribing the procedure and practice to be followed in magistrates' courts and by justices' clerks.

The Criminal Justice Act 1977, s 48, extends this by empowering the making of rules governing the provision by the prosecutor to the accused of information about the prosecution case. The Magistrates' Courts (Advance Information) Rules 1985 (SI 1985/601), which govern the making of advance disclosure in proceedings against any person for an either way offence (as to which, see annotations to s 1) were made under these provisions. As to the 1985 Advance Disclosure Rules, see para **2.18**.

Section 13 of the new Act refers to the Magistrates' Courts Act 1980, s 144(1), but not to the Criminal Justice Act 1977, s 48.

Section 84 of the Supreme Court Act 1981 (subs (1))—Section 84 confers power for rules of court to be made for the purpose of regulating and prescribing the practice and procedure to be followed in the Supreme Court. Such rules are made by the Supreme Court Rule Committee (defined by 1981 Act, s 85) and Crown Court Rule Committee (defined by 1981 Act, s 86).

Schedule 3 to the Contempt of Court Act 1981 (subs (3))—Schedule 3 to the 1981 Act provides that where proceedings are taken of the court's own motion, certain provisions of the Act shall apply as if a complaint had been made against the person against whom the proceedings are taken. The relevant provisions are the Magistrates' Courts Act 1980, s 51 (issue of summons), s 53(1) and (2) (procedure on hearing), s 54 (adjournment), s 55 (summons to witness), s 101 (onus of proving exceptions), s 121(1) and (3)(a) (constitution and place of sitting of court), s 123 (defect in process).

20 Other statutory rules as to disclosure

(1) A duty under any of the disclosure provisions shall not affect or be affected by any duty arising under any other enactment with regard to material to be provided to or by the accused or a person representing him; but this is subject to subsection (2).

(2) In making an order under section 9 of the Criminal Justice Act 1987 or section 31 of this Act (preparatory hearings) the judge may take account of anything which—

(a) has been done,
(b) has been required to be done, or
(c) will be required to be done,

in pursuance of any of the disclosure provisions.

(3) Without prejudice to the generality of section 144(1) of the Magistrates' Courts Act 1980 (magistrates' court rules) the power to make rules under that section includes power to make, with regard to any proceedings before a magistrates' court which relate to an alleged offence, provision for—

- (a) requiring any party to the proceedings to disclose to the other party or parties any expert evidence which he proposes to adduce in the proceedings;
- (b) prohibiting a party who fails to comply in respect of any evidence with any requirement imposed by virtue of paragraph (a) from adducing that evidence without the leave of the court.

(4) Rules made by virtue of subsection (3)—

- (a) may specify the kinds of expert evidence to which they apply;
- (b) may exempt facts or matters of any description specified in the rules.

(5) For the purposes of this section—

- (a) the disclosure provisions are sections 3 to 9;
- (b) "enactment" includes an enactment comprised in subordinate legislation (which here has the same meaning as in the Interpretation Act 1978).

Explanatory text—See para **2.18**.

Commencement—On Royal Assent (4 July 1996), but see s 1(5).

Duty arising under any other enactment (subs (1))—For the pre-existing position under other statutory provisions, see paras **2.18–2.19**.

Order (subs (2))—The order must be made by statutory instrument; see s 77(1)–(4).

Section 9 of the Criminal Justice Act 1987 (subs (2))—See para **2.18**.

Section 144(1) of the Magistrates' Courts Act 1980 (subs (3))—See annotations to s 19.

Expert evidence (subss (3) and (4))—PACE, s 81, authorises the making of rules regarding the disclosure of expert evidence. The Crown Court (Advance Disclosure of Expert Evidence) Rules 1987 (SI 1987/716) apply to trials on indictment. The party who is seeking to rely on expert evidence whether of fact or opinion, must furnish to the other party a statement in writing of any finding or opinion on which he proposes to rely, and, on request in writing, provide a copy of (or access to, if that is more practicable) the record of any observation, test, calculation, or other procedure in respect of which the finding or opinion is based. A failure to disclose means that the evidence cannot be adduced without the leave of the court.

Subordinate legislation (subs (5))—By virtue of the Interpretation Act 1978, s 2, 'subordinate legislation' means Orders in Council, orders, rules, regulations, schemes, warrants, byelaws and other instruments made or to be made under any Act'.

21 Common law rules as to disclosure

(1) Where this Part applies as regards things falling to be done after the relevant time in relation to an alleged offence, the rules of common law which—

- (a) were effective immediately before the appointed day, and
- (b) relate to the disclosure of material by the prosecutor,

do not apply as regards things falling to be done after that time in relation to the alleged offence.

(2) Subsection (1) does not affect the rules of common law as to whether disclosure is in the public interest.

(3) References in subsection (1) to the relevant time are to the time when—

   (a) the accused pleads not guilty (where this Part applies by virtue of section 1(1)),

   (b) the accused is committed for trial (where this Part applies by virtue of section 1(2)(a)),

   (c) the proceedings are transferred (where this Part applies by virtue of section 1(2)(b) or (c)),

   (d) the count is included in the indictment (where this Part applies by virtue of section 1(2)(d)), or

   (e) the bill of indictment is preferred (where this Part applies by virtue of section 1(2)(e)).

(4) The reference in subsection (1) to the appointed day is to the day appointed under section 1(5).

Explanatory text—See para **2.9**.

Commencement—On Royal Assent (4 July 1996), but see s 1(5).

Rules of common law (subss (1) and (2))—See paras **2.23–2.25**.

Prosecutor (subs (1))—See annotations to s 2.

Public interest (subs (2))—See paras **3.55–3.65**.

Appointed day (subss (1) and (5))—See annotations to s 1.

PART II
CRIMINAL INVESTIGATIONS

22 Introduction

(1) For the purposes of this Part a criminal investigation is an investigation conducted by police officers with a view to it being ascertained—

   (a) whether a person should be charged with an offence, or

   (b) whether a person charged with an offence is guilty of it.

(2) In this Part references to material are to material of all kinds, and in particular include references to—

   (a) information, and

   (b) objects of all descriptions.

(3) In this Part references to recording information are to putting it in a durable or retrievable form (such as writing or tape).

Explanatory text—See para **3.2**.

Commencement—On Royal Assent (4 July 1996), but see s 25(2).

Police officers (subs (1))—See annotations to s 1.

Writing (subs (3))—See annotations to s 2.

Tape (s 22(3))—See annotations to s 2.

23 Code of practice

(1) The Secretary of State shall prepare a code of practice containing provisions designed to secure—

   (a) that where a criminal investigation is conducted all reasonable steps are taken for the purposes of the investigation and, in particular, all reasonable lines of inquiry are pursued;

(b) that information which is obtained in the course of a criminal investigation and may be relevant to the investigation is recorded;

(c) that any record of such information is retained;

(d) that any other material which is obtained in the course of a criminal investigation and may be relevant to the investigation is retained;

(e) that information falling within paragraph (b) and material falling within paragraph (d) is revealed to a person who is involved in the prosecution of criminal proceedings arising out of or relating to the investigation and who is identified in accordance with prescribed provisions;

(f) that where such a person inspects information or other material in pursuance of a requirement that it be revealed to him, and he requests that it be disclosed to the accused, the accused is allowed to inspect it or is given a copy of it;

(g) that where such a person is given a document indicating the nature of information or other material in pursuance of a requirement that it be revealed to him, and he requests that it be disclosed to the accused, the accused is allowed to inspect it or is given a copy of it;

(h) that the person who is to allow the accused to inspect information or other material or to give him a copy of it shall decide which of those (inspecting or giving a copy) is appropriate;

(i) that where the accused is allowed to inspect material as mentioned in paragraph (f) or (g) and he requests a copy, he is given one unless the person allowing the inspection is of opinion that it is not practicable or not desirable to give him one;

(j) that a person mentioned in paragraph (e) is given a written statement that prescribed activities which the code requires have been carried out.

(2) The code may include provision—

(a) that a police officer identified in accordance with prescribed provisions must carry out a prescribed activity which the code requires;

(b) that a police officer so identified must take steps to secure the carrying out by a person (whether or not a police officer) of a prescribed activity which the code requires;

(c) that a duty must be discharged by different people in succession in prescribed circumstances (as where a person dies or retires).

(3) The code may include provision about the form in which information is to be recorded.

(4) The code may include provision about the manner in which and the period for which—

(a) a record of information is to be retained, and

(b) any other material is to be retained;

and if a person is charged with an offence the period may extend beyond a conviction or an acquittal.

(5) The code may include provision about the time when, the form in which, the way in which, and the extent to which, information or any other material is to be revealed to the person mentioned in subsection (1)(e).

(6) The code must be so framed that it does not apply to material intercepted in obedience to a warrant issued under section 2 of the Interception of Communications Act 1985.

(7) The code may—

(a) make different provision in relation to different cases or descriptions of case;

(b) contain exceptions as regards prescribed cases or descriptions of case.

(8) In this section "prescribed" means prescribed by the code.

Explanatory text—See para **3.4**.

Commencement—On Royal Assent (4 July 1996), but see s 25(2).

Recorded/record (subss (1),(3) and (4))—The term 'record' envisages might be regarded as requiring not only the reduction of information into a permanent form (see Geoffrey Lane LJ in *Jones* [1978] 1 WLR 195), but its incorporation into a 'record'. A record (for the purpose of Civil Evidence Act 1968, s 4) was defined by Bingham J in *H v Schering Chemicals* [1983] 1 All ER 849 as a document which 'a historian would recognise as original or primary sources ... documents which either give effect to a transaction itself or which contain a contemporaneous register of information supplied by those with direct knowledge of the facts.'
    See also: *Tirado* (1974) 59 Cr App R 80 (CA).

Material (subss (1) and (4),(6))—See s 22(2).

Criminal investigation (subs (1))—See annotations to s 1.

Police officer (subs (2))—See annotations to s 1.

Conviction or acquittal (subs (4))—See annotations to s 9.

Section 2 of the Interception of Communications Act 1985 (subs (6))—See annotations to s 3.

24 Examples of disclosure provisions

(1) This section gives examples of the kinds of provision that may be included in the code by virtue of section 23(5).

(2) The code may provide that if the person required to reveal material has possession of material which he believes is sensitive he must give a document which—

(a) indicates the nature of that material, and

(b) states that he so believes.

(3) The code may provide that if the person required to reveal material has possession of material which is of a description prescribed under this subsection and which he does not believe is sensitive he must give a document which—

(a) indicates the nature of that material, and

(b) states that he does not so believe.

(4) The code may provide that if—

(a) a document is given in pursuance of provision contained in the code by virtue of subsection (2), and

(b) a person identified in accordance with prescribed provisions asks for any of the material,

the person giving the document must give a copy of the material asked for to the person asking for it or (depending on the circumstances) must allow him to inspect it.

(5) The code may provide that if—

(a) a document is given in pursuance of provision contained in the code by virtue of subsection (3),

(b) all or any of the material is of a description prescribed under this subsection, and

(c) a person is identified in accordance with prescribed provisions as entitled to material of that description,

the person giving the document must give a copy of the material of that description to the person so identified or (depending on the circumstances) must allow him to inspect it.

(6) The code may provide that if—

(a) a document is given in pursuance of provision contained in the code by virtue of subsection (3),
(b) all or any of the material is not of a description prescribed under subsection (5), and
(c) a person identified in accordance with prescribed provisions asks for any of the material not of that description,

the person giving the document must give a copy of the material asked for to the person asking for it or (depending on the circumstances) must allow him to inspect it.

(7) The code may provide that if the person required to reveal material has possession of material which he believes is sensitive and of such a nature that provision contained in the code by virtue of subsection (2) should not apply with regard to it—

(a) that provision shall not apply with regard to the material,
(b) he must notify a person identified in accordance with prescribed provisions of the existence of the material, and
(c) he must allow the person so notified to inspect the material.

(8) For the purposes of this section material is sensitive to the extent that its disclosure under Part I would be contrary to the public interest.

(9) In this section "prescribed" means prescribed by the code.

Explanatory text—See para **3.9**.

Commencement—On Royal Assent (4 July 1996), but see s 25(2).

Material (subss (2),(3),(4) and (5))—See s 22.

Possession (subss (2) and (3))—See annotations to s 3.

Document (subss (5) and (6))—See annotations to s 4.

Public interest (subs (7))—See paras **3.56–3.66**.

25 Operation and revision of code

(1) When the Secretary of State has prepared a code under section 23—

(a) he shall publish it in the form of a draft,
(b) he shall consider any representations made to him about the draft, and
(c) he may modify the draft accordingly.

(2) When the Secretary of State has acted under subsection (1) he shall lay the code before each House of Parliament, and when he has done so he may bring it into operation on such day as he may appoint by order.

(3) A code brought into operation under this section shall apply in relation to suspected or alleged offences into which no criminal investigation has begun before the day so appointed.

(4) The Secretary of State may from time to time revise a code previously brought into operation under this section; and the preceding provisions of this section shall apply to a revised code as they apply to the code as first prepared.

Explanatory text—See para **3.2**.

Commencement—On Royal Assent (4 July 1996), but see subs (2).

Order (subs (2))—The order must be made by statutory instrument, and be subject to the affirmative resolution procedure; see s 77(1)–(4).

Criminal investigation has begun (subs (3))—See annotations to s 1.

26 Effect of code

(1) A person other than a police officer who is charged with the duty of conducting an investigation with a view to it being ascertained—

    (a) whether a person should be charged with an offence, or

    (b) whether a person charged with an offence is guilty of it,

shall in discharging that duty have regard to any relevant provision of a code which would apply if the investigation were conducted by police officers.

(2) A failure—

    (a) by a police officer to comply with any provision of a code for the time being in operation by virtue of an order under section 25, or

    (b) by a person to comply with subsection (1),

shall not in itself render him liable to any criminal or civil proceedings.

(3) In all criminal and civil proceedings a code in operation at any time by virtue of an order under section 25 shall be admissible in evidence.

(4) If it appears to a court or tribunal conducting criminal or civil proceedings that—

    (a) any provision of a code in operation at any time by virtue of an order under section 25, or

    (b) any failure mentioned in subsection (2)(a) or (b),

is relevant to any question arising in the proceedings, the provision or failure shall be taken into account in deciding the question.

Explanatory text—See para **3.18**.

Commencement—On Royal Assent (4 July 1996), but see s 25(2).

Person ... charged with the duty of conducting an investigation (subs (1))—See annotations to s 1.

Police officer (subss (1) and (2))—See annotations to s 1.

Admissible in evidence (subs (2))—This term encompasses not only rulings as to whether in law evidence can be admitted, but also whether it will be permitted to be, and thus includes the exclusionary. For this reason, a preparatory hearing ruling may be made in respect of the discretionary exclusion of evidence, eg under Police and Criminal Evidence Act 1984, s 78. See para **4.21**.

27 Common law rules as to criminal investigations

(1) Where a code prepared under section 23 and brought into operation under section 25 applies in relation to a suspected or alleged offence, the rules of common law which—

    (a) were effective immediately before the appointed day, and

    (b) relate to the matter mentioned in subsection (2),

shall not apply in relation to the suspected or alleged offence.

(2) The matter is the revealing of material—

    (a) by a police officer or other person charged with the duty of conducting an investigation with a view to it being ascertained whether a person should be charged with an offence or whether a person charged with an offence is guilty of it;

    (b) to a person involved in the prosecution of criminal proceedings.

(3) In subsection (1) "the appointed day" means the day appointed under section 25 with regard to the code as first prepared.

Explanatory text—See para **3.15**.

Commencement—On Royal Assent (4 July 1996), but see s 25(2).

Rules of common law (s 27(1))—See paras **2.23–2.25**.

Suspected or alleged offence (subs (1))—See para **3.17**.

Material (subs (2))—See s 22(2).

Police officer or other person charged with the duty of conducting an investigation (subs (2))—See annotations to s 1. There is no apparent significance in the differences between the wording of this provision and that of s 1(4) ('. . . which police officers or other persons have a duty to conduct . . .').

Appointed day (subs (3))—No day had been appointed when this book went to press.

PART III
PREPARATORY HEARINGS

Introduction

28 Introduction

(1) This Part applies in relation to an offence if—

    (a) on or after the appointed day the accused is committed for trial for the offence concerned,

    (b) proceedings for the trial on the charge concerned are transferred to the Crown Court on or after the appointed day, or

    (c) a bill of indictment relating to the offence is preferred on or after the appointed day under the authority of section 2(2)(b) of the Administration of Justice (Miscellaneous Provisions) Act 1933 (bill preferred by direction of Court of appeal, or by direction or with consent of a judge).

(2) References in subsection (1) to the appointed day are to such day as is appointed for the purposes of this section by the Secretary of State by order.

(3) If an order under this section so provides, this Part applies only in relation to the Crown Court sitting at a place or places specified in the order.

(4) References in this Part to the prosecutor are to any person acting as prosecutor, whether an individual or a body.

Explanatory text—See para **4.17**.

Commencement—On Royal Assent (4 July 1996), but see subs (1).

Transferred to the Crown Court (subs (1))—See annotations to s 1.

Appointed day (subss (1) and (2))—No day had been appointed when this book went to press.

Bill of indictment ... under ... section 2(2)(b) of the Administration of Justice (Miscellaneous Provisions) Act 1933 (subs (1))—See annotations to s 1.

Order (subs (2))—The order must be made by statutory instrument; see s 77(1)–(4).

Prosecutor (subs (4))—See annotations to s 2.

Preparatory hearings

29 Power to order preparatory hearing

(1) Where it appears to a judge of the Crown Court that an indictment reveals a case of such complexity, or a case whose trial is likely to be of such length, that substantial benefits are likely to accrue from a hearing—

- (a) before the jury are sworn, and
- (b) for any of the purposes mentioned in subsection (2),

he may order that such hearing (in this Part referred to as a preparatory hearing) shall be held.

(2) The purposes are those of—

- (a) identifying issues which are likely to be material to the verdict of the jury;
- (b) assisting their comprehension of any such issues;
- (c) expediting the proceedings before the jury;
- (d) assisting the judge's management of the trial.

(3) No order may be made under subsection (1) where it appears to a judge of the Crown Court that the evidence on an indictment reveals a case of fraud of such seriousness or complexity as is mentioned in section 7(1) of the Criminal Justice Act 1987 (preparatory hearings in cases of serious or complex fraud).

(4) A judge may make an order under subsection (1)—

- (a) on the application of the prosecutor,
- (b) on the application of the accused or, if there is more than one, any of them, or
- (c) of the judge's own motion.

Explanatory text—See para **4.18**.

Commencement—On Royal Assent (4 July 1996), but see s 28(1).

Case of such seriousness and complexity as is mentioned in section 7(1) of the Criminal Justice Act 1987 (subs (3))—See annotations to s 5.

Prosecutor (subs (4))—See annotations to s 3.

30 Start of trial and arraignment

If a judge orders a preparatory hearing—

- (a) the trial shall start with that hearing, and
- (b) arraignment shall take place at the start of that hearing, unless it has taken place before then.

Explanatory text—See para **4.22**.

Commencement—On Royal Assent (4 July 1996), but see s 28(1).

Trial shall start with that hearing (s 30)—See para **4.22**, and annotation to 'arraignment', below.

Arraignment (s 30)—Arraignment marks the start of a trial on indictment (Supreme Court Act 1981, s 77(3)), although this must be read subject to the terms of CPIA 1996, s 39(3) as well as those of s 30(a) of the 1996 Act. It comprises the putting of the indictment to the accused and the taking of pleas in respect of each count on that indictment. The terms of s 23 are thus consistent with the existing position. Arraignment must occur within the minimum and maximum time periods specified by r 24 of the Crown Court Rules 1982 (SI 1982/1109), and made pursuant to s 77(1) of the 1981 Act. Rule 24 specifies these periods as 14 days and 8 weeks respectively, unless leave for late arraignment is granted. For the changes made by the new Act, see paras **5.27–5.34**.

. It is open to a Divisional Court on judicial review to review the validity of an arraignment: *Maidstone Crown Court ex parte Clark* (1994) *The Times*, 19 December (DC). This is not a matter relating to trial on indictment for the purpose of the Supreme Court Act 1981, s 29(3). This proposition was confirmed in *Maidstone Crown Court ex parte Clark*, even though the court in that case doubted the earlier decision in *Maidstone Crown Court ex parte Hollstein* (1994) *The Times*, 4 November that an arraignment for the sole purpose of foiling the custody time-limits prescribed by the Bail Act 1976 was a sham. See para **5.29**. Even if an arraignment is quashed on judicial review, this would not appear to affect the validity of any preparatory hearing held.

31 The preparatory hearing

(1) At the preparatory hearing the judge may exercise any of the powers specified in this section.

(2) The judge may adjourn a preparatory hearing from time to time.

(3) He may make a ruling as to—

    (a) any question as to the admissibility of evidence;
    (b) any other question of law relating to the case.

(4) He may order the prosecutor—

    (a) to give the court and the accused or, if there is more than one, each of them a written statement (a case statement) of the matters falling within subsection (5);
    (b) to prepare the prosecution evidence and any explanatory material in such a form as appears to the judge to be likely to aid comprehension by the jury and to give it in that form to the court and to the accused or, if there is more than one, to each of them;
    (c) to give the court and the accused or, if there is more than one, each of them written notice of documents the truth of the contents of which ought in the prosecutor's view to be admitted and of any other matters which in his view ought to be agreed;
    (d) to make any amendments of any case statement given in pursuance of an order under paragraph (a) that appear to the judge to be appropriate, having regard to objections made by the accused or, if there is more than one, by any of them.

(5) The matters referred to in subsection (4)(a) are—

    (a) the principal facts of the case for the prosecution;
    (b) the witnesses who will speak to those facts;
    (c) any exhibits relevant to those facts;
    (d) any proposition of law on which the prosecutor proposes to rely;
    (e) the consequences in relation to any of the counts in the indictment that appear to the prosecutor to flow from the matters falling within paragraphs (a) to (d).

(6) Where a judge has ordered the prosecutor to give a case statement and the prosecutor has complied with the order, the judge may order the accused or, if there is more than one, each of them—

(a) to give the court and the prosecutor a written statement setting out in general terms the nature of his defence and indicating the principal matters on which he takes issue with the prosecution;

(b) to give the court and the prosecutor written notice of any objections that he has to the case statement;

(c) to give the court and the prosecutor written notice of any point of law (including any point as to the admissibility of evidence) which he wishes to take, and any authority on which he intends to rely for that purpose.

(7) Where a judge has ordered the prosecutor to give notice under subsection (4)(c) and the prosecutor has complied with the order, the judge may order the accused or, if there is more than one, each of them to give the court and the prosecutor a written notice stating—

(a) the extent to which he agrees with the prosecutor as to documents and other matters to which the notice under subsection (4)(c) relates, and

(b) the reason for any disagreement.

(8) a judge making an order under subsection (6) or (7) shall warn the accused or, if there is more than one, each of them of the possible consequence under section 34 of not complying with it.

(9) If it appears to a judge that reasons given in pursuance of subsection (7) are inadequate, he shall inform the person giving them and may require him to give further or better reasons.

(10) An order under this section may specify the time within which any specified requirement contained in it is to be complied with.

(11) An order or ruling made under this section shall have effect throughout the trial, unless it appears to the judge on application made to him that the interests of justice require him to vary or discharge it.

Explanatory text—See para **4.23**.

Commencement—On Royal Assent (4 July 1996), but see s 28(1).

Admissible in evidence (s 25(3),(6))—See annotations to s 26.

Question of law (s 25(3))—Ie Any matter which is decided by the tribunal of law, and from which decision an appeal may lie. It probably does not extend to rulings as to procedure. See, generally, paras **4.19–4.20**.

Prosecutor (subss (4),(5),(6) and (7))—See annotations to s 2.

Documents (subss (4) and (7))—See annotations to s 4.

The truth of the contents ... ought ... to be admitted ... and ... ought to be agreed (sub (4))—By CJA 1967, s 10, any fact of which oral evidence may be given in any criminal proceedings may be admitted for the purpose of those proceedings by or on behalf of the prosecutor or defendant, and the admission by any party of any such fact under s 10 shall as against that party be conclusive evidence in those proceedings of the fact admitted. Such an admission may be made before or at the proceedings, but if made otherwise than in court shall be made in writing. If made by an individual, they must be approved by his solicitor or counsel, and, if made on his behalf, made by solicitor or counsel. By s 10(4), an admission may be withdrawn with the leave of the court in any criminal proceedings relating to the same matter.

Written (subss (4),(6) and (7)—See annotations to s 2.

32 Orders before preparatory hearing

(1) This section applies where—

- (a) a judge orders a preparatory hearing, and
- (b) he decides that any order which could be made under section 31(4) to (7) at the hearing should be made before the hearing.

(2) In such a case—

- (a) he may make any such order before the hearing (or at the hearing), and
- (b) section 31(4) to (11) shall apply accordingly.

Explanatory text—See para **4.22**.

Commencement—On Royal Assent (4 July 1996), but see s 28(1).

33 Crown Court Rules

(1) Crown Court Rules may provide that except to the extent that disclosure is required—

- (a) by rules under section 81 of the Police and Criminal Evidence Act 1984 (expert evidence), or
- (b) by section 5(7) of this Act,

anything required to be given by an accused in pursuance of a requirement imposed under section 31 need not disclose who will give evidence.

(2) Crown Court Rules may make provision as to the minimum or maximum time that may be specified under section 31(10).

Explanatory text—See para **4.29**.

Commencement—On Royal Assent (4 July 1996), but see s 28(1).

Section 81 of the Police and Criminal Evidence Act 1984 (s 33(1))—See annotations to s 20.

34 Later stages of trial

(1) Any party may depart from the case he disclosed in pursuance of a requirement imposed under section 31.

(2) Where

- (a) a party departs from the case he disclosed in pursuance of a requirement imposed under section 31, or
- (b) a party fails to comply with such a requirement,

the judge or, with the leave of the judge, any other party may make such comment as appears to the judge or the other party (as the case may be) to be appropriate and the jury may draw such inference as appears proper.

(3) In deciding whether to give leave the judge shall have regard—

- (a) to the extent of the departure or failure, and
- (b) to whether there is any justification for it.

(4) Except as provided by this section no part—

- (a) of a statement given under section 31(6)(a), or
- (b) of any other information relating to the case for the accused or, if there is more than one, the case for any of them, which was given in pursuance of a requirement imposed under section 31,

may be disclosed at a stage in the trial after the jury have been sworn without the consent of the accused concerned.

Explanatory text—See para **4.28**.

Commencement—On Royal Assent (4 July 1996), but see s 28(1).

Such inference as appears proper (subs (1))—See annotations to s 11.

Appeals

35 Appeals to Court of Appeal

(1) An appeal shall lie to the Court of Appeal from any ruling of a judge under section 31(3), but only with the leave of the judsge or of the Court of Appeal.

(2) The judge may continue a preparatory hearing notwithstanding that leave to appeal has been granted under subsection (1), but no jury shall be sworn until after the appeal has been determined or abandoned.

(3) On the termination of the hearing of an appeal, the Court of Appeal may confirm, reverse or vary the decision appealed against.

(4) Subject to rules of court made under section 53(1) of the Supreme Court Act 1981 (power by rules to distribute business of Court of Appeal between its civil and criminal divisions)—

  (a) the jurisdiction of the Court of Appeal under subsection (1) above shall be exercised by the criminal division of the court;
  (b) references in this Part to the Court of Appeal shall be construed as references to that division.

Explanatory text—See para **4.30**.

Commencement—On Royal Assent (4 July 1996), but see s 28(1).

36 Appeals to House of Lords

(1) In the Criminal Appeal Act 1968, in—

  (a) section 33(1) (right of appeal to House of Lords), and
  (b) section 36 (bail),

after "1987" there shall be inserted "or section 35 of the Criminal Procedure and Investigations Act 1996".

(2) The judge may continue a preparatory hearing notwithstanding that leave to appeal has been granted under Part II of the Criminal Appeal Act 1968, but no jury shall be sworn until after the appeal has been determined or abandoned.

Explanatory text—See para **4.30**.

Commencement—On Royal Assent (4 July 1996), but see s 28(1).

Criminal Appeal Act 1968, section 33(1) (subs (1))—Section 33 permits an appeal to the House of Lords from the Court of Appeal following a decision of that court under Part I of the 1968 Act, or from the Criminal Justice Act 1987, s 7, preparatory hearing, or from a ruling in preparatory proceedings held under s 31 of the new Act.

Criminal Appeal Act 1968, section 36 (subs (1))—This provision is supplementary to s 33, and permits the Court of Appeal to grant bail pending determination of an appeal by the House of Lords.

Leave … under Part II of the Criminal Appeal Act 1968 (subs (2))—Part II of the 1968 Act deals with appeals from the Court of Appeal to the House of Lords. Section 33 of the 1968 Act provides that leave must be sought and granted by either the Court of Appeal or House of Lords; leave shall not be granted unless it is certified by the Court of Appeal that a point of law of general public importance is involved in the decision and it appears to the Court of Appeal or House of Lords (as the case may be) that the point is one that ought to be considered by the House of Lords.

Reporting restrictions

37 Restrictions on reporting

(1) Except as provided by this section—

    (a) no written report of proceedings falling within subsection (2) shall be published in Great Britain;

    (b) no report of proceedings falling within subsection (2) shall be included in a relevant programme for reception in Great Britain.

(2) The following proceedings fall within this subsection—

    (a) a preparatory hearing;

    (b) an application for leave to appeal in relation to such a hearing;

    (c) an appeal in relation to such a hearing.

(3) The judge dealing with a preparatory hearing may order that subsection (1) shall not apply, or shall not apply to a specified extent, to a report of—

    (a) the preparatory hearing, or

    (b) an application to the judge for leave to appeal to the Court of Appeal under section 35(1) in relation to the preparatory hearing.

(4) The Court of Appeal may order that subsection (1) shall not apply, or shall not apply to a specified extent, to a report of—

    (a) an appeal to the Court of Appeal under section 35(1) in relation to a preparatory hearing,

    (b) an application to that Court for leave to appeal to it under section 35(1) in relation to a preparatory hearing, or

    (c) an application to that Court for leave to appeal to the House of Lords under Part II of the Criminal Appeal Act 1968 in relation to a preparatory hearing.

(5) The House of Lords may order that subsection (1) shall not apply, or shall not apply to a specified extent, to a report of—

    (a) an appeal to that House under Part II of the Criminal Appeal Act 1968 in relation to a preparatory hearing, or

    (b) an application to that House for leave to appeal to it under Part II of the Criminal Appeal Act 1968 in relation to a preparatory hearing.

(6) Where there is only one accused and he objects to the making of an order under subsection (3), (4) or (5) the judge or the Court of Appeal or the House of Lords shall make the order if (and only if) satisfied after hearing the representations of the accused that it is in the interests of justice to do so; and if the order is made it shall not apply to the extent that a report deals with any such objection or representations.

(7) Where there are two or more accused and one or more of them objects to the making of an order under subsection (3), (4) or (5) the judge or the Court of Appeal or the House of Lords shall make the order if (and only if) satisfied after hearing the representations of each of the accused that it is in the interests of justice to do so; and if

the order is made it shall not apply to the extent that a report deals with any such objection or representations.

(8) Subsection (1) does not apply to—

    (a) the publication of a report of a preparatory hearing,

    (b) the publication of a report of an appeal in relation to a preparatory hearing or of an application for leave to appeal in relation to such a hearing,

    (c) the inclusion in a relevant programme of a report of a preparatory hearing, or

    (d) the inclusion in a relevant programme of a report of an appeal in relation to a preparatory hearing or of an application for leave to appeal in relation to such a hearing,

at the conclusion of the trial of the accused or of the last of the accused to be tried.

(9) Subsection (1) does not apply to a report which contains only one or more of the following matters—

    (a) the identity of the court and the name of the judge;

    (b) the names, ages, home addresses and occupations of the accused and witnesses;

    (c) the offence or offences, or a summary of them, with which the accused is or are charged;

    (d) the names of counsel and solicitors in the proceedings;

    (e) where the proceedings are adjourned, the date and place to which they are adjourned;

    (f) any arrangements as to bail;

    (g) whether legal aid was granted to the accused or any of the accused.

(10) The addresses that may be published or included in a relevant programme under subsection (9) are addresses—

    (a) at any relevant time, and

    (b) at the time of their publication or inclusion in a relevant programme;

and "relevant time" here means a time when events giving rise to the charges to which the proceedings relate occurred.

(11) Nothing in this section affects any prohibition or restriction imposed by virtue of any other enactment on a publication or on matter included in a programme.

(12) In this section—

    (a) "publish", in relation to a report, means publish the report, either by itself or as part of a newspaper or periodical, for distribution to the public;

    (b) expressions cognate with "publish" shall be construed accordingly;

    (c) "relevant programme" means a programme included in a programme service, within the meaning of the Broadcasting Act 1990.

Explanatory text—See para **4.31**.

Commencement—On Royal Assent (4 July 1996), but see s 28(1).

Great Britain (subs (1))—See general annotations.

Relevant programme/programme service, within the meaning of the Broadcasting Act 1990 (subss (1),(8) and (12))—See general annotations.

Part II of the Criminal Appeal Act 1968 (subss (4) and (5))—See annotations to s 36.

Section 37(11)—See para **4.31**.

Publish/publications (subss (8), (9), (10), (11) and (12))—See the terms of subs (12). No further definition is provided.

38 Offences in connection with reporting

(1) If a report is published or included in a relevant programme in contravention of section 37 each of the following persons is guilty of an offence—

    (a) in the case of a publication of a written report as part of a newspaper or periodical, any proprietor, editor or publisher of the newspaper or periodical;

    (b) in the case of a publication of a written report otherwise than as part of a newspaper or periodical, the person who publishes it;

    (c) in the case of the inclusion of a report in a relevant programme, any body corporate which is engaged in providing the service in which the programme is included and any person having functions in relation to the programme corresponding to those of an editor of a newspaper.

(2) A person guilty of an offence under this section is liable on summary conviction to a fine of an amount not exceeding level 5 on the standard scale.

(3) Proceedings for an offence under this section shall not be instituted in England and Wales otherwise than by or with the consent of the Attorney General.

(4) Subsection (12) of section 37 applies for the purposes of this section as it applies for the purposes of that.

Explanatory text—See para **4.32**.

Commencement—On Royal Assent (4 July 1996), but see s 28(1).

Publish/publication (subs (1))—See annotations to s 37.

Person (subs (1))—By s 5 of and Sch 1 to the Interpretation Act 1978, 'person' includes a body corporate unless the contrary intention appears. Section 43(4) makes it clear that there is no contrary intention, and the structure of s 43(1) is such as to indicate that a body corporate, like a human being falling within the description there, can be convicted of an offence without the need to have recourse to principles of vicarious liability or the identification principle of corporate criminal liability.

    By s 6 of the Interpretation Act 1978, 'persons' include 'person', and vice versa (unless there is a contrary indication which there is clearly not here).

Level 5 on the Standard scale (subs (2))—See general annotations.

PART IV
RULINGS

39 Meaning of pre-trial hearing

(1) For the purposes of this Part a hearing is a pre-trial hearing if it relates to a trial on indictment and it takes place—

    (a) after the accused has been committed for trial for the offence concerned or after the proceedings for the trial have been transferred to the Crown Court, and

    (b) before the start of the trial.

(2) For the purposes of this Part a hearing is also a pre-trial hearing if—

    (a) it relates to a trial on indictment to be held in pursuance of a bill of indictment preferred under the authority of section 2(2)(b) of the Administration of Justice (Miscellaneous Provisions) Act 1933 (bill preferred by direction of Court of Appeal, or by direction or with consent of a judge), and

   (b) it takes place after the bill of indictment has been preferred and before the start of the trial.

(3) For the purposes of this section the start of a trial on indictment occurs when a jury is sworn to consider the issue of guilt or fitness to plead or, if the court accepts a plea of guilty before a jury is sworn, when that plea is accepted; but this is subject to section 8 of the Criminal Justice Act 1987 and section 30 of this Act (preparatory hearings).

Explanatory text—See para **4.7**.

Commencement—On Royal Assent (4 July 1996), but see s 43(1).

Trial on indictment (subs (1))—See annotations to s 1.

Trial on indictment ... in pursuance of bill of indictment ... under ... section 2(2)(b) of the Administration of Justice (Miscellaneous Provisions) Act 1933 (subs (2))—See annotations to s 1.

Section 8 of the Criminal Justice Act 1987 (subs (1))—By virtue of the Criminal Justice Act 1987, s 7(1), a judge in case to which the provision applies (as to which, see annotations to s 5) considers that substantial benefits are likely to accrue from a preparatory hearing under the 1987 Act, he may so order. Section 8 of the 1987 Act provides that the trial is deemed to begin with the preparatory hearing, with the accused being arraigned at the commencement thereof. For preparatory hearings generally, see paras **4.16–4.32**.

40 Power to make rulings

(1) A judge may make at a pre-trial hearing a ruling as to—

   (a) any question as to the admissibility of evidence;
   (b) any other question of law relating to the case concerned.

(2) A ruling may be made under this section—

   (a) on an application by a party to the case, or
   (b) of the judge's own motion.

(3) Subject to subsection (4), a ruling made under this section has binding effect from the time it is made until the case against the accused or, if there is more than one, against each of them is disposed of; and the case against an accused is disposed of if—

   (a) he is acquitted or convicted, or
   (b) the prosecutor decides not to proceed with the case against him.

(4) A judge may discharge or vary (or further vary) a ruling made under this section if it appears to him that it is in the interests of justice to do so; and a judge may act under this subsection—

   (a) on an application by a party to the case, or
   (b) of the judge's own motion.

(5) No application may be made under subsection (4)(a) unless there has been a material change of circumstances since the ruling was made or, if a previous application has been made, since the application (or last application) was made.

(6) The judge referred to in subsection (4) need not be the judge who made the ruling or, if it has been varied, the judge (or any of the judges) who varied it.

(7) For the purposes of this section the prosecutor is any person acting as prosecutor, whether an individual or a body.

Explanatory text—See para **4.6**.

Commencement—On Royal Assent (4 July 1996), but see s 43(1).

Admissibility of evidence (subs (1))—See annotations to s 26.

Acquitted/convicted/decision not to proceed (subs (2))—See annotations to s 9.

Person (subs (7))—See annotations to s 38.

41 Restrictions on reporting

(1) Except as provided by this section—

- (a) no written report of matters falling within subsection (2) shall be published in Great Britain;
- (b) no report of matters falling within subsection (2) shall be included in a relevant programme for reception in Great Britain.

(2) The following matters fall within this subsection—

- (a) a ruling made under section 40;
- (b) proceedings on an application for a ruling to be made under section 40;
- (c) an order that a ruling made under section 40 be discharged or varied or further varied;
- (d) proceedings on an application for a ruling made under section 40 to be discharged or varied or further varied.

(3) The judge dealing with any matter falling within subsection (2) may order that subsection (1) shall not apply, or shall not apply to a specified extent, to a report of the matter.

(4) Where there is only one accused and he objects to the making of an order under subsection (3) the judge shall make the order if (and only if) satisfied after hearing the representations of the accused that it is in the interests of justice to do so; and if the order is made it shall not apply to the extent that a report deals with any such objection or representations.

(5) Where there are two or more accused and one or more of them objects to the making of an order under subsection (3) the judge shall make the order if (and only if) satisfied after hearing the representations of each of the accused that it is in the interests of justice to do so; and if the order is made it shall not only apply to the extent that a report deals with any such objection or representations.

(6) Subsection (1) does not apply to—

- (a) the publication of a report of matters, or
- (b) the inclusion in a relevant programme of a report of matters,

at the conclusion of the trial of the accused or of the last of the accused to be tried.

(7) Nothing in this section affects any prohibition or restriction imposed by virtue of any other enactment on a publication or on matter included in a programme.

(8) In this section—

- (a) "publish", in relation to a report, means publish the report, either by itself or as part of a newspaper or periodical, for distribution to the public;
- (b) expressions cognate with "publish" shall be construed accordingly;
- (c) "relevant programme" means a programme included in a programme service, within the meaning of the Broadcasting Act 1990.

Explanatory text—See para **4.14**.

Commencement—On Royal Assent (4 July 1996), but see s 43(1).

Great Britain (subs (1))—See general annotations.

Programme service (subs (1))—See general annotations.

Publish (subss (1), (6) and (8))—See annotations to s 37.

42 Offences in connection with reporting

(1) If a report is published or included in a relevant programme in contravention of section 41 each of the following persons is guilty of an offence—

   (a) in the case of a publication of a written report as part of a newspaper or periodical, any proprietor, editor or publisher of the newspaper or periodical;
   (b) in the case of a publication of a written report otherwise than as part of a newspaper or periodical, the person who publishes it;
   (c) in the case of the inclusion of a report in a relevant programme, any body corporate which is engaged in providing the service in which the programme is included and any person having functions in relation to the programme corresponding to those of an editor of a newspaper.

(2) A person guilty of an offence under this section is liable on summary conviction to a fine of an amount not exceeding level 5 on the standard scale.

(3) Proceedings for an offence under this section shall not be instituted in England and Wales otherwise than by or with the consent of the Attorney General.

(4) Subsection (8) of section 41 applies for the purposes of this section as it applies for the purposes of that.

Explanatory text—See para **4.16**.

Commencement—On Royal Assent (4 July 1996), but see s 43(1).

Relevant programme (subs (1)); Standard scale (subs (2))—See general annotations.

Person/persons (subs (1))—See annotations to s 37.

Written/writing (subs (1))—See annotations to s 2.

England and Wales (subs (3))—See general annotations.

43 Application of this Part

(1) This Part applies in relation to pre-trial hearings beginning on or after the appointed day.

(2) The reference in subsection (1) to the appointed day is to such day as is appointed for the purposes of this section by the Secretary of State by order.

Explanatory text—See para **4.6**.

Commencement—On Royal Assent (4 July 1996), but see subs (1).

Appointed day (subss (1) and (2))—No day had been appointed when this book went to press.

Order (subs (2))—The order must be made by statutory instrument; see s 77(1)–(4).

PART V
COMMITTAL, TRANSFER, ETC.

44 Reinstatement of certain provisions

(1) The Criminal Justice and Public Order Act 1994 shall be amended as follows.

(2) Section 44 and Schedule 4 (which provide for transfer for trial instead of committal proceedings) shall be omitted.

(3) In each of sections 34, 36 and 37 for paragraph (a) of subsection (2) (magistrates' court proceeding with a view to transfer) there shall be substituted—

"(a) a magistrates' court inquiring into the offence as examining justices;".

(4) Sections 34(7), 36(8) and 37(7) (transitional) shall be omitted.

(5) In Schedule 11 (repeals) the entries relating to the following (which concern committal, transfer and other matters) shall be omitted—

(a) sections 13(3) and 49(2) of the Criminal Justice Act 1925;
(b) section 1 of the Criminal Procedure (Attendance of Witnesses) Act 1965;
(c) section 7 of the Criminal Justice Act 1967 and in section 36(1) of that Act the definition of "committal proceedings";
(d) in paragraph 1 of Schedule 2 to the Criminal Appeal Act 1968 the words from "section 13(3)" to "but";
(e) in section 46(1) of the Criminal Justice Act 1972 the words "Section 102 of the Magistrates' Courts Act 1980 and", "which respectively allow", "committal proceedings and in other", "and section 106 of the said Act of 1980", "which punish the making of", "102 or" and ", as the case may be", and section 46(2) of that Act;
(f) in section 32(1)(b) of the Powers of Criminal Courts Act 1973 the words "tried or";
(g) in Schedule 1 to the Interpretation Act 1978, paragraph (a) of the definition of "Committed for trial";
(h) in section 97(1) of the Magistrates' Courts Act 1980 the words from "at an inquiry" to "be) or", sections 102, 103, 105, 106 and 145(1)(e) of that Act, in section 150(1) of that Act the definition of "committal proceedings", and paragraph 2 of Schedule 5 to that Act;
(i) in section 2(2)(g) of the Criminal Attempts Act 1981 the words "or committed for trial";
(j) in section 1(2) of the Criminal Justice Act 1982 the words "trial or";
(k) paragraphs 10 and 11 of Schedule 2 to the Criminal Justice Act 1987;
(l) in section 20(4)(a) of the Legal Aid Act 1988 the words "trial or", and section 20(4)(bb) and (5) of that Act;
(m) in section 1(4) of the War Crimes Act 1991 the words "England, Wales or", and Part I of the Schedule to that Act.

(6) The 1994 Act shall be treated as having been enacted with the amendments made by subsections (2) and (5).

(7) Subsections (3) and (4) apply where a magistrates' court begins to inquire into an offence as examining justices after the day on which this Act is passed.

Explanatory text—See paras 6.1–6.4.

Commencement—On Royal Assent (4 July 1996), but see subs (7).

Subs (2)—These provisions are repealed by s 80 and Sch 5.

Subss (3) and (4)—These changes are consequential on the repeal of the provisions in s 44 of, and Sch 5 to, the 1994 Act relating to transfer for trial. As amended, ss 34, 36 and 37, which concern inferences from an accused's silence, of the 1994 Act are as follows:

'**34** ... (1) Where, in any proceedings against a person for an offence, evidence is given that the accused—

(a)   at any time before he was charged with the offence, on being questioned under caution by a constable trying to discover whether or by whom the offence had been committed, failed to mention any fact relied on in his defence in those proceedings; or

   (b) on being charged with the offence or officially informed that he might be prosecuted for it, failed to mention any such fact,

being a fact which in the circumstances existing at the time the accused could reasonably have been expected to mention when so questioned, charged or informed, as the case may be, subsection (2) below applies.

(2) Where this subsection applies—

   (a) a magistrates' court inquiring into the offence as examining magistrates;
   (b) a judge, in deciding whether to grant an application made by the accused under—
      (i) section 6 of the Criminal Justice Act 1987 (application for dismissal of charge of serious fraud in respect of which notice of transfer has been given under section 4 of that Act); or
     (ii) paragraph 5 of Schedule 6 to the Criminal Justice Act 1991 (application for dismissal of charge of violent or sexual offence involving child in respect of which notice of transfer has been given under section 53 of that Act);
   (c) the court, in determining whether there is a case to answer; and
   (d) the court or jury, in determining whether the accused is guilty of the offence charged,

may draw such inferences from the failure as appear proper.

(3) Subject to any directions by the court, evidence tending to establish the failure may be given before or after evidence tending to establish the fact which the accused is alleged to have failed to mention.

(4) This section applies in relation to questioning by persons (other than constables) charged with the duty of investigating offences or charging offenders as it applies in relation to questioning by constables; and in subsection (1) above "officially informed" means informed by a constable or any such person.

(5) This section does not—

   (a) prejudice the admissibility in evidence of the silence or other reaction of the accused in the face of anything said in his presence relating to the conduct in respect of which he is charged, in so far as evidence thereof would be admissible apart from this section; or
   (b) preclude the drawing of any inference from any such silence or other reaction of the accused which could properly be drawn apart from this section.

(6) This section does not apply in relation to a failure to mention a fact if the failure occurred before the commencement of this section. ...

36 ... (1) Where—

   (a) a person is arrested by a constable, and there is—
      (i) on his person; or
     (ii) in or on his clothing or footwear; or
    (iii) otherwise in his possession; or
    (iv) in any place in which he is at the time of his arrest,
     any object, substance or mark, or there is any mark on any such object; and
   (b) that or another constable investigating the case reasonably believes that the presence of the object, substance or mark may be attributable to the participation of the person arrested in the commission of an offence specified by the constable; and
   (c) the constable informs the person arrested that he so believes, and requests him to account for the presence of the object, substance or mark; and
   (d) the person fails or refuses to do so,

then if, in any proceedings against the person for the offence so specified, evidence of those matters is given, subsection (2) below applies.

(2) Where this subsection applies—

   (a) a magistrates' court inquiring into the offence as examining magistrates;
   (b) a judge, in deciding whether to grant an application made by the accused under—

(i) section 6 of the Criminal Justice Act 1987 (application for dismissal of charge of serious fraud in respect of which notice of transfer has been given under section 4 of that Act); or

(ii) paragraph 5 of Schedule 6 to the Criminal Justice Act 1991 (application for dismissal of charge of violent or sexual offence involving child in respect of which notice of transfer has been given under section 53 of that Act);

(c) the court, in determining whether there is a case to answer; and

(d) the court or jury, in determining whether the accused is guilty of the offence charged,

may draw such inferences from the failure or refusal as appear proper.

(3) Subsections (1) and (2) above apply to the condition of clothing or footwear as they apply to a substance or mark thereon.

(4) Subsections (1) and (2) above do not apply unless the accused was told in ordinary language by the constable when making the request mentioned in subsection (1)(c) above what the effect of this section would be if he failed or refused to comply with the request.

(5) This section applies in relation to officers of customs and excise as it applies in relation to constables.

(6) This section does not preclude the drawing of any inference from a failure or refusal of the accused to account for the presence of an object, substance or mark or from the condition of clothing or footwear which could properly be drawn apart from this section.

(7) This section does not apply in relation to a failure or refusal which occurred before the commencement of this section.

37 (1) Where—

(a) a person arrested by a constable was found by him at a place at or about the time the offence for which he was arrested is alleged to have been committed; and

(b) that or another constable investigating the offence reasonably believes that the presence of the person at that place and at that time may be attributable to his participation in the commission of the offence; and

(c) the constable informs the person that he so believes, and requests him to account for that presence; and

(d) the person fails or refuses to do so,

then if, in any proceedings against the person for the offence, evidence of those matters is given, subsection (2) below applies.

(2) Where this subsection applies—

(a) a magistrates' court inquiring into the offence as examining magistrates;

(b) a judge, in deciding whether to grant an application made by the accused under—

(i) section 6 of the Criminal Justice Act 1987 (application for dismissal of charge of serious fraud in respect of which notice of transfer has been given under section 4 of that Act); or

(ii) paragraph 5 of Schedule 6 to the Criminal Justice Act 1991 (application for dismissal of charge of violent or sexual offence involving child in respect of which notice of transfer has been given under section 53 of that Act);

(c) the court, in determining whether there is a case to answer; and

(d) the court or jury, in determining whether the accused is guilty of the offence charged,

may draw such inferences from the failure or refusal as appear proper.

(3) Subsections (1) and (2) do not apply unless the accused was told in ordinary language by the constable when making the request mentioned in subsection (1)(c) above what the effect of this section would be if he failed or refused to comply with the request.

(4) This section applies in relation to officers of customs and excise as it applies in relation to constables.

(5) This section does not preclude the drawing of any inference from a failure or refusal of the accused to account for his presence at a place which could properly be drawn apart from this section.

(6) This section does not apply in relation to a failure or refusal which occurred before the commencement of this section.'

Sections 34(7), 36(8) and 37(7), which are omitted by subs (4), provided that in relation to any time before the commencement of the 1994 Act, s 34, 36 and 38, respectively, had effect as if the reference in subs (2)(a) of each section (which has now been substituted) to a magistrates' court engaged in deciding whether to grant an application for dismissal in the course of proceedings with a view to transfer for trial, was a reference to a magistrates' court engaged in deciding whether to commit for trial.

Subs (5)—

(a)   The Criminal Justice Act 1925, s 13(3) (see para **6.55**), is nevertheless repealed by the new Act, Sch 5. The Criminal Justice Act 1925, s 49(2) contains a definition of 'examining justices' for the purposes of that Act, which is preserved by the present provisions.

(b)   The Criminal Procedure (Attendance of Witnesses) Act 1965, s 1, although preserved by the present provision, is amended by s 65 of the new Act.

(c)   The Criminal Justice Act 1967, s 7, provided that an examining justice who signed a certificate authenticating one or more depositions or statements tendered under s 102 of the Magistrates' Courts Act 1980 (repealed by the new Act) was to be treated for the purposes of the requirement in the Criminal Justice Act 1925, s 13(3)(c), as having signed that deposition or statement or each of them. Section 13(3) of the 1925 Act is repealed by Sch 5 to the new Act. The repeal of s 7 is, therefore, consequential. Section 36(1) of the 1967 Act remains in force.

(d)   Consequential on the repeal of the Criminal Justice Act 1925, s 13(3), this provision is repealed by Sch 5.

(e)   These provisions are repealed by Sch 5. See para **6.11**, fn 1.

(f)   The Powers of Criminal Courts Act 1973, s 32(1)(b), which survives, provides, in respect of the enforcement of a fine or recognisance, that a fine imposed or a recognisance forfeited by the Crown Court shall be treated for the purposes of collection, enforcement and remission of the fine or other sum as having been imposed or forfeited by the magistrates' court by which the offender was committed to the Crown Court for trial or sentence. Section 32(1)(b) does not apply if the Crown Court has specified a magistrates' court in an order. In such a case, the fine (or recognisance) is treated by s 32(1)(a) as imposed (or forfeited) by that magistrates' court for the purposes of collection etc.

(g)   This simply preserves the pre-existing definition of 'committal for trial' for the purposes of general statutory interpretation.

(h)   As to s 97(1), which has been amended by the new Act, see para **7.32**. Sections 102 and 105 (see paras **6.9** and **6.10**) are repealed by Sch 5. As to s 103, see para **6.34**. As to s 106, which survives, see para **6.12**. Section 145(1)(e) has been repealed by Sch 5. The definition of 'committal proceedings' in s 150(1) survives, and so does Sch 5, para 2.

(i)   Section 2(2)(g), as preserved, provides that provisions whereby a person may not be convicted or committed for trial on the uncorroborated evidence of one witness, have effects in relation to an offence of attempt contrary to s 1 of the Criminal Attempts Act 1981 as they have effect in relation to the offence attempted.

(j)   Section 1(2), as preserved, provides that nothing in s 1(1) of the 1982 Act prevents the committal to prison of someone under 21 who is remanded in custody or committed in custody for trial or sentence.

(k)   These two paragraphs, which are preserved, continue in force the amendments made to the Supreme Court Act 1981, s 77(1) and s 81(1)(a), by paras 10 and 11 respectively of Sch 2 to the Criminal Justice Act 1987.

(l)   Section 20(4)(a) of the 1988 Act, which is preserved, provides that the magistrates' court which commits a person for trial or sentence or to be dealt with in respect of a sentence, is also competent to grant representation under Part I of the Act for the purposes of proceedings before the Crown Court. On the other hand, s 20(4)(bb) of that Act, which made similar provision in respect of a magistrates' court which has been given notice of transfer under the War Crimes Act 1991, Sch 1, is repealed consequent on the repeal of the 1991 Act, Sch 1, by the new Act, Sch 5. Section 20(5) of the 1988 Act, which provides that the magistrates' court inquiring into an offence as examining justices is also competent, before it decides whether or not to commit the accused for trial, to grant representation under Part I of the Act as respects any proceedings before the Crown Court on his trial, is preserved.

(m) Both these provisions, which related to notices of transfer under the 1991 Act, are repealed by the new Act, Sch 5.

Day on which this Act is passed (subs (7))—See 'Commencement', above.

45 Notices of transfer

(1) Section 5 of the Criminal Justice Act 1987 (notices of transfer in cases of serious or complex fraud) shall be amended as mentioned in subsections (2) and (3).

(2) In subsection (9)(a) (regulations) for the words "a statement of the evidence" there shall be substituted "copies of the documents containing the evidence (including oral evidence)".

(3) The following subsection shall be inserted after subsection (9)—

"(9A) Regulations under subsection (9)(a) above may provide that there shall be no requirement for copies of documents to accompany the copy of the notice of transfer if they are referred to, in documents sent with the notice of transfer, as having already been supplied."

(4) In Schedule 6 to the Criminal Justice Act 1991 (notices of transfer in certain cases involving children) paragraph 4 (regulations) shall be amended as mentioned in subsections (5) and (6).

(5) In sub-paragraph (1)(a) for the words "a statement of the evidence" there shall be substituted "copies of the documents containing the evidence (including oral evidence)".

(6) The following sub-paragraph shall be inserted after sub-paragraph (1)—

"(1A) Regulations under sub-paragraph (1)(a) above may provide that there shall be no requirement for copies of documents to accompany the copy of the notice of transfer if they are referred to, in documents sent with the notice of transfer, as having already been supplied."

(7) In paragraph 6 of Schedule 6 to the 1991 Act (reporting restrictions) in sub-paragraph (8) for the words "sub-paragraphs (5) and (6)" there shall be substituted "sub-paragraphs (5) and (7)".

(8) This section applies where a notice of transfer is given under section 4 of the 1987 Act or served under section 53 of the 1991 Act (as the case may be) on or after the appointed day.

(9) The reference in subsection (8) to the appointed day is to such day as is appointed for the purposes of this section by the Secretary of State by order.

Commencement—On Royal Assent (4 July 1996), but see subs (8).

Subs (2)–(6)—See 'Explanatory text', paras **7.1–7.3**.

Subs (7)—This simply corrects a typographical error in Sch 6 of the 1987 Act. The relevant provisions in Sch 6 now read:

'(5) It shall not be unlawful under this paragraph to publish or include in a relevant programme a report of an application under paragraph 5(1) above [application for dismissal of charge after a notice of transfer has been given] containing any matter other than that permitted by sub-paragraph (8) below where the application is successful.

(6) Where—
  (a) two or more persons were jointly charged; and
  (b) applications under paragraph 5(1) above are made by more than one of them, sub-paragraph (5) above shall have effect as if for the words "the application is" there were substituted the words "all the applications are".

(7) It shall not be unlawful under this paragraph to publish or include in a relevant programme a report of an unsuccessful application at the conclusion of the trial of the person charged, or of the last of the persons charged to be tried.

(8) The following matters may be contained in a report published or included in a relevant programme without an order under sub-paragraph (2) above before the time authorised by sub-paragraphs (5) and (7) above, that is to say—
  (a) the identity of the court and the name of the judge;
  (b) the names, ages, home addresses and occupations of the accused and witnesses;
  (c) the offence or offences, or a summary of them, with which the accused is or are charged;
  (d) the names of counsel and solicitors engaged in the proceedings;
  (e) where the proceedings are adjourned, the date and place to which they are adjourned;
  (f) the arrangements as to bail;
  (g) whether legal aid was granted to the accused or any of the accused.'

Appointed day (subss (8) and (9))—No day had been appointed when this book went to press.

By order (subs (9))—The order must be made by statutory instrument; see s 77(1)–(4).

46 War crimes: abolition of transfer procedure

(1) In the War Crimes Act 1991—

  (a) in section 1(4) (which introduces the Schedule providing a procedure for use instead of committal proceedings for certain war crimes) the words "England, Wales or" shall be omitted, and
  (b) Part I of the Schedule (procedure for use in England and Wales instead of committal proceedings) shall be omitted.

(2) In section 20(4) of the Legal Aid Act 1988 (power of magistrates' court to grant legal aid for Crown Court proceedings)—

  (a) the word "or" shall be inserted at the end of paragraph (b), and
  (b) paragraph (bb) (which relates to a notice of transfer under Part I of the Schedule to the War Crimes Act 1991) shall be omitted.

Explanatory text—See para **6.4**.

Commencement—On Royal Assent (4 July 1996).

47 Committal proceedings

Schedule 1 to this Act (which contains provisions about committal proceedings and related matters) shall have effect.

Explanatory text—See Chapter 6, generally.

Commencement—On Royal Assent (4 July 1996).

PART VI
MAGISTRATES' COURTS

48 Non-appearance of accused: issue of warrant

(1) Section 13 of the Magistrates' Courts Act 1980 (non-appearance of accused: issue of warrant) shall be amended as follows.

(2) In subsection (2) (no warrant where summons has been issued unless certain conditions fulfilled) for the words from "unless" to the end of the subsection there shall be substituted "unless the condition in subsection (2A) below or that in subsection (2B) below is fulfilled".

(3) The following subsections shall be inserted after subsection (2)—

"(2A) The condition in this subsection is that it is proved to the satisfaction of the court, on oath or in such other manner as may be prescribed, that the summons was served on the accused within what appears to the court to be a reasonable time before the trial or adjourned trial.

(2B) The condition in this subsection is that—

    (a) the adjournment now being made is a second or subsequent adjournment of the trial,

    (b) the accused was present on the last (or only) occasion when the trial was adjourned, and

    (c) on that occasion the court determined the time for the hearing at which the adjournment is now being made."

(4) This section applies where the court proposes to issue a warrant under section 13 on or after the appointed day.

(5) The reference in subsection (4) to the appointed day is to such day as is appointed for the purposes of this section by the Secretary of State by order.

Explanatory text—See paras **7.25–7.30**.

Commencement—On Royal Assent (4 July 1996), but see subs (4).

Appointed day (subss (4) and (5))—No day had been appointed when this book went to press.

By order (sub (5))—The order must be made by statutory instrument; see s 77(1)–(4).

49 Either way offences: accused's intention as to plea

(1) The Magistrates' Courts Act 1980 shall be amended as follows.

(2) The following sections shall be inserted after section 17 (offences triable on indictment or summarily)—

"17A Initial procedure: accused to indicate intention as to plea

(1) This section shall have effect where a person who has attained the age of 18 years appears or is brought before a magistrates' court on an information charging him with an offence triable either way.

(2) Everything that the court is required to do under the following provisions of this section must be done with the accused present in court.

(3) The court shall cause the charge to be written down, if this has not already been done, and to be read to the accused.

(4) The court shall then explain to the accused in ordinary language that he may indicate whether (if the offence were to proceed to trial) he would plead guilty or not guilty, and that if he indicates that he would plead guilty—

  (a) the court must proceed as mentioned in subsection (6) below; and
  (b) he may be committed for sentence to the Crown Court under section 38 below if the court is of such opinion as is mentioned in subsection (2) of that section.

(5) The court shall then ask the accused whether (if the offence were to proceed to trial) he would plead guilty or not guilty.

(6) If the accused indicates that he would plead guilty the court shall proceed as if—

  (a) the proceedings constituted from the beginning the summary trial of the information; and
  (b) section 9(1) above was complied with and he pleaded guilty under it.

(7) If the accused indicates that he would plead not guilty section 18(1) below shall apply.

(8) If the accused in fact fails to indicate how he would plead, for the purposes of this section and section 18(1) below he shall be taken to indicate that he would plead not guilty.

(9) Subject to subsection (6) above, the following shall not for any purpose be taken to constitute the taking of a plea—

  (a) asking the accused under this section whether (if the offence were to proceed to trial) he would plead guilty or not guilty;
  (b) an indication by the accused under this section of how he would plead.

17B Intention as to plea: absence of accused

(1) This section shall have effect where—

  (a) a person who has attained the age of 18 years appears or is brought before a magistrates' court on an information charging him with an offence triable either way,
  (b) the accused is represented by a legal representative,
  (c) the court considers that by reason of the accused's disorderly conduct before the court it is not practicable for proceedings under section 17A above to be conducted in his presence, and
  (d) the court considers that it should proceed in the absence of the accused.

(2) In such a case—

  (a) the court shall cause the charge to be written down, if this has not already been done, and to be read to the representative;
  (b) the court shall ask the representative whether (if the offence were to proceed to trial) the accused would plead guilty or not guilty;
  (c) if the representative indicates that the accused would plead guilty the court shall proceed as if the proceedings constituted from the beginning the summary trial of the information, and as if section 9(1) above was complied with and the accused pleaded guilty under it;

(d) if the representative indicates that the accused would plead not guilty section 18(1) below shall apply.

(3) If the representative in fact fails to indicate how the accused would plead, for the purposes of this section and section 18(1) below he shall be taken to indicate that the accused would plead not guilty.

(4) Subject to subsection (2)(c) above, the following shall not for any purpose be taken to constitute the taking of a plea—

(a) asking the representative under this section whether (if the offence were to proceed to trial) the accused would plead guilty or not guilty;

(b) an indication by the representative under this section of how the accused would plead.

17C Intention as to plea: adjournment

A magistrates' court proceeding under section 17A or 17B above may adjourn the proceedings at any time, and on doing so on any occasion when the accused is present may remand the accused, and shall remand him if—

(a) on the occasion on which he first appeared, or was brought, before the court to answer to the information he was in custody or, having been released on bail, surrendered to the custody of the court; or

(b) he has been remanded at any time in the course of proceedings on the information;

and where the court remands the accused, the time fixed for the resumption of proceedings shall be that at which he is required to appear or be brought before the court in pursuance of the remand or would be required to be brought before the court but for section 128(3A) below."

(3) In section 18(1) (initial procedure) after "either way" there shall be inserted "and—

(a) he indicates under section 17A above that (if the offence were to proceed to trial) he would plead not guilty, or

(b) his representative indicates under section 17B above that (if the offence were to proceed to trial) he would plead not guilty".

(4) In section 19 (court to consider which mode of trial appears more suitable) paragraph (a) of subsection (2) (charge to be read to accused) shall be omitted.

(5) In—

(a) subsections (1A), (3A), (3C) and (3E) of section 128 (remand), and

(b) subsection (1) of section 130 (transfer of remand hearings),

after "10(1)" there shall be inserted ", 17C".

(6) This section applies where a person appears or is brought before a magistrates' court on or after the appointed day, unless he has appeared or been brought before such a court in respect of the same offence on a previous occasion falling before that day.

(7) The reference in subsection (6) to the appointed day is to such day as is appointed for the purposes of this section by the Secretary of State by order.

Explanatory text—See paras **7.4–7.23**.

Commencement—On Royal Assent (4 July 1996), but see subs (6).

Age of 18 years (Magistrates' Courts Act 1980, ss 17A(1) and 17B(1))—See annotations to s 1.

Offence triable either way (MCA 1980, ss 17A(1) and 17B(1))—See annotations to s 1.

Practicable (MCA 1980, s 17B(1))—See annotations to s 58.

Subs (3)—The Magistrates' Courts Act 1980, s 18(1) now provides:

'Sections 19 to 23 [determination of mode of trial in case of either way offences] below shall have effect where a person who has attained the age of 18 years appears or is brought before a magistrates' court on an information charging him with an offence triable either way and

(a) he indicates under section 17A above that (if the offence were to proceed to trial) he would plead not guilty, or

(b) his representative indicates under section 17B above that (if the offence were to proceed to trial) he would plead not guilty.'

Subs (4)—The Magistrates' Courts Act 1980, s 19(2) now provides:

'Before so considering [whether in the case of an either way offence, the offence is more suitable for summary trial or trial on indictment], the court shall afford the prosecutor and then the accused an opportunity to representations as to which mode of trial would be more suitable.'

Subs (5)—The Magistrates' Courts Act 1980, s 128(1A), as amended by this subsection and s 52(1) below, provides that:

'Where—

(a) on adjourning a case under section 4(4), 10(1), 17C or 18(4) above the court proposes to remand or further remand a person in custody; and

(b) he is before the court; and

[(c) is omitted by s 52(1), and repealed by s 80 and Sch 5.]

(d) he is legally represented in that court, it shall be the duty of the court—

    (i) to explain the effect of subsections (3A) and (3B) below to him in ordinary language; and

    (ii) to inform him in ordinary language that, notwithstanding the procedure for a remand without his being brought before a court, he would be brought before a court for the hearing and determination of at least every fourth application for his remand, and of every application for his remand heard at a time when it appeared to the court that he had no solicitor acting for him in the case.'

The Magistrates' Courts Act 1980, s 128(3A), as amended now provides:

'Subject to subsection (3B) below, where a person has been remanded in custody and the remand was not a remand under section 128A below for a period exceeding 8 clear days, the court may further remand him (otherwise than in the exercise of the power conferred by that section) on an adjournment under section 4(4), 10(1), 17C or 18(4) above without his being brought before it if it is satisfied—

(a) that he gave his consent, either in response to a question under subsection (1C) above or otherwise, to the hearing and determination in his absence of any application for his remand on an adjournment of the case under any of those provisions; and

(b) that he has not by virtue of this subsection been remanded without being brought before the court on more than two such applications immediately preceding the application which the court is hearing, and

[(c) is omitted by s 52(1), and repealed by s 80 and Sch 5.]

(d) that he has not withdrawn his consent to their being so heard and determined.'

The Magistrates' Courts Act 1980, s 128(3C), as amended, provides:

'Where—

(a) a person has been remanded in custody on an adjournment of a case under section 4(4), 10(1), 17C or 18(4) above, and

(b) an application is subsequently made for his further remand on such an adjournment; and

(c) he is not brought before the court which hears and determines the application; and

(d) that court is not satisfied as mentioned in subsection (3A) above, the court shall adjourn the case and remand him in custody for the period for which it stands adjourned.'

The Magistrates' Courts Act 1980, s 128(3E), as amended, provides:

'(3E) Where—

(a) on an adjournment of a case under section 4(4), 10(1), 17C or 18(4) above a person has been remanded in custody without being brought before the court; and
(b) it subsequently appears—
  (i) to the court which remanded him in custody, or
  (ii) to an alternate magistrates' court to which he is remanded under section 130 below,

that he ought not to have been remanded in custody in his absence, the court shall require him to be brought before it at the earliest time that appears to the court to be possible.'

The Magistrates' Courts Act 1980, s 130(1), as amended provides:

'A magistrates' court adjourning a case under section 4(4), 10(1), 17C or 18(4) above, and remanding the accused in custody, may, if he has attained the age of 17, order that he be brought up for any subsequent remand before an alternate magistrates' court nearer to the prison where he is to be confined while on remand.'

Appointed day (subss (6) and (7))—No day had been appointed when this book went to press.

By order (subs (7))—The order must be made by statutory instrument; see s 77(1)–(4).

50 Enforcement of payment of fines

(1) In section 87 of the Magistrates' Courts Act 1980 (enforcement of fines) in subsection (3) (no proceedings unless court authorises it after inquiry into means) for the words from "authorised" to the end of the subsection there shall be substituted "there has been an inquiry under section 82 above into that person's means and he appeared to the court to have sufficient means to pay the sum forthwith."

(2) This section applies where the clerk of a magistrates' court proposes to take proceedings by virtue of section 87(1) on or after the appointed day.

(3) The reference in subsection (2) to the appointed day is to such day as is appointed for the purposes of this section by the Secretary of State by order.

Explanatory text—See para **7.39**.

Commencement—On Royal Assent (4 July 1996), but see subs (2).

Forthwith (subs (1))—Ie within a reasonable time thereafter; what is reasonable is a matter for the magistrates' court to decide in all the circumstances: *Hillingdon London Borough Council v Cutler* [1968] 1 QB 124, [1967] 2 All ER 361 (DC); *Re Muscovitch ex parte Muscovitch* [1939] 1 All ER 135.

Appointed day (subss (2) and (3))—No day had been appointed when this book went to press.

By order (subs (3))—The order must be made by statutory instrument; see s 77(1)–(4).

51 Summons to witness and warrant for his arrest

(1) In section 97 of the Magistrates' Courts Act 1980 (summons to witness and warrant for his arrest) the following subsections shall be inserted after subsection (2A)—

"(2B) A justice may refuse to issue a summons under subsection (1) above in relation to the summary trial of an information if he is not satisfied that an application for the summons was made by a party to the case as soon as reasonably practicable after the accused pleaded not guilty.

(2C) In relation to the summary trial of an information, subsection (2) above shall have effect as if the reference to the matters mentioned in subsection (1) above included a reference to the matter mentioned in subsection (2B) above."

(2) This section applies in relation to any proceedings for the purpose of which no summons has been issued under section 97(1), and no warrant has been issued under section 97(2), before the appointed day.

(3) The reference in subsection (2) to the appointed day is to such day as is appointed for the purposes of this section by the Secretary of State by order.

Explanatory text—See paras **7.31–7.35**.

Commencement—On Royal Assent (4 July 1996), but see subs (2).

Appointed day (subss (2) and (3))—No day had been appointed when this book went to press.

By order (subs (3))—The order must be made by statutory instrument; see s 77(1)–(4).

52 Remand

(1) In section 128 of the Magistrates' Courts Act 1980 (remand in custody or on bail) paragraph (c) of subsection (1A) and paragraph (c) of subsection (3A) (which restrict certain provisions about remand to persons who have attained the age of 17) shall be omitted.

(2) In section 128A(1) of that Act (power to make order allowing remand in custody for more than 8 clear days if accused has attained the age of 17) the words "who has attained the age of 17" shall be omitted.

(3) Subsection (1) applies where the offence with which the person concerned is charged is alleged to be committed on or after the appointed day.

(4) The reference in subsection (3) to the appointed day is to such day as is appointed for the purposes of this section by the Secretary of State by order.

Explanatory text—See paras **7.36–7.38**.

Commencement—On Royal Assent (4 July 1996), but see subs (3).

Subs (1)—See annotations to s 49(5).

Alleged to be committed (subs (3))—See s 75(1) and (2).

Appointed day (subss (3) and (4))—No day had been appointed when this book went to press.

By order (subs (4))—The order must be made by statutory instrument; see s 77(1)–(4).

53 Attachment of earnings

(1) In section 3 of the Attachment of Earnings Act 1971 (court's power to make order) the following subsections shall be inserted after subsection (3A)—

"(3B) Where—

    (a) a magistrates' court imposes a fine on a person in respect of an offence, and
    (b) that person consents to an order being made under this subsection,

the court may at the time it imposes the fine, and without the need for an application, make an attachment of earnings order to secure the payment of the fine.

(3C) Where—

(a) a magistrates' court makes in the case of a person convicted of an offence an order under section 35 of the Powers of Criminal Courts Act 1973 (a compensation order) requiring him to pay compensation or to make other payments, and

(b) that person consents to an order being made under this subsection,

the court may at the time it makes the compensation order, and without the need for an application, make an attachment of earnings order to secure the payment of the compensation or other payments."

(2) This section applies in relation to—

(a) fines imposed in respect of offences committed on or after the appointed day;

(b) compensation orders made on convictions for offences committed on or after that day.

(3) The reference in subsection (2) to the appointed day is to such day as is appointed for the purposes of this section by the Secretary of State by order.

Explanatory text—See paras **7.40–7.42**.

Commencement—On Royal Assent (4 July 1996), but see subs (2).

Subs (1)—The relevant parts of the Attachment of Earnings Act 1971, s 3, as amended, provide:

'(3) Subject to subsection 3A below, for an attachment of earnings order to be made on the application of any person other than the debtor it must appear to the court that the debtor has failed to make one or more payments required by the relevant adjudication.

(3A) Subsection (3) above shall not apply where the relevant adjudication is a maintenance order.

(3B) Where—

(a) a magistrates' court imposes a fine on a person in respect of an offence, and

(b) that person consents to an order being made under this subsection,

the court may at the time it imposes the fine, and without the need for an application, make an attachment of earnings order to secure the payment of the fine.

(3C) Where—

(a) a magistrates' court makes in the case of a person convicted of an offence an order under section 35 of the Powers of Criminal Courts Act 1973 (a compensation order) requiring him to pay compensation or to make other payments, and

(b) that person consents to an order being made under this subsection,

the court may at the time it makes the compensation order, and without the need for an application, make an attachment of earnings order to secure the payment of the compensation or other payments.'

Appointed day (subss (2) and (3))—No day had been appointed when this book went to press.

By order (sub (3))—The order must be made by statutory instrument; see s 77(1)–(4).

PART VII
MISCELLANEOUS AND GENERAL

Tainted acquittals

54 Acquittals tainted by intimidation etc.

(1) This section applies where—

(a) a person has been acquitted of an offence, and

(b) a person has been convicted of an administration of justice offence involving interference with or intimidation of a juror or a witness (or potential witness) in any proceedings which led to the acquittal.

(2) Where it appears to the court before which the person was convicted that—

(a) there is a real possibility that, but for the interference or intimidation, the acquitted person would not have been acquitted, and

(b) subsection (5) does not apply,

the court shall certify that it so appears.

(3) Where a court certifies under subsection (2) an application may be made to the High Court for an order quashing the acquittal, and the Court shall make the order if (but shall not do so unless) the four conditions in section 55 are satisfied.

(4) Where an order is made under subsection (3) proceedings may be taken against the acquitted person for the offence of which he was acquitted.

(5) This subsection applies if, because of lapse of time or for any other reason, it would be contrary to the interests of justice to take proceedings against the acquitted person for the offence of which he was acquitted.

(6) For the purposes of this section the following offences are administration of justice offences—

(a) the offence of perverting the course of justice;

(b) the offence under section 51(1) of the Criminal Justice and Public Order Act 1994 (intimidation etc. of witnesses, jurors and others);

(c) an offence of aiding, abetting, counselling, procuring, suborning or inciting another person to commit an offence under section 1 of the Perjury Act 1911.

(7) This section applies in relation to acquittals in respect of offences alleged to be committed on or after the appointed day.

(8) The reference in subsection (7) to the appointed day is to such day as is appointed for the purposes of this section by the Secretary of State by order.

Explanatory text—See paras **5.1–5.7, 5.9** and **5.10**.

Commencement—On Royal Assent (4 July 1996), but see subs (7).

Subs (6)—The offence of perverting the course of justice is sometimes referred to as the substantive offence of attempting to pervert the course of justice. For a description of this offence, see Card, Cross and Jones *Criminal Law* 13th edn (Butterworths, 1995), paras 16.32–16.34.

For a description of the offence under the Criminal Justice and Public Order Act 1994, s 51(1), see Card and Ward *Criminal Justice and Public Order Act 1994* (Jordans, 1994) paras 4.45–4.56.

Aiding, abetting, counselling, procuring or suborning another person to commit perjury is an offence under the Perjury Act 1911, s 7(1). For this offence the perjury must have been committed. Inciting another person to commit perjury is an offence under the 1911 Act, s 7(2). There can be liability for incitement even though the perjury incited is not committed, but, unless it is, the requirement in subs (2)(b) above would not be satisfied. As to the requirements of these offences, see Card, Cross and Jones *Criminal Law* (above) chs 16, 22 and 24.

Subs (7)—See s 75. As to the 'appointed day', no day had been appointed when this book went to press.

By order (subs (8))—The order must be made by statutory instrument; see s 77(1)–(4).

55 Conditions for making order

(1) The first condition is that it appears to the High Court likely that, but for the interference or intimidation, the acquitted person would not have been acquitted.

(2) The second condition is that it does not appear to the Court that, because of lapse of time or for any other reason, it would be contrary to the interests of justice to take proceedings against the acquitted person for the offence of which he was acquitted.

(3) The third condition is that it appears to the Court that the acquitted person has been given a reasonable opportunity to make written representations to the Court.

(4) The fourth condition is that it appears to the Court that the conviction for the administration of justice offence will stand.

(5) In applying subsection (4) the Court shall—

    (a) take into account all the information before it, but
    (b) ignore the possibility of new factors coming to light.

(6) Accordingly, the fourth condition has the effect that the Court shall not make an order under section 54(3) if (for instance) it appears to the Court that any time allowed for giving notice of appeal has not expired or that an appeal is pending.

Explanatory text—See para **5.8.**

Commencement—On Royal Assent (4 July 1996).

56 Time limits for proceedings

(1) Where—

    (a) an order is made under section 54(3) quashing an acquittal,
    (b) by virtue of section 54(4) it is proposed to take proceedings against the acquitted person for the offence of which he was acquitted, and
    (c) apart from this subsection, the effect of an enactment would be that the proceedings must be commenced before a specified period calculated by reference to the commission of the offence,

in relation to the proceedings the enactment shall have effect as if the period were instead one calculated by reference to the time the order is made under section 54(3).

(2) Subsection (1)(c) applies however the enactment is expressed so that (for instance) it applies in the case of—

    (a) paragraph 10 of Schedule 2 to the Sexual Offences Act 1956 (prosecution for certain offences may not be commenced more than 12 months after offence);
    (b) section 127(1) of the Magistrates' Courts Act 1980 (magistrates' court not to try information unless it is laid within 6 months from time when offence committed);
    (c) an enactment that imposes a time limit only in certain circumstances (as where proceedings are not instituted by or with the consent of the Director of Public Prosecutions).

Explanatory text—See para **5.9.**

Commencement—On Royal Assent (4 July 1996).

57 Tainted acquittals: supplementary

(1) Section 45 of the Offences Against the Person Act 1861 (which releases a person from criminal proceedings in certain circumstances) shall have effect subject to section 54(4) of this Act.

(2) The Contempt of Court Act 1981 shall be amended as mentioned in subsections (3) and (4).

(3) In section 4 (contemporary reports of proceedings) after subsection (2) there shall be inserted—

> "(2A) Where in proceedings for any offence which is an administration of justice offence for the purposes of section 54 of the Criminal Procedure and Investigations Act 1996 (acquittal tainted by an administration of justice offence) it appears to the court that there is a possibility that (by virtue of that section) proceedings may be taken against a person for an offence of which he has been acquitted, subsection (2) of this section shall apply as if those proceedings were pending or imminent."

(4) In Schedule 1 (time when proceedings are active for purposes of section 2) in paragraph 3 (period for which criminal proceedings are active) after "4" there shall be inserted "or 4A", and after paragraph 4 there shall be inserted—

> "4A. Where as a result of an order under section 54 of the Criminal Procedure and Investigations Act 1996 (acquittal tainted by an administration of justice offence) proceedings are brought against a person for an offence of which he has previously been acquitted, the initial step of the proceedings is a certification under subsection (2) of that section; and paragraph 4 has effect subject to this."

Explanatory text—See paras **5.11–5.15**.

Commencement—On Royal Assent (4 July 1996).

Derogatory assertions

58 Orders in respect of certain assertions

(1) This section applies where a person has been convicted of an offence and a speech in mitigation is made by him or on his behalf before—

(a) a court determining what sentence should be passed on him in respect of the offence, or

(b) a magistrates' court determining whether he should be committed to the Crown Court for sentence.

(2) This section also applies where a sentence has been passed on a person in respect of an offence and a submission relating to the sentence is made by him or on his behalf before—

(a) a court hearing an appeal against or reviewing the sentence, or

(b) a court determining whether to grant leave to appeal against the sentence.

(3) Where it appears to the court that there is a real possibility that an order under subsection (8) will be made in relation to the assertion, the court may make an order under subsection (7) in relation to the assertion.

(4) Where there are substantial grounds for believing—

(a) that an assertion forming part of the speech or submission is derogatory to a person's character (for instance, because it suggests that his conduct is or has been criminal, immoral or improper), and

(b) that the assertion is false or that the facts asserted are irrelevant to the sentence,

the court may make an order under subsection (8) in relation to the assertion.

(5) An order under subsection (7) or (8) must not be made in relation to an assertion if it appears to the court that the assertion was previously made—

(a) at the trial at which the person was convicted of the offence, or
(b) during any other proceedings relating to the offence.

(6) Section 59 has effect where a court makes an order under subsection (7) or (8).

(7) An order under this subsection—

(a) may be made at any time before the court has made a determination with regard to sentencing;
(b) may be revoked at any time by the court;
(c) subject to paragraph (b), shall cease to have effect when the court makes a determination with regard to sentencing.

(8) An order under this subsection—

(a) may be made after the court has made a determination with regard to sentencing, but only if it is made as soon as is reasonably practicable after the making of the determination;
(b) may be revoked at any time by the court;
(c) subject to paragraph (b), shall cease to have effect at the end of the period of 12 months beginning with the day on which it is made;
(d) may be made whether or not an order has been made under subsection (7) with regard to the case concerned.

(9) For the purposes of subsections (7) and (8) the court makes a determination with regard to sentencing—

(a) when it determines what sentence should be passed (where this section applies by virtue of subsection (1)(a));
(b) when it determines whether the person should be committed to the Crown Court for sentence (where this section applies by virtue of subsection (1)(b));
(c) when it determines what the sentence should be (where this section applies by virtue of subsection (2)(a));
(d) when it determines whether to grant leave to appeal (where this section applies by virtue of subsection (2)(b)).

Explanatory text—See paras **5.16–5.18** and **5.20–5.22**.

Commencement—On Royal Assent (4 July 1996), but see s 61(1).

Reasonably practicable (subs (8))—'Practicable' is defined by the Oxford English Dictionary as 'capable of being carried out in action' or 'feasible' adopted by Goddard LCJ in *Lee v Nursery Furnishings Ltd* [1945] 1 All ER 387 at 389), and by Webster's Dictionary as 'possible to be accomplished with known means or resources' (adopted by Parker J in *Adsett v K & L Steelfounders and Engineers Ltd* [1953] 1 All ER 97 at 98).

'Reasonably practicable' imposes a less strict standard than 'practicable'. It has been held, in relation to a court order to do something so far 'as reasonably practicable', that that phrase was sufficient general to embrace considerations going beyond what was physically feasible and was apt to include financial considerations (*Jordan v Norfolk County Council* [1994] 4 All ER 218 (DC)).

12 months (subs (8))—'Months' are calendar months (Interpretation Act 1978, s 5 and Sch 1).

59 Restriction on reporting of assertions

(1) Where a court makes an order under section 58(7) or (8) in relation to any assertion, at any time when the order has effect the assertion must not—

(a) be published in Great Britain in a written publication available to the public, or
(b) be included in a relevant programme for reception in Great Britain.

(2) In this section—

"relevant programme" means a programme included in a programme service, within the meaning of the Broadcasting Act 1990;

"written publication" includes a film, a soundtrack and any other record in permanent form but does not include an indictment or other document prepared for use in particular legal proceedings.

(3) For the purposes of this section an assertion is published or included in a programme if the material published or included—

(a) names the person about whom the assertion is made or, without naming him, contains enough to make it likely that members of the public will identify him as the person about whom it is made, and
(b) reproduces the actual wording of the matter asserted or contains its substance.

Explanatory text—See para **5.19**.

Commencement—On Royal Assent (4 July 1996).

Great Britain (subs (1))—See general annotations.

'Relevant programme' (subs (2))—See general annotations.

'Written' (subs (2))—See annotations to s 2.

60 Reporting of assertions: offences

(1) If an assertion is published or included in a relevant programme in contravention of section 59, each of the following persons is guilty of an offence—

(a) in the case of publication in a newspaper or periodical, any proprietor, any editor and any publisher of the newspaper or periodical;
(b) in the case of publication in any other form, the person publishing the assertion;
(c) in the case of an assertion included in a relevant programme, any body corporate engaged in providing the service in which the programme is included and any person having functions in relation to the programme corresponding to those of an editor of a newspaper.

(2) A person guilty of an offence under this section is liable on summary conviction to a fine of an amount not exceeding level 5 on the standard scale.

(3) Where a person is charged with an offence under this section it is a defence to prove that at the time of the alleged offence—

(a) he was not aware, and neither suspected nor had reason to suspect, that an order under section 58(7) or (8) had effect at that time, or
(b) he was not aware, and neither suspected nor had reason to suspect, that the publication or programme in question was of, or (as the case may be) included, the assertion in question.

(4) Where an offence under this section committed by a body corporate is proved to have been committed with the consent or connivance of, or to be attributable to any neglect on the part of—

(a) a director, manager, secretary or other similar officer of the body corporate, or
(b) a person purporting to act in any such capacity,

he as well as the body corporate is guilty of the offence and liable to be proceeded against and punished accordingly.

(5) In relation to a body corporate whose affairs are managed by its members "director" in subsection (4) means a member of the body corporate.

(6) Subsections (2) and (3) of section 59 apply for the purposes of this section as they apply for the purposes of that.

Explanatory text—See paras **5.24–5.26**.

Commencement—On Royal Assent (4 July 1996).

Persons/person (subss (1), (2) and (3))—See annotations to s 38. The structure of s 60(1) is such as to indicate that a body corporate, like a human being falling within the description there, can be convicted of an offence without the need to have recourse to principles of vicarious liability or the identification principle of corporate criminal liability.

Relevant programme (sub (1))—See general annotations.

Level 5 on the standard scale (sub (2))—See general annotations.

It is a defence to prove (sub (3))—The standard of proof is on the balance of probabilities (*Sodeman v R* [1936] 2 All ER 1138 (PC); *Carr-Briant* [1943] KB 607, [1943] 2 All ER 156 (CCA)), as opposed to proof beyond reasonable doubt, which is the standard borne by the prosecution in relation to the proof of the prohibited conduct required for an offence under s 60(1). The defence will satisfy this standard if the jury or magistrates are reasonably satisfied that one or other of the defences in s 60(3) applies or find it more probable than not that one or other of them does (*Miller v Minister of Pensions* [1947] 2 All ER 372 at 373–374).

Not aware and neither suspected nor had reason to suspect (sub (3))—'Suspicion' is something less than 'belief' (*Johnson v Whitehouse* [1984] RTR 38 (DC)). 'Suspicion in its ordinary meaning is a state of conjecture or surmise when proof is lacking' (*Shakben Bin Hussien v Chong Fook Kam* [1970] AC 442 at 948, [1969] 3 All ER 1626, per Lord Devlin).

'Reason to suspect' involves a wholly objective test. See, for example, *Young* [1984] 2 All ER 164, [1984] 1 WLR 654 (C-MAC). The only case apparently to the contrary, *Hudson* [1966] 1 QB 448, [1965] 1 All ER 721 (CCA), contains a dictum that not only must there be an objective 'reason to suspect' but also the accused himself, taking into account his mental and other capacities, ought to have suspected. However, this dictum has not been followed in any other case.

With the consent or connivance of, or to be attributable to any neglect on the part of, any director etc. (subs (4))—Where a body corporate is criminally liable under s 60(1), superior officers may be criminally liable as accomplices under the general principles relating to complicity in crime if they have assisted, encouraged or procured the commission of the offence with the relevant mens rea. However, the present provision renders it unnecessary to rely on the general law of complicity. This provision catches superior officers who would undoubtedly be guilty under that general law and also in some cases those whose guilt would be hard or impossible to prove under it. It provides that a director etc will be criminally liable for the same offence as the body corporate if it is proved that the offence was committed with his consent or connivance or to be attributable to any neglect on his part.

'Consent' to a thing connotes awareness of it and agreement to it: a person can only consent to a thing of which he is aware: *Re Caughey ex parte Ford* (1876) 1 Ch D 521 at 528; *Lamb v Wright & Co* [1924] 1 KB 857 at 864. 'It would seem that where a director consents to the commission of an offence by his company he is well aware of what is going on and agrees to it.': *Huckerby v Elliott* [1970] 1 All ER 189 at 194.

'Connivance' is generally regarded as involving wilful blindness (ie a realisation that the offence may be being committed coupled with a deliberate failure to find out); *Somerset v Hart* (1884) 12 QBD 360 (DC).

In *Lewin v Bland* [1985] RTR 171 (DC), it was held that an offence is only attributable to any neglect on the part of a director, manager or other similar officer of a corporation if he was in breach of a duty to check the conduct (which resulted in the offence) of the person who committed the offence, and that normally there is no duty to check the conduct of an experienced member of staff whom one can expect to act in accordance with one's instructions unless there is something to prompt one into checking.

Any director, manager, secretary or other similar officer (subs (4))—These are people who, along with persons mentioned in the next annotation, can be made criminally liable, as well as the body corporate, if they have consented to or connived at the commission of the offence by it. 'Manager' means someone managing in a governing role the affairs of the body corporate, as opposed to someone with a day-to-day function (*Boal* [1992] QB 591, [1992] 3 All ER 177 (CA)).

Or a person purporting to act in any such capacity—These words are necessary in view of the decision in *Dean v Hiesler* [1942] 2 All ER 340 (DC) that a director who had not been validly appointed was not liable under a provision similar to subs (4) for an offence committed by the body corporate.

61 Reporting of assertions: commencement and supplementary

(1) Section 58 applies where the offence mentioned in subsection (1) or (2) of that section is committed on or after the appointed day.

(2) The reference in subsection (1) to the appointed day is to such day as is appointed for the purposes of this section by the Secretary of State by order.

(3) Nothing in section 58 or 59 affects any prohibition or restriction imposed by virtue of any other enactment on a publication or on matter included in a programme.

(4) Nothing in section 58 or 59 affects section 3 of the Law of Libel Amendment Act 1888 (privilege of newspaper reports of court proceedings).

(5) Section 8 of the Law of Libel Amendment Act 1888 (order of judge required for prosecution for libel published in a newspaper) does not apply to a prosecution for an offence under section 60.

(6) In section 159 of the Criminal Justice Act 1988 (appeal to Court of Appeal against orders restricting reports etc.) in subsection (1) the following paragraph shall be inserted after paragraph (a)—

> "(aa)   an order made by the Crown Court under section 58(7) or (8) of the Criminal Procedure and Investigations Act 1996 in a case where the Court has convicted a person on a trial on indictment;".

Explanatory text—Paras **5.16** (fn 2) and **5.23**.

Commencement—On Royal Assent (4 July 1996).

Is committed (subs (1))—See s 75(2) and (3).

Appointed day (subss (1) and (2))—No day had been appointed when this book went to press.

By order (subs (2))—The order must be made by statutory instrument; see s 77(1)–(4).

Subs (6)—The Criminal Justice Act 1988, s 159(1) provides in consequence of this amendment:

> 'A person aggrieved may appeal to the Court of Appeal, if that court grants leave, against . . . an order made by the Crown Court under s 49(7) or (8) of the Criminal Procedure and Investigations Act 1996 in a case where the court has convicted a person on a trial on indictment.'

Evidence: special provisions

62 Television links and video recordings

(1) In section 32 of the Criminal Justice Act 1988 (evidence through television links) the following subsections shall be inserted after subsection (3B)—

"(3C) Where—

(a) the court gives leave for a person to give evidence through a live television link, and
(b) the leave is given by virtue of subsection (1)(b) above,

then, subject to subsection (3D) below, the person concerned may not give evidence otherwise than through a live television link.

(3D) In a case falling within subsection (3C) above the court may give permission for the person to give evidence otherwise than through a live television link if it appears to the court to be in the interests of justice to give such permission.

(3E) Permission may be given under subsection (3D) above—

(a) on an application by a party to the case, or
(b) of the court's own motion;

but no application may be made under paragraph (a) above unless there has been a material change of circumstances since the leave was given by virtue of subsection (1)(b) above."

(2) In section 32A of the Criminal Justice Act 1988 (video recordings of testimony from child witnesses) the following subsections shall be inserted after subsection (6)—

"(6A) Where the court gives leave under subsection (2) above the child witness shall not give relevant evidence (within the meaning given by subsection (6D) below) otherwise than by means of the video recording; but this is subject to subsection (6B) below.

(6B) In a case falling within subsection (6A) above the court may give permission for the child witness to give relevant evidence (within the meaning given by subsection (6D) below) otherwise than by means of the video recording if it appears to the court to be in the interests of justice to give such permission.

(6C) Permission may be given under subsection (6B) above—

(a) on an application by a party to the case, or
(b) of the court's own motion;

but no application may be made under paragraph (a) above unless there has been a material change of circumstances since the leave was given under subsection (2) above.

(6D) For the purposes of subsections (6A) and (6B) above evidence is relevant evidence if—

(a) it is evidence in chief on behalf of the party who tendered the video recording, and
(b) it relates to matter which, in the opinion of the court, is dealt with in the recording and which the court has not directed to be excluded under subsection (3) above."

(3) This section applies where the leave concerned is given on or after the appointed day.

(4) The reference in subsection (3) to the appointed day is to such day as is appointed for the purposes of this section by the Secretary of State by order.

Explanatory text—See para **5.48**.

Commencement—On Royal Assent (4 July 1996), but see subs (3).

Section 32 of the Criminal Justice Act 1988 (subs (1))—Section 32 states as follows:

'(1) A person other than the accused may give evidence through a live television link on a trial on indictment or an appeal to the criminal division of the Court of Appeal or the hearing of a reference under section 17 of the Criminal Appeal Act 1968 if—

(a)   the witness is outside the United Kingdom; or

(b)   the witness is a child or is to be cross examined following the admission under section 32A below of a video recording of testimony from him, and the offence is one to which subsection (2) below applies,

but evidence may not be so given without the leave of the court.

(1A) This subsection applies—

(a)   to trials on indictment, appeals to the criminal division of the Court of Appeal and hearings of references under section 17 of the Criminal Appeal Act 1968; and

(b)   to proceedings in youth courts and appeals to the Crown Court arising out of such proceedings.

(2) This subsection applies—

(a)   to an offence which involves an assault on, or injury or a threat of injury to, a person;

(b)   to an offence under section 1 of the Children and Young Persons Act 1933 (cruelty to persons under 16);

(c)   to an offence under the Sexual Offences Act 1956, the Indecency with Children Act 1960, the Sexual Offences Act 1967, section 54 of the Criminal Law Act 1977 or the Protection of Children Act 1978; and

(d)   to an offence which consists of attempting or conspiring to commit, or of aiding, abetting, counselling, procuring or inciting the commission of, an offence falling within paragraph (a), (m) or (c) above.

(3) A statement made on oath by a witness outside the United Kingdom and given in evidence through a link by virtue of this section shall be treated for the purposes of section 1 of the Perjury Act 1911 as having been made in the proceedings in which it is given in evidence.

(3A) Where, in the case of any proceedings before a youth court—

(a)   leave is given by virtue of subsection (1)(b) above for evidence to be given through a live television link; and

(b)   suitable facilities for receiving such evidence are not available at any petty sessional court-house in which the court can (apart from this subsection) lawfully sit,

the court may sit for the purposes of the whole or any part of these proceedings at any place at which such facilities are available and which has been appointed for the purposes of this subsection by the justices acting for the petty sessions area for which the court acts.

(3B) A place appointed under subsection (3) above may be outside the petty sessions area for which it is appointed; but it shall be deemed to be in that area for the purposes of the jurisdiction of the justices acting for that area.

(3C) [See new Act, above.]

(3D) [See new Act, above.]

(3E) [See new Act, above.]

(4) Without prejudice to the generality of any enactment conferring power to make rules to which this subsection applies, such rules may make such provision as appears to the authority making them to be necessary or expedient for the purposes of this section.

(5) The rules to which subsection 4 above applies are [the Magistrates' Courts Rules, Crown Court Rules and Criminal Appeal Rules].

(6) Subsection (7) of section 32A below shall apply for the purposes of this section as it applies for the purposes of that section, but with the omission of the references to a person being, in the cases there mentioned, under the age of fifteen years or under the age of eighteen years.'

For the meaning of the words in s 32(2)(a), see *Lee* [1996] Crim LR 412 (CA). Those words relate to the circumstances of the offence not the state of mind of the offender, and it did not necessarily involve threat of injury to any particular person. 'A person' did not have to be the child giving evidence.

Section 32A of the Criminal Justice Act 1988 (subs (2))—Section 32A states as follows:

'(1) This section applies in relation to the following proceedings, namely—

    (a)   trials on indictment for any offence to which section 32(2) above applies;

    (b)   appeals to the criminal division of the Court of Appeal and hearings of references under section 17 of the Criminal Appeal Act 1968 in respect of any such offence; and

    (c)   proceedings in youth courts for any such offence and appeals to the Crown Court arising out of such proceedings.

(2) In any such proceedings a video recording of an interview which—

    (a)   is conducted between an adult and a child who is not the accused or one of the accused ("the child witness"); and

    (b)   relates to any matter in issue in the proceedings,

may, with leave of the court, be given in evidence in so far as it is not excluded by the court under subsection (3) below.

(3) Where a video recording is tendered in evidence under this section, the court shall (subject to the exercise of any power of the court to exclude evidence which is otherwise admissible) give leave under subsection (2) above unless—

    (a)   it appears that the child witness will not be available for cross examination;

    (b)   any rules of court requiring disclosure of the circumstances in which the recording was made have not been complied with to the satisfaction of the court; or

    (c)   the court is of the opinion, having regard to all the circumstances of the case, that in the interests of justice the recording ought not to be admitted;

and where the court gives such leave it may, if it is of the opinion that in the interests of justice any part of the recording ought not to be admitted, direct that that part shall be excluded.

(4) In considering whether any part of a recording ought to be excluded under subsection (3) above, the court shall consider whether any prejudice to the accused, or one of the accused, which might result from the admission of that part is outweighed by the desirability of showing the whole, or substantially the whole, of the recorded interview.

(5) Where a video recording is admitted under this section—

    (a)   the child witness shall be called by the party who tendered it in evidence;

    (b)   that witness shall not be examined in chief on any matter which, in the opinion of the court, has been dealt with adequately in his recorded testimony.

(6) Where a video recording is given in evidence under this section, any statement made by the child witness which is disclosed by the recording shall be treated as if given by that witness in direct oral testimony; and accordingly—

    (a)   any such statement shall be admissible evidence of any fact of which such testimony from him would be admissible;

    (b)   no such statement shall be capable of corroborating any other evidence given by him.

(6A) [See new Act, above.]

(6B) [See new Act, above.]

(6C) [See new Act, above.]

(6D) [See new Act, above.]'

Appointed day (subss (3) and (4))—No day had been appointed when this book went to press.

63 Road traffic and transport: provision of specimens

(1) In section 7(3) of the Road Traffic Act 1988 (provision of blood or urine in course of investigating whether certain road traffic offences have been committed) after paragraph (b) there shall be inserted—

> "(bb) a device of the type mentioned in subsection (1)(a) above has been used at the police station but the constable who required the specimens of breath has reasonable cause to believe that the device has not produced a reliable indication of the proportion of alcohol in the breath of the person concerned, or".

(2) In section 31(4) of the Transport and Works Act 1992 (provision of blood or urine in course of investigating whether offences have been committed by persons working on transport systems) the word "or" at the end of paragraph (b) shall be omitted and after that paragraph there shall be inserted—

> "(bb) a device of the type mentioned in subsection (1)(a) above has been used at the police station but the constable who required the specimens of breath has reasonable cause to believe that the device has not produced a reliable indication of the proportion of alcohol in the breath of the person concerned, or".

(3) This section applies where it is proposed to make a requirement mentioned in section 7(3) of the 1988 Act or section 31(3) of the 1992 Act after the appointed day.

(4) The reference in subsection (3) to the appointed day is to such day as is appointed for the purposes of this section by the Secretary of State by order.

Explanatory text—See below.

Commencement—On Royal Assent (4 July 1996), but see subs (3).

Subs (1)—The Road Traffic Act 1988, s 7, is concerned with the provision of a specimen for analysis in the course of an investigation into specified drink-drive offences, normally after a positive roadside 'screening' breath test (or a failure by the motorist to undergo one) and arrest.

Section 7(1) provides that, in the course of an investigation into whether a person has committed an offence under s 3A (causing death by careless driving when under the influence of drink or drugs), s 4 (driving, attempting to drive or being in charge of a mechanically propelled vehicle when under influence of drink or drugs) or s 5 (driving, attempting to drive or being in charge of a motor vehicle with alcohol concentration above prescribed limit) of this Act a constable may require him—

(a) to provide two specimens of breath for analysis by means of a device of a type approved by the Secretary of State, or

(b) to provide a specimen of blood or urine for a laboratory test.

By s 7(3) a requirement under s 7 to provide a specimen of blood or urine can only be made at a police station or at a hospital; and it cannot be made at a police station unless one of a number of specified conditions is satisfied.

As enacted, the Road Traffic Act 1988, s 7(3), provided that a constable could only make a requirement at a police station for a specimen of blood or urine to be provided for analysis if one of three situations exists:

(a) the constable making the requirement has reasonable cause to believe that for medical reasons a specimen of breath cannot be provided or should not be required (s 7(3)(a));

(b) at the time that the requirement is made an approved breath analysis device or a reliable one is not available at the station or it is otherwise impracticable to use such a device there (s 7(3)(b)); or

(c) the suspected offence is one under s 3A (causing death by careless driving while unfit to drive through drink or drugs) or s 4 (driving etc while unfit) and the constable making the requirement has been advised by a medical practitioner that the condition of the person required to provide the specimen might be due to some drug (s 7(3)(c)).

Paragraph (bb), added to the Road Traffic Act 1988, s 7(3), by subs (1), provides a fourth ground under which a constable may require a specimen of blood or urine under s 7(3), viz where:

'a device of the type mentioned in [s 7(1)(a), ie a breath-analysis device of a type approved by the Secretary of State] has been used at the police station but the constable who required the specimen of breath has reasonable cause to believe that the device has not produced a reliable indication of the proportion of alcohol in the breath of the person concerned.'

The rationale for this new provision was explained by Baroness Blatch, Minister of State, Home Office (Lords' Consideration of Commons' amendments, cols 970–971), as follows:

'The new clause ensures that the police can make full use of new evidential breath testing equipment, which will shortly be available, by continuing to be able to exercise their existing discretion to require blood or urine samples from suspected drink drivers in certain situations ... The existing breath testing equipment at police stations was introduced in 1983 and we need to plan ahead for its replacement. Technology has moved on since 1983, as have the international standards on breath testing. The new equipment therefore incorporates some new software which enables it to identify and flag up automatically certain situations which are currently catered for by operational arrangements. Put simply, these cover situations where it is suspected an interfering substance may be present, or the alleged offender produces mouth alcohol or the difference between the reading for two breath samples is greater than 15 per cent. In such situations, the machine will advise the operator and the constable should then be able to require a blood or urine sample as an alternative.

The existing provisions in section 7 of the Road Traffic Act 1988 do not currently allow specimens to be required in a situation where a properly working machine indicates such readings. The new clause therefore extends the police's existing discretion to allow specimens to be taken in such situations.'

Although the Road Traffic Act 1988, s 7(3)(bb), is undoubtedly adequate to meet its intended purpose, its drafting would seem to remove the need for the courts to continue to apply a stretched construction to the wording of s 7(3)(b) in a case where a constable reasonably but mistakenly believes, after using on the occasion in question an approved breath-analysis device of any type, that it is not reliable. The wording of s 7(3)(b), especially when contrasted with s 7(3)(a) and (c), which refer to the state of mind, or knowledge, of the constable, appears to indicate that the reference in s 7(3)(b) to the absence of an approved device or of a reliable one is an objective requirement, with the result that its terms would not be satisfied where it was not proved that there was no approved device or no reliable approved device available but the constable reasonably believed that there was no approved device available at the police station or no reliable approved device available there. However, on a number of occasions, the courts have interpreted s 7(3)(b) so as to hold that it is satisfied even if there is a reliable approved device available at the police station (or it is not proved that there was not) if the constable reasonably believes that there is not (*Thompson v Thynne* [1986] RTR 293 (DC); *Stokes v Sayers* [1988] RTR 89 (DC); *Haghigat-Khou v Chambers* [1988] RTR 95 (DC)) or if the constable reasonably believes that there is no approved device available there (*Thompson v Thynne* [1986] RTR at 298).

This interpretation has obvious practical advantages. It would be unfortunate if, where a constable reasonably believed that a device was unreliable and consequently sought another mode of analysis, the results of a blood or urine analysis could be inadmissible simply because his reasonable belief was mistaken and the device was reliable.

Nevertheless, the interpretation does clear violence to the words of s 7(3) in question, and there is consequently a risk of appeals based on a literal interpretation of them being brought.

The wording of s 7(3)(bb) is appropriate to cover those cases where, as in *Thompson v Thynne* and *Stokes v Sayers*, the constable forms a reasonable belief as to the unreliability of the device after he has used it because, for example, of the results produced by it or by some other indication given by it.

Section 7(3)(bb), however, does not cover the less common type of case where, as in *Haghiget-Khou v Chambers*, the constable forms a reasonable belief as to reliability before using a device and consequently does not use it and proceeds immediately to request a blood or urine specimen, or where he forms such a belief as to the unavailability of an approved device. When a case of one of these two types arises in the future, the determination of the validity of a request for a blood or urine specimen will have to be judged by reference to s 7(3)(b), as interpreted.

Subs (2)—Part II of the Transport and Works Act 1992 applies to transport systems which are used, or are intended to be used, wholly or partly for the carriage of members of the public. Its provisions are restricted to railways, tramways, and to other *guided transport systems* specified by the Secretary of State. The guided transport systems at Birmingham International Airport; Merry Hill Centre, West Midlands; and Gatwick and Stansted Airports have been so specified.

The Act creates two offences involving drink or drugs on such transport systems which can be committed by the following workers:

(a) drivers, guards, conductors, signalmen and others who control or affect the movement of vehicles operating under one of these systems; or

(b) persons who couple or uncouple such vehicles or check that they are working properly; or

(c) persons maintaining the permanent way (or other support or guidance structures), signalling systems and power supply used by such vehicles; and

(d) supervisors of, and look-outs for, persons engaged in the functions set out in categories (b) or (c) above.

These two offences are committed where:

(1) a person in one of the above categories carries out his duties when unfit to carry out that work through drink or drugs;

(2) a person in one of the above categories carries out his duties after consuming so much alcohol that the proportion of it in his breath, blood or urine exceeds the prescribed limit (which is the same limit as prescribed by the Road Traffic Act 1988).

A constable in uniform is empowered to require a screening breath test where he has reasonable cause to suspect:

(a) that a person working on a transport system has alcohol in his body, or

(b) that a person has been working on a transport system with alcohol in his body and still has alcohol in his body.

This power is extended to circumstances in which there has been an *accident or dangerous incident* and a constable in uniform has reasonable cause to suspect that, at the time of that event, the person was working in one of the above capacities and that his act, or omission, whilst so working, may have been the cause of the accident or incident. A 'dangerous incident' means an incident which, in the constable's opinion, involved a danger of death or personal injury.

Similar powers to those under the Road Traffic Act 1988 are provided by Part II of the Act in relation to arrest and entry; the provision of specimens for analysis; the option to have a breath specimen replaced if the alcohol content in it does not exceed 50 microgrammes in 100 ml of breath; failure to comply with a request; and hospital patients. The evidential provisions contained in the Road Traffic Offenders Act 1988 in respect of specimens which have been analysed are repeated in Part II of the Act.

Section 31 of the 1992 Act deals with the provision of specimens for analysis in the same terms as s 7 of the 1988 Act. Section 31(3) and (4) correspond in identical terms with those in s 7(3) (so that s 31(4)(a), (b) and (c) correspond with s 7(3)(a), (b) and (c)), and there can be no doubt they are to be interpreted in an identical fashion. The rationale and the effect of the new paragraph (bb) added to s 31(4) is the same as in respect of the Road Traffic Act 1988, s 7(3)(bb), and consequently requires no further explanation.

Appointed day (subss (3) and (4))—No day had been appointed when this book went to press.

By order—The order must be made by statutory instrument; see s 77(1)–(4).

64 Checks against fingerprints etc.

(1) In section 63A of the Police and Criminal Evidence Act 1984 the following subsections shall be substituted for subsection (1) (checks against fingerprints etc. where a person has been arrested on suspicion of being involved in a recordable offence)—

> "(1) Where a person has been arrested on suspicion of being involved in a recordable offence or has been charged with such an offence or has been informed that he will be reported for such an offence, fingerprints or samples or the information derived from samples taken under any power conferred by this Part of this Act from the person may be checked against—
>
> > (a) other fingerprints or samples to which the person seeking to check has access and which are held by or on behalf of a police force (or police forces) falling within subsection (1A) below or are held in connection with or as a result of an investigation of an offence;
> > (b) information derived from other samples if the information is contained in records to which the person seeking to check has access and which are held as mentioned in paragraph (a) above.
>
> (1A) Each of the following police forces falls within this subsection—
>
> > (a) a police force within the meaning given by section 62 of the Police Act 1964 (which relates to England and Wales);
> > (b) a police force within the meaning given by section 50 of the Police (Scotland) Act 1967;
> > (c) the Royal Ulster Constabulary and the Royal Ulster Constabulary Reserve;
> > (d) the States of Jersey Police Force;
> > (e) the salaried police force of the Island of Guernsey;
> > (f) the Isle of Man Constabulary."

(2) This section applies where a person—

(a) is arrested on suspicion of being involved in a recordable offence,
(b) is charged with a recordable offence, or
(c) is informed that he will be reported for a recordable offence,

after the day on which this Act is passed.

Explanatory text—See para **5.45**.

Commencement—On Royal Assent (4 July 1996), but see subs (2).

Fingerprints etc (subss (1) and (2))—(PACE 1984, s 63A(1)) – Fingerprints include palm prints (PACE 1984, s 65).

Recordable offence (subss (1) and (2)—(s 54(3)) – 'Recordable offence' is defined by the National Police Records (Recordable Offences) Regulations 1985 (SI 1985/1941), as amended by SI 1989/694. These regulations make certain offences, and others of which the accused is convicted on the same occasion, recordable on the police national computer. The offences which are recordable are: all offences punishable by imprisonment; offences under s 1 of the Street Offences Act 1959 (common prostitute loitering or soliciting for the purposes of prostitution); offences under s 43 of the Telecommunications Act 1984 (improper use of public telecommunications system); offences under s 25 of the Road Traffic Act 1988 (tampering with motor vehicles); offences under s 1 of the Malicious Communications Act 1988 (sending letters etc, with intent to cause anxiety or distress); and offences under s 139 of CJA 1988 (having an article with a blade or point in a public place).

Suspicion (subs (2))—See annotations to s 60.

Witness orders and summonses

65 Abolition of witness orders

(1) Section 1 of the Criminal Procedure (Attendance of Witnesses) Act 1965 (examining justices to order witness to attend and give evidence before Crown Court) shall be omitted.

(2) In that Act the following words shall be omitted—

- (a) in section 3(1) the words "witness order or";
- (b) in section 4(1) the words "witness order or" and (where they next occur) "order or";
- (c) in the proviso to section 4(1) the words from "in the case" (where they first occur) to "witness summons";
- (d) in section 4(2) the words "a witness order or" and (where they next occur) "order or".

(3) In section 145 of the Magistrates' Courts Act 1980 (rules) subsection (1)(e) (which relates to witness orders) shall be omitted.

(4) This section shall have effect in accordance with provision made by the Secretary of State by order.

Explanatory text—See paras **5.35–5.44**.

Commencement—On Royal Assent (4 July 1996), but see subs (4).

Subsection 62(2)—See annotations to s 66.

Order (subs (4))—The order must be made by statutory instrument; see s 77(1)–(4).

66 Summons to witness to attend Crown Court

(1) The Criminal Procedure (Attendance of Witnesses) Act 1965 shall be amended as follows.

(2) The following shall be substituted for section 2 (summons to witness to attend Crown Court)—

"*Issue of witness summons on application*

2 Issue of witness summons on application to Crown Court

(1) This section applies where the Crown Court is satisfied that—

- (a) a person is likely to be able to give evidence likely to be material evidence, or produce any document or thing likely to be material evidence, for the purpose of any criminal proceedings before the Crown Court, and
- (b) the person will not voluntarily attend as a witness or will not voluntarily produce the document or thing.

(2) In such a case the Crown Court shall, subject to the following provisions of this section, issue a summons (a witness summons) directed to the person concerned and requiring him to—

   (a)   attend before the Crown Court at the time and place stated in the summons, and
   (b)   give the evidence or produce the document or thing.

(3) A witness summons may only be issued under this section on an application; and the Crown Court may refuse to issue the summons if any requirement relating to the application is not fulfilled.

(4) Where a person has been committed for trial for any offence to which the proceedings concerned relate, an application must be made as soon as is reasonably practicable after the committal.

(5) Where the proceedings concerned have been transferred to the Crown Court, an application must be made as soon as is reasonably practicable after the transfer.

(6) Where the proceedings concerned relate to an offence in relation to which a bill of indictment has been preferred under the authority of section 2(2)(b) of the Administration of Justice (Miscellaneous Provisions) Act 1933 (bill preferred by direction of Court of Appeal, or by direction or with consent of judge) an application must be made as soon as is reasonably practicable after the bill was preferred.

(7) An application must be made in accordance with Crown Court rules; and different provision may be made for different cases or descriptions of case.

(8) Crown Court rules—

   (a)   may, in such cases as the rules may specify, require an application to be made by a party to the case;
   (b)   may, in such cases as the rules may specify, require the service of notice of an application on the person to whom the witness summons is proposed to be directed;
   (c)   may, in such cases as the rules may specify, require an application to be supported by an affidavit containing such matters as the rules may stipulate;
   (d)   may, in such cases as the rules may specify, make provision for enabling the person to whom the witness summons is proposed to be directed to be present or represented at the hearing of the application for the witness summons.

(9) Provision contained in Crown Court rules by virtue of subsection (8)(c) above may in particular require an affidavit to—

   (a)   set out any charge on which the proceedings concerned are based;
   (b)   specify any stipulated evidence, document or thing in such a way as to enable the directed person to identify it;
   (c)   specify grounds for believing that the directed person is likely to be able to give any stipulated evidence or produce any stipulated document or thing;
   (d)   specify grounds for believing that any stipulated evidence is likely to be material evidence;
   (e)   specify grounds for believing that any stipulated document or thing is likely to be material evidence.

(10) In subsection (9) above—

(a) references to any stipulated evidence, document or thing are to any evidence, document or thing whose giving or production is proposed to be required by the witness summons;

(b) references to the directed person are to the person to whom the witness summons is proposed to be directed.

2A Power to require advance production

A witness summons which is issued under section 2 above and which requires a person to produce a document or thing as mentioned in section 2(2) above may also require him to produce the document or thing—

(a) at a place stated in the summons, and

(b) at a time which is so stated and precedes that stated under section 2(2) above,

for inspection by the person applying for the summons.

2B Summons no longer needed

(1) If—

(a) a document or thing is produced in pursuance of a requirement imposed by a witness summons under section 2A above,

(b) the person applying for the summons concludes that a requirement imposed by the summons under section 2(2) above is no longer needed, and

(c) he accordingly applies to the Crown Court for a direction that the summons shall be of no further effect,

the court may direct accordingly.

(2) An application under this section must be made in accordance with Crown Court rules; and different provision may be made for different cases or descriptions of case.

(3) Crown Court rules may, in such cases as the rules may specify, require the effect of a direction under this section to be notified to the person to whom the summons is directed.

2C Application to make summons ineffective

(1) If a witness summons issued under section 2 above is directed to a person who—

(a) applies to the Crown Court,

(b) satisfies the court that he was not served with notice of the application to issue the summons and that he was neither present nor represented at the hearing of the application, and

(c) satisfies the court that he cannot give any evidence likely to be material evidence or, as the case may be, produce any document or thing likely to be material evidence,

the court may direct that the summons shall be of no effect.

(2) For the purposes of subsection (1) above it is immaterial—

(a) whether or not Crown Court rules require the person to be served with notice of the application to issue the summons;

(b) whether or not Crown Court rules enable the person to be present or represented at the hearing of the application.

(3) In subsection (1)(b) above "served" means—

(a) served in accordance with Crown Court rules, in a case where such rules require the person to be served with notice of the application to issue the summons;

(b) served in such way as appears reasonable to the court to which the application is made under this section, in any other case.

(4) The Crown Court may refuse to make a direction under this section if any requirement relating to the application under this section is not fulfilled.

(5) An application under this section must be made in accordance with Crown Court rules; and different provision may be made for different cases or descriptions of case.

(6) Crown Court rules may, in such cases as the rules may specify, require the service of notice of an application under this section on the person on whose application the witness summons was issued.

(7) Crown Court rules may, in such cases as the rules may specify, require that where—

(a) a person applying under this section can produce a particular document or thing, but

(b) he seeks to satisfy the court that the document or thing is not likely to be material evidence,

he must arrange for the document or thing to be available at the hearing of the application.

(8) Where a direction is made under this section that a witness summons shall be of no effect, the person on whose application the summons was issued may be ordered to pay the whole or any part of the costs of the application under this section.

(9) Any costs payable under an order made under subsection (8) above shall be taxed by the proper officer of the court, and payment of those costs shall be enforceable in the same manner as an order for payment of costs made by the High Court in a civil case or as a sum adjudged summarily to be paid as a civil debt.

Issue of witness summons of court's own motion

2D Issue of witness summons of Crown Court's own motion

For the purpose of any criminal proceedings before it, the Crown Court may of its own motion issue a summons (a witness summons) directed to a person and requiring him to—

(a) attend before the court at the time and place stated in the summons, and

(b) give evidence, or produce any document or thing specified in the summons.

2E Application to make summons ineffective

(1) If a witness summons issued under section 2D above is directed to a person who—

(a) applies to the Crown Court, and

(b) satisfies the court that he cannot give any evidence likely to be material evidence or, as the case may be, produce any document or thing likely to be material evidence,

the court may direct that the summons shall be of no effect.

(2) The Crown Court may refuse to make a direction under this section if any requirement relating to the application under this section is not fulfilled.

(3) An application under this section must be made in accordance with Crown Court rules; and different provision may be made for different cases or descriptions of case.

(4) Crown Court rules may, in such cases as the rules may specify, require that where—

(a) a person applying under this section can produce a particular document or thing, but
(b) he seeks to satisfy the court that the document or thing is not likely to be material evidence,

he must arrange for the document or thing to be available at the hearing of the application.

Other provisions".

(3) In section 3 (punishment for disobedience to witness summons) after subsection (1) there shall be inserted—

"(1A) Any person who without just excuse disobeys a requirement made by any court under section 2A above shall be guilty of contempt of that court and may be punished summarily by that court as if his contempt had been committed in the face of the court."

(4) In section 3, in subsection (2) for the words "such disobedience" there shall be substituted "any disobedience mentioned in subsection (1) or (1A) above".

(5) In section 4 (further process to secure attendance of witness) in the proviso to subsection (1) after the word "give" there shall be inserted "evidence likely to be".

(6) Schedule 1 (application for direction that witness summons shall be of no effect) shall be omitted.

(7) This section applies in relation to any proceedings for the purpose of which no witness summons has been issued under section 2 of the 1965 Act before the appointed day.

(8) The reference in subsection (7) to the appointed day is to such day as is appointed for the purposes of this section by the Secretary of State by order.

Explanatory text—See para **5.34**.

Commencement—On Royal Assent (4 July 1996), but see subs (7).

Subs (3) and (4)—The Criminal Procedure (Attendance of Witnesses) Act 1965, s 3, as amended by s 65 and s 66, provides:

'(1) Any person who without just excuse disobeys a witness summons requiring him to attend before any court shall be guilty of contempt of that court and may be punished summarily by that court as if his contempt had been committed in the face of the court.

(1A) [See new Act, s 66(3)].

(2) No person shall by reason of such disobedience be liable to imprisonment for a period exceeding three months.'

Subs (5)—The 1965 Act, s 4, as amended, provides:

'(1) If a judge of the [Crown Court] is satisfied by evidence on oath that a witness in respect of whom a witness summons is in force is unlikely to comply with the summons, the judge may issue a warrant to arrest the witness and bring him before the court before which he is required to attend:

Provided that a warrant shall not be issued under this subsection in the case of a witness subject to a conditional witness order unless notice has been given requiring him to attend the trial, nor unless the judge is satisfied by such evidence as aforesaid that the witness is likely to be able to give evidence likely to be material evidence or produce any document or thing likely to be material evidence in the proceedings.

(2) Where a witness who is required to attend before [the Crown Court] by virtue of a witness order or a witness summons fails to attend in compliance with the order or summons, that court may—

> (a) in any case, cause to be served on him a notice requiring him to attend the court forthwith or at such time as may be specified in the notice;
> (b) if the court is satisfied that there are reasonable grounds for believing that he has failed to attend without just excuse, or if he has failed to comply with a notice under paragraph (a) above, issue a warrant to arrest him and bring him before the court.

(3) A witness brought before the court in pursuance of a warrant under this section may be remanded by that court in custody or on bail (with or without sureties) until such time as the court may appoint for receiving his evidence or dealing with him under section 3 of this Act; and where a witness attends a court in pursuance of a notice under this section the court may direct that the notice shall have effect as if it required him to attend at any later time appointed by the court for receiving his evidence or dealing with him as aforesaid.'

Appointed day (subs (7))—No day had been appointed when this book went to press.

By order (subs (8))—The order must be made by statutory instrument; see s 77(1)–(4).

67 Witness summons: securing attendance of witness

(1) In section 4(1) of the Criminal Procedure (Attendance of Witnesses) Act 1965 (judge of High Court may issue warrant to arrest witness in respect of whom witness summons is in force) for the words "High Court" there shall be substituted "Crown Court".

(2) This section shall have effect in accordance with provision made by the Secretary of State by order.

Explanatory text—See para **5.44**.

Commencement—On Royal Assent (4 July 1996).

Section 4 of the Criminal Procedure (Attendance of Witnesses) Act 1965 (subs (1))—See annotations to s 66.

Order (subs (2))—The order must be made by statutory instrument; see s 77(1)–(4).

Other miscellaneous provisions

68 Use of written statements and depositions at trial

Schedule 2 to this Act (which relates to the use at the trial of written statements and depositions admitted in evidence in committal proceedings) shall have effect.

Explanatory text—See para **5.43**.

Commencement—On Royal Assent (4 July 1996).

69 Proof by written statement

(1) In section 9 of the Criminal Justice Act 1967 (proof by written statement) in subsection (3)(a) (statement by person under 21 must give his age) for "twenty-one" there shall be substituted "eighteen".

(2) This section applies in relation to statements tendered in evidence on or after the appointed day.

(3) The reference in subsection (2) to the appointed day is to such day as is appointed for the purposes of this section by the Secretary of State by order.

Explanatory text—See para **5.43**.

Commencement—On Royal Assent (4 July 1996), but see subs (2).

Section 9 of the Criminal Justice Act 1967 (subs (1))—Section 9 permits, in any criminal proceedings other than committal proceedings, a written statement to be admissible as evidence to the like extent as oral evidence to the like effect by that person. The relevant conditions are set out in subss (2) and (3).

Order (subs (3))—The order must be made by statutory instrument; see s 77(1)–(4).

70 Indemnification of justices and justices' clerks

(1) In section 53 of the Justices of the Peace Act 1979 (indemnification of justices and justices' clerks) the following subsection shall be inserted after subsection (1)—

"(1A) So far as the duty mentioned in subsection (1) above relates to criminal matters, that subsection shall have effect as if—

(a) for the word "may" there were substituted "shall", and
(b) for the words following paragraph (c) there were substituted "unless it is proved, in respect of the matters giving rise to the proceedings or claim, that he acted in bad faith".

(2) This section applies in relation to things done or omitted on or after the appointed day.

(3) The reference in subsection (2) to the appointed day is to such day as is appointed for the purposes of this section by the Secretary of State by order.

Explanatory text—See paras **7.44–7.49**.

Commencement—On Royal Assent (4 July 1996), but see subs (2).

Criminal matters (subs (1))—Whether or not a matter is in a criminal matter depends on the nature of the proceedings to which it relates (or of the underlying proceedings or decision if the judgment is in judicial review proceedings: *Secretary of State for the Home Department ex parte Garner* (1991) 3 Admin LR 33 (CA); *Tan v Cameron* [1993] 2 All ER 493 (PC)).

The authorities show that, if the direct outcome of the proceedings may be the trial and punishment of a person by a court for a breach of the public law, they are a 'criminal matter'. (*Amand v Home Secretary and Minister of Defence of Royal Netherlands Government* [1943] AC 147, [1942] 2 All ER 381 (HL); *Hull Prison Board of Visitors ex parte St Germain* [1979] QB 425, [1979] 1 All ER 701 (CA); *DPP ex parte Raymond* (1979) 70 Cr App Rep 233 (CA); *Bonalumi v Secretary of State for the Home Department* [1985] QB 675, [1985] 1 All ER 797 (CA).

Unless it is proved (subs (1))—The civil standard of proof will apply, ie proof on the balance of probabilities. It will not be satisfied unless it is shown by those claiming the bad faith in issue that it is more probable than not that there was bad faith (*Miller v Minister of Pensions* [1947] 2 All ER 372 at 373, 374).

Appointed day (subss (2) and (3))—No day had been appointed when this book went to press.

By order (subs (3))—The order must be made by statutory instrument; see s 77(1)–(4).

71 Meaning of preliminary stage of criminal proceedings

(1) Section 22 of the Prosecution of Offences Act 1985 (power of Secretary of State to set time limits in relation to preliminary stages of criminal proceedings) shall be amended as mentioned in subsections (2) and (3).

(2) In subsection (11) the following shall be substituted for the definition of "preliminary stage"—

> "'preliminary stage', in relation to any proceedings, does not include any stage after the start of the trial (within the meaning given by subsections (11A) and (11B) below);".

(3) The following subsections shall be inserted after subsection (11)—

> "(11A) For the purposes of this section, the start of a trial on indictment shall be taken to occur when a jury is sworn to consider the issue of guilt or fitness to plead or, if the court accepts a plea of guilty before a jury is sworn, when that plea is accepted; but this is subject to section 8 of the Criminal Justice Act 1987 and section 30 of the Criminal Procedure and Investigations Act 1996 (preparatory hearings).
>
> (11B) For the purposes of this section, the start of a summary trial shall be taken to occur—
>
> > (a) when the court begins to hear evidence for the prosecution at the trial or to consider whether to exercise its power under section 37(3) of the Mental Health Act 1983 (power to make hospital order without convicting the accused), or
> >
> > (b) if the court accepts a plea of guilty without proceeding as mentioned above, when that plea is accepted."

(4) The Prosecution of Offences (Custody Time Limits) Regulations 1987 shall be amended as follows, but without prejudice to the power to make further regulations amending or revoking the provisions amended—

> (a) in regulation 2 (interpretation) for paragraph (3) there shall be substituted—
> > "(3) In these Regulations any reference to the start of the trial shall be construed in accordance with section 22(11A) and (11B) of the 1985 Act.";
> (b) in regulation 4 (custody time limits in magistrates' courts) in paragraphs (2) and (3) for "commencement" there shall be substituted "start";
> (c) in regulation 5 (custody time limits in Crown Court) for "his arraignment" in paragraphs (3)(a) and (b) and (6)(a) and (b), and for "the accused's arraignment" in paragraph (5), there shall be substituted "the start of the trial";
> (d) regulation 5(7) (when arraignment occurs) shall be omitted.

(5) This section applies in relation to—

> (a) any time limit which begins to run on or after the appointed day, and
> (b) any time limit which has begun to run and has not expired before that day,

except that it does not apply in relation to proceedings for an offence for which the accused has been duly arraigned in the Crown Court before that day.

(6) The reference in subsection (5) to the appointed day is to such day as is appointed for the purposes of this section by the Secretary of State by order.

Explanatory text—See paras **5.27–5.34**.

Commencement—On Royal Assent (4 July 1996), but see subs (5).

Section 8 of the Criminal Justice Act 1987 (subs (3))—See annotations to s 39.

Subs (4)—Regs 4(2) and (3), as amended, provides:

'(2) Except as provided in paragraph (3) below, in the case of an offence triable either way the maximum period of custody between the accused's first appearance and the start of summary trial or, as the case may be, the time when the court decides whether or not to commit the accused to the Crown Court for trial shall be 70 days. . . .

(3) In the case of an offence triable either way if, before the expiry of 56 days following the day of the accused's first appearance, the court decides to proceed to summary trial in pursuance of sections 19 to 24 of the 1980 Act the maximum period of custody between the accused's first appearance and the start of the summary trial shall be 56 days.'

Regulation 5(3) and (6), as amended, provides:

'(3) The maximum period of custody –

(a) between the time when the accused is committed for trial and the start of the trial, or
(b) where a bill of indictment is preferred against him under the said section 2(2)(b), between the preferment of the bill and the start of the trial,

shall, subject to the following provisions of this Regulation, be 112 days.

(6) Where, following a committal for trial, the bill of indictment preferred against the accused (not being a bill preferred under the said section 2(2)(b) contains a count charging an offence for which he was not committed for trial, the maximum period of custody—

(a) between the preferment of the bill and the start of the trial, or
(b) if the count was added to the bill after its preferment, between that addition and the start of the trial,

shall be 112 days less any period, or the aggregate of any periods, during which he has, since the committal, been in the custody of the Crown Court in relation to an offence for which he was committed for trial.'

Appointed day (subss (5) and (6))—No day had been appointed when this book went to press.

By order (subs (6))—The order must be made by statutory instrument; see s 77(1)–(4).

72 Fraud

Schedule 3 (which amends provisions relating to serious or complex fraud) shall have effect.

Explanatory text—See paras **4.34–4.37**.

Commencement—On Royal Assent (4 July 1996).

73 [*Applies to Scotland only.*]

74 Alibi

(1) Section 11 of the Criminal Justice Act 1967 (notice of alibi) shall cease to have effect, but subject to the following provisions of this section.

(2) Subsection (1) does not affect the application of section 11 of the Criminal Justice Act 1967 to proceedings before courts martial by virtue of section 12 of that Act.

(3) The reference in section 12 of the Criminal Justice Act 1967 to section 11 as it applies to proceedings on indictment shall be construed as a reference to it as it would apply to proceedings on indictment apart from subsection (1) of this section.

(4) In section 9(6) of the Criminal Justice Act 1987 (disclosure in cases involving fraud) in paragraph (a) for the words "section 11 of the Criminal Justice Act 1967" there shall be substituted "section 5(7) of the Criminal Procedure and Investigations Act 1996".

(5) This section applies in relation to alleged offences into which no criminal investigation, within the meaning given by section 1(4), has begun before the day appointed under section 1(5).

Explanatory text—See para **2.64**.

Commencement—On Royal Assent (4 July 1996), but see subs (5).

Notice of alibi (subs (1))—See annotations to s 5.

Section 12 [of the Criminal Justice Act 1967] (subs (2) and (3))—Section 12 applies ss 9–11 of the 1967 Act to the trial of offences by courts martial.

Proceedings on indictment (subs (3))—See annotations to s 1.

Section 9(6) of the Criminal Justice Act 1987 (subs (4))—Section 9(6) of the 1987 Act provides that a defence statement thereunder need not specify who will give evidence. Details of an alibi are an exception to this and the charge made by s 77 is consequential on s 5 of the new Act.

Criminal investigation (subs (5))—See para **2.6**.

Appointed day (subs (5))—No day had been appointed when this book went to press.

General

75 Time when alleged offence committed

(1) Subsection (2) applies for the purposes of sections 52(3) and 54(7).

(2) Where an offence is alleged to be committed over a period of more than one day, or at some time during a period of more than one day, it must be taken to be alleged to be committed on the last of the days in the period.

(3) Subsection (2) applies for the purposes of section 61(1) as if "alleged to be" (in each place) were omitted.

Commencement—On Royal Assent (4 July 1996).

76 Power of magistrates' courts

In section 148(2) of the Magistrates' Courts Act 1980 (power of court to act where another may act) the reference to that Act includes a reference to this Act.

Explanatory text—See para **7.43**.

Commencement—On Royal Assent (4 July 1996).

77 Orders and regulations

(1) This section concerns the powers of the Secretary of State to make orders or regulations under this Act.

(2) Any power to make an order or regulations may be exercised differently in relation to different areas or in relation to other different cases or descriptions of case.

(3) Any order or regulations may include such supplementary, incidental, consequential or transitional provisions as appear to the Secretary of State to be necessary or expedient.

(4) Any power to make an order or regulations shall be exercisable by statutory instrument.

(5) No order under section 25 shall have effect unless approved by a resolution of each House of Parliament.

(6) A statutory instrument containing—

(a) an order under section 78, or
(b) regulations,

shall be subject to annulment in pursuance of a resolution of either House of Parliament.

Commencement—On Royal Assent (4 July 1996).

General—This is a fairly standard provision as regards the grant to a Minister of powers to make orders or regulations. With the exceptions mentioned below, the Secretary of State must exercise his powers of delegated legislation under the Act under the 'negative resolution' procedure (subs (5)). The more rigorous 'affirmative resolution' procedure is reserved for orders under s 25 (criminal investigation code of practice), just as it is required for codes of practice under PACE by PACE, s 67, in view of the particularly sensitive matters with which it deals. On the other hand, orders made under various sections appointing 'appointed days' are not subject to either of these procedures, and are not even required to be laid before Parliament in order to be operative.

Statutory instrument (subss (4) and (6))—With regard to statutory instruments generally, see the Statutory Instruments Act 1946.

Unless approved by a resolution of each House of Parliament (subs (5))—A statutory instrument containing an order under s 25 will not come into effect unless it has been laid before each House of Parliament and been approved by a resolution of each House. No amendment by either House is possible.

Subject to annulment in pursuance of a resolution of either House of Parliament (subs (6))—A statutory instrument containing an order under s 78 or regulations made under the Act must be laid before each House of Parliament before it comes into operation, unless it is essential that it should come into operation at an earlier date (in which case a special procedure must be followed), but it may be annulled by Order in Council pursuant to a resolution of either House of Parliament, that resolution being within the period of forty days beginning with the day on which the instrument was laid: Statutory Instruments Act 1946, ss 4 and 5. Annulment does not prejudice the validity of anything previously done under the instrument: ibid, s 5(1). In reckoning the period of forty days, account is to be taken of the day on which it was laid: *Hare v Gocher*, [1962] 2 QB 641; [1962] 2 All ER 763; *Trow v Ind Coope (West Midlands) Ltd* [1967] 2 QB 899; [1967] 2 All ER 900 (CA). On the other hand, no account is to be taken of any time during which Parliament is dissolved or prorogued or during which both Houses are adjourned for more than four days: Statutory Instruments Act 1946, s 7(1).

78 Application to armed forces

(1) Subject to subsection (2) and to section 74(2) and (3), nothing in this Act applies to—

(a) proceedings before a court martial constituted under the Army Act 1955, the Air Force Act 1955 or the Naval Discipline Act 1957;
(b) proceedings before a Standing Civilian Court;
(c) any investigation conducted with a view to it being ascertained whether a person should be charged with an offence under any of those Acts or whether a person charged with such an offence is guilty of it.

(2) The Secretary of State may by order—

(a) make as regards any proceedings falling within subsection (3) provision which is equivalent to the provisions contained in or made under Part I, subject to such modifications as he thinks fit and specifies in the order;

(b) make as regards any investigation falling within subsection (4) provision which is equivalent to the provisions contained in or made under Part II, subject to such modifications as he thinks fit and specifies in the order.

(3) The proceedings falling within this subsection are—

(a) proceedings before a court martial constituted under the Army Act 1955;

(b) proceedings before a court martial constituted under the Air Force Act 1955;

(c) proceedings before a court martial constituted under the Naval Discipline Act 1957;

(d) proceedings before a Standing Civilian Court.

(4) An investigation falls within this subsection if it is conducted with a view to it being ascertained whether a person should be charged with an offence under any of the Acts mentioned in subsection (3) or whether a person charged with such an offence is guilty of it.

(5) An order under this section may make provision in such way as the Secretary of State thinks fit, and may in particular apply any of the provisions concerned subject to such modifications as he thinks fit and specifies in the order.

(6) Without prejudice to the generality of section 77(3), an order under this section may include provision—

(a) repealing section 11 of the Criminal Justice Act 1967 (alibi) as it applies to proceedings before courts martial;

(b) amending or repealing any provision of section 12 of that Act or of section 74 above.

Commencement—On Royal Assent (4 July 1996).

79 Extent

(1) This Act does not extend to Scotland, with the exception of—

(a) sections 37, 38, 41, 42, 59, 60, 61(3), 63, 72, 73, 74(2) and (3) and 78, this section and section 81;

(b) paragraphs 6 and 7 of Schedule 3, and paragraph 8 of that Schedule so far as it relates to paragraphs 6 and 7;

(c) paragraph 5 of Schedule 5;

(d) paragraph 12 of Schedule 5 so far as it relates to provisions amending section 11 of the Criminal Justice Act 1987.

(2) Section 73 extends only to Scotland.

(3) Parts III and VI and sections 44, 47, 65, 67, 68 and 71 do not extend to Northern Ireland.

(4) In its application to Northern Ireland, this Act has effect subject to the modifications set out in Schedule 4.

(5) Section 74(2) and (3) extend to any place where proceedings before courts martial may be held.

(6) Section 78 extends as follows—

(a) so far as it relates to proceedings, it extends to any place where such proceedings may be held;

(b) so far as it relates to investigations, it extends to any place where such investigations may be conducted.

80 Repeals

The provisions mentioned in Schedule 5 are repealed (or revoked) to the extent specified in column 3, but subject to any provision of that Schedule.

Commencement—On Royal Assent (4 July 1996).

81 Citation

This Act may be cited as the Criminal Procedure and Investigations Act 1996.

SCHEDULES

SCHEDULE 1

COMMITTAL PROCEEDINGS

PART I
MAGISTRATES' COURTS ACT 1980

Introduction

1 The Magistrates' Courts Act 1980 shall be amended as mentioned in this Part of this Schedule.

Amendments

2 (1) Section 4 (general nature of committal proceedings) shall be amended as follows.

(2) The following subsection shall be substituted for subsection (3)—

"(3) Subject to subsection (4) below, evidence tendered before examining justices shall be tendered in the presence of the accused."

(3) In subsection (4) for the word "given" (in each place) there shall be substituted "tendered".

3 The following sections shall be inserted after section 5—

"5A Evidence which is admissible

(1) Evidence falling within subsection (2) below, and only that evidence, shall be admissible by a magistrates' court inquiring into an offence as examining justices.

(2) Evidence falls within this subsection if it—

    (a) is tendered by or on behalf of the prosecutor, and
    (b) falls within subsection (3) below.

(3) The following evidence falls within this subsection—

    (a) written statements complying with section 5B below;
    (b) the documents or other exhibits (if any) referred to in such statements;
    (c) depositions complying with section 5C below;
    (d) the documents or other exhibits (if any) referred to in such depositions;
    (e) statements complying with section 5D below;
    (f) documents falling within section 5E below.

(4) In this section "document" means anything in which information of any description is recorded.

5B Written statements

(1) For the purposes of section 5A above a written statement complies with this section if—

    (a) the conditions falling within subsection (2) below are met, and
    (b) such of the conditions falling within subsection (3) below as apply are met.

(2) The conditions falling within this subsection are that—

(a) the statement purports to be signed by the person who made it;
(b) the statement contains a declaration by that person to the effect that it is true to the best of his knowledge and belief and that he made the statement knowing that, if it were tendered in evidence, he would be liable to prosecution if he wilfully stated in it anything which he knew to be false or did not believe to be true;
(c) before the statement is tendered in evidence a copy of the statement is given, by or on behalf of the prosecutor, to each of the other parties to the proceedings.

(3) The conditions falling within this subsection are that—

(a) if the statement is made by a person under 18 years old, it gives his age;
(b) if it is made by a person who cannot read it, it is read to him before he signs it and is accompanied by a declaration by the person who so read the statement to the effect that it was so read;
(c) if it refers to any other document as an exhibit, the copy given to any other party to the proceedings under subsection (2)(c) above is accompanied by a copy of that document or by such information as may be necessary to enable the party to whom it is given to inspect that document or a copy of it.

(4) So much of any statement as is admitted in evidence by virtue of this section shall, unless the court commits the accused for trial by virtue of section 6(2) below or the court otherwise directs, be read aloud at the hearing; and where the court so directs an account shall be given orally of so much of any statement as is not read aloud.

(5) Any document or other object referred to as an exhibit and identified in a statement admitted in evidence by virtue of this section shall be treated as if it had been produced as an exhibit and identified in court by the maker of the statement.

(6) In this section "document" means anything in which information of any description is recorded.

5C Depositions

(1) For the purposes of section 5A above a deposition complies with this section if—

(a) a copy of it is sent to the prosecutor under section 97A(9) below,
(b) the condition falling within subsection (2) below is met, and
(c) the condition falling within subsection (3) below is met, in a case where it applies.

(2) The condition falling within this subsection is that before the magistrates' court begins to inquire into the offence concerned as examining justices a copy of the deposition is given, by or on behalf of the prosecutor, to each of the other parties to the proceedings.

(3) The condition falling within this subsection is that, if the deposition refers to any other document as an exhibit, the copy given to any other party to the proceedings under subsection (2) above is accompanied by a copy of that document or by such information as may be necessary to enable the party to whom it is given to inspect that document or a copy of it.

(4) So much of any deposition as is admitted in evidence by virtue of this section shall, unless the court commits the accused for trial by virtue of section 6(2) below or the court otherwise directs, be read aloud at the hearing; and where the court so

directs an account shall be given orally of so much of any deposition as is not read aloud.

(5) Any document or other object referred to as an exhibit and identified in a deposition admitted in evidence by virtue of this section shall be treated as if it had been produced as an exhibit and identified in court by the person whose evidence is taken as the deposition.

(6) In this section "document" means anything in which information of any description is recorded.

5D Statements

(1) For the purposes of section 5A above a statement complies with this section if the conditions falling within subsections (2) to (4) below are met.

(2) The condition falling within this subsection is that, before the committal proceedings begin, the prosecutor notifies the magistrates' court and each of the other parties to the proceedings that he believes—

    (a) that the statement might by virtue of section 23 or 24 of the Criminal Justice Act 1988 (statements in certain documents) be admissible as evidence if the case came to trial, and

    (b) that the statement would not be admissible as evidence otherwise than by virtue of section 23 or 24 of that Act if the case came to trial.

(3) The condition falling within this subsection is that—

    (a) the prosecutor's belief is based on information available to him at the time he makes the notification,

    (b) he has reasonable grounds for his belief, and

    (b) he gives the reasons for his belief when he makes the notification.

(4) The condition falling within this subsection is that when the court or a party is notified as mentioned in subsection (2) above a copy of the statement is given, by or on behalf of the prosecutor, to the court or the party concerned.

(5) So much of any statement as is in writing and is admitted in evidence by virtue of this section shall, unless the court commits the accused for trial by virtue of section 6(2) below or the court otherwise directs, be read aloud at the hearing; and where the court so directs an account shall be given orally of so much of any statement as is not read aloud.

5E Other documents

(1) The following documents fall within this section—

    (a) any document which by virtue of any enactment is evidence in proceedings before a magistrates' court inquiring into an offence as examining justices;

    (b) any document which by virtue of any enactment is admissible, or may be used, or is to be admitted or received, in or as evidence in such proceedings;

    (c) any document which by virtue of any enactment may be considered in such proceedings;

    (d) any document whose production constitutes proof in such proceedings by virtue of any enactment;

    (e) any document by the production of which evidence may be given in such proceedings by virtue of any enactment.

(2) In subsection (1) above—

(a) references to evidence include references to prima facie evidence;

(b) references to any enactment include references to any provision of this Act.

(3) So much of any document as is admitted in evidence by virtue of this section shall, unless the court commits the accused for trial by virtue of section 6(2) below or the court otherwise directs, be read aloud at the hearing; and where the court so directs an account shall be given orally of so much of any document as is not read aloud.

(4) In this section "document" means anything in which information of any description is recorded.

5F Proof by production of copy

(1) Where a statement, deposition or document is admissible in evidence by virtue of section 5B, 5C, 5D or 5E above it may be proved by the production of—

(a) the statement, deposition or document, or

(b) a copy of it or the material part of it.

(2) Subsection (1)(b) above applies whether or not the statement, deposition or document is still in existence.

(3) It is immaterial for the purposes of this section how many removes there are between a copy and the original.

(4) In this section "copy", in relation to a statement, deposition or document, means anything onto which information recorded in the statement, deposition or document has been copied, by whatever means and whether directly or indirectly."

4 In section 6 (discharge or committal for trial) the following subsections shall be substituted for subsections (1) and (2)—

"(1) A magistrates' court inquiring into an offence as examining justices shall on consideration of the evidence—

(a) commit the accused for trial if it is of opinion that there is sufficient evidence to put him on trial by jury for any indictable offence;

(b) discharge him if it is not of that opinion and he is in custody for no other cause than the offence under inquiry;

but the preceding provisions of this subsection have effect subject to the provisions of this and any other Act relating to the summary trial of indictable offences.

(2) If a magistrates' court inquiring into an offence as examining justices is satisfied that all the evidence tendered by or on behalf of the prosecutor falls within section 5A(3) above, it may commit the accused for trial for the offence without consideration of the contents of any statements, depositions or other documents, and without consideration of any exhibits which are not documents, unless—

(a) the accused or one of the accused has no legal representative acting for him in the case, or

(b) a legal representative for the accused or one of the accused, as the case may be, has requested the court to consider a submission that there is insufficient evidence to put that accused on trial by jury for the offence;

and subsection (1) above shall not apply to a committal for trial under this subsection."

5 (1) Section 25 (change from summary trial to committal proceedings) shall be amended as follows.

(2) In subsections (2) and (6) for the words "may adjourn the hearing without remanding the accused" there shall be substituted "shall adjourn the hearing."

(3) The following subsection shall be inserted after subsection (7)—

"(8) If the court adjourns the hearing under subsection (2) or (6) above it may (if it thinks fit) do so without remanding the accused."

6 Section 28 (using in summary trial evidence given in committal proceedings) shall be omitted.

7 In section 97 (summons to witness and warrant for his arrest) in subsection (1)—

- (a) the words "at an inquiry into an indictable offence by a magistrates' court for that commission area or" shall be omitted;
- (b) for the words "such a court" there shall be substituted "a magistrates' court for that commission area".

8 The following section shall be inserted after section 97—

"97A Summons or warrant as to committal proceedings

(1) Subsection (2) below applies where a justice of the peace for any commission area is satisfied that—

- (a) any person in England or Wales is likely to be able to make on behalf of the prosecutor a written statement containing material evidence, or produce on behalf of the prosecutor a document or other exhibit likely to be material evidence, for the purposes of proceedings before a magistrates' court inquiring into an offence as examining justices,
- (b) the person will not voluntarily make the statement or produce the document or other exhibit, and
- (c) the magistrates' court mentioned in paragraph (a) above is a court for the commission area concerned.

(2) In such a case the justice shall issue a summnons directed to that person requiring him to attend before a justice at the time and place appointed in the summons to have his evidence taken as a deposition or to produce the document or other exhibit.

(3) If a justice of the peace is satisfied by evidence on oath of the matters mentioned in subsection (1) above, and also that it is probable that a summons under subsection (2) above would not procure the result required by it, the justice may instead of issuing a summons issue a warrant to arrest the person concerned and bring him before a justice at the time and place specified in the warrant.

(4) A summons may also be issued under subsection (2) above if the justice is satisfied that the person concerned is outside the British Islands, but no warrant may be issued under subsection (3) above unless the justice is satisfied by evidence on oath that the person concerned is in England or Wales.

(5) If—

- (a) a person fails to attend before a justice in answer to a summons under this section,
- (b) the justice is satisfied by the evidence on oath that he is likely to be able to make a statement or produce a document or other exhibit as mentioned in subsection (1)(a) above,

(c) it is proved on oath, or in such other manner as may be prescribed, that he has been duly served with the summons and that a reasonable sum has been paid or tendered to him for costs and expenses, and

(d) it appears to the justice that there is no just excuse for the failure,

the justice may issue a warrant to arrest him and bring him before a justice at a time and place specified in the warrant.

(6) Where—

(a) a summons is issued under subsection (2) above or a warrant is issued under subsection (3) or (5) above, and

(b) the summons or warrant is issued with a view to securing that a person has his evidence taken as a deposition,

the time appointed in the summons or specified in the warrant shall be such as to enable the evidence to be taken as a deposition before a magistrates' court begins to inquire into the offence concerned as examining justices.

(7) If any person attending or brought before a justice in pursuance of this section refuses without just excuse to have his evidence taken as a deposition, or to produce the document or other exhibit, the justice may do one or both of the following—

(a) commit him to custody until the expiration of such period not exceeding one month as may be specified in the summons or warrant or until he sooner has his evidence taken as a deposition or produces the document or other exhibit;

(b) impose on him a fine not exceeding £2,500.

(8) A fine imposed under subsection (7) above shall be deemed, for the purposes of any enactment, to be a sum adjudged to be paid by a conviction.

(9) If in pursuance of this section a person has his evidence taken as a deposition, the clerk of the justice concerned shall as soon as is reasonably practicable send a copy of the deposition to the prosecutor.

(10) If in pursuance of this section a person produces an exhibit which is a document, the clerk of the justice concerned shall as soon as is reasonably practicable send a copy of the document to the prosecutor.

(11) If in pursuance of this section a person produces an exhibit which is not a document, the clerk of the justice concerned shall as soon as is reasonably practicable inform the prosecutor of the fact and of the nature of the exhibit."

9 Section 102 (written statements before examining justices) shall be omitted.

10 (1) Section 103 (evidence of children in certain committal proceedings) shall be amended as follows.

(2) The following subsection shall be substituted for subsection (1)—

"(1) In any proceedings before a magistrates' court inquiring as examining justices into an offence to which this section applies, a statement made in writing by or taken in writing from a child shall be admissible in evidence of any matter."

(3) Subsections (3) and (4) (exclusion of subsection (1) and of section 28) shall be omitted.

11 Section 105 (deposition of person dangerously ill may be given in evidence before examining justices) shall be omitted.

12 In section 106 (false written statements tendered in evidence) in subsection (1) for "tendered" there shall be substituted "admitted" and for "section 102" there shall be substituted "section 5B".

13 In Schedule 3 the following shall be substituted for paragraph 2(a) (representative may make statement on behalf of corporation before examining justices)—

> "(a) make before examining justices such representations as could be made by an accused who is not a corporation;".

PART II
OTHER PROVISIONS

Criminal Law Amendment Act 1867

14 Sections 6 and 7 of the Criminal Law Amendment Act 1867 (statements taken under section 105 of the Magistrates' Courts Act 1980) shall be omitted.

Bankers' Books Evidence Act 1879

15 The following shall be inserted at the end of section 4 of the Bankers' Books Evidence Act 1879—

> "Where the proceedings concerned are proceedings before a magistrates' court inquiring into an offence as examining justices, this section shall have effect with the omission of the words "orally or"."

16 The following shall be inserted at the end of section 5 of the Bankers' Books Evidence Act 1879—

> "Where the proceedings concerned are proceedings before a magistrates' court inquiring into an offence as examining justices, this section shall have effect with the omission of the words "either orally or"."

Administration of Justice (Miscellaneous Provisions) Act 1933

17 In section 2 of the Administration of Justice (Miscellaneous Provisions) Act 1933 (procedure for indictment of offencers) in proviso (i) to subsection (2) for the words "in any examination or deposition taken before a justice in his presence" there shall be substituted "to the magistrates' court inquiring into that offence as examining justices".

Criminal Justice Act 1948

18 In section 41 of the Criminal Justice Act 1948 (evidence by certificate) the following subsection shall be inserted after subsection (5)—

> "(5A) Where the proceedings mentioned in subsection (1) above are proceedings before a magistrates' court inquiring into an offence as examining justices this section shall have effect with the omission of—
>
> (a) subsection (4), and
> (b) in subsection (5), paragraph (b) and the word "or" immediately preceding it."

Theft Act 1968

19 In section 27 of the Theft Act 1968 (evidence on charge of theft or handling stolen goods) the following subsection shall be inserted after subsection (4)—

"(4A) Where the proceedings mentioned in subsection (4) above are proceedings before a magistrates' court inquiring into an offence as examining justices that subsection shall have effect with the omission of the words from "subject to the following conditions" to the end of the subsection."

20 In section 28 of the Theft Act 1968 (orders for restitution) in subsection (4) for the words from "the depositions" to the end of the subsection there shall be substituted "and such written statements, depositions and other documents as were tendered by or on behalf of the prosecutor at any committal proceedings".

Children and Young Persons Act 1969

21 In Schedule 5 to the Children and Young Persons Act 1969, in paragraph 55 for the words "section 102" there shall be substituted "section 5B".

Criminal Justice Act 1972

22 (1) Section 46 of the Criminal Justice Act 1972 (written statements made outside England and Wales) shall be amended as follows.

(2) In subsection (1) the following words shall be omitted—

    (a) "Section 102 of the Magistrates' Courts Act 1980 and";
    (b) "which respectively allow";
    (c) "committal proceedings and in other";
    (d) "and section 106 of the said Act of 1980";
    (e) "which punish the making of";
    (f) "102 or";
    (g) ", as the case may be".

(3) The following subsections shall be inserted after subsection (1)—

"(1A) The following provisions, namely—

    (a) so much of section 5A of the Magistrates' Courts Act 1980 as relates to written statements and to documents or other exhibits referred to in them,
    (b) section 5B of that Act, and
    (c) section 106 of that Act,

shall apply where written statements are made in Scotland or Northern Ireland as well as where written statements are made in England and Wales.

(1B) The following provisions, namely—

    (a) so much of section 5A of the Magistrates' Courts Act 1980 as relates to written statements and to documents or other exhibits referred to in them, and
    (b) section 5B of that Act,

shall (subject to subsection (1C) below) apply where written statements are made outside the United Kingdom.

(1C) Where written statements are made outside the United Kingdom—

   (a) section 5B of the Magistrates' Courts Act 1980 shall apply with the omission of subsections (2)(b) and (3A);

   (b) paragraph 1 of Schedule 2 to the Criminal Procedure and Investigations Act 1996 (use of written statements at trial) shall not apply."

(4) Subsection (2) shall be omitted.

Sexual Offences (Amendment) Act 1976

23 (1) Section 3 of the Sexual Offences (Amendment) Act 1976 (application of restrictions on evidence at certain trials to committal proceedings etc.) shall be amended as follows.

(2) The following subsection shall be substituted for subsection (1)—

"(1) Where a magistrates' court inquires into a rape offence as examining justices, then, except with the consent of the court, no restricted matter shall be raised; and for this purpose a restricted matter is a matter as regards which evidence could not be adduced and a question could not be asked without leave in pursuance of section 2 of this Act if—

   (a) the inquiry were a trial at which a person is charged as mentioned in section 2(1) of this Act, and

   (b) each of the accused at the inquiry were charged at the trial with the offence or offences of which he is accused at the inquiry."

(3) In subsection (2) for the words "evidence or question" (in each place) there shall be substituted "matter".

Police and Criminal Evidence Act 1984

24 The following shall be inserted at the end of section 71 of the Police and Criminal Evidence Act 1984 (microfilm copies)—

"Where the proceedings concerned are proceedings before a magistrates' court inquiring into an offence as examining justices this section shall have effect with the omission of the words "authenticated in such manner as the court may approve."

25 In section 76 of the Police and Criminal Evidence Act 1984 (confessions) the following subsection shall be inserted after subsection (8)—

"(9) Where the proceedings mentioned in subsection (1) above are proceedings before a magistrates' court inquiring into an offence as examining justices this section shall have effect with the omission of—

   (a) in subsection (1) the words "and is not excluded by the court in pursuance of this section", and

   (b) subsections (2) to (6) and (8)."

26 In section 78 of the Police and Criminal Evidence Act 1984 (exclusion of unfair evidence) the following subsection shall be inserted after subsection (2)—

"(3) This section shall not apply in the case of proceedings before a magistrates' court inquiring into an offence as examining justices."

27 In Schedule 3 to the Police and Criminal Evidence Act 1984 (computer records) at the end of paragraph 9 there shall be inserted the words "; but the preceding provisions of this paragraph shall not apply where the court is a magistrates' court inquiring into an offence as examining justices."

Criminal Justice Act 1988

28 In section 23 of the Criminal Justice Act 1988 (first-hand hearsay) the following subsection shall be inserted after subsection (4)—

"(5) This section shall not apply to proceedings before a magistrates' court inquiring into an offence as examining justices."

29 In section 24 of the Criminal Justice Act 1988 (business etc. documents) the following subsection shall be inserted after subsection (4)—

"(5) This section shall not apply to proceedings before a magistrates' court inquiring into an offence as examining justices."

30 The following shall be inserted at the end of section 26 of the Criminal Justice Act 1988 (statements in certain documents)—

"This section shall not apply to proceedings before a magistrates' court inquiring into an offence as examining justices."

31 The following shall be inserted at the end of section 27 of the Criminal Justice Act 1988 (proof of statements contained in documents)—

"This section shall not apply to proceedings before a magistrates' court inquiring into an offence as examining justices."

32 In section 30 of the Criminal Justice Act 1988 (expert reports) the following subsection shall be inserted after subsection (4)—

"(4A) Where the proceedings mentioned in subsection (1) above are proceedings before a magistrates' court inquiring into an offence as examining justices this section shall have effect with the omission of—

(a) in subsection (1) the words "whether or not the person making it attends to give oral evidence in those proceedings", and
(b) subsections (2) to (4)."

33 In section 32A(10) of the Criminal Justice Act 1988 (video recordings) the words "notwithstanding that the child witness is not called at the committal proceedings" shall be omitted.

34 In section 40 of the Criminal Justice Act 1988 (power to join in indictment count for common assault etc.) in subsection (1) for the words from "in an examination" to the end of the subsection there shall be substituted "to a magistrates' court inquiring into the offence as examining justices".

Road Traffic Offenders Act 1988

35 In section 11 of the Road Traffic Offenders Act 1988 (evidence by certificate as to driver, user or owner) the following subsection shall be inserted after subsection (3)—

"(3A) Where the proceedings mentioned in subsection (1) above are proceedings before a magistrates' court inquiring into an offence as examining justices this section shall have effect with the omission of—

   (a) subsection (2), and

   (b) in subsection (3), paragraph (b) and the word "or" immediately preceding it."

36 In section 13 of the Road Traffic Offenders Act 1988 (admissibility of records as evidence) the following subsection shall be inserted after subsection (6)—

"(7) Where the proceedings mentioned in subsection (2) above are proceedings before a magistrates' court inquiring into an offence as examining justices this section shall have effect as if—

   (a) in subsection (2) the words "to the same extent as oral evidence of that fact is admissible in those proceedings" were omitted;

   (b) in subsection (4) the word "and" were inserted at the end of paragraph (a);

   (c) in subsection (4), paragraphs (c) and (d) and the words "as if the accused had appeared and admitted it" were omitted."

37 In section 16 of the Road Traffic Offenders Act 1988 (specimens) the following subsection shall be inserted after subsection (6)—

"(6A) Where the proceedings mentioned in section 15(1) of this Act are proceedings before a magistrates' court inquiring into an offence as examining justices this section shall have effect with the omission of subsection (4)."

38 In section 20 of the Road Traffic Offenders Act 1988 (speeding etc.) the following subsection shall be inserted after subsection (8)—

"(8A) Where the proceedings for an offence to which this section applies are proceedings before a magistrates' court inquiring into an offence as examining justices this section shall have effect as if in subsection (8) the words from "and nothing" to the end of the subsection were omitted."

PART III
COMMENCEMENT

39 Parts I and II of this Schedule shall have effect in accordance with provision made by the Secretary of State by order.

Section 68   **SCHEDULE 2**

STATEMENTS AND DEPOSITIONS

Statements

1 (1) Sub-paragraph (2) applies if—

   (a) a written statement has been admitted in evidence in proceedings before a magistrates' court inquiring into an offence as examining justices,

   (b) in those proceedings a person has been committed for trial,

   (c) for the purposes of section 5A of the Magistrates' Courts Act 1980 the statement complied with section 5B of that Act prior to the committal for trial,

   (d) the statement purports to be signed by a justice of the peace, and

   (e) sub-paragraph (3) does not prevent sub-paragraph (2) applying.

(2) Where this sub-paragraph applies the statement may without further proof be read as evidence on the trial of the accused, whether for the offence for which he was

committed for trial or for any other offence arising out of the same transaction or set of circumstances.

(3) Sub-paragraph (2) does not apply if—

  (a) it is proved that the statement was not signed by the justice by whom it purports to have been signed,
  (b) the court of trial at its discretion orders that sub-paragraph (2) shall not apply, or
  (c) a party to the proceedings objects to sub-paragraph (2) applying.

(4) If a party to the proceedings objects to sub-paragraph (2) applying the court of trial may order that the objection shall have no effect if the court considers it to be in the interests of justice so to order.

Depositions

2 (1) Sub-paragraph (2) applies if—

  (a) in pursuance of section 97A of the Magistrates' Courts Act 1980 (summons or warrant to have evidence taken as a deposition etc.) a person has had his evidence taken as a deposition for the purposes of proceedings before a magistrates' court inquiring into an offence as examining justices,
  (b) the deposition has been admitted in evidence in those proceedings,
  (c) in those proceedings a person has been committed for trial,
  (d) for the purposes of section 5A of the Magistrates' Courts Act 1980 the deposition complied with section 5C of that Act prior to the committal for trial,
  (e) the deposition purports to be signed by the justice before whom it purports to have been taken, and
  (f) sub-paragraph (3) does not prevent sub-paragraph (2) applying.

(2) Where this sub-paragraph applies the deposition may without further proof be read as evidence on the trial of the accused, whether for the offence for which he was committed for trial or for any other offence arising out of the same transaction or set of circumstances.

(3) Sub-paragraph (2) does not apply if—

  (a) it is proved that the deposition was not signed by the justice by whom it purports to have been signed,
  (b) the court of trial at its discretion orders that sub-paragraph (2) shall not apply, or
  (c) a party to the proceedings objects to sub-paragraph (2) applying.

(4) If a party to the proceedings objects to sub-paragraph (2) applying the court of trial may order that the objection shall have no effect if the court considers it to be in the interests of justice so to order.

Signatures

3 (1) A justice who signs a certificate authenticating one or more relevant statements or depositions shall be treated for the purposes of paragraphs 1 and 2 as signing the statement or deposition or (as the case may be) each of them.

(2) For this purpose—

  (a) a relevant statement is a written statement made by a person for the purposes of proceedings before a magistrates' court inquiring into an offence as examining justices;

(b) a relevant deposition is a deposition made in pursuance of section 97A of the Magistrates' Courts Act 1980 for the purposes of such proceedings.

Time limit for objection

4 Without prejudice to section 84 of the Supreme Court Act 1981 (rules of court) the power to make rules under that section includes power to make provision—

(a) requiring an objection under paragraph 1(3)(c) or 2(3)(c) to be made within a period prescribed in the rules;

(b) allowing the court of trial at its discretion to permit such an objection to be made outside any such period.

Retrial

5 In Schedule 2 to the Criminal Appeal Act 1968 (procedural and other provisions applicable on order for retrial) in paragraph 1 for the words from "section 13(3)" to "before the original trial" there shall be substituted "paragraphs 1 and 2 of Schedule 2 to the Criminal Procedure and Investigations Act 1996 (use of written statements and depositions) shall not apply to any written statement or deposition read as evidence at the original trial".

Repeals

6 (1) Section 13(3) of the Criminal Justice Act 1925 (which relates to depositions taken before examining justices and is superseded by paragraph 2 above) shall be omitted.

(2) Section 7 of the Criminal Justice Act 1967 (which is superseded by paragraph 3 above) shall be omitted.

Commencement

7 This Schedule shall have effect in accordance with provision made by the Secretary of State by order.

Section 72   **SCHEDULE 3**

FRAUD

Introduction

1 The Criminal Justice Act 1987 shall be amended as provided by this Schedule.

Preparatory hearings

2 In section 7 (power to order preparatory hearing) subsections (3) to (5) (power to make order that could be made at the hearing) shall be omitted.

3 (1) Section 9 (the preparatory hearing) shall be amended as follows.

(2) In subsection (7) (warning of possible consequence under section 10(1)) the word "(1)" shall be omitted.

(3) In subsection (10) for the words "at or for the purposes of a preparatory hearing" there shall be substituted "under this section".

4 The following section shall be inserted after section 9—

"9A Orders before preparatory hearing

(1) Subjection (2) below applies where—

    (a) a judge orders a preparatory hearing, and

    (b) he decides that any order which could be made under section 9(4) or (5) above at the hearing should be made before the hearing.

(2) In such a case—

    (a) he may make any such order before the hearing (or at the hearing), and

    (b) subsections (4) to (10) of section 9 above shall apply accordingly."

5 The following section shall be substituted for section 10 (later stages of trial)—

"10 Later stages of trial

(1) Any party may depart from the case he disclosed in pursuance of a requirement imposed under section 9 above.

(2) Where—

    (a) a party departs from the case he disclosed in pursuance of a requirement imposed under section 9 above, or

    (b) a party fails to comply with such a requirement,

the judge or, with the leave of the judge, any other party may make such comment as appears to the judge or the other party (as the case may be) to be appropriate and the jury may draw such inference as appears proper.

(3) In deciding whether to give leave the judge shall have regard—

    (a) to the extent of the departure or failure, and

    (b) to whether there is any justification for it.

(4) Except as provided by this section no part—

    (a) of a statement given under section 9(5) above, or

    (b) of any other information relating to the case for the accused or, if there is more than one, the case for any of them, which was given in pursuance of a requirement imposed under section 9 above,

may be disclosed at a stage in the trial after the jury have been sworn without the consent of the accused concerned."

Reporting restrictions

6 The following sections shall be substituted for section 11 (reporting restrictions)—

"11 Restrictions on reporting

(1) Except as provided by this section—

    (a) no written report of proceedings falling within subsection (2) below shall be published in Great Britain;

    (b) no report of proceedings falling within subsection (2) below shall be included in a relevant programme for reception in Great Britain.

(2) The following proceedings fall within this subsection—

    (a) an application under section 6(1) above;

    (b) a preparatory hearing;

(c) an application for leave to appeal in relation to such a hearing;

(d) an appeal in relation to such a hearing.

(3) The judge dealing with an application under section 6(1) above may order that subsection (1) above shall not apply, or shall not apply to a specified extent, to a report of the application.

(4) The judge dealing with a preparatory hearing may order that subsection (1) above shall not apply, or shall not apply to a specified extent, to a report of—

(a) the preparatory hearing, or

(b) an application to the judge for leave to appeal to the Court of Appeal under section 9(11) above in relation to the preparatory hearing.

(5) The Court of Appeal may order that subsection (1) above shall not apply, or shall not apply to a specified extent, to a report of—

(a) an appeal to the Court of Appeal under section 9(11) above in relation to a preparatory hearing,

(b) an application to that Court for leave to appeal to it under section 9(11) above in relation to a preparatory hearing, or

(c) an application to that Court for leave to appeal to the House of Lords under Part II of the Criminal Appeal Act 1968 in relation to a preparatory hearing.

(6) The House of Lords may order that subsection (1) above shall not apply, or shall not apply to a specified extent, to a report of—

(a) an appeal to that House under Part II of the Criminal Appeal Act 1968 in relation to a preparatory hearing, or

(b) an application to that House for leave to appeal to it under Part II of the Criminal Appeal Act 1968 in relation to a preparatory hearing.

(7) Where there is only one accused and he objects to the making of an order under subsection (3), (4), (5) or (6) above the judge or the Court of Appeal or the House of Lords shall make the order if (and only if) satisfied after hearing the representations of the accused that it is in the interests of justice to do so; and if the order is made it shall not apply to the extent that a report deals with any such objection or representations.

(8) Where there are two or more accused and one or more of them objects to the making of an order under subsection (3), (4), (5) or (6) above the judge or the Court of Appeal or the House of Lords shall make the order if (and only if) satisfied after hearing the representations of each of the accused that it is in the interests of justice to do so; and if the order is made it shall not apply to the extent that a report deals with any such objection or representations.

(9) Subsection (1) above does not apply to—

(a) the publication of a report of an application under section 6(1) above, or

(b) the inclusion in a relevant programme of a report of an application under section 6(1) above,

where the application is successful.

(10) Where—

(a) two or more persons are jointly charged, and

(b) applications under section 6(1) above are made by more than one of them, subsection (9) above shall have effect as if for the words "the application is" there were substituted "all the applications are".

(11) Subsection (1) above does not apply to—

(a) the publication of a report of an unsuccessful application made under section 6(1) above,
(b) the publication of a report of a preparatory hearing,
(c) the publication of a report of an appeal in relation to a preparatory hearing or of an application for leave to appeal in relation to such a hearing,
(d) the inclusion in a relevant programme of a report of an unsuccessful application made under section 6(1) above,
(e) the inclusion in a relevant programme of a report of a preparatory hearing, or
(f) the inclusion in a relevant programme of a report of an appeal in relation to a preparatory hearing or of an application for leave to appeal in relation to such a hearing,

at the conclusion of the trial of the accused or of the last of the accused to be tried.

(12) Subsection (1) above does not apply to a report which contains only one or more of the following matters—

(a) the identity of the court and the name of the judge;
(b) the names, ages, home addresses and occupations of the accused and witnesses;
(c) any relevant business information;
(d) the offence or offences, or a summary of them, with which the accused is or are charged;
(e) the names of counsel and solicitors in the proceedings;
(f) where the proceedings are adjourned, the date and place to which they are adjourned;
(g) any arrangements as to bail;
(h) whether legal aid was granted to the accused or any of the accused.

(13) The addresses that may be published or included in a relevant programme under subsection (12) above are addresses—

(a) at any relevant time, and
(b) at the time of their publication or inclusion in a relevant programme;

and "relevant time" here means a time when events giving rise to the charges to which the proceedings relate occurred.

(14) The following is relevant business information for the purposes of subsection (12) above—

(a) any address used by the accused for carrying on a business on his own account;
(b) the name of any business which he was carrying on on his own account at any relevant time;
(c) the name of any firm in which he was a partner at any relevant time or by which he was engaged at any such time;
(d) the address of any such firm;
(e) the name of any company of which he was a director at any relevant time or by which he was otherwise engaged at any such time;

(f)   the address of the registered or principal office of any such company;

(g)   any working address of the accused in his capacity as a person engaged by any such company;

and here "engaged" means engaged under a contract of service or a contract for services, and "relevant time" has the same meaning as in subsection (13) above.

(15) Nothing in this section affects any prohibition or restriction imposed by virtue of any other enactment on a publication or on matter included in a programme.

(16) In this section—

(a)   "publish", in relation to a report, means publish the report, either by itself or as part of a newspaper or periodical, for distribution to the public;

(b)   expressions cognate with "publish" shall be construed accordingly;

(c)   "relevant programme" means a programme included in a programme service, within the meaning of the Broadcasting Act 1990.

11A Offences in connection with reporting

(1) If a report is published or included in a relevant programme in contravention of section 11 above each of the following persons is guilty of an offence—

(a)   in the case of a publication of a written report as part of a newspaper or periodical, any proprietor, editor or publisher of the newspaper or periodical;

(b)   in the case of a publication of a written report otherwise than as part of a newspaper or periodical, the person who publishes it;

(c)   in the case of the inclusion of a report in a relevant programme, any body corporate which is engaged in providing the service in which the programme is included and any person having functions in relation to the programme corresponding to those of an editor of a newspaper.

(2) A person guilty of an offence under this section is liable on summary conviction to a fine of an amount not exceeding level 5 on the standard scale.

(3) Proceedings for an offence under this section shall not be instituted in England and Wales otherwise than by or with the consent of the Attorney General.

(4) Subsection (16) of section 11 above applies for the purposes of this section as it applies for the purposes of that."

7 In the list in section 17(2) (provisions extending to Scotland) after the entry relating to section 11 there shall be inserted "section 11A;".

General

8 (1) This Schedule applies in relation to an offence if—

(a)   on or after the appointed day the accused is committed for trial for the offence,

(b)   proceedings for the trial on the charge concerned are transferred to the Crown Court on or after the appointed day, or

(c)   a bill of indictment relating to the offence is preferred on or after the appointed day under the authority of section 2(2)(b) of the Administration of Justice (Miscellaneous Provisions) Act 1933 (bill preferred by direction of Court of Appeal, or by direction or with consent of a judge).

(2) References in this paragraph to the appointed day are to such day as is appointed for the purposes of this Schedule by the Secretary of State by order.

SCHEDULE 4
[*Applies to Northern Ireland only*]

Section 80   ## SCHEDULE 5

REPEALS

1. REINSTATEMENT OF CERTAIN PROVISIONS

Chapter	Short title	Extent of repeal
1994 c. 33.	Criminal Justice and Public Order Act 1994.	Section 34(7). Section 36(8). Section 37(7). Section 44. Schedule 4. In Schedule 11, the entries mentioned in note 1 below.

1 The entries in Schedule 11 to the 1994 Act are those relating to the following—

  (a) sections 13(3) and 49(2) of the Criminal Justice Act 1925;

  (b) section 1 of the Criminal Procedure (Attendance of Witnesses) Act 1965;

  (c) section 7 of the Criminal Justice Act 1967 and in section 36(1) of that Act the definition of "committal proceedings";

  (d) in paragraph 1 of Schedule 2 to the Criminal Appeal Act 1968 the words from "section 13(3)" to "but";

  (e) in section 46(1) of the Criminal Justice Act 1972 the words "Section 102 of the Magistrates' Courts Act 1980 and", "which respectively allow", "committal proceedings and in other", "and section 106 of the said Act of 1980", "which punish the making of", "102 or" and ", as the case may be", and section 46(2) of that Act;

  (f) in section 32(1)(b) of the Powers of Criminal Courts Act 1973 the words "tried or";

  (g) in Schedule 1 to the Interpretation Act 1978, paragraph (a) of the definition of "Committed for trial";

  (h) in section 97(1) of the Magistrates' Courts Act 1980 the words from "at an inquiry" to "be) or", sections 102, 103, 105, 106 and 145(1)(e) of that Act, in section 150(1) of that Act the definition of "committal proceedings", and paragraph 2 of Schedule 5 to that Act;

  (i) in section 2(2)(g) of the Criminal Attempts Act 1981 the words "or committed for trial";

  (j) in section 1(2) of the Criminal Justice Act 1982 the words "trial or";

  (k) paragraphs 10 and 11 of Schedule 2 to the Criminal Justice Act 1987;

  (l) in section 20(4)(a) of the Legal Aid Act 1988 the words "trial or", and section 20(4)(bb) and (5) of that Act;

  (m) in section 1(4) of the War Crimes Act 1991 the words "England, Wales or", and Part I of the Schedule to that Act.

2 The repeals under this paragraph (reinstatement of certain provisions) have effect in accordance with section 44 of this Act.

2. War Crimes

Chapter	Short title	Extent of repeal
1988 c. 34.	Legal Aid Act 1988.	Section 20(4)(bb).
1991 c. 13.	War Crimes Act 1991.	In section 1(4) the words "England, Wales or". Section 3(2). Part I of the Schedule.

3. Either Way Offences

Chapter	Short title	Extent of repeal
1980 c. 43.	Magistrates' Courts Act 1980.	Section 19(2)(a).

This repeal has effect in accordance with section 49 of this Act.

4. Remand

Chapter	Short title	Extent of repeal
1980 c. 43.	Magistrates' Courts Act 1980.	In section 128, subsections (1A)(c) and (3A)(c). In section 128A(1) the words "who has attained the age of 17".

These repeals have effect in accordance with section 52 of this Act.

5. Specimens

Chapter	Short title	Extent of repeal
1992 c. 42.	Transport and Works Act 1992.	In section 31(4) the word "or" at the end of paragraph (b).

This repeal has effect in accordance with section 63 of this Act.

6. Witness Orders

Chapter	Short title	Extent of repeal
1965 c. 69.	Criminal Procedure (Attendance of Witnesses) Act 1965.	Section 1. In section 3(1) the words "witness order or". In section 4(1) the words "witness order or" and (where they next occur) "order or". In the proviso to section 4(1) the words from "in the case" (where they first occur) to "witness summons". In section 4(2) the words "a witness order or" and (where they next occur) "order or".
1971 c. 23.	Courts Act 1971.	In Schedule 8, paragraph 45(1).
1980 c. 43.	Magistrates' Courts Act 1980.	Section 145(1)(e).

These repeals have effect in accordance with provision made by the Secretary of State by order under section 65 of this Act.

7. Summonses to Witnesses

Chapter	Short title	Extent of repeal
1965 c. 69.	Criminal Procedure (Attendance of Witnesses) Act 1965.	Schedule 1.
1971 c. 23.	Courts Act 1971.	In Schedule 8, paragraph 45(2) and (5).

These repeals have effect in accordance with section 66 of this Act.

8. Preliminary Stages

Number	Title	Extent of revocation
S.I. 1987/299	Prosecution of Offences (Custody Time Limits) Regulations 1987.	Regulation 5(7).

This revocation has effect in accordance with section 71 of this Act.

9. ALIBI

Chapter	Short title	Extent of repeal
1967 c. 80.	Criminal Justice Act 1967.	Section 11.
1980 c. 43.	Magistrates' Courts Act 1980.	In Schedule 7, paragraph 64.
1987 c. 38.	Criminal Justice Act 1987.	In Schedule 2, paragraph 2.
1994 c. 33.	Criminal Justice and Public Order Act 1994.	In Schedule 4, paragraph 15(3). In Schedule 9, paragraphs 6(2) and 7.

These repeals have effect in accordance with section 74 of this Act.

10. COMMITTAL PROCEEDINGS

Chapter	Short title	Extent of repeal
1867 c. 35.	Criminal Law Amendment Act 1867.	Section 6. Section 7.
1972 c. 71.	Criminal Justice Act 1972.	In section 46(1) the following words— "Section 102 of the Magistrates' Courts Act 1980 and"; "which respectively allow"; "committal proceedings and in other"; "and section 106 of the said Act of 1980"; "which punish the making of"; "102 or"; ", as the case may be". Section 46(2).
1980 c. 43.	Magistrates' Courts Act 1980.	Section 28. In section 97(1) the words "at an inquiry into an indictable offence by a magistrates' court for that commission area or". Section 102. Section 103(3) and (4). Section 105. In Schedule 7, paragraph 2.
1988 c. 33.	Criminal Justice Act 1988.	In section 32A(10) the words "notwithstanding that the child witness is not called at the committal proceedings". In Schedule 15, paragraph 68.

These repeals have effect in accordance with provision made by the Secretary of State by order under Schedule 1 to this Act.

11. Statements and Depositions

Chapter	Short title	Extent of repeal
1925 c. 86.	Criminal Justice Act 1925.	Section 13(3).
1965 c. 69.	Criminal Procedure (Attendance of Witnesses) Act 1965.	In Part I of Schedule 2, the entry relating to the Criminal Justice Act 1925.
1967 c. 80.	Criminal Justice Act 1967.	Section 7.
1980 c. 43.	Magistrates' Courts Act 1980.	In Schedule 7, paragraph 63.

These repeals have effect in accordance with provision made by the Secretary of State by order under Schedule 2 to this Act.

12. Fraud

Chapter	Short title	Extent of repeal
1987 c. 38.	Criminal Justice Act 1987.	In section 7, subsections (3) to (5). In section 9(7), the word "(1)".
1988 c. 33.	Criminal Justice Act 1988.	In Schedule 15, paragraph 114.
1990 c. 42.	Broadcasting Act 1990.	In Schedule 20, paragraph 47.

These repeals have effect in accordance with Schedule 3 to this Act.

APPENDIX 2

Draft Code of Practice

Introduction

1.1 This code of practice is issued under Part II of the Criminal Procedure and Investigations Act 1996 ('the Act'). It applies in respect of criminal investigations conducted by police officers which begin on or after the day on which this code comes into effect. Persons other than police officers who are charged with the duty of conducting an investigation as defined in the Act are to have regard to the relevant provisions of the code, and should adapt them to reflect their own operating procedures as necessary.

1.2 Nothing in this code applies to material intercepted in obedience to a warrant issued under section 2 of the Interception of Communications Act 1985, or to any copy of that material as defined in section 10 of that Act.

Definitions

2.1 In this code:

- a **criminal investigation** is an investigation conducted by police officers with a view to it being ascertained whether a person should be charged with an offence, or whether a person charged with an offence is guilty of it. This will include

  - investigations into crimes that have been committed;

  - investigations whose purpose is to ascertain whether a crime has been committed; and

  - investigations which begin in the belief that a crime is about to be committed, for example when the police keep premises or individuals under observation for a period of time;

- charging a person with an offence includes laying an information and issuing a summons;

- an **investigator** is any police officer involved in the conduct of a criminal investigation. All investigators have a responsibility for carrying out the duties imposed on them under this code, including in particular recording information, and retaining records of information and other material;

- the **officer in charge of an investigation** is the police officer responsible for directing a criminal investigation. He is also responsible for ensuring that proper procedures are in place for recording information, and retaining records of information and other material, in the investigation;

- the **disclosure officer** is the person responsible for examining the records created during the investigation, revealing material to the prosecutor during the investigation and any criminal proceedings resulting from it, disclosing it to the accused, and certifying where necessary that action has been taken in accordance with the requirements of this code;

– the **prosecutor** is the authority responsible for the conduct of criminal proceedings on behalf of the Crown. Particular duties may in practice fall to individuals acting on behalf of the prosecuting authority;

– **material** is material of any kind, including information and objects, which is obtained in the course of a criminal investigation and which may be relevant to the investigation;

– material may be **relevant to the investigation** if it appears to an investigator, or to the officer in charge of an investigation, or to the disclosure officer, that it has some bearing on any offence under investigation or any person being investigated, or to the surrounding circumstances of the case, unless it is incapable of having any impact on the case;

– **sensitive material** is material which an investigator, or the officer in charge of the investigation, or the disclosure officer believes it is not in the public interest to disclose;

– references to **primary prosecution disclosure** are to the duty of the prosecutor under section 3 of the Act to disclose material which is in his possession or which he has inspected, and which in his opinion might undermine the case against the accused;

– references to **secondary prosecution disclosure** are to the duty of the prosecutor under section 7 of the Act to disclose material which is in his possession or which he has inspected, and which might reasonably be expected to assist the defence disclosed by the accused in a defence statement given under the Act;

– references to the disclosure of material to a person accused of an offence include references to the disclosure of material to his legal representative;

– references to police officers and to the chief officer of police include those employed in a police force as defined in section 3(3) of the Prosecution of Offences Act 1985.

General responsibilities

3.1 The functions of the investigator, the officer in charge of an investigation and the disclosure officer are separate. Whether they are undertaken by one, two or more persons will depend on the complexity of the case and the administrative arrangements within each police force. Where they are undertaken by more than one person, close consultation between them is essential to the effective performance of the duties imposed by this code.

3.2 The chief officer of police for each police force area is responsible for putting in place arrangements to ensure that in every investigation the identity of the officer in charge of an investigation and the disclosure officer is recorded.

3.3 The officer in charge of an investigation may delegate tasks to another investigator or to civilians employed by the police force, but he remains responsible for ensuring that these have been carried out and for accounting for any general policies followed in the investigation.

3.4 In conducting an investigation, the investigator should pursue all reasonable lines of enquiry, whether these point towards or away from the suspect.

3.5 If the officer in charge of an investigation or the disclosure officer believes that other persons may be in possession of material that may be relevant to the investigation, he should inform them of the existence of the investigation, and the disclosure officer should inform the prosecutor that they may have such material. However, the officer in charge of an investigation and the disclosure officer are not required to make speculative enquiries of other persons: there must be some reason to believe that they may have relevant material.

3.6 If, during a criminal investigation, the officer in charge of an investigation or disclosure officer for any reason no longer has responsibility for the functions falling to him, either his supervisor or the police officer in charge of criminal investigations for the area must assign someone else to assume that responsibility. That person's identity must be recorded, as with those initially responsible for these functions in each investigation.

Recording of information

4.1 If material which may be relevant to the investigation consists of information which is not recorded in any form, the officer in charge of an investigation must ensure that it is recorded in a durable or retrievable form (whether in writing, on video or audio tape, or on computer disk).

4.2 Where it is not practicable to retain the initial record of information because it forms part of a larger record which is to be destroyed, its contents should be transferred to a durable and more easily stored form before that happens.

4.3 In some cases, negative information (for example a series of persons present in a particular place at a particular time who state that they saw nothing unusual) may be relevant to the investigation and should be recorded.

4.4 Where information which may be relevant is obtained, it must be recorded at the time it is obtained or as soon as practicable after that time. This includes, for example, information obtained in house-to-house enquiries, although the requirement to record information promptly does not require an investigator to take a statement from a potential witness where it would not otherwise be taken.

Retention of material

5.1 The investigator must retain material obtained in a criminal investigation which may be relevant to the investigation. This includes not only material coming into the possession of the investigator (such as documents seized in the course of searching premises) but also material generated by him (such as interview records). Material may be retained in the form of a copy rather than the original if the original was supplied to the investigator rather than generated by him and is to be returned to its owner.

5.2 Where material has been seized in the exercise of the powers of seizure conferred by the Police and Criminal Evidence Act 1984, the duty to retain it under this code is subject to the provisions on the retention of seized material in section 22 of that Act.

5.3 If the officer in charge of an investigation or the disclosure officer becomes aware as a result of developments in the case that material previously examined but not retained (because it was not thought to be relevant) may now be relevant to the investigation, he should, wherever practicable, take steps to obtain it or ensure that it is retained for further inspection or for production in court if required.

5.4 The duty to retain material includes in particular the duty to retain material falling into the following categories:

- crime reports (including crime report forms, relevant parts of incident report books or police officers' notebooks);

- records of telephone messages (for example, 999 calls) containing descriptions of an alleged offence or offender;

- final versions of witness statements (and draft versions where their content differs in any way from the final version), including any exhibits mentioned (unless these have been returned to their owner on the understanding that they will be produced in court if required);

- interview records (written records, or audio or video tapes, of interviews with actual or potential witnesses or suspects);

- communications between the police and experts such as forensic scientists, reports of work carried out by experts, and schedules of scientific material prepared by the expert for the investigator, for the purposes of criminal proceedings;

- any material casting doubt on the reliability of a confession;

- any material casting doubt on the reliability of a witness;

- any other material which may fall within the test for primary prosecution disclosure in the Act.

5.5 The duty to retain material falling into these categories does not extend to items which are purely ancillary to such material and possess no independent significance (for example, duplicate copies of records or reports).

5.6 The duty to retain draft versions of witness statements does not extend to draft statements of opinion prepared by expert witnesses: earlier versions tend to be based on incomplete information, and evolve as further information comes to light and additional expert contributions are obtained.

5.7 All relevant material must be retained until a decision is taken whether to institute proceedings against a person for an offence.

5.8 If a criminal investigation results in proceedings being instituted, all relevant material must be retained at least until either:

- the prosecutor decides not to proceed with the case;

- the case results in an acquittal;

- the case results in a conviction, and the time limit for an appeal has expired with no appeal being lodged; or

- an appeal against conviction is determined, in cases where the appeal is lodged within time.

5.9 The chief officer of police for each police force must develop a policy on the length of time for which material is retained if a criminal investigation does not result in charges and also after the conclusion of any criminal proceedings if the investigation has resulted in charges. In developing the policy he may take into account the following criteria among others:

- the seriousness of the offence;

- the plea entered by the accused;

- whether a retrial is likely, if the proceedings resulted in an acquittal;

- the length of any custodial or community sentence imposed, if the proceedings resulted in a conviction;

- whether an appeal against conviction or sentence is pending or is expected;

- the possibility that a complaint or civil action against the police might follow (particularly if an investigation has not resulted in charges);

- the retention policies developed or likely to be developed by chief officers of police in other force areas;

- any statutory requirements for the retention of material imposed other than under this code.

5.10 It is open to the chief officer of police to decide either to retain all material for a certain period, or to set differing retention periods according to the criteria set out above.

Preparation of material for prosecutor

6.1 The disclosure officer must ensure that a schedule listing material which has been retained and which does not form part of the case against the accused is prepared in the following circumstances:

- the accused is charged with an offence which is triable only on indictment;

- the accused is charged with an offence which is triable either way, and it is considered either that the case is likely to be tried on indictment or that the accused is likely to plead not guilty at a summary trial;

- the accused is charged with a summary offence, and it is considered that he is likely to plead not guilty.

6.2 In respect of either way and summary offences, whether a person has admitted the offence, and whether a police officer witnessed the offence, may be relevant to the consideration of whether a schedule is likely to be needed.

6.3 If it is believed that the court will proceed to summary trial and that the accused is likely to plead guilty, it is not necessary to prepare schedules in advance. If, contrary to this belief, it is decided that the offence is to be tried on indictment, or the court proceeds to summary trial and the accused pleads not guilty, the disclosure officer must ensure that a schedule is prepared as soon as reasonably practicable after that happens.

6.4 The disclosure officer must state on the schedule that he does not believe that the material listed on it is sensitive. Any material which is believed to be sensitive must be either listed on a sensitive schedule (paragraph 6.8 below) or, in exceptional circumstances, revealed to the prosecutor separately (paragraph 6.9 below).

6.5 The disclosure officer should ensure that each item of material is listed separately on the schedule, and is numbered consecutively. The description of each item should make clear the nature of the item and should contain sufficient detail to enable the prosecutor to form a judgement on whether the material needs to be disclosed.

6.6 In some enquiries it may not be practicable to list each item of material separately. For example, there may be many items of a similar or repetitive nature. These may be listed in a block and described by quantity and generic title.

6.7 Even if some material is listed in a block, the disclosure officer must ensure that any items among that material which might meet the test for disclosure are listed and described individually.

6.8 Subject to paragraph 6.9 below, the disclosure officer must list on a sensitive schedule any material which he or the officer in charge of an investigation or an investigator believes it is not in the public interest to disclose, and the reason for that belief. Depending on the circumstances, examples of such material may include the following among others:

- material relating to national security;

- material received from the intelligence and security agencies;

- material relating to intelligence from foreign sources which reveals sensitive intelligence gathering methods;

- material such as telephone subscriber checks which is supplied to an investigator for intelligence purposes only;

- material given in confidence;

- material relating to the identity or activities of informants, or under-cover police officers, or other persons supplying information to the police who may be in danger if their identities are revealed;

- material revealing the location of any premises or other place used for police surveillance, or the identity of any person allowing a police officer to use them for surveillance;

- material revealing, either directly or indirectly, techniques and methods relied upon by a police officer in the course of a criminal investigation, for example covert surveillance techniques, or other methods of detecting crime;

- material whose disclosure might facilitate the commission of other offences or hinder the prevention and detection of crime;

- internal police communications such as management minutes;

- communications between the police and the Crown Prosecution Service;

- material upon the strength of which search warrants were obtained;

- material containing details of persons taking part in identification parades;

- material supplied to an investigator during a criminal investigation which has been generated by an official of a body concerned with the regulation or supervision of bodies corporate or of persons engaged in financial activities, or which has been generated by a person retained by such a body;

- material supplied to an investigator during a criminal investigation which relates to a child witness and which has been generated by a local authority social services department or other party contacted by an investigator during the investigation.

6.9 In exceptional circumstances, where an investigator considers that material is so sensitive that its revelation to the prosecutor by means of an entry on the sensitive schedule is inappropriate, the existence of the material must be revealed to the prosecutor separately. Examples are where, if the material were compromised, that would be likely to lead directly to the loss of life, or directly threaten national security.

6.10 In such circumstances, the responsibility for informing the prosecutor lies with the investigator who knows the detail of the sensitive material. The investigator should act as soon as is reasonably practicable after the file containing the prosecution case is sent to the prosecutor. The investigator must also ensure that the prosecutor is able to inspect the material so that he can assess whether it needs to be brought before a court for a ruling on disclosure.

Revelation of material to prosecutor

7.1 The disclosure officer must send the schedules to the prosecutor. Wherever practicable this should be at the same time as he sends the file containing the material for the prosecution case (or as soon as is reasonably practicable after the decision on mode of trial or the plea, in cases to which paragraph 6.3 applies). The schedules should be signed and dated by the disclosure officer.

7.2 The disclosure officer should draw the attention of the prosecutor to any material an investigator has retained (whether or not listed on a schedule) which may fall within the test for primary prosecution disclosure in Act, and should explain why the investigator has come to that view.

7.3 In addition to listing material on the schedule, the disclosure officer must give the prosecutor, at the same time as he gives him the schedule, a copy of any material which falls into the following categories:

- records of the first description of a suspect given to the police by a potential witness, whether or not the description differs from that of the alleged offender;

- information provided by an accused person which indicates an explanation for the offence with which he has been charged;

- any material casting doubt on the reliability of a confession;

- any material casting doubt on the reliability of a witness;

- any other material which the investigator believes may fall within the test for primary prosecution disclosure in the Act.

7.4 If the prosecutor asks to inspect material which has not already been copied to him, the disclosure officer must allow him to inspect it. If the prosecutor asks for a copy of material which has not already been copied to him, the disclosure officer must give him a copy. However, this does not apply where the officer in charge of an investigation or disclosure officer believes that the material is too sensitive to be copied and can only be inspected.

7.5 If material consists of information which is recorded other than in writing, whether it should be given to the prosecutor in its original form as a whole, or by way of relevant extracts recorded in the same form, or in the form of a transcript, is a matter for agreement between the disclosure officer and the prosecutor.

Subsequent action by officer in charge of investigation and disclosure officer

8.1 At the time a schedule is prepared, the officer in charge of an investigation or disclosure officer will not know what defence the accused is to set out in a defence statement under Part I of the Act. After a defence statement has been given, the disclosure officer must look again at the material which has been retained and must draw the attention of the prosecutor to any material which might reasonably be expected to assist the defence disclosed by the accused; and he must reveal it to him in accordance with paragraphs 7.4 and 7.5 above.

8.2 Section 9 of the Act imposes a continuing duty on the prosecutor, for the duration of criminal proceedings against the accused, to disclose material which meets the tests for disclosure (subject to public interest considerations). To enable him to do this, any new material coming to light should be treated in the same way as the earlier material.

Certification by disclosure officer

9.1 The disclosure officer must certify to the prosecutor that to the best of his knowledge and belief the duties imposed under this code have been complied with. It will be necessary to do this not only at the time when the schedules and accompanying material are submitted to the prosecutor, but also when material which has been retained is reconsidered after the accused has given a defence statement.

9.2 Where an investigation has been conducted jointly by police officers and officers of another investigating agency, the disclosure officer will be able to certify only in relation to the activities of the police officers.

Disclosure of material to accused

10.1 If material has not already been copied to the prosecutor, and he requests its disclosure to the accused, the disclosure officer must disclose it to the accused in the following circumstances:

 – in the opinion of the prosecutor, the material might undermine the prosecution case; or

 – the accused has given the prosecutor a defence statement, and the material might reasonably be expected to assist the defence which the accused has disclosed; or

 – the court has ordered the disclosure of the material after considering an application from the accused under Part I of the Act.

10.2 If material has been copied to the prosecutor, and it is to be disclosed, whether it is disclosed by the prosecutor or the disclosure officer is a matter for agreement between the two of them.

10.3 The disclosure officer must disclose material to the accused either by giving him a copy or by allowing him to inspect it. If the accused person asks for a copy of any material which he has been allowed to inspect, the disclosure officer must give it to him, unless in the opinion of the disclosure officer that is either not practicable (for example because the material consists of an object which cannot be copied) or not desirable (for example because the material is a statement by a child witness in relation to a sexual offence, and it is believed that the accused may give the statement to persons unconnected with the proceedings).

10.4 If material which the accused has been allowed to inspect consists of information which is recorded other than in writing, whether it should be given to the accused in its original form or in the form of a transcript is a matter for the discretion of the disclosure officer. If the material is transcribed, the disclosure officer must ensure that the transcript is certified to the accused as a true record of the material which has been transcribed.

10.5 If a court concludes that it is in the public interest that an item of sensitive material must be disclosed to the accused, it will be necessary to disclose the material if the case is to proceed. This does not mean that sensitive documents must always be disclosed in their original form: for example, the court may agree that sensitive details still requiring protection should be blacked out, or that documents may be summarised, or that the prosecutor may make an admission about the substance of the material under section 10 of the Criminal Justice Act 1967.

INDEX